THE FAMILY MATTERS HANDBOOK

A JANET THOMA BOOK

THOMAS NELSON PUBLISHERS
Nashville

Published in Nashville, Tennessee, by Janet Thoma Books, a division of Thomas Nelson, Inc., Publishers, and distributed in Canada by Word Communications, Ltd., Richmond, British Columbia, and in the United Kingdom by Word (UK), Ltd., Milton Keynes, England.

Library of Congress Cataloging-in-Publication Data
The Family matters handbook.
p. cm.
Includes bibliographical references.
ISBN 0-7852-8278-5
1. Family—Religious life. 2. Parenting—Religious aspects—Christianity. 3. Marriage—Religious aspects—Christianity. I. Thomas Nelson Publishers.
BV4526.2.F332 1994
248.4—dc20
93-31980
CIP

Printed in the United States of America

1 2 3 4 5 6 — 99 98 97 96 95 94

Contents

The Growing of God's Family Tree

The tree of life indeed grows in your own back yard, your own living room, bedroom and kitchen. It is your family tree. Our children are, by far, the greatest, vast resource we have in America today. And you, Mom and Dad, have been commissioned by God to protect and nurture His precious resource. It is your heart that tills their soul, your hand that keeps them healthy, your words that keep them secure.

A tree knows only one thing: to grow to be the best tree it can be, whether it must tough its way through stony soil, grow around obstacles, or stretch to find the light. Your family tree is a living, growing thing too. You must take care to nourish it every day. You must water it every night if it wants a drink before it goes to bed. You must nurture it through the thunder rumbles of divorce, the lightning crashes of anger. There are times you must be strong to trim it back with loving discipline in order for it to bear fruit.

In this book we have put together some nutrients, wonderful nuggets of wisdom from some of the Christian community's most respected authors. The ministry of these people is the care and nurture of God's family tree. Millions of readers in this country and all over the world have learned to depend on their insight and expertise; millions of Christian mothers and fathers have learned to depend on their love and caring devotion to God's Word and God's children. Now they have come together to create this handbook on the growing of a loving, accepting, secure family, which will protect our country's most natural resource. They are here to contribute their knowledge to the care of your family tree.

There may be some new growth for your family tree in this book; we hope you will consider some new insights to see if they can be incorporated in the healthy growing of your family. Keith Fournier asks you to live in your family as you would in church. Charles Swindoll speaks to the "bents" God gave each of your children before He gave them to you that you would train them up in their way, not yours. Dr. Kevin Leman and Randy Carlson will help you look to your past childhood memories to help you with the future of your own children. Linda Dillow and Claudia Arp offer ideas on physical and fun fitness that will nurture your family tree to be the best tree it can be.

In today's world, we parents must see the forest *and* the trees. Where yesterday the greatest problems in schools were gum-chewing and spitting, today your children face drugs and alcohol. For the care and raising of your teenagers, Josh McDowell, Paul Borthwick, Drs. Frank Minirth, Brian Newman, and Paul Warren, and Dr. Grace Ketterman minister to the special needs of this oft-harried group of young people trying their best to make the leap from childhood to adulthood. They offer information for your use on the serious issues of teenage depression, drug use, alcoholism, sexuality, and suicide.

If your family tree has been split by the disease of divorce, you'll receive support for raising children in a one-parent home, learn how to maintain communication with your ex-spouse, and learn how to handle your own emotional upheaval to grow into your new life.

As your family tree begins to mature, Bill and Vonette Bright, Ron and Judy Blue, Gary Smalley and John Trent, Ph.D., and others will help you and your spouse deal with issues such as financial planning for your children, the empty nest, parenting your elderly parents, and blessing your older children.

You may do no other great deeds in your lifetime,
but if you have raised a whole, loving, giving
son or daughter of God,
you have accomplished the greatest of deeds.
You have accomplished the growing of God's family tree.

Homes That Gave the Blessing to Children

- *We were often spontaneously getting hugged even apart from completing a task or chore.*
- *They would let me explain my side of the story.*
- *We went camping as a family. (This response was repeated often.)*
- *They would take each of us out individually for a special breakfast with Mom and Dad.*
- *My father would put his arm around me at church and let me lay my head on his shoulder.*
- *I got to spend one day at Dad's office, seeing where he worked and meeting the people he worked with.*
- *My mother always carried pictures of each of us in her purse.*
- *My parents made sure that each one of us kids appeared in the family photos.*

- *My parents would make a special Christmas ornament for each child that represented a character trait we had worked on that year.*
- *They were willing to admit when they were wrong and say "I'm sorry."*
- *They had a "king or queen for a day meal" for us that would focus individual attention on each child.*
- *As a family we often read and discussed the book The Velveteen Rabbit, which talks about how valuable we are.*
- *I saw my parents praying for me even when I didn't feel I deserved it.*
- *My folks wrote up a special "story of my birth" that they read to me every year.*
- *We read Psalm 139 as a family and discussed how God had uniquely and specially designed each of us children.*

The Gift of the Blessing
Gary Smalley and John Trent, Ph.D.

PART ONE

Roles, Rules, and Relationships

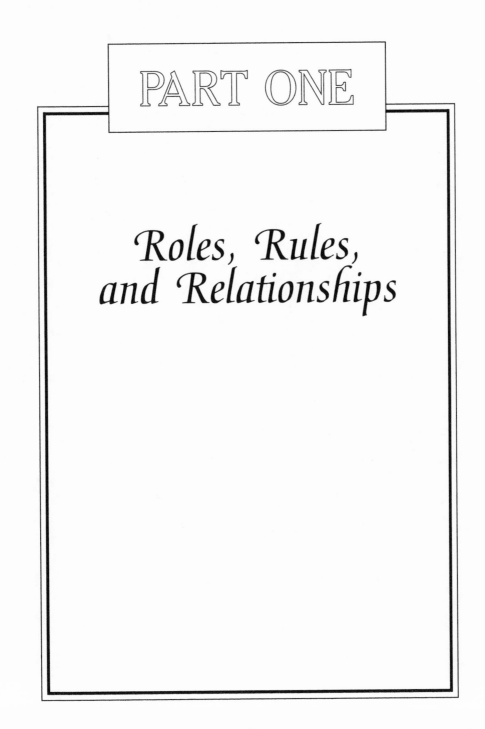

Chapter

I

The Roles of a Mother

Our roles as a mother often run together so much we never take the time to distinguish and define them all. In this chapter from my book, Mothering, *I wanted to show you the wide, colorful variety of hats a mother wears. She wears the crisp, white cotton cap of nurse and dietician; a bright lavender organdy chapeau as social coordinator and fashion expert; the black cap with black and white checked hat-band when she is taxi driver and chauffeur; the green eyeshade of the comptroller; and anything she wants to wear while she is "the Boss."*

A mother does all this and more, and through it all she must seek to maintain balance—always—to take care of herself as much as she takes care of others. It's a tough job—one that only a mother can do.

For you new mothers who are just starting your family, you can look forward to all this. For those of you who are getting to be old hands at this mothering job, now is the time to stop and realize all the important jobs you fill. Fathers, we hope you will take the time after reading this chapter to say a word of recognition and appreciation to your wife if you haven't already done so today. And for you single fathers—this is now you.

Dr. Grace Ketterman
Mothering

Today I sat around a table with eight mothers. While we ate lunch, we discussed our work as people helpers and mothers. Most of us are also wives, active in a church, children's schools and other activities, and various groups. I was, by far, the oldest, and the others looked to me for some answers my years had discovered. Despite some progress over time, I had to admit that I still search for the balances that make life bearable. As we shared and thought together, we arrived at some conclusions I'll convey to you.

To begin to balance our loads, we had to find and believe in our individual worth. Most of us had tried (and some are still trying) to prove we were good women by the many good deeds we accomplished. That is an endless cycle because it just doesn't work. So start with discovering who you are inside and your capabilities that want to be expressed.

We had to stop worrying about what others thought of us. Several of us were slaves to our children's, husbands', or parents' constant approval. It became clear that when children discover that mothers need their approval, they capitalize on that. They learn very quickly how to make moms feel guilty and gain a variety of benefits from that guilt.

A central function of stopping the search for others' constant approval is learning to say no. Out of habit, if nothing else, we all agreed that was most difficult at first, but it does get easier. On the other hand, as we grow in the knowledge of ourselves and discover new interests and abilities, there are many more things clamoring at us. So the art of saying no becomes quite complex and difficult.

We had to schedule our time. Accomplishing all that *must* be done along with all we *want* to do demands organization. By keeping a flexible daily calendar, we found we accomplished more, forgot less, and could even work in some leisure time now and then.

Delegating responsibilities also helped. We agreed that children not only must not lay guilt trips on us, but they can feel important and needed when we ask for their help. That is not to make excuses for abandoning your children. Children and mothers need plenty of time together, but kids can sometimes become selfish and demanding, and out of feeling guilty, mothers can spoil and pamper them. Children need not become tyrants.

Most of us knew that children can sense and need to understand why moms are working. A child's worst fear is that of abandonment: "What if Mom doesn't love me and wants to get away from me? Maybe I'm a terrible burden to her." We could all think of a rare mother who acted as if that might be true. But most of the moms we knew had to work to help overburdened husbands.

A few loved their children genuinely but were so depressed or bored with housework that they were irritable, grouchy mothers. We decided that children could understand that feeling and could be proud of their mother's abilities and services. Many times, I have been asked to thank my children for relinquishing me for an evening's event. I have tried to always communicate the appreciation of others for whatever help I could be to them. I believe my children know that I could not have been effective in my work had I felt guilty of neglecting them. The other side of that was that I did limit my time away and I adored them every hour I was with them (well, almost!).

Teamwork with husbands was our last big discussion. When mom is gone now and then while dad is home, children require his attention. If mother is there, children are drawn to her by sheer habit, allowing dad to slide into the role of sleeping stranger. Most of these mothers had to work a few evening hours, and they learned that their husbands really became fathers while they were gone. Most of them learned to love putting children to bed, reading stories, or even tutoring homework. They had the family under control when moms arrived home tired.

I realize all men are not that cooperative, but it was reassuring to learn that they can be. Perhaps both moms and dads will learn, in these economically difficult times, to become a supportive, loving team.

For some months I have kept a list of the many roles mothers fill in their families. I have been amazed at its length, and you may have more activities to add.

DIETITIAN

It is your job from their conception to nourish your children. Through their likes and dislikes, growth spurts and lags, the diet fads and fashions of teens, consider your challenges in planning and preparing meals. And do you have the trouble I had getting them all to the table?

The balance to find in this role is that of noticing the children's special likes and dislikes of certain foods, then serving mainly those healthy foods they need and do like with an occasional offering of something they hate. Children often eat out with friends and relatives, and it is rude to refuse a dish the hostess has worked to prepare. Teach them to eat just a little bit of everything. Rarely do children hate all healthy foods unless eating has become a battleground. Keep serving balanced meals, expect them to eat enough, and don't fight over it. Our bodies have an amazing capability of creating an appetite for the food elements they need, over time.

Make mealtimes pleasant, friendly, and happy. Save good and funny topics for mealtime, and reserve reprimands or discipline to a private time later.

NURSE

I've already described what a wonderful nurse my mother was. When children are small, sickness can be a frightening and exhausting experience. Choose a pediatrician in whom you have great confidence, and find a friend who will help you when you reach the end of your strength. A mother or sister can be a wonderful ally during such times.

As children reach age two or three, they become quite independent, and you may miss the cuddling you loved when they were babies. When they are sick, most children love to be held and rocked, read to, and entertained. Enjoy doing all of those things because most childhood illnesses don't last long. With effective medicines and a few days' time, sick children bounce back to wellness.

A few chronic illnesses, however, will challenge you to the maximum. A friend faced a long period of bed rest for her seven-year-old son. He had a disease of his hip joint that was not too painful, but it was essential that he lay with that leg and hip straight. He was an extremely active boy, used to running and climbing, and the enforced bed rest was totally unacceptable to him. He was eventually demanding and even refused to stay quiet.

Darlene learned a unique balance as his nurse. She had to be firm and require his cooperation. And she had to find activities that he could do to make life bearable. Her tough love did the former, and her creativity enabled her to do the latter. Her excellent nursing brought her son through the trying episode.

PLAYMATE

When I work with a child who doesn't know how to play with other children, I've learned to ask, "Mom, did you play with this child when she was a toddler?" Many times mothers don't know how to (or even that they should) play with young children. They buy toys for them and may show them how to use them, but then they go about their other duties. And sometimes that's okay. Babies really don't need to be entertained all of the time. But you need to play with them enough to teach them healthy interaction.

Roll a ball with a one-year-old, teach building with blocks to a two-year-old, and play "let's imagine" with a three- or four-year-old. Run with them; play hide-and-seek or any game you can create. Doing such activities will be a happy way of saying, "I love to play with you!" And your children will learn to play harmoniously with others. They will become the best playmates in the neighborhood. And by teaching these wholesome games, you will find the neighborhood children less likely to get into undesirable activities.

I suggest you also play with your preschool child's friends. Some of them will not be blessed with mothers who have taught them what you are teaching your child. Being near them or interacting with them can be a wonderful influence on them, and you can be sure no aggressive or sexual activities harm them.

With school-age children, I suggest you be around them, but usually they will not want you to play with them. Offer a snack or a drink now and then, and quietly help settle the arguments children will have. They may need you to play "Monopoly" or "Clue," and if you can, I think that's wonderful.

Adolescents are all too often totally unsupervised, so you will travel troubled waters with your teens. Due to the degree of freedom many teens are allowed, yours are likely to feel angry and embarrassed if you restrict them. But they will also feel safe and protected. So once again, balance their quest for independence with enough restrictions to keep them out of danger. Once in a while, they will enjoy having fun with you. Keep recreational events pleasant, and don't use them to lecture or vent frustrations. There are times for doing that, but don't mix that with playing together.

PROTECTOR

Infants and toddlers would never survive without constant protection. One psychologist said that up to one year, no child should be out of sight of the mother except when asleep. And up to two years, the mother should be within hearing distance at all times. I tend to agree with him, but the balance in this role lies in the fact that you do not need to touch a child all the time.

Development of a healthy child demands enough freedom to explore within the limits of the child's physical coordination. Teach your child how to manage stairs, but be beside him until you are certain of the ability to avoid falls. And be sure the stairs are enclosed on both sides to prevent a tumble off the edge. Allow your child to climb where it is safe, but make any area for which she is not ready off limits. Your ability to establish and maintain those limits is an absolute necessity in protecting your child.

Encourage your children to learn to swim, skate, ski, climb, hike, bicycle, and take part in sports. Every skill they can master adds to their confidence, broadens their social options, and can keep them from the boredom of idleness. Be involved and cheer them on in their pursuits.

The worst periods of my life were my children's first weeks of driving alone. I wanted to go with them, and I wanted to keep them at home. I dreaded their exposure to the traffic of the city. They all survived with only a rare fender bender, and so did I. I could no longer be there to personally protect them.

Nor could I go away to college with them and tell them how to live and select friends. I couldn't choose their spouses or dictate their lives. Letting go meant quitting my role as protector.

My adult daughter was a school psychologist, and occasionally, she had to visit the homes of students. Many times she told me of interrupting family fights by her visit or finding parents high on drugs. How I wanted her to come home and not be exposed to such dangers!

During these times, my faith comes into focus most comfortingly. I know I will not restrict my adult children's careers or limit their choices. But I know the Father who loves them so much more than I ever can will care for them. Even if harm comes, I know He will see us all through any eventuality. The ultimate protection lies in His hands.

TEACHER

Today I met with a middle-aged woman who is going through a divorce, has endured the slowly emptying nest, and is immeasurably sad. As we probed carefully into her tender areas, some interesting facts surfaced. She had grown up in a family where it was taught that everyone had to be happy. Ever-so-gentle but extremely painful words were rooted in this woman's very heart: "Now, Pam, you're not really angry with your sweet little sister! Tell her you're sorry you yelled at her. You know Jesus wouldn't like that!" Under the threat of her mother's disapproval and that of Jesus Christ Himself, Pam was powerless. She learned to deny her real and understandable feelings and to pretend a surface set of proper emotions, as defined by her mother.

Don't repeat this sort of mistake. Instead teach deep-down honesty and a solution-finding philosophy. Help your children learn how to be real so that the way they look, the way they talk, and the way they feel will all be congruent—they will match up.

The way you act becomes the blueprint. Your genuineness gives the basic permission to be honest to your family. And how kindly you can express your honesty makes it bearable and useful in their lives—another example of the importance of balance.

Your role as teacher involves lessons on each child's individuality, the environment in which they move, and the others whom they will encounter in their world. Help them find the balances in having self-esteem but not being ego-centered; being exuberant over their world but assuming responsibility for taking care of it; exhibiting friendliness to others but using caution regarding those who cannot be trusted.

DISCIPLINARIAN

A disciplinarian teaches right from wrong and some guidelines for discerning what makes any given act or thought right. To be effective, discipline must include establishing healthy controls, not denial as Pam above experienced but recognizing and staying in charge of one's feelings and impulses. Ultimately, each child must internalize the practices we have discussed as effective discipline.

Making such a process one's very own, believing and doing it, requires four techniques: (1) teaching and modeling clearly and consistently; (2) requiring compliance for a period of time; (3) relinquishing your authority gradually, and allowing children to explore on their own how to do it; and (4) monitoring and giving positive feedback on how they're doing with correction as needed.

Good discipline always explores a child's possibilities, expects the best she can do within her limits, and offers praise and appreciation for her efforts. It never condemns, labels, or destroys a child's self-respect or dignity. You don't need to do negative things to offer effective discipline. Give your child blessing, not cursing.

TAXI DRIVER

From the loftiness of philosophy, let's move to the practical functions you must perform. Taking children where they need to go makes you feel, many times, as if you're running a taxi service. From school in the morning through music lessons after school, and finally to and from Scouts at night, you are constantly on the move. Fighting traffic and meeting deadlines can wreck your peace of mind. Among all the scheduled activities there are the unexpected trips to the grocery store, library, and church.

Let me tell you a true story. My last child was involved in many activities, and her older brother was rarely around to help, so once again, I was a frequent taxi driver. She made our trips a great pleasure by deliberately using them as our sharing time. She would tell me many thoughts, feelings, and experiences, yet it seemed I could never hear enough. And she asked me to share some of my life with her. She never betrayed a confidence, and we became intimate friends on those many excursions.

When she turned sixteen, she was ready to obtain her driver's license, but she really never was pushy about it and even delayed getting it for a day or two. One day she stated, "Mom, I kind of wish I didn't have to drive myself now. I'm gonna really miss our times for talking in the car." That comment made it all worthwhile.

You can make the choice. You can take your children where they need to go but be resentful and grouchy; they'll grow up hardly able to wait to drive so they can get free of you. Or you can turn those times into the private joy of sharing with each other.

You can set some limits on how many trips you will make each day. It's easy to try too hard to please your child. By doing so, you can make a tyrant of him—one who controls your life and also tries to boss teachers and friends in ways that are downright obnoxious. Schedule with your child enough activities to enrich his life but not so many that both of you are overburdened. Balance your desire to provide for your child's needs with the reality of teaching her to think ahead and plan for items needed in school or for other aspects of life. Once in a while going without that new tablet or pencil for a day can teach a lesson in organizing and planning ahead.

If your children forget lunch or homework on a regular basis, you *really* need to avoid becoming a delivery woman. Children who know mom will always come to the rescue never need to grow up and become responsible for themselves. Think ahead. You can save a significant number of trips for your "taxi," and you can teach your children responsibility as well.

COMFORT AND GRIEF EXPERT

Not long ago I had lunch with a church staff member who was trained as a religious educator for children. She was gracious and intelligent, but one extremely important facet of childhood had eluded her attention. She had never thought about the many losses and grief experiences of children. She wanted to keep children stimulated, growing, learning, and happy. And all of these are vital concerns for children.

Yet many adults forget children's recurrent disappointments and hurts. When I lost my mother's approval as a child, I would find comfort in one of two places—with my soft, gentle collie or on that amazingly soft cover folded at the foot of Grandmother's bed. There, alone, I could cry, talk, or just be quiet. Grandma's coverlet was called a comforter, and so indeed it was.

Every mother needs to be like that comforter during children's pain—always available, soft, absorbent of tears, and usually quiet. While children are in acute pain, they need no lectures, no distractions, no reassurances of how great tomorrow will be. They need to be able to talk and be heard, to cry and find soft absorbency, to even yell or hit something and find a resilient shock absorber. It takes great strength to be that comforter.

After the acuteness of the grief is over, you may well offer a few words of caring and tell of a time when you, too, experienced pain and some ideas about ways to get out the strong emotions of grief.

Some losses children endure are small, but many are huge. All offer a significant opportunity to teach your child how to survive them and cope with grief. The most common losses are toys that break or are lost; friends who move away; less parental attention due to the arrival of a new brother or sister; the loss of certain freedoms and dependency when they are replaced by responsibilities (not a fair trade!); grandparents who die; the loss of a familiar environment when the family moves; the loss of a loved teacher when a child is promoted; the loss of friendship through a fight or misunderstanding; the loss of a child's whole world through a divorce; the loss of self-esteem through failure or excessive punishments; the loss of wishes and dreams when a young person can't make the groups for which he or she competes. In each case, the responses are the same, and the reassurance needed does not change.

Master those stages of grief—denial, anger, blame, pain and preoccupation, guilt and remorse. And when all of them are expressed, comfort is received, and healing is complete, joy can return. Your presence, caring, comfort, and quiet optimism will help your child survive the most tragic loss and find hope and courage for the next day and beyond.

Your comfort must also be balanced. Too much can teach your child to almost enjoy a dramatic grief episode. Too little can allow her to feel insignificant and abandoned. Look for the center of the road—warm caring, availability, suggestions for help, and enough privacy so your child can learn to cope on his own in due time.

MEDIATOR

I have a dear friend who is a negotiator in labor-management disputes. He is good because he stays clear-headed and impartial and listens extremely well. Many times a week, you need to fill this role. Your children will argue or even fight with one another. They will have squabbles with their playmates, and very often, they will disagree with you.

Years ago, the noted psychologist Haim Ginnott (author of many books on adult-child communications) lectured in my community. His philosophies were so wise I have used them many times. Sorry to say, his books are now out of print and difficult to find. One of his techniques applied to school-age children who were at odds. He suggested separating them and giving each a paper and pencil. Each was to pretend to be a lawyer and write out the case in point. Mother served as judge and staged a hearing, listening wisely and impartially to both arguments.

Usually, each child became tired of writing, decided the fight was not too important, and happily resumed playing. If the cause was really important, he would insist on staying with the task and completing the hearing. Mother could often tell by her child's attitude, therefore, who was really at fault. At any rate, the process gives both mother and children time to clarify and present issues and determine guilt and consequences.

Much more essential than determining guilt is having the opportunity to interpret the needs and feelings underlying various actions. When an older child can see, for example, that his little sister is bothering him because she craves his attention, he can feel complimented. If he fails to have Mom point this out, however, he may see his sister only as a bother who wants specifically to annoy him.

The balance in helping children settle disputes is crucial in avoiding sibling rivalry. Your approach can make it seem that you love everyone equally or that you favor one over the other. Be careful that both your love and your approval are equal for each child. Work to gain that deep understanding of every child's underlying needs and modes of expression. Then you can be like my friend Bob, the negotiator, restoring harmony in your home.

FASHION EXPERT AND SEAMSTRESS

When my older daughter went off to college, she and her roommate visited a campus clothing outfitter. They asked the manager for help, and he wisely focused their shopping with one question: "Which group do you belong to?" Being freshmen, they really didn't know about groups, and the man advised, "Wait till you look over the campus. Some dress one way, and others wouldn't be seen dead in such outfits. When you decide where you fit, come back. I'll have just the clothes for you!" I never saw that man, but I loved him for saving us money.

Not only do children's fashions need to fit somewhat with those of their friends, they also need to fit their physical makeup. The height, weight, and coloring of a young person have everything to do with styles and colors that are attractive and comfortable on them.

My older daughter is five one and tiny. My younger one is five seven and has very different proportions. When they were younger, Wendy wanted to copy the styles that were just right for her older sister. On her, they appeared grotesque. We both learned quickly what would be attractive on her, not just on the racks in stores.

Teaching children what colors go well with their eyes and hair, what styles suit them, and what colors can be mixed and matched is a challenge, and it can also be fun. It is easier, of course, if you start when they are young and trust your judgment. They will learn to like things that fit comfortably and accent their best features. They are more likely to receive compliments from friends, and when those reaffirm yours (and hopefully they will), you look all the more wise in your children's eyes.

If your child is older and resists your advice on a shopping trip, you can put your foot down and demand your choice or *no* new clothes at all, almost sure to build resentment and create rebellion. You can suggest looking or thinking further, and hope for a wise salesperson's help. Or you can allow what you consider a bad choice. Sometimes moms are mistaken, and the item may work out. If you were right, your child's friends will make that apparent by their comments. In such an instance you must avoid rescuing your child from her bad decision. Let the consequences teach her. Sympathize with her genuinely, suggest something she could do to salvage some use for it, but do *not* buy a replacement.

Expensive clothing has become a status symbol for young people, and I deplore that! Only a week ago I shopped with my twelve-year-old grandson. The name-brand sports shoes he really wanted cost $95. Even the ordinary ones were $50 to $60, and at most, he could wear them for several months.

One answer my husband and I discovered early on was to give each child a fixed clothing budget. It was as fair as we could make it and clearly defined. We began this in the early teen years, so they could shop, compare prices, and decide for themselves what they could afford. The plan saved countless arguments and taught them good economics.

All three of our children decided they could have more clothes if we made some of them, so I had the fun of helping design some really attractive garments. My son, who is nearly thirty-four years old, still wears a wardrobe of down-filled jackets and vests that I made when he was a teenager. I took pride in doing them, he saved a great deal of money, and the process was my way of saying, "Son, you are important to me, and I want to show you how much I love you by sewing this jacket for you." I might add, that was a *lot* of love because those projects were very complex.

My grandmother would darn socks with holes, restore torn blouses to nearly new, replace buttons from her stack of infinite types, and neatly mend ripped seams. So did my mother, and so did I! I hope my children will pass on these skills and the love they demonstrate to their children.

The balance for me has not been easy to achieve. I love to sew and design, while my children do not share that interest. It is easier for me to do those tasks than for them to master the skills. I hope you will do better than I. Teach your sons and your daughters the basic sewing and mending skills by not doing so much for them.

SOCIAL COORDINATOR

From your first child's first birthday party to your golden wedding celebration, one of your jobs is to plan parties. Balance in this area is indeed vital. It can be tempting to overlook certain events due to fatigue or lack of knowing how to organize and complete such an event. Or you may make even the smallest celebration so elaborate that it wears you out. Find your best balance by keeping entertaining simple but enjoyable.

For that first birthday, the fun lies in the photographs of a child smeared with frosting and a cake with fingerholes poked throughout. Invite a few relatives and friends without too many other children, take the photos, and send everybody home so you can clean up the mess! Later on, by age three or four and thereafter, a few of your child's good friends and their mothers can create a memory and make a birthday tradition to last.

By age seven or eight, a child may invite a friend to spend the night. I recommend that you help your child plan these events. Screen the friends carefully. Before bedtime, I had to return more than one frightened, homesick child who was not ready to be away from parents. Plan the snacks and food so your home will not get beyond repair, and be prepared to supervise games and work out arguments.

Even nine- or ten-year-old children tend to sneak friends of the opposite sex into slumber parties, and I strongly recommend you do not allow that. Girls need time with one another to giggle, talk, and play. And boys seem to relish group events with just fellows. They need to fully identify with their own sex before they're ready for too many activities with the opposite sex. I resent the kids' organizations that have moved to coed status in early elementary school. There is much confusion at that time regarding sexual role definition. Having many social activities geared to just boys or just girls can clarify some of that uncertainty.

Special holidays are made to be fun social events. If you have friends of another religion, invite them to share your religious holidays. If they return that hospitality, take advantage of that. I have been profoundly inspired in lovely ways by sharing Passover with Jewish friends.

Balance parties with special family events, going out to eat with preparing special meals at home, and having large groups with inviting only a few close friends. Allow your children to attend parties elsewhere, but be certain you know where they are and how they will be conducted. I consider many teenage events unwise and even seriously risky. Large "keg" parties where alcoholic beverages are available are all too common. Parents with the best of intentions can be outnumbered and lose control of these events. And some parents won't even stay on the premises.

I urge you to unite with other parents. Many share the concern of keeping teen activities wholesome and harmless. Before the teens are lost forever, organize parties with fun games and a safe environment. Be creative, energetic, and positive. Many young people are ready to learn how to enjoy healthy fun, but they need someone to show them how.

Teach social skills to your child. Playing tennis, swimming, skating, and skiing are examples of physical skills that can offer activity sharing with friends in a structured and safe setting. But balance the need for friends with the value of family time and opportunities to be alone and discover oneself. In the exciting developments of the teen years, your child may become too adult too soon. Once he enters into adult activities, it is difficult or impossible to return to the world of adolescence.

A divorced couple wanted to give their son a memorable sixteenth birthday party. He had not been doing well in school and was on the verge of serious rebellion. But they believed he would appreciate the occasion and really would "straighten out" after he turned sixteen. The parents rented some rooms in a hotel with access to the pool and recreational facilities. Both food and alcoholic beverages were unlimited because the parents were there to chaperone.

At midnight, the father left to return in an elegant convertible. Ceremoniously, he gave the keys to his son. What an exciting and enviable event! But the following week, the son and a convertible full of his friends skipped school. He received a ticket for speeding and narrowly escaped an accident. His father wondered why.

If you don't teach social responsibility to your kids, who will? Will it be the police, a judge, or our justice system? Please, let it be you!

VOLUNTEER COORDINATOR

On my bedroom mantel is a framed piece of white velvet. On that velvet, my daughter carefully pinned my medals. There are several nice ones, but I cherish most those I earned by serving as Scout den mother and Camp Fire leader. I also taught Sunday school classes for many years, and I even worked one hectic week as a counselor at a youth camp.

I chose those volunteer activities because I believed in the values those organizations stood for and because of the opportunities I found to be with my children and their friends. We did many activities that were fun, learned some meaningful rituals, and cemented some lifelong friendships. I wish I could have served even more time, but over fifteen years probably were enough.

Countless needs in every community are best served by volunteers—people who care enough to *give* themselves and demonstrate a special definition of love. Children often have too little quality time with an adult, so I hope you will find some avenue through which to give to them. Teach them about heroes, about values, about nature, and about giving themselves. Include your children, and they, too, will learn the value of giving. When one is blessed, she has an attendant responsibility to bless others.

Volunteer work can, in its own right, become too demanding, leaving you drained of time and energy for yourself and your family. Keep the balance. Give *only* what you can afford to give; take care of yourself and your family because no one else will do that. Then give as freely as you like of whatever is left over. Living within balances is a comfortable lifestyle.

STUDY HALL SUPERVISOR

I have already written about the importance of learning. You have a vital part in communicating that value to your children. Review the establishment of a studious environment. Remove distractions, make lighting convenient, have supplies available, and above all, be there and be free to help. Most children need encouragement. Almost all of them need you to give spelling words, drill them with metric flash cards, and quiz them on history and science.

Keep your mind active and growing. As you discuss new concepts or ideas you have discovered through reading or thinking, you will inevitably enhance your child's interest and motivation to learn.

Above all, never ask your child if she has homework. You are the one who knows she does. He can never learn all he needs to know in any class time. Instill the love of learning in your child, and he will learn all of his life.

VALUES CLARIFIER

In today's society, no one is doing much teaching of values. The schools fear trying to do so because of the vast differences in families' beliefs. Many children never attend church, and most parents seem to have forgotten that they need to teach values.

A young friend came to me in tears. She had made plans for a fun activity with a friend. She needed a break from her child and house and was eagerly anticipating an outing. On the morning of the event, her friend called and blithely canceled their plans. She preferred to do something else that had just occurred to her. My friend felt rejected; she was hurt and angry. She knew her friend would call her the next time she needed a favor, but she was insensitive to the needs of another.

When my children were small, I passed along the value of fairness and integrity. When you make a plan with a friend, that plan comes first. No matter what opportunity knocks later, the first commitment stands. That policy prevented a lot of trouble and hurt feelings.

Seeing the far-reaching impact of policies and the values they teach can help you lay good foundations. But begin today if you missed the earlier opportunity. First, think about the values you hold most dear. Honesty, kindness, tolerance, compassion, humor, generosity, adventure, spirituality, excellence in work, relaxation, beauty—these are just a beginning.

Next, look at yourself. Do you live these values? Which ones would come first if you prioritized them? How can you demonstrate them even more convincingly in your life? And how can you teach them to your children?

During the years of the depression, there were many homeless people. Men would leave home to look for jobs and would walk the country roads, hoping a farmer might need their help. They were dirty, desperate, defeated men. Often they came by our house and asked for food. They found the right house because my mother could always provide them with a plateful. She would give them a washbasin to wash their hands and faces, good food, and a prayer for their needs. Her example taught me compassion, generosity, kindness, respect for the down-and-out, and spiritual values.

Talk about your values only when your lifestyle demonstrates them. Tolerance for people of other faiths became real to me when Mother invited the Jewish apple peddler, who regularly visited our home, to dinner. We understood he didn't eat pork and respected his preference.

COMPTROLLER

Families vary in their task assignments, and few issues are as controversial as money management in regard to who assumes responsibility. Frankly, it seems to me that money is everybody's business. Unless you have an unlimited supply, you need to understand how to handle money, and you need to teach this skill to your children.

The basic philosophy about taking care of the economics of your family is simple. The demands must not exceed the supply. How do you achieve such a simple balance?

The best word I can think of to describe good communication is openness.

Be very clear about your total income. Never assume that a raise will be coming or that you will get an income tax refund. When those good fortunes happen, you can easily cope with them.

Be equally clear about all of your regular expenses. The biggest mistake in this category is forgetting the large bills that come due once a year, such as house and car insurance. Be certain you know them all.

Allow some flexibility for unexpected costs. Replacing an appliance or repairing a leaking roof can be costly.

Avoid using credit cards when at all possible. The interest you pay on them could startle you. The only way they are useful to you is when you can pay them completely every month so interest does not accumulate.

Now match your regular expenditures with your income. I hope that you have enough to save some, spend a bit on fun and foolishness, or expand an area of your budget that is too cramped.

You may need to reduce your lifestyle at times. As extra expenses arise that you must meet, you can often curtail a clothing budget, give up eating out for a while, and cut down your food budget a bit. The poverty-level families in our communities may go without meat for a while and rarely enjoy the luxuries many of us consider necessary. Be prepared to live now and then as if you, too, were on a poverty-income level.

Yesterday I met with a friend and his pastor. They were concerned over a growing number of parishioners who recently lost jobs and income. The blow to the pride of these men, in an affluent community, could not be measured. And the constricted budgets created problems for not only the families but the entire church.

I urge you to prepare for an economic emergency such as these families are enduring. Rather than spend the extra money from a raise or a bonus, save it. Make yourself regularly put even small amounts of money into a secure spot. Learn different skills. If you or your husband should lose a job, do you have a basis for finding a new one in a different occupation? Read about the job market and where there may be an emerging possibility for your skills to be put to work.

Learn to sew and garden. Raising some of your own vegetables can be fun, offers a project for your family to share, and really helps your food budget.

I believe in giving children allowances. Our country has enjoyed unusual prosperity for four or five decades with fairly minor setbacks. Most children have grown up receiving the majority of the things they ask for and many things they haven't even thought about asking for. Because such prosperity is unlikely to last forever, children need to learn money management just as adults do. An allowance is a made-to-order tool for teaching kids.

Start with a five-year-old, perhaps, with fifty cents a week. Teach him to give 10 percent to church—only a nickel, but it's his very own. Next I recommend that she put 10 percent in a piggy bank. She will need a pencil or tablet for school. The tablet will take several weeks' allowance, but she could buy her own pencil. She may want some sugarless gum, so her own money may buy that. You see, you are teaching your children generosity, saving, responsibility, and enjoyment. He will keep track of his pencil if he pays for it out of his own pocket, too.

As a child grows and evidences the ability to be responsible with money, you can enlarge the allowance. But with that, you must remember to also enlarge the areas in which he is to be responsible for spending it. Allowances are not all for pleasure. They are for learning that original principle of supply and demand. If your child overspends, don't rescue him. If she spends all of it the first day, she must wait for the next "payday." Don't let them start borrowing unless you want to teach them about bankruptcy. And don't be late in giving the allowance.

An allowance, in its best function, is not pay for helping the family. Family members help one another out of love and respect. There are times, however, when a child may need to earn extra money. He may want an item that is okay to have but beyond the limits of his allowance. If you can, I recommend you keep a list of extra-tough jobs he may do to earn money. Be sure you do not overpay or underpay. Make certain the job gets done well, and add your commendation to the pay when it's done. Someday, your child's spouse will love you for teaching the way to balance a budget.

THE "BOSS"

Many children reach school without ever dealing effectively with authority. They wheedle or bully their way with their parents and try the same tactics with teachers. You are doing everyone a huge favor by teaching your child you are in charge. There is no license for a mother to be a dictator, controlling or dominating her child. But when a child is out of control, unable to choose wisely or exert sufficient willpower to learn responsibility, your job is to help him or her do that. You may use different discipline methods, but just know how essential your authority is. Your child will respect and love you all the more when you master the skill of requiring compliance. You will feel confident, and your family will be enjoyable.

ANIMAL TRAINER

Growing up on a farm, I knew the value of pets. Not only was my dog my comforter, but a pet chicken, a lamb, and even a calf became fun for my sisters and me. Many parents obtain pets in the erroneous belief that they will teach their kids to be responsible. Nothing could be further from the truth! You are the one responsible for pets, like it or not. Once that truth is established, I will agree that pets can teach children many things, especially love and loyalty.

Last week a family who are friends of mine came nearly to blows about the cat and the dog who make messes regularly in their house.

Each is waiting on the other to "do something about it." You must train your pet, delegate the job, or live in a smelly, ugly house. Animals were created to live outside, to hunt and forage for food, to scratch and cover their feces, and to fend for themselves. If you expect them to live in a house, you must go against all of their natural instincts and train them in what you want them to do. In training a pet, you can also learn some basic principles about training children. These include consistency, rewards and consequences, love and follow-through.

After your pet is trained, you can train your children to care for it. Children can provide food and water as well as exercise. They can stroke and hug the pet and even groom it if they are taught. If you want your child to become responsible for a pet's care, you must avoid reminding him. Instead, establish a plan with consequences. Unless the dog is fed, you do not have dinner. If you failed to clean the litter box, you must clean up the mess on the floor. And your child's activities stop until those jobs are done. Reminding becomes nagging, and nagging creates resistance, not cooperation.

Enjoy your pet, but remember that it will often be a nuisance and a problem. If you can cope with that fact with some equanimity, you are a great mom!

In all of your roles and responsibilities, you have burdens and opportunities, challenges and privileges. As you understand what these are, you can shoulder them effectively. But always look for both extremes—too much, too little; too early, too late; too angry, too patient; expecting too much or too little; being too strict or too lenient. To find the balance, you must explore those extremes, and in doing so you will make many mistakes. That's okay. As long as you are in love with your children, they will know you are doing your best, and they will gladly forgive your mistakes.

Chapter

2

Dad's Kid Goes to School

What is a Daddy? Daddy is the guide and wagon scout for his child on the trail through life—first for his preschooler, then when his child goes to school. Just like the wagon scout on the Oregon Trail who used his expert knowledge of weather, Indians, water holes, and campsites—and to which whole families entrusted their lives, their fortunes, and their futures—your grade schooler still looks to you as the Daddy-who-knows-all. In this chapter from The Father Book, *you'll also meet Daddy the Great Protector, Daddy the Skills-Enabler, Daddy the Great Encourager, and even the dreaded Daddy the Competitor. Watch Carl Jefferson (who sells mud) and his fathering technique in this chapter—but BEWARE the parenting style of Arnold the swooping eagle who sits high on his perch with his head in the clouds only to swoop down in a great flurry if something looks wrong or he gets annoyed (usually by something his son Miles has done).*

Dr. Frank Minirth
Dr. Brian Newman
Dr. Paul Warren
The Father Book

Carl Jefferson sold mud.

"It's a dirty job, but somebody's gotta do it," he loved to say, of course.

Jefferson Mud was his one-man company's name. Carl's mud was expensive, as dirt goes. It was the specially formulated flux that petroleum drillers pump down oil wells. Carl traveled widely, prowled well sites, hobnobbed with roughnecks, and bandied about such arcane terms as fishtails, kellies, cuttings, and monkey boards. He was occasionally called as a consultant to oil fields in Australia, South America, and Asia. For a guy who grew up making mud pies, his was a wonderful life.

His wife, Ivy, sold weeds.

Weeds and Ivy, she called her sole proprietorship. She provided dried plant materials such as teasel and pearly everlasting to florists and others who used them in arrangements, decorations, and parade floats. She maintained a stock of over two hundred varieties, nearly a hundred of which she raised herself. For a kid who picked dandelion bouquets for Mom, hers was a wonderful life.

Their girls, Cathy, four, and Janey, eight, were just precious. Everybody said so, and Carl was proud as a peacock. A local college student baby-sat part-time, permitting Ivy and Carl a lot of freedom and flexibility. Carl and Ivy Jefferson had it made.

Well, not exactly. They used to have it made, until Ivy was stricken by peritonitis. She spent over nine weeks in the hospital, at a time when Carl's business particularly demanded his attention. The college student could help, but not nearly enough. Carl had to quit traveling. He had to give up a lot of his field work, and with it went a lot of his income.

Carl chafed. His was not the only mud in the world, and with the petroleum industry in a major slump, he had to hustle if he were to stave off the competition and make a buck. But here he sat around the house, coloring pictures with the preschool Cathy and waiting for Janey to walk in the door from second grade. And Ivy so sick . . . Life had turned gray.

Here Janey came up the sidewalk. She slammed the front door. Carl had pulled her fine, dark hair up into a neat ponytail this morning. Now the ponytail hung in disarray, with flyaway wispies sticking out all over. Her clothes were a disaster too—a big smudge on her shirt, grass stains, and a rip in the knees of her jeans. Another successful day at school, obviously.

"Is Mommy home yet?"

"Not yet, Sugar. Next week maybe." Carl gave her a hug and thought about all the mud he could be selling now.

She clung, so he clung. "Promise you won't get mad at me, Daddy?"

"What kind of question is that? Okay. I promise."

"Don't get mad at me for saying this, okay? I'm sorry Mommy's sick. I don't mean I like Mommy being sick. But I'm glad you're home. It's so great! This is the best time I ever had in my life."

THE NEW CHILD OF THE WORLD

Janey Jefferson wasn't overstating anything. Certainly she loved her daddy, but it was more than that. By having her daddy home, she literally had her wagon guide waiting in the house for her as she returned from the outside world. His role as scout was not diminishing in the least.

A few years ago, he had colored with Janey as he was coloring with Cathy now. They drew pictures and crayoned in coloring books, talking about the flowers and animals and scenes, discussing dreams, and telling stories. Through that seemingly inane process, Carl was actually introducing Janey to the world beyond the front door. When she went off to kindergarten she entered that world. For several hours a day she was not with Mommy; she was not with Daddy; she was not with Melody, the baby-sitter.

She came under the discipline and guidance of a total stranger who became another god in her life, Mrs. Bromley, her teacher. Then Mr. Matthews in first grade. And now Mrs. Stitt in second. People not related to the family. People carrying just as much authority as her parents. When you think about it, these were giant steps for Janey.

The preschooler is curious about the outside world; the grade schooler is beginning to actually experience it. In between lies an important transition stage: The kindergartner learns and prepares to do things away from home.

My, How the Child Has Grown!

How specifically does a grade schooler differ from the preschooler? Were Carl to compare his Cathy with his Janey, he'd see these differences:

Preschooler	Grade Schooler
Activity is random; movement and play may seem without purpose to adults.	Purposeful activity; play a game, do something, build, explore.
Play symbolic; play items can be symbols (a stick for a person, Playskool people; a block may represent an iron).	Play becomes increasingly realistic; play items must look like what they represent (Tonka Toys, mini animals, Lego and Lincoln Logs, Barbie dolls).
Playmates optional. Child plays in company of other children but often independently.	Playmates very important; "best friends." Group games and activities flourish.
Play is fairly selfish; not much cooperation or competition.	Play, even when cooperative, is highly competitive. Child constantly compares self to others.
Child needs Mommy and Daddy's approval.	Child needs approval of peers, of parents, of other adults. Achievement and recognition immensely important.

Carl would probably respond to these differences instinctively, as do you. It pays, though, to understand the way a child is changing, the better to communicate and guide.

As his little one becomes a child of the world, Daddy's role shifts considerably. Mommy has a special place. But even when he's filling Mommy's role, as Carl did temporarily, Daddy has a special place that is not Mommy's. He will, as before, model maleness. He will, as before, serve as protector and skills-enabler. He will, as before, encourage and affirm. But he'll do all this in new dimensions.

THE GREAT PROTECTOR

At this age, protecting and skills-enabling go hand in hand. Even as Dad the protector encourages his little one to make friends and play sports and games, he will supervise. His supervision may be obvious and direct, as when he becomes a Scout leader, a coach, a Sunday school teacher. It may be surreptitious and indirect, as when he simply looks up from his work now and then to make sure the kids aren't drawing blood.

For hours of each day, Mom and Dad have no supervision over

their children. The school assumes part of that responsibility. And frankly, Dad the protector will keep an eye on the school. When something blows up between his kid and the teacher, he will monitor. He will make himself the child's backup support, but not the child's alibi.

The swooping eagle tends to respond badly in those situations of discord between child and school. For example, when Miles was in the fourth grade, he and two buddies were found out in a certain matter concerning a stink bomb. In his school, a stink bomb automatically bought you a three-day suspension, no ifs, ands, or buts, and a five-percent grade reduction.

Arnold swooped down on the school, going from teacher through principal to superintendent to get his kid off the hook. He pulled every string he could grab. When he got home, he swooped on Miles as well, with a spanking, a grounding, and a loss of privileges.

Arnold, typical of swooping eagles, did not let cause and effect play out. As a result, his son Miles lost the opportunity to learn a valuable lesson in personal responsibility. Arnold had only to hold Miles accountable, and the lesson would have been made effectively.

The swooping eagle, because he is not well-connected with his children, tends to stick bandages on problems; it's all he knows to do. Too, appearance means much. The eagle is very concerned about whether the child is making him look good. He is desperate to fix it before someone notices it was broken, be "it" his reputation as a father or the light in which his child has cast the family. The eagle does not know his child well enough to be concerned about whether the child is internalizing the necessary lessons of life.

Thus, the eagle works hard to avert the school's penalty, lest his child's infraction be made glaringly public and he himself be cast in a dubious light. Then, because he is humiliated and angry, the eagle will probably turn around and overdo the punishment. Not only does the child lose out on the lesson of natural cause and effect, he or she is subjected to a more severe discipline than the case warrants. That's not good protection, for it does not prepare the child for the future.

How could the eagle use the incident to better value?

"The penalty, smart boy, is suspension and grade slash. You knew that. You broke the rule and tried to pull a funny anyway. Now you can suffer the consequences."

Action. Consequence. That the kid understands.

Increasingly now as the grade schooler goes out and about, he or she spends blocks of time essentially unsupervised. And that is as it should be. The child is becoming more independent. The child wanders farther afield, secure in the knowledge that home is still the haven, still available.

If Dad is to protect this increasingly independent little person, he must help his child internalize the protection, just as an internalized conscience works when external guidance is absent. What should the child do, exactly, if a stranger approaches or tries to entice him or her into a car? No theory, here. The child is not yet into blotting up theory and putting it into practice when needed. He or she needs exact, clear courses of action. Dad should rehearse the child through specific actions.

These true incidents were taken from the police blotter of a major western city over a three-month period. We do not include them here to scare you or point a finger of blame should your child be victimized. We believe they offer some interesting and useful instruction.

· **On a weekday after school:** A boy, seven, was crossing a parking lot on the way home from school. A man in his forties snatched the boy up and carried him quickly toward a car. The boy began instantly to scream and flail. The man told an approaching teen male that this was his son, about to be punished for disobeying. The child fought harder and begged help. Wisely, the teen intervened. The man dropped the child, bolted to his car, and drove away.

The boy's father had taught him to make a noise if any person frightened him—the louder and more boisterous the ruckus, the better.

· **On a Saturday afternoon:** A man claimed to have lost a puppy in a dense woodlot near the home of a boy, also seven. The child followed him into the thickets to help locate the dog. Under the cover of the woods, he mutilated and sodomized the boy and left him to wander out on his own.

The child had been told, "never talk to strangers," but because of the puppy angle, he thought this was different. He had never play-acted a safety lesson.

· **On the way to school:** About eight A.M., two men in their twenties stopped a car beside a thirteen-year-old girl and asked directions. When she turned away from them they made lewd and obscene requests. She dropped her books and ran back home. The mother called the police immediately, and the girl was able to provide enough description that the young men were apprehended twenty minutes later. They were held on previous charges.

Mom and Dad had both impressed safety rules upon her.

· **During an early morning house fire:** A boy, twelve, led his three younger siblings to safety by crawling the length of a hall on hands and knees with the youngest riding piggyback. They gathered at a prearranged place of safety. Their parents barely escaped from a second-floor window.

Dad had led the family in rehearsed fire drills.

· **Early morning while the mother and an uncle still slept:** Playing with a butane lighter, a girl, three, accidentally set fire to a living room chair. When the blaze spread, she and her sister, four, hid in a closet. Both died of smoke inhalation.

What else can be said?

· **In a wooded county park:** A boy, nine, playing near his family's campsite, became disoriented and wandered away. He sat down on a stump and was found two hours later. (Police were involved from the outset because of foul play in the area a few days earlier. The parents, however, made the find.)

The child had received his school district's "hug a tree" training. His father reinforced the lessons with play-acting at home. The boy was embarrassed by the childish play-acting, but participated.

In that same city within a span of three years, grade school-aged children won heroism medals for rescuing playmates, for resisting persons with alleged criminal intent, and in the case of one eleven-year-old, for performing resuscitation on a near-drowning victim. (The child had tagged along with Dad, a volunteer fire fighter, to Dad's annual CPR recertification course, picking up enough knowledge to be able to assist the person's breathing.)

Certainly, we know that not every incident is going to have a happy ending simply because the child was instructed on what to do. Tragedy happens despite the best teaching, for even with all the training in the world, children are still essentially helpless, totally vulnerable. And a good many well-trained children will never encounter a situation in which such training is needed. Still, by exercising his role as protector, Dad can raise the chances that, should his child encounter difficulties when he or she is outside of Dad's supervision, that child will be able to act wisely in a positive manner.

Some Things To Do With Your Child

Talk about these generalized situations and play-act various actions and responses. Talk about responses. Talk about the child's capabilities and strong points (speed, agility) and short points (lack of strength, size).

Are you going to unnecessarily terrify your kid? Not as much now as if the child were still a preschooler. Preschoolers' imaginations, untrammeled by reality, are likely to build wrong pictures. By grade school, kids have a more accurate understanding of the world. Their imaginations are more disciplined because they have a broader base of factual knowledge with which to build mental pictures. Kids today know that evil lurks out there.

Talk with your child about:

1. Getting lost. In rural situations (forests, campgrounds, fishing lakes), teach kids to stop as soon as they think they're lost. Wait. Hug a tree. Don't panic. Yell now and then. Let Mom and Dad come to them. In town, such as in a mall or store, review how to identify salespersons and uniformed public safety officers (police, fire, etc.). As in the woods, kids lost in malls should not go wandering.

2. Being accosted by a stranger. Teach kids to run. Observe. Kick and scream if grabbed. Cause a scene, a ruckus, and if the stranger threatens, yell louder. Kids have a strong sense of fair play now. They think if an adult says something it's true—that if the adult makes a promise ("Be quiet or I'll hurt you!") they mean it. They might. But they're so big and strong they don't have to. One of the best forms of protection a father can convey is to help the child understand that a threatening adult is going to do what he or she wants regardless of the child's actions.

3. Being approached by someone known. By talking about it, help the kids know what's acceptable and what's private. Too, teach them to never keep secrets except for happy ones, such as birthday surprises, no matter what the person says.

4. Fire. Practice leaving the house from any room. Have regular fire exit drills. Teach them the safest moves; to stay low, to check doors for heat before opening them. Identify a safe place away from the house where everyone is to gather as soon as they get out, and stress that they shouldn't go back in for any reason. Teach them how to call the fire department from a neighbor's phone.

5. Health emergencies. Every grade schooler should know how to summon help—aid units, fire department, ambulance. Visit the fire house or emergency room and know what goes on there. Get a CPR (cardiopulmonary resuscitation) card yourself and take your grade schoolers along. They might even pick up good pointers from a first aid class.

6. On the road. You and your child take the bike apart and put it back together, so the child can perform minor repairs, such as untangling a fouled chain. Practice reading street signs and maps. At the airport, even a six-year-old can learn to read arrival and departure monitors.

Ask the father hovering protectively over his children if he would ever fight his grade school-aged kid, and he'd exclaim, "Never!" But in a subtle way, some fathers may do just that. Encouragement and competition are poles apart in their effects, yet they arise in similar circumstances. The good father encourages.

Were you to ask Arnold if he competed with his son, he'd bluster, "Me? Compete with Miles? He's a kid, for crying out loud!" Loosely translated, that response would mean, "Of course not." And yet, in a subtle way, Arnold did that throughout Miles's childhood. And Miles subconsciously picked up on it.

THE GREAT ENCOURAGER/COMPETITOR

Encouragement and competition both start out the same. The child is reaching out into new dimensions, learning new things, suffering new pains, and experiencing new joys. Ideally, his wagon scout walks beside him, guiding and instructing. One form of encouragement is to help children fulfil their need to achieve.

Feeding the Child's Need to Achieve

This need to achieve, and to be recognized for the achievement, is a major milestone in a grade schooler's development. Achievement and winning help the child define who he or she is, what he or she can do, where the limits are. All are important lessons learned now or probably not at all. Personal achievement is, to use the technical term, a step in individuation.

You'll recall dad is the main font of socialization and individuation. Dad can advance the need to achieve a great deal by encouraging with words and actions.

"That's a great birdhouse you made."

"Great play in left field, kid!" with a side-to-side hug.

"You're coming along all right with your trumpet lessons."

"I watched you tooling around the corner on your bike. You can really handle that thing."

"Thanks for being polite to your sister when she was behaving badly toward you. I appreciate that."

"I appreciate you."

Occasionally the achievements are weighty; usually they are not. No matter. The child must receive recognition for something. The child need not display athletic prowess, or musical genius, or diplomatic savvy. The child need only be affirmed for efforts and for whatever degree of accomplishment is earned.

Arnold snorted. "So what should I have done when Miles screwed up? Lie to him? Praise incompetence? That kid can turn a simple job into a Pentagon nightmare."

The answer to that: constructive criticism. What are the differences between constructive and nonconstructive?

Constructive criticism praises a job and tactfully suggests ways to make a good thing better. Nonconstructive—which is a polite way of saying destructive—criticism cuts the job down. Constructive criticism identifies first the achievement and second whatever the problem is. Constructive criticism then gently suggests a possible solution to the problem. Nonconstructive criticism blurts out, "You did it wrong." Translation: *You failed again.*

Constructive criticism is actually a part of encouragement because it validates that the child has achieved. With constructive criticism, Dad makes the point that he recognizes the child's efforts.

Carl mowed the lawn as, ahead of him, Janey and Cathy picked up sticks and chased the garter snakes. Carl then raked those areas of the lawn where the mower left thick rows of clippings. He asked Janey to gather the raked piles of clippings and dump them in the compost bin while he made lunch.

She did so, but a ring of loose grass clumps marked where each of the piles had been. It was, by adult measure, a sloppy job. Carl praised the several aspects of her work. No sticks left when he went through, and no chopped snakes. Good job there. She dumped quite a big heap into the compost pile; look at all that grass she moved! "Let's see if we can add even more to the heap." Eagerly, Janey went through again, cleaning up the rings of clumps to dump still more grass into the bin. Only then did Carl praise the neat, clean yard.

He had recognized her achievements, and then had called upon her emergent sense of competition to improve her work. When the yard was properly clean, he praised that performance too.

A few simple twists of meaning, a few words placed in a different sequence, make all the difference to children. They hear literally. They do not hear pride if it's not spoken. They do not hear praise if it's not bestowed. When delivering praise and criticism, never for a minute believe that your child understands your true feelings. You have to express them. Nicely.

If that is so, why don't kids hear unspoken sentiments of praise and admiration? Because of that competitiveness. Too, kids are naturally self-deprecating. They are constantly thinking the worst of themselves, in part because their little-kid reality does not match the larger-than-life nonreality of adults and fictional heroes. It isn't hard to undermine a child's sense of worth and achievement.

Undercutting the Child's Sense of Achievement

Destructive criticism? "What you did is not good enough." With that voiced message comes the unspoken message, "You can't do it as well as I can." Competitive.

"You're never going to amount to anything. You're lazy." The nonverbal meaning: "You'll never be as good as I am. I get to point out that you're lazy because I'm not."

Dad can encourage his child profoundly by taking part in the child's hobbies.

Again, there's that sense of competition. When Dad says that sort of thing he's not meaning to compete with his little kid; neither is he realizing how the messages are being absorbed. The child is preoccupied with competitiveness anyway. He or she will hear everything said in that light.

As he was growing, Miles never managed to be a complete success in his father's eyes, no matter what he did. The paint job on his airplane model was sloppy; a decal crooked. No matter that he was eight when he built it. His father never failed to point out the flaws.

For Miles's own good, of course. You can't do better if you don't hear that you need to do better, right?

"You're not as good as your sister."

"Why can't you be more like your brother?"

More competition. Damaging competition.

Much about competition is good at this age. In fact, certain competition is necessary and excellent. Comparisons of the above sort are not.

"Words are so very powerful!" claims Frank Minirth. "We find time and again that the father is the most accurate prophet of what the children are going to be. When he says, 'You're never going to make it. You're a bumbler; you always mess up' and that kind of thing, sure enough, that usually comes true."

Even the father saying those things doesn't want to give his child that heritage any more than you do.

Conversely, when Dad inspires a "can do" spirit through his words and actions, that comes true as well.

Encouraging Through Deeds

Kids hear words, but just as effectively, they hear actions. Fathers encourage their new children of the world by their presence, their interest, and their involvement in their children's lives. Actions are like those motivational and self-improvement tapes you sometimes hear about, with subliminal messages laced in here and there. In theory, the mind picks up the messages even though the eyes and ears do not. Similarly, the minds of neither father nor child realize what Dad says with his actions, but the messages register all the same.

Share Hobbies

To an adult, hobbies are recreation. Fluff stuff. To a child, hobbies are work just as important and consuming as school or anything else.

Dad can encourage his child profoundly by taking part in the child's hobbies. Sharing in that way is actually very important at this age, this being the age of achievement. Building a model, collecting baseball cards, running Matchbox cars, shooting off rockets—what is your kid into?

To Carl's chagrin, Janey is into ballet. Carl in a tutu? Not in a million years. But he encourages in other ways. While she practices at the barre, he notices and praises. Daddy's rock-solid hand holds hers, helping her balance as she masters tours and arabesques. His attendance at recitals hasn't been perfect, but he tries.

Carl's involvement, even at the most casual level, builds Janey's self-esteem incredibly. His participation says, "You are special. God made you. I like you and the way God made you, and I like being with you as we pursue this hobby." If Carl is particularly astute, he will voice all that verbally as well, and not just once. Janey will profit immeasurably by hearing the spoken message as well as the actions.

While we're talking here about grade school, children of any age benefit from Dad's participation, although as children grow and relate more and more to the world outside the family, Dad's part even in hobbies diminishes.

Things to Think About

When I was a kid I was interested in these hobbies and sports (not just the usual—model building, softball, collecting—but the not-so-usual such as running a trapline in the woods behind the property, volunteering at the arboretum . . .):

1. ______________________________

2. ______________________________

3. ______________________________

These interests shaped my adulthood in these ways (yes or no):

____ I am in a line of work related to one or more childhood interests.

____ I now pursue a hobby or hobbies related to those of my childhood.

____ I married a spouse whose interests reflect my own childhood pursuits.

____ I find myself encouraging my child to pursue sports or hobbies that were prominent in my own childhood.

____ Other ______________________________

____

My own child has these interests that I know of:

1. ________________________________

2. ________________________________

3. ________________________________

I can encourage those interests in these specific ways (actual participation; observation such as at recitals, games; verbal and financial encouragement):

1. ________________________________

2. ________________________________

3. ________________________________

Share Activities

Says Brian Newman, "I can't overemphasize the value of men being involved in kids' activities at this age. I don't mean just hobby interests but the broader activities: Sunday school, Scouting, sport coaching. It's not so much what the father does as a Scout leader or whatever, but that he participates as a father. And you don't have to be the area president, or be the best there is, or make everyone go 'gee whiz' about how good you are. Be there. Help. That's the important part."

Paul Warren agrees heartily. "But there's a caveat. I meet a lot of dads who participate in Scout troops, for instance, who are driving their kids crazy. Accomplish, accomplish, accomplish. Their involvement is actually for the fathers themselves; they are trying to reap benefits. Involvement is important; your kid making Eagle Scout is not."

Involvement, both men emphasize, means Dad's presence. At the soccer game, at the school play, Dad is there.

DEEDS OF TRUST

After several weeks of being both Mom and Dad to his girls, Carl Jefferson received the help of a neighbor, Jean Maxwell. Jean's girls were in the fourth and sixth grades. Jean took Carl's girls in during those times when he was out of town. What a godsend! Now Carl could get out on his business trips again. Carl was back to selling mud, and he loved it, not that he didn't love being full-time Daddy.

He thought the arrangement was great. But the moment he returned from his first out-of-town trip, waved good-bye to the Maxwells, and loaded the girls into the car, Janey exploded. "Daddy, don't make us stay there! Mrs. Maxwell isn't fair!"

"Make sure your seatbelt's snug. Why isn't she?" Carl pulled out onto the beltway.

"Her kids get to stay up 'til ten, and I hafta be in bed at nine. And she made Cathy go to bed at eight! Clear in bed! No story or anything!"

"Cathy's supposed to be in bed then, and you need your sleep."

"But her kids get to stay up."

"They're older."

"It's not fair! She says we're like her own kids to her. So she should treat us alike."

Children in grade school suddenly develop an intense sense of fair play.

It's No Fair!

The theme song of the grade schooler. Children in grade school suddenly develop an intense sense of fair play. They can tell if one kid gets thirty seconds more attention than another, and they don't need a stopwatch to see it. They know if one kid is served seven lima beans and the other child only has to eat six. "Johnny down the street gets to watch scary movies and I don't. It's no fair!"

This sense of fairness constantly rankles kids more than it reassures them. To quote that misanthropic little philosopher Calvin of the *Calvin and Hobbes* cartoons, "I know the world isn't fair, but why isn't it ever unfair in my favor?"

In a way, this yearning for exquisite balance and equity among peers is an extension of the hunger for competition. Through competition, children prove themselves and develop their identity. Fairness, they believe, provides a level playing field (actually, what they really hope for is a field tilted a little bit their way).

Janey was bent out of shape that the Maxwell children had another hour in the evening, despite the fact that they were two and four years older than she. How should Carl handle the fair play issue, knowing that children cannot compete fairly on a level playing field? Their skills and needs vary too much.

With his deeds and with words, Carl, the wagon guide to the world, can teach his children that life, though not fair, ought to be just. Justice actually provides a more level playing field for competition than does fairness, for justice takes the child's age and abilities into account.

It is just that the older children be allowed to stay up later, even as it is just that tiny Cathy should go to bed before second-grader Janey. Like Calvin, kids rarely notice when fair play or justice swings in their favor. They note only the injustices and slights—and bring them to your attention instantly.

Carl, as Dad, has one other essential lesson to teach in the matter of what is fair and just. That lesson is: *You can trust me, your father, to act in your best interest.*

Carl will build trust in his girls in several ways. For Janey, he will explain why he's acting unfairly. For both girls, he will snuggle them in his lap, read to them, hold them, carry them on his shoulder, feed them, listen to them. All these seemingly random actions say "I love you. I am trustworthy." Those actions, more than anything else Carl can do, will build his children's trust in him.

As Janey and Cathy get older, he will convey trust by being careful not to go back on his word. Janey will remember instantly if he made a promise he does not keep. Carl, of course, will keep his promises not to build trust but because of his own integrity; they are promises. The lesson is effective, regardless the motive.

Now and later, when Carl issues a distasteful edict:

- "No, you cannot stay all night at So-and-so's; their family's lifestyle is not amenable to ours."
- "No, you cannot ride the Whoop-De-Doo at the amusement park. It's too dangerous for a kid your age. In a couple of years, ask again."
- "No. I'm delighted that your best friend at school has a St. Bernard, but our place isn't big enough. He wouldn't get enough exercise."
- "Yes, you do have to eat broccoli because it has a lot of vitamins and it's on sale this time of year. I don't care what the president thinks of broccoli."

Grade schoolers can understand reasons for rules and edicts, even though they may rail bitterly against them. Dad has a valid reason. He has the child's best interests at heart. Those are the inferred messages that build trust.

THE ULTIMATE MESSAGE

Miles's dad and wagon guide Arnold, in his own life, never learned a crucial lesson that he must teach Miles. It is this: Worth is not based on what you do; it is based on what you are. Until Arnold masters that basic precept, Miles cannot. Swooping eagles, for whom appearance is everything, have a hard, hard time with any worth not based on behavior.

Worth is not based on what you do; it is based on what you are.

"The stereotypical father having problems with his kids, the father I see so very, very frequently in counsel, is a good man. He's a very good man. And he sees himself as a good father because he works hard and makes money. He considers that his contribution to the family, and he wants the family to look good in return, just as he looks good," says Paul Warren.

"We're not talking about surface appearances here. I mean he wants the family to be good. Toe the mark and present a wholesome face before the world. He won't rest easy until he realizes 'Worth is who I am, a child of God.' He can't teach his kid that until he's secure with it himself."

A CHILD OF GOD

Janey Jefferson draws pictures of God (which puts her in the same league with Michelangelo, who drew God in the wet plaster of the Sistine Chapel). Michelangelo put loose robes on God; Janey always draws a hat on His divine head. In her mind, the hat places Him a cut above everyone else. After all, police officers, state troopers, Smokey Bear, fire fighters, pizza chefs, cowboys, and other prominent people all wear hats.

During her grade school years, Janey's perception of God will change rapidly. The God of the sixth grader is light years beyond the God of the first or second grader. Her daddy will shape those changes by modeling the heavenly Father, and by one-on-one spiritual instruction.

Age Appropriate Discipline

Infant

A simple "no" with voice sharp but not raised.

NEVER shaking.

NEVER striking or spanking.

Toddler

Clear, one-word commands; nothing complex.

Physically redirect child to a permissible activity.

Time out.

Preschooler

Simple explanations for the why's of rules and no-no's as well as actual discipline.

Physical punishment controlled, restrained.

Always convey love along with correction.

Time out.

Grade Schooler

Limited physical punishment.

Simple grounding (no play at neighbors').

Restriction of privileges.

Restrictions, groundings brief—few days at most.

Restitution included in correction.

Junior and Senior High Schooler

No more physical correction (spanking inappropriate).

More elaborate grounding and restrictions.

Restrictions can extend over longer period of time; weeks.

Restitution a major part of correction.

The Father Book
Dr. Frank Minirth
Dr. Brian Newman
Dr. Paul Warren

Chapter

3

Developing a Parenting Style that Works

God has designed a parenting style just for you and your child. It is built into "mother's intuition"; and it is supported by dad's role as the spiritual leader of the family who is involved in the parenting. Your first step into your all-important roles as mothers and fathers is to learn to know your child, and that begins when he or she is just a baby. In this chapter from my book, Christian Parenting and Child Care, *I would like to share what I feel are the most important beginnings for any new baby—what I call "attachment parenting." Attachment parenting is a parenting style that helps you develop your God-given intuition to know your child, to get in harmony with your baby and build a trust relationship that will fulfill God's design for the father-mother-child relationship in your family.*

Dr. William Sears
Christian Parenting and Child Care

In the first few weeks of your parenting career you will be bombarded with a barrage of conflicting advice on how to care for your baby. All of your well-meaning friends and relatives are going to offer you their personal how-tos of baby care. Caring for your baby is known as "developing a parenting style." I like to think of a parenting style as a relationship that develops naturally with your baby.

From this relationship the how-tos automatically unfold. My dear parents, bear in mind that because you love your baby so much you will be vulnerable to any advice that may claim to make you a better parent or your baby a better child. In this section you will find suggestions on how to evaluate baby-care advice.

My opinion is that God loves us so much that He gives each parent a special intuition to know how to care for and to enjoy his or her child. Implied in this divine design is the law of supply and demand: as long as a parenting style is practiced that allows this intuition to develop, God will supply as much intuition as the child's needs demand. Some parents feel less confident than others, and some children have higher needs than others. I strongly believe that each parent's intuition for child care will match his or her child's needs—but only if the parent allows this relationship to grow according to God's design.

The purpose of this chapter is to help new parents develop a parenting style that is in accordance with God's design. The term *Christian parenting style* means a series of relationships between you and your child that will give you a greater chance of achieving the three primary goals of Christian parenting: (1) knowing your child, (2) helping your child feel right, and (3) leading your child to Christ.

A flurry of books and articles on parenting styles has surfaced in the past twenty years. Titles such as *Choices of Parenting Styles* and *Options for the Busy Parent* convey that new parents can choose a system of child care that fits most conveniently into their own lifestyles. According to these parenting options, parents should identify what lifestyle makes them happiest and then conform their children to it "because children are resilient." I do not feel this style of convenience parenting is in accordance with God's design. Be mindful of the Father's advice, "Train up a child in the way he should go . . ." (Prov. 22:6), meaning the way God has ordained for this child. Seek to determine God's way for your baby. Then help your child grow up in that way even though it may not be the most convenient way.

Another parenting style that is commonly recommended is what I call "restraint parenting." The catch phrases of restraint parenting are: "Don't be so quick to pick up your baby every time he cries"; "Don't let your baby manipulate you"; "What? You're still nursing? You're making him too dependent"; "Don't let your baby sleep with you; she may get into the habit"; "You're going to spoil her"; "You've got to get away from that kid." These common admonitions from trusted advisors to vulnerable new parents only detach parents and babies. Restraint parenting keeps you from knowing your child, keeps your child from feeling right, and ultimately keeps you from fully enjoying your child. Detachment or restraint parenting is not in accordance with God's design.

ATTACHMENT PARENTING

The style of parenting I sincerely believe is God's design for the father-mother-child relationship is a style I call "attachment parenting." My dear Christian parents, my feelings about conveying this style of parenting to you are so strong that I have spent more hours in prayerful thought on this topic than on any other topic in this book. Attachment parenting is not just my own theory. It is a parenting style I have derived from (1) parenting our own seven children, (2) observing and recording my patients' parenting styles throughout the past twenty years, and (3) becoming involved in parenting organizations whose principles I respect. I have a deep personal conviction that this is the way God wants His children parented. It works!

When discussing attachment, I refer mostly to the mother, not because I feel the father has a minor role in parenting, but because I feel God prefers greater maternal involvement in the first few months of a child's life. However, let me say to fathers that mother-infant attachment is difficult to achieve unless the father is the spiritual leader in a supportive environment. Most of the problems in the parent-child relationship are not a fault in the design or the Designer; they are a result of a total breakdown of the support system that allows a mother to follow God's design.

What is attachment? Mother-infant attachment is a special bond of closeness between mother and baby. This is a unique relationship designed by the Creator to enable the young of the species to reach their fullest potential. I feel that God placed within each mother a type of programming we call "mother's intuition." Some mothers naturally have a more developed intuition; others have to work at developing it, but it is there!

When your child is born, he or she comes complete with a unique set of characteristics we call "temperament." This child also is born with specific needs that, if met, will help modify this temperament and benefit the child's total personality. Some children have higher needs than others. Some children have different sensitive periods for different needs. No two children come wired the same way.

It logically follows that God would not give a certain mother a child whose needs she cannot meet. This is in keeping with what I believe the concept of the Creator to be. God's matching program is perfect; God's law of supply and demand will work, but only if parents develop a parenting style that allows God's design for the parent-child relationship to develop. If parents care for their children according to the divine design, they have a greater chance of claiming the promise, "Train up a child in the way he should go, / And when he is old he will not depart from it" (Prov. 22:6).

Attachment means that mother and baby are in harmony with each other. Baby gives a cue; mother, because she is open to baby's cues, responds. Baby likes the response and is further motivated to give more cues (because he or she learns he or she will get a predictable response), and the mother-baby pair enjoys each other. They get used to each other. As one attached mother told me, "I'm absolutely addicted to her." Once this happens, the mother's responses become more spontaneous and the how-tos naturally flow. How do you know when you get that attached feeling? When your baby gives you a cue and you respond, if you have a feeling of rightness about your response, and if you are continually sensitive to your baby, you are there. The attachment style of parenting helps you build up your sensitivity.

Why is attachment parenting preferable to restraint parenting? Compare these two styles and the effects they have on parent-child relationships.

Attachment Parenting Advice	*Restraint Parenting Advice*
"Be open to your baby's cues."	"Don't let your baby run your life."
"Take your baby with you."	"You've got to get away from that kid."
"Throw away the clock and the calendar."	"Get that baby on a schedule."
"Respond promptly to cries."	"Let your baby cry it out."
"Travel as a unit."	"You and your husband need to get away."
"Sleep wherever you all sleep best."	"Don't let your baby sleep in your bed; she'll get used to it."
"Let your baby sleep when he is tired."	"Put him down at 7:00, and let him cry; he'll learn to sleep."

"Wean when both of you are ready."	"What, you're still nursing?"
"Let her decide when she is ready to be independent."	"You're making her dependent."
"Allow discipline to flow naturally from harmony with your baby."	"You're spoiling him; he'll never mind."
"Let authority flow from trust."	"She's controlling you."

Attachment Parenting Results	*Restraint Parenting Results*
You develop trust and confidence in your parenting intuition.	You do not trust your instincts, and you rely on outside advice.
You know your child better.	You and your baby have a strained relationship.
You develop realistic expectations.	You compare your baby to other babies.
You adjust more easily to your new lifestyle.	You suffer burnout more easily.
You enjoy your baby more.	You seek alternative fulfillment.
You find discipline to be easy.	You find discipline to be strained.
You find spiritual training to be rewarding.	You find spiritual training to be stilted.
You are more discerning of advice.	You are vulnerable to unwise advice.
You keep pace with your child.	You play catch-up parenting.

Attachment Parenting Results for Your Child	*Restraint Parenting Results for Your Child*
Your child trusts care-givers.	Your child doesn't learn trust.
Your child forms attachments easily.	Your child resists new relationships.
Your child feels right, acts right.	Your child is anxious and dissatisfied.
Your child becomes loving and giving.	Your child becomes withdrawn and restrained.
Your child separates from you easily because he or she was attached to you early.	Your child separates from you with difficulty.

Your child has a good model for his or her own parenting.	Your child is confused about his or her role as a parent.

An objection to attachment parenting is, "I'm not going to let this tiny baby dominate me; I'll get her on *my* schedule rather than listen to her needs." Being open to your baby's cues does not mean that you are losing control. Being open simply provides the conditions for fully developing your God-given intuition. Openness implies trust in three relationships: (1) you trust your baby to give you the cues to tell you what he needs; (2) you trust yourself and your ability to respond to your baby's cues appropriately; and (3) you trust that God's design for a mother-baby communication network will work if allowed to operate as designed. When your baby cries in the middle of the night (for the third time) and you respond, don't feel you are "giving in"; you are simply giving.

It is important for you to realize that God would not have designed a system of child care that does not work. If you are a mother who says, "I don't feel I have any intuition," respond consistently to your baby without restraint and you will find your shaky intuition maturing. Try to see parenting as a stimulus-response relationship. For example, your baby cries, you pick him up; your baby is restless at night, you sleep with him; your baby enjoys nursing, you don't wean him before his or her time. By freely exercising this stimulus-response relationship, you become more confident in the appropriateness of your response.

What if you are confident in your intuition but are blessed with a very demanding baby? Again, the law of supply and demand works. Your intuitive response and your perseverance level increase in proportion to your baby's needs. You stay in harmony, in sync, with each other. However, if you succumb to outside pressure not to be open to your baby, you soon restrain your responses, trust yourself less, and eventually lose harmony with your baby. Restraint parenting leads to a strained parent-child relationship.

Because of the great variability in family situations, you may not be able to practice all of the disciplines of attachment parenting all the time. However, the more these parenting styles are practiced, the greater your chances are of truly enjoying your child.

A Harmonious Relationship

What attachment parenting does for you may be summed up in one word, *harmony*. A harmonious relationship allows you and your baby to be more in sync with each other, to become sensitive to each other. You, too, will become addicted to your baby.

A "Hormoneous" Relationship

Attachment parenting also permits you to have a sustained chemical change in your body. Breastfeeding stimulates the hormone prolactin (the milk-producing hormone). This hormone can give you the added boost you need during trying times. I suspect this hormone may be part of the divine design of mother's intuition.

By now, you may be feeling that this attachment style of parenting is all giving, giving, giving. To a certain extent, this is true. Parents are givers and babies are takers; that is how God designed them. Baby's turn to give will come later, and better takers make better givers. But because of this "hormoneous" relationship, baby still can give something back to mother—more prolactin. This mutual giving is a beautiful example of the divine design: mothering stimulates more mothering.

There are nearly two thousand references to "giving" in the Bible. Isn't that what Christianity is all about? Parenting according to God's design helps both parents and children grow to be giving persons.

WHAT CAN YOUR CHILD EXPECT?

Children who experience attachment parenting exude a feeling of rightness, the basis for a strong self-esteem. If your child feels right about himself, he will be a source of great joy to you. Attachment parenting can give you a better opportunity to enjoy your child.

Attachment parenting also can give your child an appropriate model to follow when he or she becomes a parent. Remember, you are parenting someone else's future husband or wife, father or mother. How your child was parented will influence how he or she parents. The lack of definite models is what causes confusion in many young parents today.

Attachment parenting's real payoff is in caring for what I call the "high-need child." This child goes by many names—the fussy baby, the demanding baby, the strong-willed child—but I prefer the term *high-need child* because it more accurately describes the level of parenting this temperament requires.

God's law of supply and demand works especially well for the high-need child. Attachment parenting increases your parenting energies as your child's needs increase, and you stay in harmony with each other. Restraint parenting may cause you to go out of sync with your baby so that you do not enjoy this special child.

Practicing attachment parenting does not guarantee that your child will not later depart from your teachings. It simply increases the chances that your child will turn out to be a blessing to you. There are three reasons why you cannot claim full credit or blame for your child's future: (1) every child comes wired with a unique temperament; (2) throughout life, your child will be continually bombarded with outside temptations and alternative lifestyles; and (3) God has given your child a free will. Comparing child-rearing with planting a seed may help you understand this concept. Certain styles of care give a seed a better chance of bearing good fruit. However, each seed is unique, and the fruit it bears will be vulnerable to the forces of nature. Your child is subject to forces beyond your control including his or her free will. You can understand why the most well-attached child may bend a bit.

Because God knew children would have erring, human parents, I feel He builds into each child an ability to adjust to a wide range of parenting styles. Most children have a wider acceptance of parenting styles than parents have of their behavior. However, the closer your style of parenting is to God's design, the less your children will tap into their reserves of resilience. As a result, certain undesirable behaviors of childhood that I call "diseases of detachment" are less common (anger, tantrums, depression, withdrawal, distancing).

Attachment parenting lays the foundation for discipline and spiritual training within the first two years of your child's life. Because you know your child better, you are able to assess his or her behavior more accurately and can respond to it more appropriately. Because your child feels right, he or she is more likely to act right. Such an attitude in your child makes punishment seldom necessary, and when necessary, it is administered more appropriately. Because of the attachment you have, both you and your child trust each other. Trust is the basis of authority, and authority makes the final goal of parenting, spiritual training, more effective.

FATHER FEELINGS AND MOTHER-INFANT ATTACHMENT

Occasionally, fathers share these feelings with me: "She's too attached"; "All she does is nurse"; "I feel left out"; "We need to get away alone." These are real feelings from real fathers who sincerely love their children, but feel displaced by them. If you are a father who is feeling displaced, let me assure you that your father feelings and your wife's attachment are very usual and very normal. Perhaps an understanding of God's design for mother-infant attachment and the changes that happen in your wife after birth may help you understand her apparent preference for your baby.

Before she gives birth, a woman's sexual hormones dominate her maternal hormones. After she gives birth, the reverse is true. The maternal hormones increase and stay at high levels for at least six months, during which time a woman's maternal urges may appear to take priority over her sexual urges. This shift of hormones may be part of the divine design to ensure that His young get mothered. A new mother also may feel drained by the incessant demands of her baby, so that by evening she has no sexual inclinations. Mothers commonly describe this feeling as being "all touched out."

A new mother is programmed to be attached to her baby physically, chemically, and emotionally. This does not mean that the father is being displaced by his baby but that some of the energies previously directed toward him are now being directed toward his infant. In time, these energies will be redirected toward the father. Let me share with you an investment tip I have learned in my practice and in my own family: if you are a caring, involved, and supportive husband during this early attachment period, these energies will return to you at a higher level.

I call the early attachment period a "season" of the marriage, a season to parent. If the harvest of this season is tended with care, the season to be sexual will again return.

THE OVERATTACHMENT SYNDROME

Be sensitive to the needs of your husband. God designed the family to function as a father-mother-child unit, not as a mother-child unit separate from the father. If you do not have a stable, fulfilled Christian marriage, the father-mother-child relationship ultimately will suffer.

You should not have to choose between your marriage and your child. If both relationships are kept in perspective, both will operate on a higher level. A child should not divide a marriage; a child should be a catalyst to bring husband and wife closer together, if their marriage is God-centered.

The following is a common story about what I call the "overattachment syndrome." Mary and Tom had a reasonably good marriage, but their relationship still needed a lot of maturing and it was not well-founded on Christ. After their baby arrived, Mary tried very hard to be a good mother. Tom was somewhat uncomfortable about handling babies, but he loved his little daughter very much. Mary sensed Tom's uneasy father feelings and was afraid to trust him to comfort the baby when she cried for fear he might upset the baby more. Tom felt more and more left out, and gradually they drifted down separate paths, Mary into her mothering and Tom into his work.

As Mary became more attached to the baby, Tom became more attached to his job and eventually made a few "attachments" of his own. Finally, Mary found herself in her pediatrician's office wondering why her marriage was disintegrating. "But I tried to be such a good mother," she said. "My baby needed me. I thought Tom was a big boy and could take care of himself." This common scenario occurs when there is fundamental breakdown in God's order for the family.

Watch out for "red flags" in your attachment relationship: Is the stress causing a division in your marriage? Are you spending less and less time with each other? Is Dad working more and enjoying fathering less? If these red flags are occurring, bring prayer and consultation into your relationship before the diseases of detachment take hold.

Pray daily for your child, for your marriage, and for your parenting relationship. If you bring Christ into your marriage and your parenting relationships, you have a head start toward the attachment mothering and the involved fathering that I sincerely believe are God's order for the Christian family.

A PERSONAL EXPERIENCE

I chose the most attached mother in my practice and asked her to tell what mother-infant attachment has meant to her. The following is what she wrote.

Before birth, a mother and infant are totally attached to each other. Within minutes, birth makes a drastic change in their physical attachment, but in every other way the attachment changes only gradually over a period of years. In some ways, such as emotionally and intellectually, the attachment actually increases. In other ways—

functionally and biologically—the attachment takes new forms and gradually lessens.

Immediately after birth the baby and the mother need to remain physically together. Although the physical link between them is severed, the necessity for closeness is intense. The baby needs to be surrounded by familiarity, to be warmed and suckled. The mother needs to be assured that the tiny kicks she had become accustomed to from inside are still there, and that the pregnancy she has "lost" is very surely "found" in the squirming little baby placed on her abdomen. She needs to envelop with her arms and drink in with her eyes and ears the feel, sight, sound, and smell of her newly born child. She needs to marvel at the miracle God has wrought in the depths of her body.

In the first days after birth, the attachment shows itself in new ways. The slightest whimper, the subtlest change in breathing rhythm, or the least shifting of the little body brings the mother to immediate attention. She very quickly responds by drawing her baby close to her, and she feels a rightness flood over her body and mind.

She begins to sleep with "one eye open" in case her baby needs her. If her baby is in a separate room for the night, she sleeps fitfully. She wakes often to listen for his or her cries and often goes in only to find the baby sleeping quietly.

As she performs her daily routine, she keeps her baby near her. If by some chance she discovers her baby has been crying, she is full of remorse that she was not there the instant the baby needed her. The discomfort this brings to her increases her vigilance and her determination that it not happen again. As she settles down to soothe her baby by holding, stroking, crooning, or nursing, a warm feeling of rightness melts away the pain and dismay in a flood of maternal emotions.

As the weeks pass, a pattern of attachment develops that is custom-made for the mother and her baby; it is a secret code known and trusted only by the two of them. The father knows and understands this attachment only in part by watching it unfold before him. He develops an attachment of his own to the baby, but it doesn't seem to ease the feeling he has sometimes of being left out of the inner circle around mother and baby. How good it is when he feels secure enough not to interfere with their closeness and not to feel threatened by it.

The father eventually becomes intrigued with the fine tuning he sees between his wife and their baby. "How did you know?" he'll ask, incredulous that such a subtle clue from the baby (indiscernible to himself) could be so completely and accurately understood by the baby's mother. The mother herself is amazed by her sixth sense about what the baby needs. He doesn't have to cry to let her know he wants to nurse or be picked up or shifted to a change of scene. The baby has a language of gestures, glances, and tiny noises that communicates his needs. The mother and baby are so close, so attached, that the baby seldom cries. The mother has learned to read her baby.

The attachment brings daily discoveries to the mother about herself and about her baby. She finds that if her baby takes an unusually long nap, she begins to yearn for her baby to wake up. She tingles with excitement when she finally notices him or her stirring awake; she has missed her baby and it is good to be reunited.

She makes another discovery in the church nursery debating with herself whether or not to leave the baby for the first time. She watches other babies being handed over to the nursery workers and put into their assigned slots—one in a swing, one in a crib, one in an infant seat. She pictures herself handing her baby over and considers what instructions she will give. But it doesn't feel right. She watches for a while longer and feels a growing conviction that she should keep her baby with her. As she leaves the nursery with her baby still in her arms, she is relieved the separation hasn't happened.

Another day she discovers that the baby has a finely developed sense of attachment in terms of measuring acceptable distances. As long as she is within touching distance or within seeing or hearing distance, the baby feels OK. Depending on the baby's need at a particular moment, he or she can tolerate lesser or greater amounts of distance between himself or herself, and his or her mother. Her constant availability enables the baby to develop a trusting nature.

As the baby gets older, the mother feels less urgency in responding to her baby's expressions of need. She feels OK about hurrying through a task, calling "Momma's coming," rather than dropping her work instantly to tend to him or her. Their attachment is now strong enough to handle a slight delay: the mother knows just how long the baby is able to wait before he or she will push the panic button. And these panics rarely occur now that she has learned so much about her baby and about herself as a mother.

A major milestone has been reached, and there will be many others. The attachment that started out to be so total and so intense has changed and will change even more, but there will be one constant thread throughout: the mother and child have a bond that will last a lifetime; it will serve the divine order for both their lives. The mother will have nurtured and the baby will in his or her turn nurture. Their attachment has given birth to human love for generations to come and has guaranteed the fulfillment of God's design for His children.

FROM ONENESS TO SEPARATENESS

Timely separation is a very important concept. A child must be filled with a sense of oneness with the mother before he or she can develop separateness. A baby must first learn attachment before he or she can handle detachment. A baby must first have a strong identity with his or her mother before he or she can evolve into his or her own self-identity. The age at which babies go from oneness to separateness varies tremendously from baby to baby.

Going from oneness to separateness according to God's design enhances child development. When a baby is securely attached at one stage of development, he more easily progresses to the next stage of development. Eventually the natural desire for independence stimulates the baby to begin to detach gradually from the mother. *It is important that the baby detach from the mother, not the mother from the baby.* For example, a toddler who is just learning to walk cruises farther and farther from his or her mother but periodically turns toward home base to check in. He or she feels secure detaching because his or her mother is there. However, if mother leaves during this separation-sensitive stage, the toddler might become less secure in exploring because home base is gone. Dependence actually fosters independence as long as it happens according to divine design.

Realizing that healthy attachment makes separation easier is good protection against those who insist attachment parenting makes your baby too dependent. Exactly the opposite is true. The baby who is the product of attachment parenting is actually less dependent later. Over the past ten years, research has confirmed what mothers have intuitively known—that early attachment fosters later independence. (I have summarized these scientific studies in my book *Growing Together,* published by La Leche League International, Franklin Park, Illinois, 1987.) The concept of oneness to separateness has long been appreciated in secular books on child care.

Unfortunately, it has not been understood among writers of Christian childcare books.

When Can I Leave My Baby?

If your attachment parenting has been practiced according to divine design, you will not want to leave your baby. You will probably experience some withdrawal symptoms the first time you leave your baby. For example, I see new mothers peering through the window the first time they leave their babies in the church nursery. They are not being possessive, which means keeping a child from doing what he needs to do because of some personal need. They are simply being attached. If you are a new mother and you feel a continual urge to get away from your baby, I advise you to pray and seek counsel because very often this desire implies some departure from God's design. You should enjoy being with your baby so much that, although an occasional outing may seem necessary, you really have difficulty being away from him or her.

How often and at what age a mother leaves her baby depends on many variables, including her need to get away. You may honestly feel you need occasional relief. If you feel a need to be refilled by some outside interest, follow your desire; an empty mother is no good to anyone, especially her baby. Oftentimes your restlessness will not be the need to get away from your baby, but the need for a change of scenery. Consider taking your baby along. You may feel you're not the stay-at-home type. "Home" to a tiny baby is where his mother is; take your baby out. God's design is for mother and baby to be tied together, not tied down. The divine design is a bond, not a bondage. When planning a time to be apart from your baby, the following questions need to be considered.

How separation-sensitive is your baby?

Some babies separate more easily than others because of their individual temperaments.

What is your baby's need level?

High-need babies separate with difficulty; they are designed that way.

Who is the substitute care-giver?

When you leave your baby, be sure to give explicit instructions on how you want your baby mothered in your absence. For example, tell the care-giver, "When she cries, I want you to pick her up immediately and comfort her." If possible, try to leave your baby during his or her prime time, which is the mornings for most babies. Try not to leave your baby during fussy times when he or she needs your nurturing.

Chapter

4

Your Marriage: On the Rock or On the Rocks?

The best way to begin to be good parents is to be good partners—to build your marriage on the Rock that can help you withstand all life's storms. When Mom and Dad show they love each other, the children feel more secure. You'll find that by investing in each other, you are investing in your children's future. In this chapter from Dad, Do You Love Mom?, *I'd like to share some pointers that I hope will help you and your family become winners through the power of Jesus Christ, the Rock.*

Jay Strack
Dad, Do You Love Mom?

In the Sermon on the Mount (Matt. 7:24–27), Jesus talked about two men who built houses: one on the sand and one on the rock. When the storms came, the house on the sand fell flat while the house on the rock stood firm. The same storms hit both homes, but only one could withstand the onslaught—the one on the rock. Then Jesus likened Himself to the rock and encouraged everyone to build their lives on Him. When people do, they are building on the only Rock which will stand forever—the powerful Son of God.

When I was a boy growing up in Florida, we could always tell when a storm was coming. The clouds would darken, the wind would pick up, the tides would shift, and we would all scurry for cover. But today, while the storm clouds gather, the winds of criticism blow, and the tides of indifference shift, people go right on living for themselves and building their lives on the shifting sands of human opinion.

"But, Jay," you may say, "what difference does it make if the same storms hit us all? Why bother if we all must struggle with life's difficulties?" The answer is that our efforts to build on Christ will result in a home that can withstand life's storms. Without Him as the foundation, our home will collapse under the strain, and "great [will be] the fall of it."

Happily married people are healthier and live longer. And spiritually committed people are happier people. The two go hand in hand: God and marriage.

When you build your home on the right foundation, your family can withstand any storm, but when you build it wrong, it is bound to fall. The foolish man, who built his house on the sand, reminds me of Abraham and his nephew Lot. Their stories are told in the book of Genesis. Both were wealthy and blessed by God, but Lot became selfish and his selfishness destroyed him and his family too.

While the Bible speaks much of Abraham's faith in God, it never mentions anything about Lot's beliefs. Though Abraham built many an altar to worship God, there is no record that Lot ever built an altar. Abraham built an altar and pitched his tent. But Lot built his tent and pitched the altar! Like all foolish men, Lot thought he could do it all himself.

He was weak in his devotions. Though he believed in God, he never had any time for God. As a result, his wife became indulgent, his sons-in-law indifferent, and his daughters immoral.

He was worldly in his desires. The Bible records that Lot made selfish choices and eventually "pitched his tent toward Sodom." Soon, he moved into that wicked city, and its ungodly influence took its toll on his family.

He was wrong in his decisions. Somehow Lot became the victim of his own selfish decisions. Before it was all over, he lost his wife, his children, his home, and his testimony. Today, he is remembered as a failure rather than as a success.

If you really want to make your life and marriage count, let God have control. Do not be afraid to admit you have failed. Turn it all over to Him. Do not let the hurts and wrongs of the past keep you from a wonderful future in Christ. Now is the time to turn to Him and let Him take control of your life. You and your family will never be the same.

Just before my mother passed away in 1980, she asked God's forgiveness for her sins and placed her trust in Christ as her personal Savior. Though she is gone now, I know she is in a far better place than she ever knew here.

As the years have passed, my father and I have been able to communicate about the scars of the past. It has been a thrill to watch him overcome his alcoholism and reach out to others who struggle with the same addiction.

God has done a great work in our family. He can do the same in yours! Let Him take control. You will never regret it.

GOOD PARTNERS MAKE GOOD PARENTS

The key concept that runs through my book like a scarlet thread is the fact that good partners make good parents. The more you are willing to work on your relationship as a couple, the better prepared you will be for the challenges of parenting. When things are going wrong in a marriage, they tend to influence and distort everything else in the family.

The more Dad and Mom love each other, the more secure their children will feel. Kids need to be reassured that their little world is not going to fall apart because Mom and Dad are going to split up. The security of a loving and stable family is vital to a child's own stability, success, and maturity.

The more Dad and Mom love each other, the more secure their children will feel.

The more you as a couple are willing to invest in each other, the more you are ultimately investing in the future of your children. Do not make the mistake of putting all your attention on the kids and neglecting each other. The time you spend rekindling the flame of your marriage is ultimately time invested in your children. Becoming a winner at marriage will automatically qualify you to become a winner at parenting. While the two do not necessarily equate, the one is built on the other. If you want to make a significant difference in your family's future, try the following suggestions:

Put the past in the past. What's done is done. Stop beating yourself with the club of the past and get on with the present. What you do right now will change your future and that is really all that matters.

Stop making excuses. Don't make excuses for what went wrong in your family and don't play the "if only . . ." game. Excuses do not lessen guilt; they only keep the issue alive when it should be buried and forgotten.

Turn your family over to God. Confess that you are a confused spouse and parent, and let God handle the things you cannot. Don't worry on your knees, however; learn to pray and leave your concerns in God's hands.

Rebuild your life and testimony. No matter how much time it takes, rebuilding is always worth the effort. Rebuild your relationship with your mate and your kids. Rebuild your testimony and reputation in your community. Apologize to people you may have wronged and let them know you are beginning again.

Don't become easily discouraged. If you fail again after your new beginning, don't assume you are an impossible case. Don't *quit!* God will see you through. Rebuilding is hard work.

Stay away from temptation. Don't go back to the places, habits, and people who set—or kept—you on a wrong course in the beginning. Keep your life and heart morally pure.

Establish positive goals. At the end of one week, ask your spouse how you're doing in his or her eyes. At the end of one month, call a family meeting and ask how things have changed and how they can still change for the better.

Determine that you and your family will be winners through the power of Jesus Christ. Reach out for others who can help: counselors, church members, Bible teachers, deacons, and pastors. I love the words to this song:

You say, "Winners don't need a crutch
Only losers could believe in such"
You don't need God, you don't need
anything
You'll face life alone
You take what the future will bring
You think I've missed what success can
bring
I miss success like trees miss cold in spring
You think that all is far too much to give.
But that's what Jesus gave
So that this loser could live
Here's to all the losers
That lose all guilt and sin
Here's to life in Jesus
All of the losers win.

"All the Losers Win," Words by Ed DeGarmo and Dana Key,

Will you and your family be winners? Or will you succumb to the pressures that surround all of us and sadly quit the game?

YOUR HOME: HEAVEN ON EARTH

Most of all, fathers and mothers, God has a ministry for you in your home. You may also have a ministry outside your home, but God wants you to first dedicate yourself to the home He has placed within your reach. What greater challenge is there?

If you have children, Scripture admonishes you to perform the following duties of parents:

Teach (Deut. 6:7). Teach your children about the things of God when you sit at home, when you walk together, when you gather around the dinner table, and when you put the kids to bed.

Train (Prov. 22:6; Deut. 4:9). Train your children as they grow and in ways appropriate to their age level.

Provide life's necessities (2 Cor. 12:14). Few parents neglect to provide life's physical requirements such as food and clothing, but how many parents provide the proper emotional and spiritual requirements necessary for a healthy child? Do you give unconditional love, or is a price tag attached to your approval? Does your child understand that he is a spiritual being?

Nurture (Col. 3:21). Do not criticize or hopelessly break the spirit of your children, but lovingly bring them up in the training of the Lord.

Discipline (1 Tim. 3:4,12). A child with no discipline and no limits knows no boundary of love. Boundaries are important for your child's security. (See also Prov. 13:24; 19:18; 22:15; and 23:13.)

Love (Titus 2:4). Few people need to be reminded to love a beautiful baby, but how have you loved your teenager today? Have you spent time with him or her? Have you spoken words of praise, or have you given nothing but nagging reminders? Have you led your child today to an awareness of God?

"See then that you walk circumspectly, not as fools but as wise, redeeming the time, because the days are evil. Therefore do not be unwise, but understand what the will of the Lord is" (Eph. 5:15–17).

Make a conscious decision each morning: "Today I will love my partner and my kids to the best of my ability."

How can you establish a happy home in an age when the nuclear, two-parent family seems to be an anachronism? How can you raise teenagers when "adolescence" is practically a social disease? How can you teach your children to be morally pure when the pregnancy rate for American teens is more than twice that of any other industrialized country?[1] How can you honor your marriage vows at work when the boss promises you a promotion for sexual favors?

You can follow God's will and know that He will bless you. Your "Paradise Lost" can become "Paradise Regained." How? Make your home a place of affection, protection, and imitation.

Give your spouse and your children *affection.* Love them and accept them for what they are. Choose a new way to express your love each day. Make a conscious decision each morning: "Today I will love my partner and my kids to the best of my ability."

Make your home a place of *protection.* Relieve stress from your marriage partner by not adding to his or her problems when you meet again after the day's work. Protect your children from influences that would harm them. Know what movies, television programs, and music they are watching or hearing. Do these things honor Christ? Are they beneficial? If not, keep them out of your home.

Make your home a place of *imitation.* Children learn by observing their parents, so make your model worthy of emulation. Do you want your children to pick up your habits? Should your children spend their time as you spend yours? If your children treat their marriage partners as you treat your spouse, will their homes be happy?

The chances are great that if you hate carrots, your kids do too! If you like basketball, your kids probably join you for the game in front of the television. If you are indifferent to spiritual things and do not go to church, it is highly likely that your son and daughter will feel the same way.

Coach Price coached the University of California in the 1929 Rose Bowl. On New Year's Day the California team met Georgia Tech on the playing field. Emotions were running high.

On one crucial play there was a fumble, and during the chaos that ensued Roy Riegels of California grabbed the ball and began running *the wrong way.* It took a determined effort for his own bewildered and stunned teammates to bring him down, but they did—just short of a goal. Georgia was quick to turn the gained yardage into a touchdown, and Riegels was not only embarrassed, he was devastated.

In the locker room at half time, everyone expected Coach Price to rant and rave about Riegels' stupid mistake. But the room was deadly silent. Riegels stripped off his jersey and sat sobbing in a corner with a blanket around his shoulders.

When the break was over, Coach Price stood and said simply, "I want the same team that started the game out on the field now." The team stood and ran back out to play—everyone, that is, except Roy Riegels. "Didn't you hear me, Roy?" asked the coach.

"I can't go back out there," said the player. "I've ruined myself, I've ruined the game, I've ruined the college's reputation. I'd rather die than face that crowd again."

Coach Price drew himself up and said sternly, "Boy, the game is only half over. Get out there and play."

California lost that game eight to seven, but those who watched Riegels play during the second half say that they've never seen anyone play football with as much heart.[2]

Be like Roy Riegels and correct your mistakes. Even though you may have been running the wrong way, you can still turn the game around and play your heart out. Riegels could only play on one chilly day in January, but you have an entire lifetime in which to change direction and really love your family.

FOR MEN ONLY

I believe the Bible makes clear what roles men are to take in the family. Husband, your wife needs your help. Dads, your children need your leadership. Here are four things you can do that will go a long way toward making your home a better place to live.

Be a provider. Most men understand their role as a financial provider but forget that they are to provide not only materially, but also emotionally and spiritually to their family's well-being. Men get their needs satisfied quickly and, therefore, often forget to be sensitive to the needs of their wives and children. You may even have to say *no* to your "toys" in order to better meet your family's needs.

Be a protector. Every Mary needs a Joseph. Remember, she rode while he walked. Your wife and children deserve the security of a responsible husband and father who will do whatever is necessary to protect his family from spiritual danger as well as from physical harm. As a spiritual leader in your home, be sure to keep out harmful influences that will pull you away from your commitment to live for Christ.

Be a priest. Perhaps as never before, men are needed who are willing to be spiritual leaders in their own homes. Pray with your wife and children. Read the Bible together. Worship God as a family practice in your home. Don't let your wife have to be the one to insist on asking the blessing or reading devotions. You do it!

Be a pal. Become your wife's best friend. Remember, the friendship factor is the greatest insulator against divorce. Develop common interests and a strong friendship. Make sure you give plenty of time to your wife in order to grow in your relationship. First Peter 3:7 tells you to *know* your wife, *honor* her, and *share* the grace of life with her. Take time to smell the roses. Life will go better if you do.

FOR WOMEN ONLY

The Bible also clearly prescribes a woman's role in marriage. Women, if you want your husbands to become better leaders, you will have to become better followers.

Be supportive. Support his dreams. Don't tell him why he can't, tell him why he can! Treat him like a king and he will treat you like a queen. Become his biggest fan and cheer him on to success. Let him know you are there to help, not hinder. Men often walk out of a marriage claiming they were not appreciated. Give him all the attention and admiration you can.

Be submissive. Meet his needs without being asked. Remember, relationships work both ways. The more you follow his leadership, the more he will be willing to lead. If you do not meet his needs, someone else will.

Be spiritual. Don't neglect your own spiritual growth. Determine to become more Christ-like in all your attitudes and actions. Learn to be positive and uplifting. Encourage spiritual growth; don't discourage it.

Be smart. Keep up with your husband's interests, hobbies, and education. Read and improve yourself. Keep your attractability high. Look sharp, think deep, and develop your full potential in every area of your life.

Remember, marriage is what you make it. The divorce rate just indicates that some are not trying very hard. God can make a difference in your life, and you, in turn, can make a difference in your marriage. And that difference will spell security, high self-worth, and unconditional acceptance, not only to your mate, but to your children as well. They will thrive under the love Mom and Dad show to each other.

What are you waiting for? Help your children answer yes to the questions, Dad, do you love Mom? and Mom, do you love Dad? The first step begins with you.

Chapter

5

Children: Making the Right Impression

It has often been said that children learn what you live, not what you teach. How you live your life and how you live it with them is what is important. As you love your children, so shall you also set an example for them. The impressions you set upon your children can be of lasting value or no value. This short chapter from Walking with Christ in the Details of Life, *I hope, will remind you to impress upon your children the way of the Lord—to make a lasting impression that may not be so obvious, but whose value will stay with them for a lifetime.*

Patrick M. Morley
Walking with Christ in the Details of Life

After retiring ten years ago, Ed expected a low-key, quiet life. But his two daughters didn't marry wisely, and he spends some of each day fretting over the unhappiness of his two girls, both with children of their own, one divorced and the other unhappily married.

No matter how unhappy you are today, it is nothing compared to how unhappy you will be if your children have unhappy lives later. No matter how happy you are today, if your children grow to be unhappy adults, you, too, will bear much grief.

Can you think of anything that matters to you more than the

salvation and happiness of your children? What can we do to give our children the spiritual heritage we long for them to have?

When my wife was a teenager, she walked down the hall toward her room one evening past the slightly cracked door of her parents' darkened bedroom. When she absently glanced inside, she saw her father kneeling next to the bed in prayer. Fifteen minutes later she skipped back up the hall and was astonished to see her dad still in the same position, kneeling in prayer. I can't begin to tell you the number of times she has mentioned this experience; it made an indelible impression on her.

The Bible tells us to *impress* the commands of God upon our children—to inculcate His values. Teaching our children is not a collection of clever homilies, but a lifestyle—thousands of individual impressions that shape the values and beliefs of our children, like Patsy's father on his knees.

The only lasting possessions your children will take with them when they leave home are their value system and their belief system.

When your children walk out the door that last time to establish their own household, what will they take with them? The only lasting possessions your children will take with them when they leave home are their value system and their belief system. Whatever else they have will wear out or rust away within a few brief years, but the values and beliefs you impress upon them will guide them, for better or for worse, until they rest in their graves. Based on how it has been going so far, with what heritage will your children begin their own families? And the conspicuous question, what can be done?

AVAILABILITY VERSUS STRUCTURE

Availability is more important than structure. In other words, doing anything with your kids is more important than trying to devise a structured teaching moment. Let the activity provide the teaching opportunity.

My son wanted to help change a flat tire on my car. He couldn't loosen the lug nuts. He ran out of energy to unscrew them all. He couldn't lift the old tire off nor put the new one on. Once the new tire was on, he tried to get away with only putting on every other lug nut. It took twice as long with his help.

While he couldn't help me as much as he thought he could, he went away thinking he had helped me more than he did. The experience made a large spiritual impression on him. His self-esteem grew by a mile, and now he understands the concepts of diligence and excellence in a deeper way. Those are Biblical values, and I impressed them upon my son in a way that was natural, not contrived. I wasn't teaching him how to change a flat tire; I was teaching him how to be a man of God.

A LIFESTYLE

Impressing the way of the Lord is a lifestyle, not an event. "Talk about them when you sit at home and when you walk along the road, when you lie down and when you get up. Tie them as symbols on your hands and bind them on your foreheads. Write them on the doorframes of your houses and on your gates" (Deut. 6:7–9 NIV).

Whether at home or at the mall, whether over breakfast or after dinner, talk about the Lord. In the home where Christ is reserved for Sunday, He is an event, not a lifestyle. Memorize Scripture, repeat it, teach it, put up plaques, read your Bible, pray in secret often enough that you are accidentally discovered.

Can you think of any earthly pain more devastating than for your children to be unhappy? To be godly parents is no guarantee that your children will turn out right; that they will follow the Lord and lead happy, productive lives. But to be ungodly parents is a virtual guarantee that they will turn out wrong. And if you don't do your part and by God's grace they turn out right, you will have had little to do with it.

APATHY VERSUS ERROR

Children are harmed more by our apathy than our error. It is not the mistakes we make with them that devastate their lives; it is the neglect. Have you impressed your children with the values necessary to lead a happy, productive life? Have you impressed them with the beliefs to lead them to eternal life? Make the decision to make a difference in the lives of your children now; it may be the source of your greatest joy later.

I Surrender

Father, I confess that I have not sensed
the gravity of how I am to impress
my children with Your ways.
Teach me that I may teach
them. Spare my children
from the grief and pain
of wrong values and beliefs.
Equip me that I may
equip them. Amen.

Chapter

6

I Remember Mama—and Daddy, Too

This chapter's for your life. It's from our book, Unlocking the Secrets of Your Childhood Memories. *And we're inviting you to take a look at your own childhood family atmosphere because, just like a bad penny, your family atmosphere will turn up again and again in your life. Did you grow up in an authoritarian home? a perfectionistic family atmosphere? an overly permissive climate or a martyred atmosphere? More than likely it is affecting your parenting style.*

Looking at your earliest childhood memories—along with some insightful information on birth order—can help you sort out the reason why you are the way you are and why you are the type of parent you are. If you want to build happy childhood memories for your children, the best way to do it is to work out the problems from your childhood.

Dr. Kevin Leman and Randy Carlson
Unlocking the Secrets of Your Childhood Memories

According to Shakespeare, "All the world's a stage, / And all the men and women merely players. . . ."[1] That's all too true, and the curtain goes up very early in life. Like everyone else you accumulated your childhood memories on a very special stage—your family setting. To unlock the deepest secrets of your memories, you need to get a better understanding of how that setting affected you.

Mom and Dad were the king pin and queen pin of your family theater troupe. They set the stage, and each family member had a part in the play. The scripts were written as you went along, and the entire improvised production of "Days of Your Childhood" was under the direction (good or bad) of your parents.

While you acted out your roles on your family's stage, you learned early what would work and not work for you. Studies have shown that learning can occur even while a child is in the womb, and once an infant hits life's stage and gets that first "hand of recognition," he or she learns very fast indeed.

Actually, we don't give tiny babies enough credit. They're anything but the helpless little darlings we make them out to be in ads for Pampers or Michelins. For example, a normal baby with deaf/mute parents soon concludes that making noise to get his way doesn't work, so he becomes an expert at "crying" in pantomime, contorting his little red mug, pumping his arms and legs like little windmills, but never making a sound! Later he may learn to stomp on the floor during tantrums so his parents can "hear" the vibrations.[2]

One psychologist did studies that showed it's possible to teach a toddler to read with comprehension, take dictation, and even operate an electric typewriter.[3] Tiny tots aren't quite ready to bail out that poor boss in the television commercial ("She can't type!"), but they are ready to take an active role in creating their own personalities. That's exactly what you did when you were born. As you sorted out what worked and what didn't, you created a life "plan" that developed into a unique style of living—yours.

In this chapter we want to focus on the family stage where you played your own starring role. It is here that your memories were made. We will look at that stage from two perspectives: (1) The "climate control" set up by your parents, who created a certain family atmosphere that influences you to this day; (2) your birth order, the limb where you landed on the family tree.

Although we know generalizations can be dangerous, research has shown that individuals with similar personalities and problems tend to come from similar family atmospheres. This is as true for those who come from encouraging, nurturing families as it is for those from critical, chaotic, and abusive environments. To see how family atmosphere dovetails with memory exploration, let's look at the emotional climates of typical homes and the life-molding memories they produced.

"AS LONG AS YOU LIVE IN THIS HOUSE . . ."

Carl was the only child of immigrant parents. The family lived in an apartment behind the family-run business they all (kids as well as Mom and Dad) worked in. Carl recalls this memory from when he was eight:

Early one morning, just before time to leave for school, my father handed me a box of merchandise and told me to hurry and put it all out on the store shelves. When he came to check on me a few minutes later, I'd stopped to look at a book; only half the box had been emptied. My father was so angry he took me into the storeroom and ordered me to stand in the corner until he came back.

The hours ticked by but I never moved. It seemed as if my dad was gone for *days.* When he finally did come back, it was three o'clock in the afternoon! He'd forgotten all about me! And I'd missed school. I'd had to go to the bathroom so bad, but I hadn't dared move because I was afraid my father would come back and whale the daylights out of me.

What kind of family atmosphere was this? Carl obviously grew up in an *authoritarian* home, where the parents—especially his father—were the boss and no questions were asked. Carl's dad was from the Old Country. He had grown up in an authoritarian atmosphere, and his own home was exactly the same.

Carl told Kevin this early memory when he came in for counseling after he became miserable in his high-paying job in microbiology. He had gone to postgraduate programs for seven years to obtain science degrees. Now his job was good, but his life was in the pits. His wife had just left him because she couldn't handle his perfectionistic ways any more.

Carl was so prescriptive in his thinking that before his wedding he read several books on "how to be married." Unfortunately, they didn't cover "Thou shalt not nit-pick thy wife." She managed to put him through school and hoped things would be better once he got his degree, but they weren't. Finally his constant criticism caused her to pack up her belongings and their two children and leave.

When Carl and Kevin explored that early memory together, the light went on. He realized that he had sweated through college and graduate school to do something, not for himself, but for his authoritarian father who wanted him to get the education and high-paying job he never had. Carl decided to quit that high-paying job and totally change careers. Today he is a well-adjusted—and contented—operator of a salvage yard. On Kevin's advice, he is taking his time about remarrying and is trying to be more aware of his habit of nit-picking and criticizing as he develops new relationships.

Carl is a good example of a child who grew up in an authoritarian atmosphere and knuckled under. By sharp comparison, a client named Bruce knuckled up. He came to Randy for consultation because he was having so much trouble dealing with those who had authority over him at work. Together they discovered a series of Bruce's childhood memories that all centered on how he rebelled against his father's authoritarian ways:

> My dad would use his belt on me all the time, even when I was small. By the time I was eight or nine, we were practically at each other's throats. We just never got along. I remember one day my dad thought I had done something wrong and he wouldn't listen to me when I tried to explain. All he said was, "None of your mouth—you can spend the rest of the day in your room without lunch or dinner." I was so mad I crawled out of my bedroom window and went over to a friend's house to play for the afternoon. I wasn't about to submit to my dad's punishment.

Bruce also remembered loving rock music by the time he was eleven or twelve and playing it "just loud enough" to set his dad off. And he clearly remembered the time his father told him, "Son, your grades are lousy. If you don't pass this next test, you're grounded for a week." Bruce deliberately failed the test and recalls thinking, "It's worth it just to show Dad."

As we counsel with families, one of the most serious causes of chaos and misery that we deal with is authoritarian parenting. Research shows that children from authoritarian homes display the following characteristics:

- Often rebel in later life or when free of authority
- Likely to be inconsiderate of others, quarrelsome, unpopular, emotionally unstable
- Often very sensitive to praise and blame
- May be polite, "respectful," and proper, but shy and timid
- Often unable to solve problems without the help of an authority

- Often lack creativity, spontaneity, and resourcefulness
- May resort to passive-aggressive strategy such as lying and stealing
- Can "go wild" when shifted to a more permissive atmosphere or when living on his or her own[4]

Look again at the list of characteristics above. Do any of them fit you today? Look back on your own family atmosphere. Was either of your parents authoritarian? In what ways? Mine your memories a little to see if you can come up with some brief videotapes that may shed light on your habits or hang-ups.

"LET'S BE SURE WE GET IT RIGHT THIS TIME!"

Perhaps you're saying, "My parents weren't really hard-core authoritarians. I got a few spankings, sure, but what I remember more is the criticism—the constant demand to measure up."

If your childhood memories center on those constant demands to measure up or jump a little higher, you probably grew up in a *perfectionistic* family atmosphere. Victims of this kind of environment are also frequent visitors to our counseling offices. For example, first-born Brenda, discouraged and finally broken by years of feeling like a failure, finally sought some help. Here are two samples of her early childhood memories that told Randy a lot about her childhood family atmosphere and why she's having problems today:

At six I was a big girl—bigger than the others in my class. I was also clumsy. I always wanted to play with the other girls on the playground, but no one would pick me for their team. In fact, I remember one day a girl telling me I wasn't good enough to be on her team.

Another time, my dad took me to watch my younger sister play softball. I must have been nine or ten at the time. I recall his words as though it were yesterday. "Brenda, maybe someday you'll learn to try as hard as your sister does." I was crushed.

Brenda's parents, like most perfectionistic parents, set high standards to encourage their children to succeed. But Brenda ended up feeling she could never measure up. While her younger sister and baby brother always seemed to exceed the goals set for them,

Brenda always landed a few feet short in the broad jump of life. The harder she worked, the farther behind she fell.

It didn't help Brenda any to be first-born. She already had one foot in the perfectionist's swamp of despair, trying to measure up to all those high standards Mom and Dad set for their first child. People raised in a perfectionistic atmosphere show many highly recognizable characteristics:

- That feeling of never measuring up, always believing they could do much better
- Low self-esteem
- Feeling like a failure with no real hope of ever being a success
- Strong feelings of self-criticism, lashing themselves for even the slightest error or mistake
- Biting off more than they can chew and never being able to finish on time
- Procrastinating because "there isn't enough time to do it right anyway"

Like a bad penny, your family atmosphere follows you through life. Whom did Brenda marry? A flaw picker, of course. Brenda's husband, Gary, was also a first-born whose job as an accountant called for meticulous attention to every percentage point. At home, every burnt piece of toast, every cold cup of coffee, every wrinkled shirt was held up to his unwavering, critical gaze. But while he commented on all of Brenda's flaws, he seldom noticed or praised any of her strengths or successes. So Brenda wound up playing the same familiar role in her marriage that she had played on her childhood family stage.

Do you struggle with perfectionism? Look over that list of characteristics above, and then flip on your memory video to see if anything starts to make sense. You may find memories where you're being unfavorably compared to a brother or sister. Or perhaps you will recall the sting of a remark made when you failed a test or struck out in the last of the ninth in the Little League championship game. Maybe your video will show you being frustrated, feeling hopeless.

On the other side of the coin, perhaps your memories center on personal achievements and successes. Maybe you build your life around how well you perform, and so far you've gotten away with it. But the performance treadmill gets old. You may already be getting a bit tired. You can't change your perfectionist grain, but there is a lot you can do to counter the demands of those critical parents who flicker across your memory screen.

"WELL, I GUESS JUST ONE MORE TIME WON'T MATTER. . . ."

At the other end of the spectrum from authoritarian and *perfectionistic* atmosphere is the family where the climate is *permissive.* Barbara, thirty-eight-year-old mother of three and last-born in a family where she had three older brothers, came to see Kevin. She complained of frustration, friction with her husband and children, and being discriminated against at work by being passed over for promotions while men who weren't as capable got better jobs.

As she and Kevin probed her early childhood memories, several scenes came up, all of which featured Barbara, the baby princess at the center of attention. But Barbara's most revealing memory of all was this:

> Neither one of our parents was much for discipline. My three older brothers were terrors, but when I came along, they really let down all the fences because they had wanted a girl so very badly. I got whatever I wanted and can still remember the time we were all headed out for burgers and fries—something my brothers really loved. But I stamped my feet and insisted that we go to Guiseppe's for pizza. They all tried to talk me out of it, but I wouldn't budge. I wanted pizza, and that was that! My parents gave in, much to my brothers' disgust, and we all went out for pizza. But on the way home they did stop and buy all the guys milkshakes—and one for me, of course. Our parents were always giving in to us like that.

As Kevin probed a little deeper, Barbara's problem became plain. She had always gotten her way, and now, as a married mother of three, she was running into problems. She wanted to be permissive with the children, but her husband, Jim, had come from an authoritarian atmosphere and had radically different ideas. They clashed constantly on how to discipline their two sons and daughter.

As for friends, Barbara had few at work or at church. People tended to stay clear of her because of her quick wit and biting tongue. "My office is filled with male chauvinist pigs," she said bitterly. "I'm twice the salesperson any of the men are, but I know two cases where men were moved up to manager and I am still where I started."

Kevin worked hard with Barbara to show her how her parents had raised her in a permissive atmosphere that had never helped her learn self-discipline and compromise. Not surprisingly, none of her memories revealed her having to give in to anyone. She always got her own way. Now, in her late thirties, Barbara revealed characteristics that are standard in a person reared in an overly permissive family:

- A lack of consideration for others
- Compulsive behavior, like overspending, overeating, or overdrinking, typical of someone whose family atmosphere lacked direction and boundaries
- A quick and caustic tongue that doesn't spare the feelings of others
- The inability to delay gratification, the overwhelming drive to "want what I want when I want it, which is now"
- An ability to be charming on the surface, but lack of ability to maintain lasting friendships

If your memory videos reveal these characteristics, you probably were reared in a permissive family atmosphere. Maybe it didn't seem too permissive to you at the time because you never knew what toeing the mark was like, but a look at some early childhood memories will be consistent with the difficulties you are having today.

"I KNEW IT WOULDN'T WORK OUT . . ."

A family climate that leads children to see life with the glass half empty is the *martyred* atmosphere that Nels grew up in. His parents lived through the Depression years and lost, within a few weeks, the savings and accumulations of a lifetime. From this traumatic experience, they concluded that all they could expect from life was to be taken advantage of by "the system." Naturally, they passed this attitude along to first-born Nels as we can see in this typical memory he shared with Randy:

I recall the time my third-grade teacher gave me an F on a work paper because I forgot to do the problems on the back side—which I hadn't noticed when I was working on the assignment. Now that didn't seem fair to me.

Children like Nels, raised in a martyred atmosphere, often:

- Conclude life doesn't hold much promise for them
- Become self-righteous and judgmental toward others
- Try to control others through guilt and manipulation

You can see some strong similarities between the martyred child and the overprotected one. The martyr isn't just timid and afraid of risks. He is basically pessimistic. He knows life just isn't going to work out and the glass is always half empty, never half full.

While martyrs feel pessimistic about their own roles in life, they still look down on others, whom they blame for all their suffering. Often this blaming shifts to control or manipulation. They say, "Just look at all I've been through. Surely you can see I need you to help me out, or at least feel sorry for me or be impressed by my noble suffering."

Do any of the above traits fit you at all? If you're in the habit of throwing pity parties for yourself today, you might want to look through your childhood memories for any scenes that came out of a martyred family atmosphere, scenes that taught you pessimism, negativism, prejudice, or a judgmental attitude.

It isn't comfortable to admit that you might be something of a martyr, but be honest. To be a martyr for a worthy cause may get you into history books; to be a martyr without a cause may get you into counseling.

ATMOSPHERIC CONDITIONS CAN OVERLAP

After looking at several examples of family climate control (or more correctly, families where the climate is out of control), you may be unsure that the family of your childhood could be described by any of these labels. Because families include human beings, they seldom fit totally into nice neat categories. Whenever we speak about a category like "authoritarian family," we are pointing only toward certain trends or characteristics that may be prevalent. And there are many other nuances or idiosyncrasies in families that could be called "atmospheres."

In *the overprotective or pitying atmosphere,* excessive sympathy is given to the misfortunes and losses of the child. These atmospheres are close cousins to families that are permissive, but the emphasis is on going overboard to help the child, comfort him when he is hurt, and give him the best care possible.

In *the competitive atmosphere,* one family member's performance is compared and contrasted to the others in a constant attempt to see "who can be the best." It is similar in many ways to the perfectionistic atmosphere and, in some cases, the authoritarian. Some fathers, for example, are frustrated jocks who drive their kids to see the world as a competitive battleground where nice guys finish last.

In *the neglecting atmosphere,* the parents are so preoccupied with their own problems or interests they have no time for the child. The neglecting parent is often pictured as a criminal or drug addict. Sometimes that is true. Very often, however, neglecting parents are workaholics who are so busy with their jobs or their duties they have little awareness of or interest in their child's needs.

In *the materialistic atmosphere,* the acquisition and control of things, money, and power are sought after.

In *the hurried atmosphere,* all family members are caught in the fast lane of life, and the children are exposed to adult lifestyles and adult pressures that force them to become older than their years too quickly. This can start as early as preschool where the kids get shoved into kiddy college, while Mom and Dad hurry off to high-pressure jobs, a commuter's hour or so away. Obviously, the materialistic or hurried atmospheres can help contribute to making children feel neglected.

If you're getting the idea that family atmospheres can overlap, you're right. Many family atmospheres are variations of the ones we've described or combinations of two or more.

CAN A FAMILY'S ATMOSPHERE BE CHANGED?

While our book *Unlocking the Secrets of Your Childhood Memories* is not intended to be a parenting guide, you may be getting obvious hints about some changes you need to make in your own parenting style. As you explore your own memories and remember the family atmosphere in which you grew up, it's natural to ask yourself: "How can I build healthier childhood memories for my kids?" The best way is to build good-time memories that come out of an atmosphere of mutual self-respect.

One other question may have popped into your mind as we have described some examples of family atmosphere: "If a family atmosphere is such a strong determinant of a person's personality, why can children from the same family atmosphere turn out to be so different from each other?"

A big part of the answer to that one lies in the fact that two children reared by the same parents in the same house can each perceive and/or respond to the family atmosphere very differently. For example, take Greg and his younger sister, Peggy, who grew up in what could be judged an overprotective family. Yet, there's an obvious difference in their memories. Greg recalls:

> One day when I was four, I wanted to go across the street to the park, but my parents said no. I would have to wait until one of them could go along. It made me mad that I wasn't allowed to do something by myself. That happened a lot. I felt my parents never trusted me.

Greg's sister, Peggy, however, has a series of memories that show the family "protective" atmosphere in another light. For example:

> Our parents were always concerned about taking care of us and protecting us from danger. I remember one day when I was five or six. I was riding my bike in the street by our home when my dad yelled at me to get off the street "NOW!" I wasn't allowed to ride my bike for a week. I felt terrible that I had disobeyed my dad.

First-born Greg viewed his family atmosphere as oppressive, and he responded by resenting it and wanting to break loose. His younger sister saw the same atmosphere as protective and responded by feeling guilty if she did not abide by her parents' wishes.

All of this simply says that it's not just the family atmosphere that shapes a child's personality. The child's perception of his family—how he sees himself fitting into the atmosphere of his home—has a powerful impact. And a lot of it has to do with the child's birth order—his or her particular limb on the family tree.

Memories Are Born as Well as Made

We could spend a whole book chronicling the impact your birth order has on who you are and why you do what you do. In fact, that's just what Kevin does in *The Birth Order Book*. So we're not going to go through all that in great detail, but we do want to cover it briefly to show how it ties in with family atmosphere to mold your early memories.

Birth order theory holds that the order of your arrival in your family strongly influences who you are today. Basically, there are four birth order categories: only child, first-born, the middle child, and the last-born or baby. Each group commonly exhibits distinct characteristics.

First-Borns Get Too Much Attention

First-born children are guinea pigs without cages for novice parents to experiment on. They're usually the recipients of high expectations, too much attention, considerable criticism, and other examples of over-parenting.

But it's not all bad by any means. First-borns discover right from the start that the world is a challenging place and everything they do is a "big deal" to Mom and Dad and the grandparents. They quickly learn the ground rules for fitting into the forest of adult kneecaps around them. They tend to take life seriously and grow up to be reliable and conscientious—seekers of approval who want to win as many good citizenship awards as possible.

Lonely Onlies Are a Special Breed

A special breed of first-born is the only child. In fact, an only child is simply a first-born in spades, diamonds, clubs, and hearts. Lonely onlies can often be critical of everyone, including themselves. They grow up with few friends or playmates, and their most frequent contacts are with Mom and Dad. When they get older, they often have a hard time relating to their peer group. They get along far better with people who are much older or much younger.

If you're a first-born or only child, your early childhood memories are likely to reflect:

- Mistakes, goof-ups that really bothered you
- Times of achievement (in school or athletics)
- Self-discipline (being the "good" one)
- Concern about the approval of others
- Being afraid—especially of being hurt or falling
- Doing things right
- Authority figures

- Lots of detail
- Stressful or lonely times

Because only children and first-borns get huge amounts of attention, glory—and pressure—they share a common burden: the tar baby of perfectionism. If things don't go just right, the first-born or only child can get very uptight. We call perfectionism "slow suicide," and so it is. You don't have to be a first-born or only child to be a perfectionist, but our case loads often bear out this characterization.

The Middle Child Is Much More "Iffy"

Predicting the path for middle children is a much "iffier" proposition than it is with first-borns or babies. The personalities of middle children are less predictable because they are subject to pressures coming from more than one direction. To understand the middle child, you usually have to look at who is above and below.

One of the few rules you can cite for middle children is that they are likely to be the opposite of their first-born brother or sister. If big brother is an A student, the middle child may opt for athletics. She reasons: "Why fill a spot that is already taken? I'll carve my own niche in life."

Because they feel squeezed between the older and younger ones in the family, middle children get that "fifth-wheel" feeling. They go outside the home to spend time with friends more than anyone else in the family. In fact, friends are very important to middle-born kids. It's among friends that the middle-borns find recognition and feelings of acceptance.

Another typical characteristic of the middle child is the ability to negotiate. Many middle-born children are excellent diplomats who grow up to be mediators and go-betweens. They can also be quite manipulative, skilled in the art of compromise and working out conflicts through negotiation because they have to deal with both the older and younger siblings.

If you're a middle-born, your early childhood memories may well reflect:

- Feelings of not belonging
- Having lots of friends, and hearing Mom call you home from next door because you're late for dinner, again
- Feeling sensitive about being treated unjustly

· Compromising—being good at negotiation and "working things out"

Randy recalls counseling a thirty-three-year-old mother who specialized in smoothing the waters for her entire family, especially keeping peace between her husband and the in-laws. She clearly remembered the time when she was eight, and the entire family was going out for ice cream. Her older and younger sisters began pushing and fighting in the back seat, and her father threatened to cancel ice cream for everyone if they didn't shape up.

Marian clearly remembers saying, "Hey, if you knock it off, you can play with my Barbie dolls when we get back home." Because both sisters loved that Barbie doll collection, they quickly settled down and a good ice cream time was had by all.

Babies Love the Limelight

Last-born children, "babies," are often the attention-getters and comedians in their families. They love to be the life of the party—carefree, vivacious, and outgoing. Babies of the family love the limelight and can become self-centered because they want all the attention.

Kevin's early memories paint a clear picture—maybe it's a clear caricature—of a typical baby of the family. After he got the nickname "Cub," he made the most of it with attention-getting behavior that ranged from cute and amusing to boisterous and obnoxious.

If you're a baby of the family, your early childhood memories may well reflect:

· Being cute, getting attention with your antics
· Celebrating birthdays and Christmas and receiving gifts
· Having other people do things for you because you were "too little"
· Wanting to show those bigger, older kids you could do it, too
· Feeling that you always had to prove you could be trusted because you were youngest or "littlest"

Randy recalls counseling a last-born gentleman who clearly remembered being told when he was about six: "You can't climb up that ladder. Be sure to stay away from the ladder." Naturally, the little last-born waited until no one was around and went scampering up the ladder to the roof, where he screamed, "Hey, look at me." His parents came rushing out and almost had dual heart attacks on the spot. Naturally, the little last-born had to be rescued, something else that babies love.

BIRTH ORDER IS ONLY A PARTIAL PICTURE

This brief sketch of birth order may have left you feeling a bit confused. You may be a first-born who acts more like a middle child, but there are usually very good reasons for that. Every family tree grows with different branches. The correct psychological term is *constellation,* but family tree is more descriptive. (In some homes, family zoo comes even closer.) Different factors affect the assembly of each family, especially *spacing,* the number of years between each child. One important birth order rule of thumb says any gap of five or more years between children starts the entire system over.

Suppose, for example, you had this kind of family combination:

First-born male

Four-year gap

Second-born male

Six-year gap

Third-born male

Does this family of three boys with several years between each child sound familiar? You may remember Randy had two big brothers—one six years older and the other ten years ahead of him. Yes, Randy was last-born in his family, but instead of reflecting baby characteristics, he comes across with many first-born or only child traits. He's conscientious, serious, organized, cautious, and orderly. He wouldn't think of coming to work without his coat and tie, while Kevin often shows up to tape our radio show wearing tennis shoes, shorts, and a sport shirt. He would probably come in even less, but the station put up a sign just for him: "No shoes or shirt, no show!"

It's not hard to see why Randy came out more first-born than baby. With six and ten years between his older brothers and himself, he didn't spend that much time with them. In fact, he admits that he grew up as something of a loner, trying to avoid trouble and embarrassment. He recalls being the funniest child in the family, but not to get attention. Instead, he did it to keep the peace or relieve tension.

A subtle but important thing to remember about birth order is that the entire family changes with the birth of each child. Besides spacing, birth order can be affected by other forces:

The birth order of parents can make a real difference. For example, if two perfectionistic first-borns get together, they're going to rear their children a lot differently than two babies would.

A handicapped sibling can flip-flop everything and make a younger or older sibling do a complete role reversal to help care for a child who is handicapped.

A traumatic event or the death of a sibling can have a strong effect. So can physical differences like height, weight, and looks. For example, little first-born Dickie, who is ten years old, an even five feet tall, and ninety pounds dripping wet, is going to have his hands full with his second-born brother who is half a head taller, thirty-five pounds heavier, and answers to the name of "Moose."

And stepsiblings are an entirely different ball game. Many of today's Brady bunches are finding that they have at least two family constellations to work with, sometimes more.

Birth order is just part of the personality puzzle. The more pieces you can find that fit, the better you will understand yourself. And childhood memories are critical to your finding more pieces to the puzzle. As Kevin says, "Childhood memories are even more reliable than birth order as an indicator of 'why you are the way you are,' since these memories are the tapes you play in your head, which determine your response to everyday living."

Remember the analogy picturing a family enacting a drama on a stage? As you play your own role, you discover, by trial and error, what works and doesn't work—for you. It is here that your memories were made, and out of the scenes that made your memories, you developed your own unique style of living, or what is called your personality.

Chapter

7

Discipline—The Key to a Positive Kid's Greatness

And now we come to discipline—teaching and training, setting boundaries, training up a child in the way he is to go. The only way to raise positive kids is to be a positive parent. Discipline is not a negative thing, but an expression of your love for your children. I know it's tough to raise positive kids in today's negative world. Sometimes it's even harder to discipline them. That's why I've chosen this particular chapter from my book, Raising Positive Kids in a Negative World, *to give you a little help and support. You can see how important I think discipline is if you're trying to raise a positive kid. It's the key to his potential greatness, to his being a happy, healthy, creative, well-adjusted, and morally sound adult human being.*

Zig Ziglar
Raising Positive Kids in a Negative World

Discipline: "training or experience that corrects, molds, strengthens, or perfects."

A TRULY HANDICAPPED CHILD

Handicapped children come in many forms. For example, Freddie is a seriously handicapped child. I met him a number of years ago when I was in a home in South Carolina making a call on his family to sell a set of cookware. Just looking at him, you would seriously question my observation that he is handicapped. He was a precocious nine year old with beautiful blond hair and blue eyes. He was a little large for his age, and his dad said he was a "natural athlete." He made good grades in school and gave every indication of being a bright student. Yet I can honestly say he was one of the most handicapped youngsters I've ever met. He was handicapped behaviorally.

Freddie was rude, thoughtless, selfish, demanding, and inconsiderate, and he had a temper he used to manipulate and intimidate his family. At school he was not popular with his teacher or his classmates. When his parents visited friends, he was not exactly welcome because he took over and got the lion's share of whatever the host and hostess offered in the form of refreshments. He took the kids' toys and demanded to have his own way in everything. Later on in life when Freddie goes out to get a job, he's probably going to be faced with the same basic rejection he gets now when he goes places.

However, it's not Freddie's fault. He is simply doing exactly what he's been taught to do. His parents have indulged and spoiled him, maintaining they love him so much they just can't say no to him. By not saying no to his whims, demands, temper, boorishness, selfishness, and thoughtlessness, they're forcing the business, academic, and social communities to say no to the son they seldom said no to as he was growing up. How tragic, especially since Freddie, like *all* kids, really wanted to be loved enough to be disciplined.

I believe it is human nature for all of us from time to time to resist authority. At each stage of a child's life, he is going to take those steps of resistance. As a parent interested in raising a positive child, you need to understand that his resistance or rebellion does not mean he wants to win or that he wants you to surrender to him. He is simply testing you. What he wants is reassurance that you are firm and strong but still loving. He needs and must have boundaries within which he can operate and a loving authority to whom he can go with the confidence he's going to get the direction necessary to succeed in life.

SECURITY THROUGH DISCIPLINE

If you won't let your child open his mouth one day, but permit him to get away with murder the next day by talking back and being "sassy," you create incredible inner turmoil and problems for him. Dr. Bruno Bettelheim, the world-famous psychologist from the University of Chicago, says that any time a parent permits a child to talk back or put the parent down, to belittle or degrade him, serious damage is done to the child. The child's security is wrapped up in a parent he can trust and look to for strength and guidance. When the child belittles or degrades the parent, the child has no one to look up to. Consequently he loses his security.

One of the saddest things about overt permissiveness, when a parent lets a child "run loose" and do everything he wants to, is that it sets up expectancy in the child's mind that others should and will treat him the same way. That is both unreasonable and unrealistic. When an overindulged child visits or goes to play in other homes, and especially when he gets into school, as we would say down home, he is going to have a "long row to hoe."

This is certainly poor preparation for survival in our world today. Over the long haul, this leads to serious problems for both child and parents because many of the parents' best friends will not welcome the intrusion into their home of a little monster (as they see him) who is destructive, selfish, bad mannered, and ill-tempered and who abuses their own children. This causes the undisciplined one to feel rejected and certainly damages his ego and self-acceptance.

Discipline and order are part of the natural laws of the universe. The child who has not been disciplined with love by his little world (the family) will be disciplined, generally without love, by the big world.

PARENTS—NOT BUDDIES—BADLY NEEDED

Some parents work hard at becoming their children's "buddies," permitting the children to call them by their first names and treating the children as equals. In reality, there is nothing equal about a five year old and a thirty year old.

The obvious question is, If you become a pal to your child, when the need arises for you to discipline, instruct, or require certain conduct and performance from your child, why should he obey a pal's orders? After all, you're equal. At least that's the view you've created in his mind by becoming his buddy instead of his mom or dad—the one he can look to for protection, counsel, guidance, and loving discipline.

WHAT IS DISCIPLINE?

Discipline is teaching a child the way he should go. Discipline, therefore, includes everything you do to help your child learn. Unfortunately it's one of the most misunderstood words in the English language. Most people generally think of it as punishment or as something unpleasant. However, both Greek and Hebrew words denoting discipline include the meaning of chastening, correction, rebuke, upbringing, training, instruction, education, and reproof. The purpose of discipline is positive—to produce a whole person, free from the faults and handicaps that hinder maximum development.

One of the synonyms for discipline is *education.* The word *discipline* comes from *disciple,* who is "a follower of a teacher." A disciple should not follow his teacher out of fear of punishment, but out of love or conviction. Certainly positive, loving parents will want their children to follow them and their rules because they love and trust them, rather than because they fear them.

The child who has not been
disciplined with love
by his little world
will be disciplined,
generally without love,
by the big world.

The reality is that whether you do or don't discipline your child, you educate him to a particular set of values. Realistically, if you don't administer loving but fair discipline to the child, you can be certain society sooner or later *will,* but not always in a loving, fair manner. Perhaps that's the reason a 1980 Gallup Poll revealed that over 90 percent of the graduating high school seniors wished their parents and teachers loved them enough to discipline them more and require more of them. Maybe these young people instinctively knew that in the real world they would be entering (where the report card is a paycheck), they were going to need the knowledge, confidence, and discipline they had not received while they were in school. They know that winners are not developed on feather beds.

DISCIPLINE—WANTED, NEEDED, AND DEMANDED

I love this thought: "No man ever became great doing as he pleased." Little men do as they please; great men submit themselves to the laws governing the realm of their greatness.

When you teach a child discipline, you are giving him one of the most important tools for his future success and happiness. Instinctively children seem to know this. For example, in families where there is a divorce and the child is given a choice of which parent to live with, he almost always chooses the parent who is the disciplinarian—the one who has been the most firm and demanding of him. The child *knows* that real discipline is an expression of love and is in his long-range best interests.

The disciplined person is the one who does what needs to be done when it needs to be done. He is a practical pragmatist who does the things necessary and not just the things he wants to do. Show me someone who has accomplished anything of any significance, and I will show you a disciplined person.

NONE OF THEM ARE HAPPY

One summer when the Redhead and I were in Colorado on a "working vacation," we happened to see a well-known interviewer and commentator on TV. At that time this person undoubtedly knew more celebrities in Hollywood than anyone else. The discussion was about the death of comedian Freddie Prinz, whom some of you will undoubtedly remember. Freddie had just taken his own life, and the commentator was asked, "Do you know of any other superstar in athletics, music, entertainment, the television industry, or movies who might also be in danger of either deliberately or accidentally taking his own life?" After a moment's reflection, she answered with one of the saddest statements I've ever heard. "I don't know of anyone who is famous and in these fields who is not in danger of either deliberately or accidentally taking his own life, because I don't know a single one who is happy."

That's really tragic, isn't it? In most cases these people have more money than they can use, often spending more on a wardrobe in a month than the average person will spend in a span of years. Private jets take them anywhere they want to go; they receive an enormous amount of publicity; many of them have so much charisma they have to hire bodyguards to keep members of the opposite sex away from them. They're idolized and eulogized on a daily basis, and yet not a single one is happy. It becomes more evident every day that what you have is not going to make you happy—*it's what you are.* That's why in *Raising Positive Kids* I stress repeatedly that the qualities of life you teach your children are far more important than the "things" you give them.

SOME PRACTICAL TIPS FOR PARENTS

Mrs. Johnson came into young Billy's room to find him bandaging his thumb.

"What happened?" she asked.

"I hit it with a hammer."

"But I didn't hear you cry."

"I thought you were out."—A. H. Berzen*

This little "funny" is so true of life. To raise a positive kid, parents and grandparents need to ignore the child occasionally. I'm comfortable with the statement that virtually all parents have observed that when little Johnny or Mary falls, if Mom and Dad rush forward to pick him or her up, extend all sorts of sympathy, offer reassurances that everything's all right, and kiss away the hurt, they establish a pattern. Every time anything happens, little Johnny and little Mary cry, and Mom and Dad are on their way to raising a crybaby who will be dependent on them for too long.

Don't misunderstand. If your child falls and really *is* hurt, then obviously he needs your attention. But with our four, I can tell you their mother and I have seen them on many occasions "hurt" themselves. As we watched from the corners of our eyes, it was obvious that their reaction—crying and demanding attention or going on about their business—was entirely dependent upon whether or not we rushed forward to kiss away their hurts. I'll admit that after our first one, we became a little more discerning with the other three.

* Reprinted with permission from The Saturday Evening Post Society, A Division of BFL&MS, Inc. © 1984.

One little technique we developed was to watch the immediate reaction of our little girl. If she couldn't decide whether to laugh or cry, we would say, "Come over here and I'll pick you up." If she got up and came to us, we were comfortable she was going to survive.

On one memorable occasion when granddaughter "Sunshine" was four years old, she was crying about some imagined physical or emotional hurt. I took a very large mixing bowl from the cabinet and told her that her tears were far too valuable to lose and she must put all of them in the mixing bowl. We both got tickled, so that ended the tear-collection process.

Another event that begs to be ignored is the childhood squabble. When your child and another child get involved in one of the 28,211 squabbles they're going to have, you should usually maintain a discreet distance, assuming they are of roughly the same age and size. I'm not talking about permitting your child to injure or mutilate another, nor am I talking about permitting your child to be injured. I'm simply saying that when two four-year-olds have their differences about playing with a toy or being first in the sandbox, they are inevitably going to have countless little altercations. If parents get involved, the incidents are blown out of proportion, and the kids may stop playing together. Both of them, as well as their parents, lose as a result.

You might well ask, "How can you tell when to pick your child up when he falls?" or "How can you tell when is the time to intercede in childhood squabbles?" Those are questions no book can answer for you. You have to rely on that plain common sense and instinctive judgment God gives you as parents. Obviously, as you and the kids get older, you will become more adept at making the decisions that are best for you and your child.

DON'T BE A "UPAS TREE" PARENT

Though the advantages and benefits of Mom's staying home to raise the children have been dealt with at length, I want to stress that she needs to teach the children to be self-sufficient and not completely dependent on their parents. The worst possible mistake parents can make is to devote all of their time, attention, and energy to the children. That's what "upas tree" parents do. Let me explain.

The upas tree grows in Indonesia. It secretes poison and grows so full and thick that it kills all vegetation growing beneath it. It shelters, shades, and destroys. "Upas tree" parents smother their children, and although they don't actually choke off life itself, they effectively hinder growth and keep their children "babies" all their lives. Here's an example of how to be a upas tree parent.

Because of space limitations and because of their desire to be available to take care of the new baby, many young parents place the crib in their bedroom. Also, some couples make the mistake of starting to put their babies in bed with them "for the night." Both actions are unnecessary unless the baby is sick or extremely fretful and the mother feels the baby needs the comfort and reassurance of her presence. Among other things, there is always the danger that mom or dad will roll over and injure the baby. Whether anything happens physically or not, if this situation continues, it will destroy the normal life-style and relationship between husband and wife. (P.S.: I'm not talking about the small child getting up in the early morning hours and occasionally sneaking into bed with Mom and Dad for some extra snuggling and hugging.)

Of considerable significance is the fact that the child will grow accustomed to sleeping with the parents and will soon be unable or unwilling to sleep anywhere else. When this happens, you, your child, and your marriage are facing a rocky road ahead, which means the little one has to get out of your bed and bedroom.

It is true that your child might not sleep as well the first night he is alone, but it is also true that by the fourth or fifth night he will sleep pretty well. And you will sleep much better, which will make you better parents.

START THE TEACHING PROCESS EARLY

Start teaching your children to do things at an early age, provided, of course, there is no physical danger involved, such as using a knife, a power lawn mower, or some other potentially harmful tool. But things like sweeping the floor, taking out the trash, making the bed, and so on are appropriate activities for youngsters.

Frankly it would be much simpler for you to go ahead and do those things. You can do them so much better and faster, and actually with less effort than it takes to spend some time persuading and teaching the child how to do them. The problem is that a four year old is often unaware of his limitations, and at that stage of the game he believes he can do just about anything and is anxious to give it a shot. When you put the child aside and say, "Here, let Dad or Mom do it," you are sending a message.

The message is, "You can't do it very well, but Dad or Mom can." You will probably need some time to convince him of it, but by the time the child is nine or ten years old, you will have totally convinced him that you are much better at doing everything than he is. As a result, the child not only will "let" you do everything but also will obstinately refuse to help you around the house. Either that or he will do it so grudgingly that you come to the conclusion that you were right all the time. Of course, you will send a child into the world both unprepared and unwilling to tackle anything difficult or distasteful.

You raise positive kids by teaching *and* requiring them early on to do the *little* things around the house. Step by step they naturally progress into accepting more and more responsibility until the happy day arrives when they will be able to do many things better than either parent. That's when you will know that discipline pays.

DOUBLE-BARRELED BURDEN

"It hurts me worse than it hurts you!" That statement has been handed down through the generations. No doubt many a kid has heard that and wondered to himself, *Oh, yeah? Well, why don't we just trade places for awhile!* When they're on the receiving end of such consolation, you can bet that kids aren't feeling sorry for their parents, but it is one of the toughest parts of parenting. I call that dilemma the "Double-Barreled Burden." It's like a double-barreled gun that shoots in both directions. You've got to think about it before you start shooting.

The way you reprimand your kids is a very sensitive aspect of parenting, because the method you use will have an effect on their esteem. You should reprimand and criticize the action, not the person who committed the action. When you have an understanding with your kids, they know what's expected of them. If they don't do what's expected and agreed upon, they expect, even demand, a reprimand. Not to follow through is to weaken and negate the possibility of future effective follow-through in regard to your other requirements. When kids do something wrong and get by with it, they feel guilty. The only way to relieve that guilt and to reinforce your authority and your rules is to effectively deal with the problem.

The disciplined person
is the one who does
what needs to be done
when it needs to be done.

SHOULD YOU ACTUALLY SPANK THEM?

Speaking on parental discipline, Billy Graham once told of the time his two-year-old son spat at him in a fit of anger. He said, "I don't know where he learned such an ugly habit, but one thing I know for certain: If that boy chews tobacco when he grows up, he'll swallow the juice. After what I did to him, he'll never spit again."

Question: Is physical discipline (spanking) necessary?

Answer: Yes, it is, for several reasons. Primarily, children between the ages of about two and twelve live out a decade in life when they lack the maturity to listen to, understand, and responsibly follow their parents' instructions. Part of the fabric of humanity is a matter of individual will. Kids come into the world, into the family, and into society without any controls on that will. One of the most significant aspects of maturity is learning to be self-controlled or self-disciplined. A young child simply will not have this kind of maturity. Discipline literally means "to train," and youngsters need a lot of training; most of it should be of a verbal or spoken nature, but some of it will have to be of a firm, physical nature.

As a rule of thumb, when your child is "willfully disobedient" toward you, that's when physical action is necessary. It could be the swiftest, surest way to get your message across. If a kid continues approaching something of danger after several verbal warnings about the danger—playing in the street, standing on chairs or on top of kitchen counters, climbing on the roof of the house, playing with matches or with household appliances—then it is imperative that you react swiftly. A little heat on the bottom should instantly communicate what you mean.

Kids will "ask for it," but they don't always understand what they are asking for. It might take a few instances of willful disobedience, followed by instant corrective action, before they understand and follow your parental guidance. You must not fail to give them what they're asking for. It is critically important that you give your kids a spanking if they challenge you. You must realize that your decision to spank will be met with protest. You must also realize that kids don't always want what they're asking for, but they usually need it.

USE WITH CARE

When approaching corporal discipline, you must recognize first of all that spanking is only one means of discipline. It should be used with careful discretion, primarily when willful disobedience is involved. When there is a need to spank, the way you do it is also important. Never spank your child when you are angry. Kids can and will do things that will make you absolutely furious. *That's not the time to spank them.*

My good friend psychiatrist John Kozek suggested that if you are overly angry because of your child's disobedience and it calls for a spanking, wait a few moments to calm yourself. You need to be certain that the intensity of your discipline fits the offense and that it's not related to the intensity of your anger. Dr. Kozek recommended that, if possible, the other parent should be present and your discipline should be followed by expressions of love with lots of hugging and holding and explanations of the reasons for the spanking. This is probably the most important thing to convey to your kids —that you love them—and because you love them and because of their disobedience, you discipline (spank) them.

Your spanking conveys a message of care, concern, and love and helps them to eliminate feelings of guilt. Psychologists will tell you that guilt is very destructive, but it is harmful only if it is not dealt with. When a child rebels or disobeys a parent, there is a feeling of guilt, and the guilt is real. The spanking will serve to remove the guilt, and as Chuck Swindoll says, the child's tears flush out his guilt and clear his conscience.

But how often do you spank? How often is it needed? There will be periods in the growth and development of your child when you will have to spank more often than at other times. As he reaches grade school age, if proper discipline has been administered in the early years, the need to spank diminishes. That need is something for the parent to decide; no one can really judge but you.

However, let's think about some reasonable guidelines. Until children can understand your words and can comprehend your "redirection" of their close calls with danger and difficulty (about fifteen to eighteen months of age), your maturity as an adult must prevent you from taking physical action.

BE CAREFUL HOW YOU DISCIPLINE

The "shaken-infant syndrome" is now being reported around the country. Parents, otherwise well-meaning in their behavior, have shaken their infants so severely that brain damage has resulted. Usually the parents are trying to stop their infants from crying or to punish a baby for a perceived misdeed, which most often is merely childish clumsiness. Not only are such efforts fruitless with infants, because they are too young to understand what is required of them, but the tragedy could have been averted if parents understood more about what to expect from young children. Shaking a baby is not discipline—it is abuse.

Infants are going to cry when they're hungry, hot, cold, uncomfortable, wet, or sick. Toddlers are going to be clumsy. When a child spills, damages, or "destroys" something because of childish clumsiness, spanking is only confusing, because it is for the wrong reason. You don't spank because a kid has black hair and not brown hair, or because he has freckles and not dimples. Neither do you spank because of childish, immature ways.

But what if it's dinner time and two-year-old Billy won't stay in his chair? An appropriate application to the backside should do the job, especially if you leave the ruler or other spanking object in plain view of the child.

As a child approaches kindergarten and school age, he continues to need to be disciplined for his willful disobedience, but he also needs to be instructed about the motivation behind his behavior. Other means of discipline, such as restrictions and deductions of allowance and other privileges, become more effective.

That raises another important question concerning what you will use to spank your child. A very definite rule is that you use a "neutral" object such as a light ruler or yardstick rather than your hand. The main concern is that it must not be a heavy object that would cause injury. That would be a tragedy. The object used must deliver enough "warmth" to the backside that it does what it is intended to do. As the old saying goes, "No pain, no gain."

When the need to discipline comes, it is imperative that you use not your hand but a neutral object that will not be associated with you personally. If the situation is really critical (as with a small child and immediate danger) and you must use your hand to quickly swat him a time or two to get his attention, that is fine. However, when disciplinary action is seen as necessary for repeated or serious defiance of parental direction, then a more "formal" approach, meaning privacy with the child in the home and with appropriate disciplinary action, is the course to take.

CAREFUL ABOUT THE WHEN AND WHERE

Another thing about the way you use corporal, "of the body," discipline is that you never strike a child, young or old, upon the face. If you've ever tried to pet a "whupped dog," a defenseless, cowering critter that was regularly slapped by his master, then you understand why slapping a child would literally destroy the spirit rather than channel and redirect the spirit and will, which is what appropriate discipline does. The interesting thing about it all is that the body is equipped with a sensitive but naturally well-padded "point of disciplinary contact." That's right—the backside is the place to deliver the discipline called for.

The sweet joys of family life will be wisely salted from time to time with some form of firm, corporal discipline. It is a part of the normal way of life and parenting. It is to be used sparingly, with very careful restraint, but it most certainly will be used by those seeking to raise positive kids. Child discipline revolutionaries will cry that such things strike at the foundation of a child's personality. Just as a master's chisel strikes to carve the rough edges off a block of stone to ultimately reveal his masterpiece, so the brief shock of corporal discipline tears at the personality of a child—tears him away from his immaturity and selfish recklessness and propels him toward the toughness and maturity needed to face a negative world and win!

God's discipline
produces strength,
not weakness.

A WARNING FOR ALL PARENTS

Sometimes there is a thin line between spanking and child abuse. If you ever get carried away and so completely lose control that you spank (beat) your child too hard, you *must* forever abandon corporal punishment as a method of disciplining your child. If his body (bottom) carries welts, bruises, cuts, or abrasions an hour later, you have overdone the punishment. *This is the most important paragraph in this book.*

"PERMISSIVE" VERSUS "AUTHORITARIAN"

In his book, *How to Make Your Child a Winner,* Dr. Victor Cline, a professor of psychology at the University of Utah in Salt Lake City, states that a major disaster occurred in a large number of American families starting in the 1950s. Called by many names, most frequently "permissiveness" and "family democracy," it was a noble experiment based on the mistaken notion that young children are basically wise and good and perfectly able to determine their own destinies. Exerting control over your children was called "authoritarian" and "antidemocratic." Spanking, even in love, was seen by certain "experts" as a form of child abuse. Being a good parent meant letting your kids "do their own thing." Dr. Cline states he is in complete disagreement with almost all of those premises of the fifties. He points out that by setting reasonable limits on your child's behavior and enforcing them, you're helping your child establish his own inner controls over his antisocial impulses.

Psychologist James Dobson, the author of *The Strong-Willed Child,* states "It is certain that I will make mistakes, but I cannot abandon my responsibility simply because I lack infinite wisdom and insight. Besides, I do have more experience and a better perspective on which to base decisions than my children do. I've been where they're going."

In a series of studies conducted by psychologist Stanley Coopersmith, he found children with high self-esteem have parents who run a tight ship with a clearly defined and comprehensive set of rules, zealously enforced. These findings suggest that parents who have definite values, who have a clear idea of what they regard as appropriate behavior, who make their beliefs known to their children are more likely to rear children who value themselves highly, develop their own sense of ethics, and have greater respect and affection for their parents.

If parents don't assume this responsibility, if they don't set and consistently enforce reasonable limits, the child is apt to interpret this as parental indifference. This makes the child anxious and reduces his capacity to develop inner controls.

Discipline is necessary and good. You can't raise successful children without it, but discipline should not repress or tyrannize. Discipline should lead to powerful habits of direction, work, and good judgment. Good discipline produces strength, not weakness; creativity, not banality; responsibility, not self-indulgence. It can also help shape the character out of which a capacity to love and sacrifice can emerge.

Chapter

8

Managing a Child's Anger

Anger is a scary emotion—for parents and children. Do you often speak tensely to your children? Do you give in too easily, wanting peace at any cost? Do you feel you have to defend your disciplinary actions excessively? These are all signs of hidden anger; and if you were not taught as a child how to manage your anger in healthy ways, more than likely you are unable to teach your child. Mismanaged anger is then compounded and passed from generation to generation. Your children are going to have trouble with anger also—their own and yours.

In The Anger Workbook, *we help you as an adult identify the underlying causes of your anger—unmet needs, feeling controlled, fear, pride, loneliness, or inferiority feelings—and resolve them. It is by dealing with your own anger that you are able to better deal with your children's anger, recognize its causes and respond correctly.*

In this chapter, we want to look specifically at how you can teach your children to manage their own angry emotions. With these insights and a little work, we can keep from passing on anger from generation to generation.

Dr. Les Carter
Dr. Frank Minirth
The Anger Workbook

Ideally, healthy anger management is learned during childhood and refined as the stages of life unfold. Unfortunately, most parents were not properly guided in using anger during their own childhoods, and their accumulated bad habits are then passed along to the next generation. It can be an ever-perpetuating cycle until someone steps forward and says, "The buck stops here."

One such person was Patricia. When she came for counseling she was in her early forties, the mother of a fifteen-year-old boy and a ten-year-old girl. She had sought help because her emotions were ruling her life. She admitted she was causing so much tension, her family was coming apart.

In an early visit with Dr. Carter she said, "Either I get a grip on my tension or I'm going to lose my husband. And if that happens, my children will surely turn against me. They're tired of my constant irritability."

She began a series of counseling sessions that trained her to minimize her emotional ups and downs. After incorporating the insights she had learned and significantly reducing her level of anger, she stated, "I don't want my children to enter adulthood with the same baggage I had. Starting now I want to give them some tips about handling their emotions successfully. Jason is fifteen, so I don't have a lot of time left with him, but I know he would be receptive. Jennifer is ten and she's just like I was at that age, sweet in public but sour in private."

"By reflecting on your own childhood experiences perhaps you can remember what it's like to be their ages, having emotions but not feeling certain what to do with them," Dr. Carter suggested.

"Oh, I know what they are going through. They've seen me on my emotional roller coaster often enough to be confused. Sometimes they bottle up their frustrations, which become seeds for discontent and resentment. Other times they jump right in and slug it out."

"Are they openly argumentative with you?"

"Sometimes they are. Jason wants to be very independent so he usually resists restrictions I put on him. He has a real temper when pushed. Jennifer is more of a pouter and whiner. When she's angry she becomes cranky. She really knows how to push my buttons."

"It's going to require some consistency and discipline on your part," said Dr. Carter, "but with persistence you can become the guide they need."

KEYS TO HANDLING YOUR CHILD'S ANGER

Perhaps the greatest error parents make is letting the child set the agenda for how emotions are managed in the family. Parents may have good intentions about being firm or fair-minded, but when the child fails to respond as expected those good intentions go right out the window. This is what we call a reactor mentality in the parent. To counter this tendency, parents need to go on the initiative. Rather than wondering, *How can I get the child to behave so I can be composed?* they can ask themselves, *How can I be composed so I can get the child to behave?*

There are several ways to accomplish this. In this chapter, we'll share six ideas we've found to be effective: don't be threatened by your child's anger, let choices and consequences shape the child, don't preach, don't major on the minors (meaning don't let minor problems deplete your parenting energy supply), share your own experiences, and incorporate spiritual insights delicately. Let's look at each of these suggestions separately.

Don't Be Threatened by Your Child's Anger

Sometimes anger can be caused by unresolved fears that are manifested as defensiveness. Do you ever think of yourself as being *afraid* of your child's anger? If you get easily caught in power plays or if you often speak tensely to your child, you may be exhibiting this kind of defensiveness and revealing how threatened you are. Subconsciously, the child reacts with manipulation.

Dr. Carter sensed that Patricia worried too much about her son's responses to her discipline. "When Jason balks at your discipline, it seems to spark a tense reaction in you. It's as though you're thinking, *How dare he disagree with my wisdom!*"

"Well, in a sense that's exactly what I'm thinking," she replied. "I can't figure out why he has to be so contrary. For example, last Saturday he wanted to spend the entire day with his friends, then go out again that evening. I made him stay home in the afternoon to finish some chores. By his reaction you would have thought I was the Wicked Witch of the West. I don't know what to do when he gets into these moods, but they have got to stop."

"I can appreciate the annoyance you felt," said Dr. Carter, "but let's look at something very basic. Kids Jason's age want to be with their peers. In fact, it would be abnormal if he didn't want to hang out with his buddies. So when Mom says he needs to stay home he's going to interpret that as a real insult. Now you and I both know you have sound reasons for your decision, but he hasn't taken the time to consider your viewpoint. And he probably won't consider your viewpoint deeply for many years to come. So it's no surprise he would balk."

"You're saying I am too easily shocked by his anger when I really should just accept it as a normal teenage reaction?"

"That's right. Children have an ongoing internal conflict about authority. At one level they know they need the guidance, but on another level they're preoccupied with themselves and they want zero input. So his response is hardly surprising. He's playing out his conflict with you.

"My suggestion is," Dr. Carter continued, "don't be threatened by his anger. He's just being normal. This doesn't mean you shouldn't maintain your boundaries. But don't feel like you have to immediately squelch his irritation. That's not your job."

Parents who are easily threatened by a child's anger respond in several common ways. Check the following responses that apply to you.

_____ You say yes when you know it is best to say no.

_____ When a child challenges your ideas you immediately speak with greater force.

_____ You give excessive explanations for choosing a discipline.

_____ Inwardly you think, *How dare my child speak to me in that tone of voice.*

_____ You are not sure your child takes you seriously when you say something.

_____ You give in too easily to a child's whining or fussing, wanting peace at any cost.

Recall some examples of times you have been threatened by your child's anger? *(For instance, I responded very heavy-handedly when my daughter talked back to me.)*

When we respond in fear to a child's anger, we communicate, *You are a very powerful force in my life and I have to overwhelm you to teach you anything.* It is an invitation to battle. And any time a parent battles the child, everyone loses.

So what is the alternative? First, let your child be human. You've had moments of irritability, too, and you probably don't respond all that well when someone attempts to scold you for your emotions. Allow your child the same latitude. Second, quietly hold firm to your rightful authority, even if the child eyes you with skepticism. If your words make sense and your discipline is fair, let them stand on their own merits. Don't attempt to sell a child something that needs no salesmanship.

When you lose your shock over a child's anger, the result is increased objectivity and the ability to relate with reason and fairness. Stability and logic, rather than knee-jerk emotion, will be your guide. A calm firmness will permeate your character, prompting the child to realize the futility of power plays.

Dr. Carter explained to Patricia, "When you are not threatened by your child's anger you can use the 'nonetheless' approach to discipline."

She smiled as she responded, "I'm not sure what you mean by the 'nonetheless' approach, but I'm all ears."

"Suppose you tell your son, 'If you are going out with your friends tonight I'll need you to stay home this afternoon to help me clean the garage.' He protests angrily and complains how unreasonable you are for making him do slave's labor."

"Have you been looking in my windows? That sounds just like some of the conversations we have."

"At that point you are susceptible to being threatened by his anger, and you feel compelled to defend your decision by explaining why he should not be feeling as he does."

"I do that all the time, but it never seems to get me anywhere."

"Patricia, your explanations only fuel his fire. So it's time to drop them in favor of a 'nonetheless' statement. You can say, 'Jason, I know you're frustrated because you'll have to alter your plans. Nonetheless, the garage needs to be cleaned this afternoon.' "

"But Dr. Carter, what if he continues to protest? He's not going to just fall in line based on one calm statement I make."

"Don't be threatened by his protest. Continue your course. You can say again, 'Nonetheless, the garage needs to be cleaned so you can go out this evening.' And if he protests again, tell him the same thing again with no pleading or persuasion. It's your way of communicating that you are confident enough in your decision that you can withstand his angry reaction. Eventually he'll get the picture and lower his anger level."

As you consider being more confident in yourself and less threatened by your child's emotions, think of adjustments you could make when your child responds irritably to you. *(For instance, when my daughter complains about her supper, I can calmly tell her, "I know you're disappointed because this is not what you were hoping for tonight; nonetheless, this is what we're having for supper and this is what you get to eat.")*

By recommending that you drop your sense of shock and be less defensive about your decisions, we are not suggesting that you never explain your reasoning to the child. Sometimes it can be quite helpful for the child to know why you make the decisions you do. But if your explanations rapidly deteriorate into a useless debate, it is time to allow the child to feel frustrated while you hold your ground with calm firmness.

Let Choices and Consequences Shape the Child

We parents can be impatient for our children to learn important lessons. For example, if a child is rude or disruptive to a sibling we want the child to stop behaving so intolerably. So what do we do? We tell the child how to think. We give lectures and follow up with threats. And how does this affect the child? He or she becomes angrier and inwardly vows that no one will tell him or her what to do. It is not the instruction itself that the child is angry about, it is the fact that the adult is not letting the child have choices.

In one of her early counseling sessions with Dr. Carter, Patricia revealed how she typically succumbed to ineffective responses when her ten-year-old daughter Jennifer would whine about something trivial. For example, Jennifer commonly griped about not having enough clothes to wear or not having anything to do to fill her free time. Patricia's typical response would be, "How can you possibly think those things? Your closet is full of clothes and the cabinet has more games in it than you'll ever play! You can't say you've got it bad."

Dr. Carter responded with a smile and a sly question, "When you say that to Jennifer, how many times does she reply with, 'Hey, Mom, thanks for pointing that out, I guess I needed the perspective'?"

Laughing, Patricia said, "Never! We just get drawn further into a hole of anger."

"Your mistake," said Dr. Carter, "is trying to think for your daughter. Rather than doing the mental work for her, let her choose for herself how she'll handle her tension. For example, when she says she has nothing to wear to school, let her know she can select whatever is in her closet. Then be quiet and allow her choices to unfold."

"But if I tell her that, she might make a poor choice. I'm not going to let her go to school looking totally inappropriate."

"I can appreciate your concern," said Dr. Carter, "although I caution you against being too finicky about the choices you'll allow. My point is that you are doing her no favors by trying to think for her. She needs the experience of struggling with her own emotions. Right now her decisions are relatively harmless, but ten years from now when she is living on her own, she'll need to know how to sift through opinions about more complex matters and make the best choice. Now is the best time for her to develop strategies for managing her emotions. But she won't become proficient if you get in the way."

Take a moment to write on a separate sheet of paper some common situations when you try to think for your child and steer him or her emotions your way. *(For instance, when my son complains that his friends are mean, I tell him to quit worrying about it and play with someone else.)*

Children need to feel competent to manage their own anger. With that in mind, parents can toss the ball into their court by asking questions such as, "What do you think can be done about this?" or "What opinions do you have?" In this subtle way, the parent communicates confidence in the child.

"Let's take a common situation," suggested Dr. Carter, "and I'll show you what I mean. Let's assume Jennifer complains that her brother is rude to her. She comes whining to you about the problem, prompting you to grope for ways to solve their tension. Is that a fairly common scenario in your home?"

"All too common. Jennifer can really make life miserable when Jason puts her in a foul mood."

"It's at times like this when you'll be tempted to think for Jennifer. So let's be careful about deciding how you'll respond. Normally, you might say, 'Well, just stay away from Jason and quit fighting.' Right?"

"Right. It doesn't usually work, but you've got me pegged."

"Well, let's try a different approach, one that encourages Jennifer to take greater responsibility for her emotions. Throw the problem back into her lap by telling her, 'I see you're feeling frustrated because Jason shows you no respect. What options do you have to manage this frustration?' "

"Dr. Carter, she'll probably continue whining and say, 'I don't know.' "

"Don't take her bait; instead, tell her, 'This won't be an easy problem to solve, but you always have choices. You can argue back with Jason, you can hold a grudge, you can go to a different part of the house. Which choice makes the most sense to you?' Keep putting it back into her lap."

"What if she chooses to go back to Jason and scream?"

"Let her know that is, indeed, an option, but it carries a consequence, perhaps no play time for the rest of the afternoon. She'll soon learn to pick a different option."

Make a list of areas you could more freely offer choices to your children. *(For instance, I could let them choose the time of day they complete their homework assignments.)*

Using choices and consequences can be more time-consuming for parents than merely telling the child what to do. But the child becomes more responsible and is forced to think about the direction of his or her emotions. It causes the child to struggle to come to terms with who he or she will be. Ultimately, the child becomes an initiator of healthy behavior rather than just one who lives according to someone else's dogma.

Don't Preach

To teach our children to handle their anger correctly, we adults must model healthy communication. That means avoiding such ironic responses to a child's anger as warning, "You'd better get your act together or I'll give you something to be mad about." The irony is the condescending anger this adult shows while he or she tells the child to stop being angry. The child responds more to the tone of the message than to the message itself.

Adults are more effective in helping children handle their anger when they give a low-key performance in the authority-figure role. To put it another way, the top dog who barks too loudly is ultimately regarded as an insecure nuisance.

To determine if you lean too heavily on an authoritative style, check the level of persuasion in your speech. Do you debate fine points with your child? Do you offer rebuttals to your child's point of view? Do you work extra hard to convince the child of the validity of your opinion? Do you accuse your child of insubordination and induce guilt for being different?

Jot down ways you may carry out the authority-figure role too heavy-handedly. *(For instance, I raise my voice when my child disagrees with me; I make too many threats.)*

Patricia admitted, "I know I'm less effective with my kids when I'm heavy-handed; it only increases their anger. But it's hard to resist the temptation to come on strong when one of them is contrary."

"From personal experience, I know that to be true," Dr. Carter nodded. "But I want you to focus on a subtle but powerful truth: Our greatest impact on people is not in the words we speak but in the way we deliver those words. Our manner can convey many unspoken messages about our respect and trust for the other person and about our confidence in ourselves. When we speak too strongly it implies disrespect, lack of trust, and personal insecurity."

Our greatest impact on people is not in the words we speak but in the way we deliver those words.

"You're implying then that I should respond to my kids' anger with an even tone of voice. That's easier said than done."

"That's so true," Dr. Carter replied. "But if you can keep an even tone, you are showing your children how to disagree without being disagreeable. You are showing them that differentness does not have to result in an adversarial relationship."

Learn to recognize the meaning of your child's anger. Many times anger is linked to self-preservation instincts. When you speak to a child in a way that emphasizes your authority over his or her worth, you keep the anger alive in that child. But when you speak respectfully, even in disagreements, you diffuse the reason for the anger.

Don't Major in the Minors

Have you noticed how children get upset over the most trivial things?

- An eight-year-old girl is mad because her mother makes her wear pants on a cold day rather than the skirt she prefers.

· A fifteen-year-old boy complains that he has to be home at night thirty minutes earlier than his buddy.

· A group of fifth-graders moan about the extra math homework the teacher assigned.

· An eager young boy pouts because his mother won't let him ride his bike on a stormy afternoon.

Children are not faced with the same issues that confront their parents. Their big dilemmas are small in comparison to worries about inflation, health care, rising crime, etc. Nonetheless, it is necessary for them to resolve the problems that seem major. They feel just as irritated about an insult on the school playground as we feel about business matters that cause financial strain. And their maturity is slowed when adults don't know how to respond to their emotions.

In most cases, when minor problems affect our children, we parents make the mistake of giving them too much attention. In doing so we increase the child's anger. For example:

· When an eleven-year-old girl says she wants to buy an item that costs three dollars more than her mother wants to spend, the mother reacts with extreme agitation and putdowns.

· When a sixteen-year-old son forgets to fill the car with gas as his dad requested, the father grounds him for two weeks.

· When a seven-year-old spills a drink on the kitchen floor the parent complains repeatedly about the child's clumsiness, warning it cannot be tolerated.

Sound absurd? It is. But too often we expend excessive energy on issues of little significance, thus perpetuating an atmosphere of unnecessary anger.

On a sheet of paper write ways you have majored on the minors. *(For instance, I gave my son the silent treatment for several hours when he told me he forgot to bring a book home from school.)*

Why do we do this? Our overemphasis on trivia represents a shallow understanding of the purpose of relationships. When we respond this way, the important matters of relationships—respect, encouragement, and empathy—take a backseat to perfectionism, selfishness, impatience, and petty preferences.

Check the following statements you can agree with:

____I'd rather let a child make minor errors and learn from those mistakes than insist on a mistake-free life.

____In our home, differentness is not only allowed, it is often encouraged.

____I prefer to save my discipline for issues that really matter.

____When a child becomes upset over simple things, I can be objective and not get pulled into the emotions of the moment.

____I can chuckle or smile to myself about some of the little worries that bother kids.

____I am not obliged to fix every minor problem my child presents to me.

When we focus too heavily on minor issues we teach children to be imbalanced in their anger. But when we let minor issues remain minor, the emotions are minimized.

Share Your Own Experiences

Children are at a disadvantage because they are not as aware of adult struggles as we are of their problems. When they become angry or insecure their emotions are on display for all the world to see. But when adults become angry or insecure, those feelings are often hidden. Or worse, children easily see the adult's emotion but they are not allowed to discuss their reactions to it. This leaves the child with a negative feeling of differentness that ultimately increases irritability.

Children need openness and honesty with their parents if they are to develop emotional composure, and this openness should not be a one-way window into the child's feelings. Children need to see the insides of their parents too.

Patricia raised an eyebrow when Dr. Carter suggested that openness with Jason and Jennifer would go a long way toward helping them contain their emotions. "I'm not sure it would be best to confess my problems to my children. For their own security they need to think I've got it together."

"Let's look at an interesting idea," Dr. Carter responded. "Your children are insightful enough to know you have mood swings just as they do. But it creates more questions than it solves when you are secretive about them. You'll show your level of inner confidence when you can freely discuss your own emotions with them. You'll become more believable and thus more approachable. Ultimately this removes the pressure for them to be perfect, and their own emotions are less severe."

The next week she reported, "I tried what we discussed and was amazed at the result. Jennifer was complaining about being rejected by a friend at school and I shared with her a similar experience I had when I was her age. As I told her my story her mood shifted noticeably. She was more relaxed, and several times in the next couple of days she asked follow-up questions."

"So when you shared with her, she felt less isolated," said Dr. Carter. "Your self-disclosure created an opportunity for cohesion. I imagine her pain then became less severe."

Take a moment to think of what keeps you from being open in your parent-child communications. Write some of these in a journal, or on a sheet of paper. *(For instance, my parents never spoke about personal matters with me; I stay too focused on performances.)*

When parents refuse to be vulnerable with their children, they create an atmosphere of phoniness and false superiority, and the children resent it. Ultimately, the parents' authority position is weakened. But when parents are willing to be authentic, family communication opens significantly. The child thinks, *Hey, you really do know what the score is. I can relate to you now.*

Think of a time in your own experiences when a friend or relative made himself or herself vulnerable and shared a very personal matter with you. Were you put off by it? Were you offended? Or were you appreciative? Did your respect for that person rise? If managed appropriately, that relationship was probably strengthened substantially, much as it would be if you injected deep sharing into your relationship with your child.

How would you respond to the following sentences?

When I tell my child of a struggle similar to his, he is likely to feel

____.

If I refuse to expose my humanness to my child, our relationship will probably ____.

The reward for self-disclosure would be ___________________________.

Incorporate Spiritual Insights Delicately

Anger management is ultimately a function of spiritual maturity. When we are in a right relationship with God, living consistently in His plans, we find the strength to overcome adversities that might otherwise seem paralyzing. The prophet Isaiah explained, "You will keep him in perfect peace, / Whose mind is stayed on You" (Isa. 26:3).

Spiritual insights are necessary for each child who seeks emotional peace. But how well are these insights taught? Most children's exposure to spiritual life consists of hearing interesting Bible stories and learning a long list of do's and dont's. That's it. But beyond the objective facts, they need guidance to incorporate solid Christian truths into their daily lives. The process of teaching spiritual insights to a child is not complex, but it requires great delicacy. That is, truths about grace or forgiveness or respectful confronting can be woven into everyday communication as common circumstances arise.

Consider some of the prominent spiritual truths you want your child to incorporate and write those on a sheet of paper. *(For instance, I want my child to know the merits of forgiveness; I want my child to be less self-serving and more sensitive to others.)*

Now ask yourself, *How do I go about teaching these truths to my child?*

Patricia was particularly eager to pass along good spiritual instructions to her children. She told Dr. Carter, "I guess I've lectured my kids dozens of times about the advantages of spiritual commitments. They both have accepted Christ as their Savior, but I'm not sure they understand how He can guide them in daily matters."

"Let me hazard a guess that you usually tell Jason and Jennifer what truths they should know without asking about those truths' impact on them."

"I've never thought about it much, but I think you're right. So what are you getting at?"

"Once the children have been taught the basic rules of right and wrong," Dr. Carter explained, "your role can shift from instructor to facilitator. Take common situations and ask them to apply spiritual values to those situations."

Here are examples of how Patricia learned to communicate in deeper ways:

· Jason was aware that some of his friends had experimented with alcohol, so Patricia mentioned, "You've heard me talk about maintaining a good witness for the Lord, but I'm curious to know how you can do this with these friends."

· When Jennifer expressed anger toward a friend who had been rude, Patricia asked, "Do you suppose you can forgive even when a friend does nothing to deserve it?"

Children will not always apply spiritual truths maturely. They can be wildly erratic (as adults can) in remembering what they've learned. The parents' goal is not to force spiritual perfection but to keep contemplative thinking alive. In time, children can fine-tune their religious concepts as they gain understanding of God's plan for their lives. By encouraging an inquisitiveness about biblical truths, their beliefs are less legalistic and more personally meaningful.

PART TWO

The Growing Family: Mind and Spirit

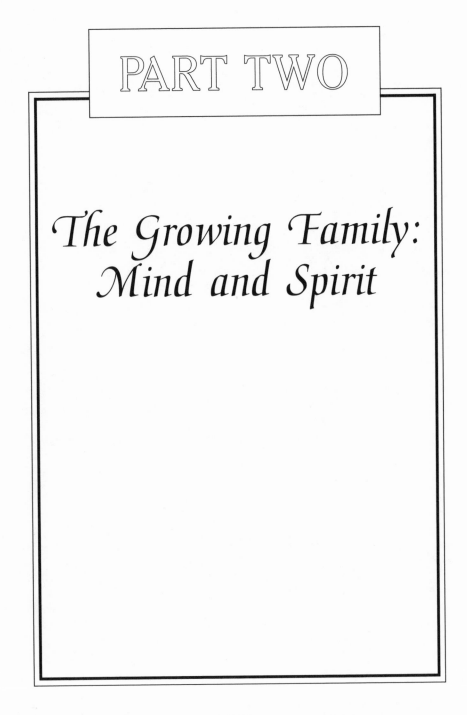

Chapter

9

Self-Esteem: I Feel Like Such a Failure at Times

You can get most experts to agree on this: Self-esteem is one of the most important, life-giving factors you can instill in your children. And what influences your ability to nurture self-esteem in your children? You guessed it—your own positive self-esteem! Self-esteem is an essential building block of a good family, one I have discussed in my book Single Mothers Raising Sons.

I want to encourage you first to be gentle and kind to yourself as you develop, protect, and maintain your own positive self-image. Then I would like to contribute some very concrete, practical ideas for creating and developing a healthy self-esteem in your children—from keeping a "Life Notebook" with your child to family nights together.

Bobbie Reed
Single Mothers Raising Sons

A few years ago I decided to buy a personal computer and a printer. Because I didn't know much about the different models, I relied heavily on the advice of a couple of friends who had worked with computers for some time and were satisfied with what they had purchased. I ended up with very good bargains, a Brand A computer and a Brand B printer. The price was right and I was assured that the

Brand B printer worked with the Brand A computer. I was told they were "compatible."

In the next few weeks I experienced a tremendous amount of frustration. Often I regretted ever buying a computer. I even went so far as to pack up the computer and printer intending to return them. They wouldn't do what I wanted them to! What I wanted was to bring home my new "toys," unpack them, quickly scan the instruction manual, and be able to start using them immediately. In reality, things went differently.

First, I learned that while the printer was "compatible" with the computer, I had to get a new software program that would translate the signals from the computer to this particular printer. The computer had to learn some new ways of communicating in order to be understood by the printer.

Second, if I wanted the computer and printer to do my bidding, I had to learn the commands to give and the buttons to push in correct sequence. When they did what I wanted, I was thrilled with my machines. But when they didn't, not only was I upset but I also discovered that it was usually my fault. I had done something wrong; I'd either forgotten or not known how to do the right thing.

One day I realized how similar my expectations and responses to my computer and printer were to those I had for my sons. Somewhere along the way I had picked up some strange ideas. What I seemed to have wanted was to have a son, bring him home, set him up in his room, and immediately start to see him do what I wanted, when I wanted it, the way I wanted it done!

At first, being a young mother with a baby in the house was great fun, though exhausting. Nevertheless, as the years went by, I had to learn new ways to communicate, new ways to present my commands, and new sequences for getting what I needed from my son. When he did what I wanted, I was happy and proud. When he didn't, I was frustrated and angry, sometimes fantasizing about wanting to "send him back."

There are three major differences in these experiences, however. First, when the computer and printer failed to do my bidding, it was usually my error; but when my son failed to do my bidding, it might have been my error, his error, or no one's error. People, both old and young, think for themselves and make choices about what to do or not to do.

Next, my child is not a possession who exists solely to do my bidding. He is a person, entrusted to my care for me to train to become a mature, independent adult. He will never, nor should he, become my clone.

Last, if I was particularly frustrated with trying to use my machines I could cover them up and ignore them until I was ready to try again. But when things aren't going well with my son, I still have to keep trying to connect, because it usually isn't appropriate to just stop communicating for a week or two. That's not to say, however, that a little psychological space isn't needed at times to regain a perspective and reduce the intensity of a conflict.

The conflict between mother and son tends to focus on the differences in who each person is and what is wanted or valued by each. When my son doesn't make the choices I want him to, I experience a loss of self-esteem and feel that I must have failed as a parent. When he feels that I disapprove of him simply because he isn't everything I want him to be, he also experiences a loss of self-esteem.

One afternoon when Jon was about nine, he came home late for dinner, and I was waiting with a lecture. How could he scare me that way? Didn't he know that I always came home and prepared dinner right away? Didn't he care how hard I tried to do things for him? How could he forget to check the time just because he was at a friend's house playing? I was just getting wound up, when he looked at me with his big brown eyes and explained, "Mom, I can't help it if I'm not perfect. I'm just a little boy!"

He was right. Sometimes I couldn't help feeling inadequate trying to raise my sons alone, because I never was a little boy! How was I to understand how a little boy felt or thought or why he behaved the way he did?

DON'T THINK OF YOURSELF AS INADEQUATE!

Develop a positive self-esteem: the way you feel about yourself, your overall judgment of how well you like your own particular person. As a parent you want to do everything you can to assist your son in developing a healthy self-esteem, which is linked to the mental picture you have of yourself.

Josh McDowell talks about this mental image in his book *His Image, My Image.* He says that some of us have photos of ourselves we are pleased with, which we display in silver frames on top of the piano. But many of us also have different pictures of ourselves that we hide in our wallets and only show when required to do so to cash a check, because we hate the way we look in that photo. All too often the inner mental picture we carry around looks more like the driver's license photo than the one in a silver frame. Our mental image (sometimes called our self-image) reflects what we tell ourselves about ourselves.

Your son's self-image will influence his choice of friends, how he interacts with others, whom he chooses to marry, and how productive he will be in society. It will affect his stability, his integrity, and even his creativity. In fact, his self-image has a direct bearing on all aspects of his life. Knowing how important a self-concept can be to your son, you will want to do everything you can to help him to develop *positive self-images.*

WHERE DOES SELF-ESTEEM COME FROM?

Our self-esteem has two foundations, as explained by Maurice Wagner in *The Sensation of Being Somebody.* One is *functional* and has three aspects. The aspect of *appearance* is how well we look and appear to others. The aspect of *performance* is how well we do things, our levels of skills, knowledge, and abilities. The aspect of *status* is the level of respect or importance we have from our jobs, friends, education, or family name.

The best basis for a positive self-image is a spiritual one.

The second foundation is much more significant to us because it contains our *feelings,* three of which are most important: *belongingness, worthiness,* and *competence.* Belongingness is a sense of being wanted, accepted, and cared for. Feelings of worthiness are the result of doing what we know to be right in the eyes of others. Competence is feeling adequate in a given situation because of a proven ability in similar instances.

The problems with using this approach alone in developing a positive self-image are many. Our inherent value as a human being isn't based on what we look like, how well we perform, or what status we have achieved. Belongingness depends on the voluntary acceptance of others, which may be capriciously withheld at times. Worthiness is dependent upon proper self-appraisal and approval. And competence demands success in prior endeavors. So on any given day, we can feel good or bad about ourselves based on what we think that day and how others are responding to us.

The best basis for a positive self-image is a spiritual one. We can feel great about ourselves when we come to recognize that we belong to God who has *accepted* us (see Eph. 1:6). We are considered *worthy* because Jesus Christ came to teach us about love and to pay the price for our shortcomings (see 1 Peter 1:18–19). We are *competent* because God gives us the strength for any task (see Phil. 4:13; Deut. 33:25). Each of us has unique gifts and abilities that make us special (see 1 Cor. 12:7).

WAYS TO ENCOURAGE YOUR SON TOWARD SELF-ESTEEM

An old friend we hadn't seen in several years came to dinner one evening when Michael was about twelve. As the conversation drifted into "remember when's," Michael took an unusually active part. In fact, he became so animated he nearly took over the conversation completely. Our friend kept expressing genuine surprise that Michael could remember so far back, even events that we adults had forgotten. After about an hour when our friend went to the restroom, I whispered to Michael that he should not talk so much and bother our friend.

"But, Mom," he explained excitedly, "I'm not bothering him, I am *amazing* him!"

I understood. I relaxed and let Michael share all he wanted to. It is one of life's rare, great thrills to have another person genuinely impressed with or admiring of us. Approval is such a treat! We all need to be affirmed and encouraged because it not only builds self-esteem, but it also reinforces a positive self-image.

Be An Affirming Mom

Not only do we need to ensure that our sons develop the spiritual aspects of a positive self-image, but we need also to provide for their identified needs for approval. Ways to affirm your son include praise, giving physical affection, listening, spending time together, allowing input into family decisions, and many other actions that we will explore more fully.

1. One Characteristic at a Time

Sally worked out a terrific plan for herself and her three sons. She made a list of twelve positive characteristics she wanted to develop in their family: love, joy, peacemaking, kindness, patience, self-control, gentleness, cheerfulness, assertiveness, consideration, dependability, and honesty. Then she assigned one, starting with kindness, to each of the twelve months. First, she and the boys discussed what kindness was and ways they could be kind to others. Then she explained that every evening at dinner for the next month they would share ways they had been kind to someone.

The first few days were the hardest. One or the other of the three would have forgotten to do a specific kind deed. But by the end of the week, all three had a story to share. "Sometimes the stories were comical, but I couldn't laugh," Sally remembered. "One day eight-year-old Kyle said he had been standing in the lunch line at school when he remembered that he needed to do something kind, so he stepped out of line and let everyone else go in first just so he could do his kind deed!"

When Sally added the second characteristic, patience, the next month the boys still shared about the kind deeds they had done. But now they included ways they had practiced patience.

We all need to be affirmed and encouraged because it not only builds self-esteem, but it also reinforces a positive self-image.

Sally's plan was terrific. It gave family members a chance to share good things about themselves and be affirmed by other family members. It promoted healthful, positive conversation at dinner and encouraged new, good habits. Psychologists tell us that if we do a new behavior everyday for twenty-one days, we will develop a habit. Sally planned to develop twelve good "habits" in each family member's life over a period of a year.

You might decide to use Sally's idea. Look through the Scriptures and list characteristics Christians are supposed to develop. Then practice them with your sons. Both you and the boys will be growing spiritually.

2. Setting Goals

Betty developed a "Life Notebook" with her son, Lance. When he was thirteen they made a list of everything he needed or wanted to learn to do in order to live on his own by age eighteen. The list included cooking, cleaning, washing clothes, balancing a checkbook, applying for jobs, driving a car, developing a budget. They wrote each item on the list on a separate sheet of notebook paper and put them all in a binder. They spent weeks organizing the notebook, setting dates for the mastering of each skill, noting ways to achieve each goal, and clarifying how they would know when each skill was acquired (e.g., did family wash for one month without wrinkling the wash and wear, mixing the colored and white clothes, or having any laundry mishaps). It was a great experience just to plan the notebook, but even more fulfilling was to work through the plan and see her son develop the skills. Each time he could write Done on a page, his self-concept grew to include that skill. How's that for bringing home *management by objectives* principles!

You may not want to be quite that elaborate, but it is wise to assist your son in setting and achieving goals. Goals provide a direction and purpose for channeling activity. Achieving goals provides a sense of accomplishment that is a wonderful boost to one's self-esteem. Remember how good it feels to check off the completed items on your Saturday to-do list? Help your son learn the joy of accomplishment by encouraging him to set and achieve good goals.

Working on goals together will give you and your son opportunities to get to know one another better as people and not just as parent and child. Spending positive time with someone is also a good way of affirming worth as an individual and further builds self-esteem.

Before setting goals together as a family, take time to read the Bible together to get God's goals in mind. There are lots of instructions in the Word that give straightforward guidelines, but almost any passage can be used to identify God's standards for His children. For our children, the stories are sometimes easier to identify with than direct instructions. First Corinthians 10:11–13 tells us that we can learn from the experiences of the Israelites. Read a story together and then discuss how the characters behaved and the consequences of their choices. Discuss how the same types of choices are presented to us each day. Help your children decide on proper choices and then try to find ways to practice the new, correct choices.

3. Family Night Activities

"I'd love to go to the party with you, Diane," Sharon told her friend. "But I can't. I'm already committed for Tuesday. That's family night at our house."

"Family night! That's only for your kids. Can't you change it just this once?" Diane coaxed teasingly.

"No. Family night is a priority in our home," Sharon answered seriously.

Having a family night at your house can be a very special way of becoming, or staying, close to your children. Plans for fun things to do for family nights can be found in many books and magazines at bookstores or libraries if you run short of ideas yourself.

When you first start having family nights, you may find the new schedule difficult, but if you don't give up and keep your commitment to developing your family uppermost in your mind, you will soon find that you wouldn't miss family nights for the world! Besides, the nights are affirming if you give them priority, because you are saying by your actions that your children are important to you. And they will know and feel that they are loved.

4. By Word and Deed

"Sometimes I feel as if I never have anything positive to say to my children," Ellen said. "Between the 'don'ts,' the 'no's,' and the 'stop that's,' I rarely get a chance to catch my breath, let alone tell my children how well they are doing!"

If we want to act as loving guides and affirm the development of our sons, we need to be truly committed to being available when needed, to offering support and encouragement when the going gets tough, and to providing the discipline that is needed. Here are a few suggestions others have found helpful:

· Find one thing each day to affirm in your son. At first this may be difficult if you are not used to complimenting your son, but the affirmation need not be something major, just something you appreciate: a clean room, the outfit chosen to wear to school, helping with the dishes, taking out the trash, or cheerfully running an errand.

· Express your personal confidence in the child. At least three or four times a week express your belief that your son can accomplish something. This is best if it is something the child has set as a goal, but it is also valuable if it is about something the child doesn't think is possible. Be sure to be honest so that your confidence in the child becomes something to be trusted, not false praise. "You can do it" and "You did that very well" are wonderful affirmations, if they are true. Reflect on how good you feel when a friend believes that you can successfully take on a big project, or the boss entrusts you with a special job. You seem to grow with and rise to the occasion. You feel increased self-esteem as you recognize that someone else has confidence in you. Give your son that same experience.

· Don't be too hasty with a no. If your first instinct is to say no when your child asks to do something different, try a few more yeses. Risk taking is a part of growing up and your child should not be deprived of stretching and growing. This, of course, does not mean you shouldn't take proper safety precautions, if indicated.

· Allow your son the freedom to fail without heaping incriminations on his head. Part of risking is learning to take failures in stride.

As the two of you focus on the positives, you will find that your son will begin to develop more independence and maturity, which is one of the goals of parenting. And most likely, along the way, you will have grown a bit yourself.

5. Listen

Nancy shared, "I find that when Donny has something on his mind and I invite him to share, he really appreciates my listening. I mean, I stop what I am doing and sit down so I can give him my full attention. That is one way I can let him know how much I care."

Nancy is right. Attentive listening is an important way to build another person's self-esteem, to show that he or she is valued. Nancy continued, "Whenever I am tempted not to give Donny my full attention, I remember an experience I had with a girl friend. When we used to talk on the telephone it was like talking to her whole family, including the dog. She would turn away from the phone and carry on a conversation with one or the other or both of her children, laugh at the dog's antics, and seem to pay attention to everyone else except me. I used to feel as if I weren't important enough for her to give me her full attention for the few minutes we were talking on the telephone. I don't want my son to feel that way about me."

6. Recognize His Right to Be Unique

"Every once in a while I have to remind myself that Fred has a right to be his own person," Patricia said. "We don't have to like the same clothes, music, television shows, movies, books, jokes, friends, or foods. I have a lot of friends who don't like some of the same things I do and that's okay. It needs to be okay for my son not to as well."

Why is it so hard for us to acknowledge the differences between us and our sons? I believe the reason is that we think people will judge us by our children's choices—and they may! But each one of us is unique, an unrepeatable miracle, designed to be different. So unless our sons' choices are harmful to themselves or others, we must let them do the choosing.

We must begin to appreciate the individual differences in our sons in order to appreciate them fully. We are not alike, but we can complement one another and form a strong, working, family team.

PROTECT YOUR OWN SELF-ESTEEM

You will find that as you consciously do the things described in this chapter to build your son's self-esteem, in the process you will have begun to feel good about yourself as a parent. However, don't let all your self-esteem depend upon your role as a parent, for you are a total person. You will recognize that you are a loving, caring, kind, understanding, affirming, achieving, wonderful person!

If that's true, then why is it that we sometimes feel as if we are failures? Perhaps we haven't taken care of some of our own support and *belonging* needs. It helps to join a singles group, get involved in activities at church, participate in the PTA or other community activities, get a job, and cultivate a few good friendships, particularly with other single moms.

Maybe you need to work on your feelings of *worthiness* by reflecting on the many ways you are doing the best you know how as a person and a parent. Share with good friends about difficult areas in your life where you are sticking to your guns regardless of the cost, and reflect on the people who depend on you for something in their lives, such as friendship, shelter, joy, laughter.

You may need to reassure yourself of your *competence* by setting and achieving goals and reminding yourself of positive accomplishments, by reviewing the many areas in which you have been successful, and by making a list of your strengths.

Most of all, you need a strong personal faith and an active spiritual life to maintain a proper self-image. In addition, there are other things you can do.

Take Time Alone

A common fantasy of single moms with custody of their children is having some uninterrupted time alone! How that time would be spent varies from individual to individual. You may dream of reading, relaxing, sitting on the patio, studying, working on a favorite hobby, sleeping, or just doing nothing. When asked about the obstacles to living out such fantasies, several moms cited guilt about being selfish, having too many other priorities, or not having anyone to watch the children. And so, failing to overcome such obstacles, too many of us dutifully focus on our parenting role to the exclusion of other areas of our lives.

There is a time when I dreaded going home after work because I was always greeted at the door by both boys, each making several demands at once. Finally, I resolved this problem by negotiating with the kids. They agreed that for the first thirty minutes after I came home they would leave me alone. No questions, no demands. The second half hour I would talk with and listen to them. That quiet thirty minutes each day made a significant difference in our relationships.

Whether it is thirty minutes a day, one evening a week, or even an occasional weekend without the children, you must decide what will meet your needs. Then work out the details.

Get a Hug

When was the last time you received a friendly bear hug when you needed it? More and more single adults are discovering the value of friendly hugs. That comforting, affirming, nonsexual touch from another adult often says, You can do it! I care! I understand! Hang in there!

Words of encouragement are important. A sympathetic ear is comforting. But there's nothing like being held. Become a hugger.

Each time you give a hug, you get a hug back. So, the more you give, the more you get. Learn to tell a good friend that you need a hug.

If you are one of those people who aren't comfortable with physical touching, you can "get in touch" with others in different ways. You can call a friend and go out together for coffee. Or you can send cards or write letters.

Even if you don't enjoy physical closeness with other adults, you are probably affectionate with the children. You will want to express your love in the family with a lot of touching, particularly during tough times. A hug or a hand on the shoulder says much more than words can. If you have never developed the habit of affectionate touching within your family, start now. It may take a while, but you will soon become comfortable.

You and your sons can give each other an affirming "touch" by playing physical contact sports, romping, mock wrestling, giving piggyback rides, brushing one another's hair. Perhaps you will want to trade backrubs, crowd into a hottub, or cuddle up under a blanket and tell scary stories.

We need one another. We are social beings. So as the familiar advertising jingle says, "Reach out and touch someone."

Get Professional Assistance if Needed

There were times when I needed professional help, so I called a counselor to make an appointment. When the frustration, pain, and uncertainty made me question my approach, I went for help, confirmation, and advice.

When you are facing specific major problems or can't seem to cope with the consistent realities of single-again life, a counselor's office is usually the best place to go for advice, guidance, and assistance. One of the most frequent reasons single moms consult counselors is that there are problems with the children. Discipline is a big issue because children who have not sorted out their feelings, adjusted to the breakup, or developed the skills to cope with trauma, may act up as a result of those fears, hostilities, or insecurities.

It is important to remember that whenever one family member has a problem of this nature, it becomes a family problem. No one suffers alone. Most of these behaviors or symptoms are a cry for help or a response to a situation that is perceived as intolerable. Don't let these problems make you feel that you are a failure as a parent. Don't let your self-image slip down. And don't let a lack of money prevent you from seeking professional assistance if it is needed by you or your children. Get help.

Several resources are probably available to you. School districts often have free family counseling services. Your medical insurance may cover counseling. Many pastors or lay church leaders serve as volunteer counselors. The local social services department may be of assistance. There may be a women's center in your town.

Seeking professional assistance when needed is the wisest move a mom can make when the family experiences troubled times. It is not a sign of weakness, but one of strength.

Develop a Strong Personal Relationship with the Lord

Your secret strength, not only for the parenting job but also for being successful in life, is to develop a strong, personal relationship with the Lord. You need His guidance every day in your life, and you need the Word on a daily basis. Become involved in a Bible study program either on Sunday or during the week. Take time for personal devotions. Seek the fellowship of other Christians, particularly single moms raising sons alone. These can give you the strength, the wisdom, the support, and the joy you need to be a good, Christian mom.

Most of all, be gentle with yourself. You are doing the best that you can. If there's something you don't really like about your approach to parenting, start now to change. Do it slowly, one step at a time. As human beings we have the ability to choose to make changes. We can learn and grow.

Chapter

10

Don't Allow Your Kids to Be Self-Critical

You offer the greatest gift to your child by believing in her. You'll be instilling both a high self-esteem and a confidence in herself. After all, if Mom and Dad believe in her, she knows she must be super.

Do you know how much you communicate your belief in your child by merely asking her opinion on something—and listening closely to her answer? Or correcting her self-critical comments about herself? Here are two small chapters from my book, 52 Simple Ways to Build Your Child's Self-Esteem and Confidence, *that I hope you will incorporate into your everyday living to show your little boy or girl—or even your big boys and girls for that matter—how much you believe in them.*

Jan Dargatz
52 Simple Ways to Build Your Child's Self-Esteem and Confidence

In building self-esteem, a child's criticism of his or her own actions is acceptable. Criticism of "self" is not.

Watch your child's responses when he or she experiences failure. These actions will tell you a lot about your child's level of self-esteem.

"I'm just a dummy," said Kevin after he lost five successive games of tic-tac-toe. "Dummy, dummy, dummy."

Kevin learned those negative responses from someone, somewhere, at some time. The sadder implication, however, is that Kevin has started equating his performance in one area of life with his value as a human being. He was not only criticizing his performance, he was criticizing himself. At that point a parent or other caring adult needs to step in.

A few months ago, I witnessed a phenomenal event. I saw Rob swing and miss at forty-eight consecutive pitches from an automatic ball-pitcher at the local batting range. Several friends and a couple of adults stood nearby offering encouragement, advice, cheers when he came close, and dismay when he missed by a mile. Eleven-year-old Rob had lots of witnesses for his forty-eight swings. Six rounds at twenty-five cents each and not one hit! Not even a foul ball.

He didn't seem remotely concerned. "Tough deal," I said as he walked out of the cage.

"Yeah," he said as he sat down beside me. "I've been trying for two years to hit one. I can hit the softball pitches," he added matter-of-factly. "And I can hit about half the slow-speed pitches. But I haven't got any of the medium-speed ones, yet."

Two years. I couldn't get over the fact that Rob had tried and failed for two years to hit a medium-speed pitch. He must have swung at several thousand balls hurled at him from that unseen machine. Furthermore, he displayed no intent to give up. Everything about his attitude said he'd be at that range every weekend until he mastered the medium-pitch.

I was equally impressed with the fact that Rob could be so matter-of-fact about his failure. He certainly didn't consider himself "stupid" or "dumb" for missing those pitches—not even in the presence of friends and family.

"But, children do make mistakes," you may say. "They do perform badly. Isn't it wrong to ignore errors?"

Yes, children fail. In fact, they often fail at a task many more times than they succeed. A child's failures at certain tasks, however, do not mean that the child is a failure as a child!

What are some positive responses that an adult can make when a child acknowledges failure?

"Did you hear me miss that chord?" said Rachel after a single flub in an otherwise flawless piano recital performance. "I really blew it."

"Yes," I agreed. "You blew four out of 1,302 notes. Pretty good percentage, I'd say." Rachel might not even know what "percentage" means, and I wasn't certain there were 1,302 notes of music in the piece she played. The point was, we both knew she failed at one small part of one task, and that it was incidental to her personal worth.

"I couldn't hit the side of a barn today," said Jeff after being removed from the pitcher's mound in the sixth inning. "A small barn or a big barn?" I asked. He grinned. We both knew he had experienced an off day, yet we wouldn't let this setback diminish his self-image.

Sure, kids err. They can and should acknowledge their mistakes, but we must make certain they keep their self-criticism limited to the realm of actions, not of self.

When adults allow children to criticize themselves they think, *You agree with me. I must really be stupid. I must really be a dummy.* Allowing your child to transfer an unsuccessful performance into a negative sense of self-worth prompts the thought, *You think my worth as a person is tied up in my ability to perform well.*"

Both conclusions can destroy self-esteem, if they go uncorrected. No child should be allowed to criticize *who* he or she is, and never should a child be allowed to equate mistakes or failure to self-worth.

Chapter

11

Ask Your Child's Opinion

A big part of a child's self-esteem is rooted in the feeling that his or her feelings and thoughts are valuable and important to a parent, to the family, and to his or her community of friends and schoolmates.

"What do you think?"

"What's your idea?"

These are questions adults take for granted as common fare in our relationships, especially in our workplace or in daily conversation with spouses and friends. But how uncommon these questions often are in relationships between adults and children! Not that children don't have thoughts, opinions, or ideas to express. It's just that adults rarely ask. Perhaps even worse, adults often cut short a child's attempts to convey ideas and feelings.

Do you really know your child's opinion? Do you know what he or she is thinking, or imagining? Have you asked lately?

Even at very early ages, children begin to form opinions, largely in the form of likes and dislikes. They respond favorably to some things, reject others. As they experience their world, some events stand out, others don't. They have ideas about the way things ought to be. Often, their ideas are rooted in fantasy rather than reality. Still, they've got an idea and from their perspective, it's a worthy idea.

Boosting a feeling of self-value in a child can be done simply when an adult, especially a parent, turns to a child in the middle of a conversation, and says, "And what about you? What do you think? How do you feel about this? Do you have any ideas?"

Include your child in dinner time conversation. Take time to hear out his or her ideas.

Don't criticize your child's opinions. As opinions, they are as valid as anyone's. Let your child know that whatever his or her opinion, it's OK to express it.

Don't make fun of your child's ideas. Don't hack away at your child's lack of logic or the "unworkableness" of your child's ideas. The process of telling and exploring ideas is, after all, the way your child comes to form ideas and, eventually, to come up with better ideas. Ask your child, "What do you think would happen if we did that?" Or, "Do you think this would work all the time, or just in this particular case?" You may be surprised at the creative twists and turns such a conversation can take!

Don't totally discount the validity of your child's opinion, even if it's ill-founded. Avoid declaring with a tone of finality, "That's rubbish." Instead, say to your child, "I'll consider that," or "I'll take that under advisement." In nearly all cases, a child isn't nearly as concerned that an idea be enacted as he or she is delighted that the idea has been expressed.

The most important result of establishing conversation between adult and child is that a child might remain willing to express his or her thoughts and feelings throughout life. A child who is rarely or never asked for an idea or an opinion is highly unlikely to emerge as a teenager willing to talk freely with a parent about drugs, sex, God, or life goals! A child whose ideas and feelings are never explored or appreciated is unlikely to become an adult who freely expresses opinions to parents.

The child with high self-esteem and confidence is a child who can look in the mirror and say, "My ideas have merit. My opinions have validity. My thoughts are worth expressing." All of these statements are translated within the spirit of the child as: "I have value." And *that* feeling is at the very heart of self-esteem!

Chapter

12

Giving Your Children a Hug from God

How do your children see God? They see Him through the kind of person you are and the kind of parent you are. Do your children see God as a demanding, impatient, condemning, explosive God—or a God that hands out hugs frequently and loves unconditionally? If your children are to see an image of God as all-loving, all-accepting, and forgiving, they must first see it in you.

This chapter from my book Please Let Me Know You, God, *offers some real-life scenarios that may look all too familiar. Let me share with you the Ten Steps to Building a Healthy Image of God in your children by creating a home environment that truly represents God in all His loving-kindness. You are God's representative here on earth. It is up to you to give your children a hug from God every day.*

Dr. Larry D. Stephens
Please Let Me Know You, God

A couple took their three-year-old son to church to be dedicated. During the dedication service, the pastor told the boy that *dedication* means that his mommy and daddy are promising to raise him to know Jesus and to have God living in his heart. The boy listened with wide-eyed attention.

The next morning the boy bounced down to breakfast with an

excited expression on his face and his hand tucked under his pajama shirt. "God is in my heart!" he announced. "I can feel Him bumping around in there!"[1]

This story, told by comedian Dick Van Dyke in his book *Faith, Hope and Hilarity,* illustrates the challenge and the joys of teaching our children about God—who He is, how we can know Him, how we can have Him living inside our hearts. Van Dyke—the veteran star of Broadway, TV, and films such as *Mary Poppins*—is also a father of four and a former Sunday school teacher, so he has given a lot of thought to the question, "How can parents help shape a healthy image of God in their children?"

"Have you ever tried to tell a child about God?" he writes.

> Grown-ups take it for granted that God is all-powerful, all-wise, all-perfect, all this and all that, but to children this is pretty exciting stuff. This God, whoever He is, must be the biggest hero of them all: smarter, braver, and stronger than any of those guys in the comic strips and on TV. He's probably flying round up there in Heaven with a cape and a big "G" on His chest, as He zaps all the villainous evildoers. As one boy explained to his smaller buddies, "God is greater than Superman, Batman, and The Lone Ranger put together."[2]

In his book, Van Dyke collected stories from parents and Sunday school teachers across the country. Several of these stories amusingly illustrate the powerful influence of fathers in shaping their children's image of God. "A four-year-old," writes Van Dyke, "was sure he knew exactly what God looks like: 'Just like my Daddy, only lots bigger.'"[3]

How do you explain to a child what God—this invisible, omnipresent, all-seeing Being—is like? One mother tried to explain God to her three-year-old daughter, with entertaining results. "God is everywhere," said the mother. "You can't see God, but He can see you."

The little girl's face came alight. "Let's guess where He's hiding!"[4]

Other snippets of kid theology from Van Dyke's book range from the fanciful ("God has a big fat tummy, and we're in it") to the frightening ("God is a giant who is on a mountain and hits people with a stick if they are bad").[5] These words underscore the responsibility that is ours as Christian parents, charged with the awesome task of raising our children in the nurture and admonition of the Lord.

CHILDREN RUNNING ON EMPTY

The Minirth-Meier Clinic book *Love Is a Choice* contains a diagram we often use at the clinic to illustrate the love relationship God planned to exist between parents and their children. We call it the "Love Tank" diagram.[6]

All of us have a reservoir of love, which is graphically represented as a heart-shaped love tank. Imagine having a love tank deep within yourself and a fuel gauge showing how much love is stored there. When we are born, that tank is empty, and the gauge reads "E." God's plan is for our parents to pour love into our love tanks out of the reservoir of their love tanks. As we grow, our inner love tanks fill, little by little. By the time we reach adulthood, our love tanks should be full enough that we can fill the tanks of our children.

In functional families, each generation pours love into the love tanks of the next generation, and that generation passes its love to the next, and on and on in a beautifully cascading cycle of love. Children grow up secure in the love they have received from their parents, and secure in the love of God. (These heart-shaped tanks are shown less than completely full because being imperfect human beings, we can never have perfectly full tanks; the only love tank that is ever 100 percent full is God's.)

In dysfunctional families, children do not receive the filling of their emotional love tanks as God intended. They may receive neglect instead of nurturing; unpredictable outbursts of rage instead of steady, firm, loving discipline; absence instead of involvement and availability; coldness and criticism instead of acceptance and affirmation.

How do we fill the love tanks of our children? What are our specific acts and behaviors that fill up their inner reservoirs with the sense of love and security God intended them to have? We give our children our time and attention. We give them our availability. We give them our affirmation, affection, and forgiveness. We give them all the gifts God has given us through His Son Jesus Christ.

Children deprived of these ingredients grow up with an undersupply of love and security. They may attempt to fill the gnawing emptiness in their love tanks with any number of false love-substitutes: drug abuse, alcohol abuse, or food abuse; sexual promiscuity; workaholism; religious legalism; or some other compulsive behavior. Adolescents or young adults with an aching emptiness in their love tanks are also easy prey for cults and the occult. Their image of God is distorted, and the New Age and other false religious systems are quick to exploit their need for security and belonging that has never been met in childhood.

The Child's View of God chart shows the contrast between the child with a well-filled love tank and the child with an empty love tank—and how each child tends to perceive God.

A CHILD'S VIEW OF GOD

Child with a Well-filled Love Tank	**Child with an Empty Love Tank**
Present and available	Absent and unreal
Loving and caring	Neglectful and unconcerned
Holy, just and fair	Unjust, unfair, and biased
Stable and reliable	Touchy, unpredictable, and untrustworthy
Kind and merciful	Uncaring and vindictive
Gracious	Demanding
Generous, the Giver of good gifts	Malicious, the One who stomps out enjoyment
Affirming	Impossible to please

As you compare and contrast the traits, consider which set you tend to display toward your children. Which column most represents your character and your parenting style? In what areas do you need to improve to better exemplify a healthy example of Christian character and the image of God?

When Jesus was on the earth, He invited the little children to come to Him. He embraced them and spoke lovingly to them. When Jesus hugged them, they were getting—in a very direct sense—a hug from God. Jesus no longer walks the earth as a flesh-and-blood man. God is spirit, and children cannot go to a spirit for a warm flesh-and-blood hug and a gentle word of affirmation. The affection and the unconditional love of God are real, but they are mediated through human parents. It is our job as parents to give our children a hug from God every day.

If we are neglectful, impatient, explosive, condemning, and/or legalistic, we will build our children's image out of these same raw materials. It won't matter very much what we *tell* our children about

God or what they learn about Him in Sunday school or church. We will have already imprinted our distortions of God's character in their minds and emotions by our sinful and dysfunctional behavior.

It is our job as parents to give our children a hug from God every day.

Our goal as Christian parents is to fill the love tanks of our children, day by day, cupful by cupful. As their inner reservoirs of love and security rise to the brim of their hearts, their relationship with God will grow strong, reliable, and secure.

America's Saddest Home Videos

Here is a story that took place a short time before Carrie Bishop came to me for counseling. In fact, the incident was one factor that caused Carrie to see that she needed help in dealing with her emotional and spiritual issues.

Carrie stood in the bleachers of the junior high gymnasium, a camcorder whirring away in her hands, her right eye glued to the eyepiece, the camera lens focused on the hardwood court below. Her thirteen-year-old son Jeremy had just been fouled by a player on the opposing team, so he was taking his place in the center of the key. As she peered at the black-and-white image of her son in the viewfinder, Carrie grinned tensely. "Okay, Jer, this is it!" she called hoarsely. "It's a one and one, Jer! Don't miss the first one!"

Jeremy ran one hand through his brown hair as he placed the toes of his shoes against the charity strip. He bounced the ball twice on the floor. He could hear his mother shouting his name, urging him to make the shot. He eyed the hoop. It seemed like it was a million miles away. His stomach felt constricted, as if it were tied in a knot. His hands shook as they clutched the ball. He sucked in a deep breath, held it, and launched the shot.

The ball sailed in a high parabola. From the stands, Carrie's camcorder followed its flight. The ball thudded against the backboard, a little left of center, and fell onto the rim of the hoop. It rolled once around the rim. It dropped.

But not through the net. No point. And no second shot.

Carrie took the camcorder away from her face, which had become a contorted mask of fury. "Jeremy!" she bellowed. "Jeremy Mark Bishop, what is the matter with you!"

On the court, Jeremy turned, white-faced, and saw his mother stalking down the bleachers, oblivious to the shocked faces of parents and students who watched the game. Jeremy knew what was coming, and he also knew he could do nothing to stop it. But the ball was back in play, and he had to bear down and get back in the game.

So Jeremy played. Legs pumping, lungs straining, a lump of shame in his throat bigger than any basketball, Jeremy moved up and down the court with his teammates. At the same time, his mother stormed up and down the sidelines, screaming, "Jeremy, that was so *stupid!* That was the easiest point you ever could have made! How could you blow an easy shot like that?"

After the game, Carrie drove her son home. Jeremy spent the first couple of miles looking out the passenger-side window. Finally, he spoke. "How could you do that, Mom?"

"Do what?"

"Holler at me like that," he answered. Both anger and tears seemed to be fighting for control of his face. "In front of the guys and the coach and everybody. That was so awful."

"Jer, I was just trying to encourage you to do better, that's all!" Carrie said defensively. "You're my kid and I love you. I just want you to do your best." She reached out and put her hand on her son's arm, but he shook it off angrily.

"Don't touch me!" he growled.

Not another word was said for the rest of the drive home.

The next day was Carrie's day off from work. After she drove Jeremy to school, she came home, rewound the videotape she had taken of Jeremy's game, and began to watch. She came to the place where Jeremy missed the shot from the free throw line—but the tape didn't stop there. She had forgotten to press the red button on the camcorder. There, on the TV screen, was jerky video footage of her shoes, the bleachers, the gym floor. The pictures might have been funny, like something from that TV show with Bob Saget, but the soundtrack was not funny at all.

Horrified, Carrie heard her voice: "Jeremy Mark Bishop, what is the matter with you! That was so *stupid!* How could you blow an easy shot like that?"

She stopped the tape, dropped her head in her hands, and began to weep. "Jeremy, Jeremy, what am I doing to you?" she cried.

THERE *IS* HOPE

Carrie was raised with a near-empty love tank. Her father was sexually abusive and her mother was emotionally abusive. One way Carrie learned to compensate for the imperfections of her childhood was to become a ruthless perfectionist. She maintained the perfect image, kept her house perfectly clean, dressed her son in the perfect clothes, and demanded complete perfection in everything he did, from his grades in school to his sports activities.

Today, Carrie realizes that one reason she has been so driven to live through the achievements of her son is that she has long felt her life was worthless. In an attempt to build a "perfect" life for her son, she was destroying him emotionally.

Several months after that incident, during one of Carrie's early visits to my office, I could plainly see the fear in Carrie's eyes as she asked, "How do I fill my son's love tank when my own is completely dry?"

Perhaps you can identify with Carrie's fear. Perhaps you, too, feel trapped in the cycle of intergenerational pain. You have grown up with a distorted image of God, now you see yourself inflicting similar pain on your children, and you feel helpless to stop yourself.

That's how Carrie felt, but after she watched the videotape and heard the hurtful things she yelled at her son, she cried out to God for help. And God showed her what to do.

That afternoon, Carrie picked up her son from school as usual. He sat sullen and silent all the way home. When they got to the door, Carrie opened it and let Jeremy enter first. From the front door, he could see into the dining room. Taped to the dining room wall was a big hand-painted sign that read: JEREMY, I'M SO SORRY, PLEASE FORGIVE ME. I LOVE YOU SO MUCH. MOM On the table was a plate of Jeremy's favorite thing in the whole world: oatmeal cookies with chocolate chips and M & M's.®

"I made them myself," said Carrie, "with extra M & M's.®" And she began to cry. "Oh, Jer, I'm so sorry—"

The hug her son gave her told her everything was all right. Carrie had created a memory to last a lifetime in the heart of her young son —the memory of a parent who says, "I'm sorry."

There *is* hope. Carrie's story proves that you are not doomed to repeat the patterns inflicted on you by your parents. The fact that you are reading this book shows you are aware that you need to deal with your image of God issues. Here are some steps you can take:

1. Get the help you need. If you are dealing with emotional and spiritual issues arising from your family-of-origin, please take the step of seeking the help appropriate to your need—a Christian counselor, psychologist, or psychiatrist; your pastor; a support group or a recovery group. If you don't know where to turn for help, your pastor can refer you to the help you need.

If you are abusing your children—physically, sexually, or emotionally—you must get help *immediately*. Don't wait. Don't try to "get better" on your own. If you truly love your children, don't hesitate for another second to get the help you urgently need.

2. Communicate honestly with your children. As human beings, parents make mistakes. Even the best parents will yell, discipline inappropriately, say hurtful things, or act thoughtlessly from time to time. When you do, you have a duty as a Christian parent to honestly admit your mistakes to your kids. You may be reluctant to humble yourself before your children and say, "I was wrong. Please forgive me." But if you fail to admit the wrongs you do to your children, they will grow up feeling that *they* are to blame for your inappropriate behavior.

When you communicate honestly with your children, admitting your wrongs and asking their forgiveness, you break that cycle of intergenerational pain. You tell your children, in effect, "I just did something I'm sorry for. That is not the example I want to set for you. That is not the kind of person I want to be. That is not the kind of person God is." Honest communication—including confession of your faults—helps to erase the distortions of your sins and mistakes from your children's image of God.

3. Spend time with your children, talking, praying, and singing about God's love. This is good therapy not only for your children but also for *you*. As Jesus said on more than one occasion, the path to spiritual wholeness lies in becoming as little children.[7] So cultivate a childlike faith within your heart. Sit down with your children and sing songs about God's love: "Jesus Loves Me," "Jesus Loves the Little Children," "Jesus Loves the Little Ones Like Me, Me, Me."

Tell your children stories about God's love. Either paraphrase the stories of the Bible, or get one or two children's Bible storybooks. Read, pray, and sing with your children at a special time each day—say, at breakfast or at bedtime. Don't make it a deep time of solemn religious instruction; make it *fun!* You will find that the time you spend building a healthy image of a loving God in your children's hearts will also bring healing in your image of God.

TEN STEPS TO BUILDING A HEALTHY IMAGE OF GOD IN YOUR CHILDREN

As Christian parents, we want to raise our children to have a positive image of God. Scripture charges us with the solemn responsibility to raise our children in the training and admonition of the Lord, not to provoke them to wrath and leave them with an emotional residue of bitterness and anger.[8] Here are some specific things you can do to build an emotional foundation in your children that leads to a healthy image of God:

1. Create a home environment where feelings—including feelings of anger—can be appropriately expressed. Children and parents should be continually learning to express anger and other emotions in ways that do not hurt other people. When children are allowed to explode in uncontrollable anger, they become baby tyrants, controlling the mood of the entire family. In a similar way, unpredictable and disproportionate flareups of *parental* anger can terrorize a family and shake children's sense of security.

When children become angry, they are likely to scream, hit, kick, or otherwise act in an inappropriate way (to put it mildly!). As a parent, your tendency is to try to change their behavior—to stop the screaming, the hitting, and the kicking. Unfortunately, many parents also have a tendency to suppress or minimize the very real feelings that prompted the inappropriate behavior.

One way you can fulfill the biblical admonition to "not provoke your children to wrath" is to make a genuine effort to understand their feelings. "What are you angry about?" you might ask. "I'm not going to allow you to yell and hit people, but I do want to understand why you are angry. It's okay for you to tell me you feel angry. But I want you to express your anger in a way that doesn't hurt yourself or other people."

When children are unhappy or afraid, you cannot turn off those feelings by denying them. If you say to children, "Don't feel unhappy," or "You have no reason to be afraid," all you do is make them feel ashamed of their feelings. Instead, you should encourage your children to talk about their feelings, honestly and openly.

2. Be an open, approachable parent. Make a conscious effort to be the kind of parent children can approach with any issue, any problem, any feeling—and always feel *safe.* There should be no off-limits topics and no out-of-bounds issues.

That doesn't mean you never discipline or say tough things to your children. But even tough things can be said in a firm, gentle way, surrounded by unconditional love. No matter how tough the issue, your kids should never feel unsafe or wary around you, as if they have to tiptoe on eggshells in your presence.

3. Forgive and receive forgiveness. Never hold a sin over children's heads. Once the matter is dealt with, forgive it and forget it. Don't remind the children of a sin you forgave a week ago or a year ago. If you do, you didn't really forgive.

When you do something that hurts your children, admit what you did, tell them you are sorry, and ask them to forgive you. As you build the concept of God's forgiving grace into the minds and hearts of your children, they will grow to healthy adulthood, able to forgive and receive forgiveness as God intended, free of the poisonous emotion of shame.

4. Never use God as a threat. Telling children that God will hurt or kill them if they sin can distort their view of God for life. I've counseled many people who were threatened in this way when they were children. Now, in their thirties, forties, and beyond, they see God as an enemy, ready to punish them any moment. Always portray God as loving and forgiving. If you use God as a threat against children, you slander the character of God.

5. Respect your children's emotional boundaries. The most extreme forms of violating children's emotional boundaries include sexual and physical abuse. Children who are abused learn to see the victim role as normal, and they grow up expecting to be abused by other people and by God Himself.

But there are also subtler forms of violating children's emotional boundaries. Some parents dominate their children emotionally. They make their decisions for them, choose (or pass judgment on) their friends, rescue them from every difficulty, manipulate their feelings, and cling to them when they approach the stage of maturity where they should be let go.

As a Christian parent, you naturally want to be involved in your children's lives. You want the best for them. You want to give them your time, show you are interested in their lives, and demonstrate an appropriate level of affection. But to raise healthy kids with a healthy image of God, you must also give them the right to be themselves, think their thoughts, feel their feelings, and develop as individuals separate and distinct from you. If you live through your children or smother their personhood with your control, they will grow up with areas of severe distortion in their emotions and in their relationship with God.

6. Help children make healthy attributions to God. Sometimes your children approach you with tough questions: "Why does God allow people to steal and hurt other people?" or "Why does He allow so many people to starve in other countries?" Or a child may say, "I don't like God! He could have kept Grandma well, but He let her die!"

These are normal questions and feelings. Whenever children ask these questions or express these feelings, you have an opportunity to help them build a more realistic and reliable image of God. You should be unshockable and accept what they are feeling without condemning or scolding them. After listening to the children express their feelings, you should explain God's character as best you can in a way that is appropriate to their level of understanding.

For example, to the child who blames God for world hunger, you can say, "I know you are feeling that God is unfair to allow people to die of hunger. But you know, the Bible says that God loves the whole world and does not want anyone to suffer and perish. If you look closely at the situation in a country like Ethiopia or Cambodia, you find out that it is not God but sinful people who have caused all that suffering. Some sinful people want to have power so they can lord it over everyone else, and that causes wars and hunger and a lot of suffering.

"The only way God could stop these things from happening would be to take away our human free will, and He chooses not to do that. We cannot understand everything that God does or allows, but we know that God wants us to choose, in our own free will, to follow Him and to help other people. Instead of being angry with God for allowing people to go hungry, why don't you start setting aside some of your allowance each week so you can give it to help hungry people find food and find Jesus?"

7. Build warm memories. Some of the richest, most lasting memories of our lives are built during childhood. A child's thinking is more emotional than cognitive, and a child's memory is triggered by strong emotions. In other words, a child's memory is much more strongly affected by *feelings* than by *facts*. Every day, your children experience emotions—feelings of love, joy, and security, or feelings of pain, sadness, and shame—and they will carry those feelings in the inner being for a *lifetime*. If you want to care for children spiritually, you must nurture them emotionally.

The best times to build a child's image of God are those times when emotions are warm and pleasant, when there is a sense of excitement, discovery, and fun. You can use those golden moments to plant an idea, a feeling, a rich sense of God's pervasive presence and love toward us.

During a visit to Disneyland, a brief comment can transform a fun experience into something meaningful in the lives of children: "If you think this is fun, imagine what heaven must be like!" A vacation in the mountains or at the seashore can be used as an object lesson in God's wisdom and creative power. A beautiful sunset or a rainbow can be described as a gift of God's love to us.

Any spare moment in the day can be an opportunity for you and your children to pray together, simply and briefly: "Thank You, God, for the gift of this day. We're really enjoying our time together. Amen." Keep prayers short and personal—not poetic, lengthy, or religious sounding. Pause and give thanks to God for that special report card or that letter from Grandpa. Or take a moment in the middle of the day to pray together for a special need: "Please help Evan not to be afraid of visiting the dentist," or "Please help Molly find her missing library book."

Make time to be a friend to your children. Read stories to them. Sing with them. Play with them. Put your grown-up fingers in the modeling clay or the finger paints. Make drawings alongside your children, using their crayons and colored markers. Show them that you enjoy their company, and while you're at it, tell your children how Jesus enjoyed playing with children. These activities are beautiful opportunities not for teaching deep theological lessons but for making your love relationship with God a natural part of your fun times, your happy moments, your daily life.

8. Become involved in your children's spiritual education. Church, Sunday school, and vacation Bible school are important influences on your children's image of God. Dick Van Dyke writes,

> Many parents got their kids interested in the Bible at home only to have a dull [Sunday school] class turn them off again. A mother in Los Angeles told me what happened after she read some Bible stories to her children one day. Her four-year-old girl said, "Isn't God wonderful? I just love Him." Her brother, age six, said "Wait until you go to Sunday school. You'll hate God."

Van Dyke knows that bringing the Bible alive for kids, week after week, can strain even the talents of the star of *Mary Poppins.* He taught twelve- and thirteen-year-olds in the Dutch Reformed Presbyterian Church of Long Island, New York. "Teaching Sunday school is one of the most important jobs there is, because it's training for life itself," he observes.

> The first lesson I learned as a Sunday school teacher had more to do with show business than theology: get their attention and keep them interested while you're doing your act. . . . I found the kids seemed to get more out of a lesson if we dramatized it. I'd bring along a tape recorder and some scripts, and the kids would play the roles of such biblical characters as Jacob and Esau.[9]

Involve yourself in your children's spiritual education at church. Make sure the Christian education experience is stimulating, lively, and engaging for their active minds. Then reinforce their spiritual education at home.

Explain the meaning of Bible stories to them in terms they can understand and relate to. Help your children identify with the person in the story. If a child is a preschooler or grade-schooler, select stories featuring children and young people. Be alert to any misconceptions your children might gain from the stories they hear at Sunday school or at home. Some well-meaning teachers and parents have done a lot of harm to their children's image of Jesus by reading from the King James Version and not explaining what those Shakespearean-era words mean. For example, what do these words of

Jesus—as translated in 1611—say to children of the "Sesame Street" generation: "Suffer the little children . . ."?

9. Discipline with love and consistency. A major source of spiritual distrust is parents who display conditional love, who punish their children out of anger, and who practice discipline that varies according to their internal tension barometer. Inconsistent and unloving discipline causes children to live in fear, never knowing what will set Mom or Dad off, never sure if their next step will earn them a rap in the mouth, a harsh rebuke, or no response at all. Those who felt wary around their parents in childhood tend to feel wary around God in adulthood. They expect God to have the same erratic temper as their parents, and they are continually fearful of God's unexpected anger and retaliation.

Consistency in affirming and reinforcing children is crucial. Love should always be offered freely and unconditionally, even in the face of tough discussions, bad behavior, and bad report cards. Children must know where the boundary lines are, which consequences follow which actions. Parents can't always be 100 percent fair, but children should know that their parents always *try* to be fair.

What about the old adage "spare the rod and spoil the child"? Ross Campbell, in his book *How to Really Love Your Child,* replies,

> Yes, I have seen children who were raised by the rod [of punishment] become Christians. But because they were raised primarily by punishment instead of unconditional love, these unfortunate people seldom have a healthy, loving, warm relationship with God. They tend to use their religion punitively against others under the guise of "helping" them. They use biblical commandments and other scriptural statements to justify their own harsh, unloving behavior. . . .
>
> It is possible, of course, for any child to eventually find his way into God's loving arms and to accept His love. With God anything is possible. Unfortunately, a child's chances are markedly diminished if his parents have not given him a loving foundation. . . .
>
> There are two requirements essential to helping a child spiritually: A parent's personal relationship with God, and a child's assurance that he is unconditionally loved.[10]

The most profound biblical teaching on discipline can be summed up in the words of Ephesians 6:4: "Do not provoke your children to wrath, but bring them up in the training and admonition of the Lord." In other words, don't inflict emotional wounds on your children that will make them feel angry and bitter for the rest of their lives. Instead, nurture them. Train them. Meet their emotional needs. When you do that, you are raising them to have a healthy relationship with their loving heavenly Father.

10. Most of all, give your children the gift of your time—and yourself. Spend time alone with your children—focused time, fun time, intimate time. Make eye contact with them as you talk to them about God and His love. Meet your children's emotional as well as spiritual needs. Bedtime is a valuable time for building their image of God, for at bedtime your children are especially eager to cuddle and interact with you. Use those moments to build memories and a sense of truth and security.

Share your spiritual pilgrimage with your children in terms appropriate to their ages and understanding. Talk about how you came to know the Lord, how Jesus is a friend to you, how you can talk to God anytime you want, in any words you want, not just at meals or at bedtime. Let your children hear you praying for them, thanking God for them, and praying for their future. Let them hear you address God as a loving heavenly Father, who loves, forgives, and is the Giver of good gifts.

Pray very specifically for your children's hurts, needs, and fears, no matter how trivial they may seem from an adult perspective. Remember how large those issues loom in the minds and emotions of children.

How to Lose a Son

Randy Sullivan was raised in a respected Christian home in the suburbs. His parents had their careers (Dad was an attorney, Mom a nurse practitioner). They were also very involved in the church (he was an elder, and she was Sunday school superintendent).

Randy had been vaguely unhappy for several years, though he could not articulate *why* he was unhappy. The Sullivans were affluent enough, and there was nothing Randy wanted that he didn't already have. Randy's folks were slow to notice when his grades began to slide and he began staying away from home for long periods of time. After all, they were not home very much themselves.

When, at the age of fifteen, Randy announced he didn't want to go to church anymore, Mr. Sullivan didn't bother to ask his son *why* he didn't want to go. He just gave Randy the same answer he had given many times before: "As long as you're living under my roof, eating my chow, with clothes I paid for on your back, you'll go to church and do anything else I tell you to!"

As his father went into the old refrain, Randy mockingly chimed in on the chorus: "Living under my roof, eating my chow . . ."

Mr. Sullivan then promised to "wipe that smirk" off his son's face. From there, things inevitably escalated into a full-blown shouting match. Later, after things quieted down, Randy's father grumbled to his wife, "Where does he get that stuff? Why does he think all I ever do is yell at him? Lately, it seems I hardly ever talk to him at all, much less yell at him!"

Randy's dad was closer to the truth than he realized, but he still couldn't see it. He had become almost absent as a father, busily taking care of the office business and the church business while neglecting the business of his own home. When did he ever talk to Randy anymore? Only when things went wrong, and then only at the top of his lungs.

Over the next few months, Randy sank even deeper into sullenness and depression. Mr. and Mrs. Sullivan had no idea who his friends were or how he spent his time. They would have been horrified to hear the heavy metal music he was listening to—and the discussions he was having with his friends about the meaning of life.

"Santa Claus, the Easter Bunny, Jesus Christ, what's the difference?" said Randy's friend Scott, who was dressed in black pants and a black Slayer T-shirt. "No more myths for me, man. I create my own reality. You can't find God in church, Randy. The only God there is, is is-ness itself."

"Scott's right, Randy," added Shannon, Scott's girlfriend. With her frosted black hair and heavy eye makeup in shades of bruise black and livid purple, she looked like a refugee from the Addams family. "Your folks still want you to go to church and learn about their Christian God, right? Well, I don't have to visit my god in church."

The three of them—Randy, Scott, and Shannon—were sitting in the basement recreation room of the Sullivans's home, listening to Twisted Sister screaming the lyrics to "Burn in Hell" on the CD player. Randy didn't expect his folks to be home for hours, so he invited Scott and Shannon over for some music and talk. Randy lapped up every word his friends said. The idea of a god who was completely unlike his parents' God captured his imagination. He wanted nothing to do with the God his parents worshiped.

"I worship two kinds of deities," Shannon continued, "the ones whose energies are already a part of me, and the ones who are alien energies from outside myself. Lately, I've been working a lot with Gaia, the earth goddess."

"Church'll just mess up your head, Randy," added Scott. "I get my insight straight from my spirit guides. I concentrate on deep breathing, and I visualize myself inhaling white light. The light pours into me, and I let it flow through me. You should try it, man."

And Randy did try it. Soon, he was receiving messages from spirit guides too. At first, it was exciting to know he had tapped into a power beyond his imagining. But as the weeks passed, he began to feel haunted and afraid. His sleep was troubled by night-terrors and bad dreams. He experienced strange, powerful compulsions—to cut himself, burn himself with cigarettes, or kill himself.

Randy's parents had no idea what he was into until they came home from church one Wednesday night. From somewhere in the house, a stereo was shrieking rock at maximum volume. "Randy!" called Mr. Sullivan as he entered the screaming, shuddering house. "Randy! Answer me! Where are you?" There was no answer. Looking for the blaring source of the music, the Sullivans descended the stairs to the rec room and found their son Randy on the floor. He was unconscious.

Mr. Sullivan lifted his son, carried him to the car, and rushed him to the hospital, where his stomach was pumped. He had swallowed a large number of Quaaludes along with some liquor his friend Scott had given him. Today, Randy and his parents are in counseling with a Christian psychologist and their pastor. Mr. and Mrs. Sullivan came within a whisker of losing their son—and their son may well have come equally close to losing his eternal soul. God only knows.

Randy is not out of the woods yet—his psychological and emotional wounds are too deep for any quick fix. But Randy *is* making progress. He has begun to look to God for his ultimate reality—not to spirit guides. Randy's parents have resigned from the majority of their time-consuming church duties so they can spend more time with their son. If only they hadn't waited until they nearly *lost* their son to make time to *find* him!

Randy's parents have learned a painful lesson. So has Carrie Bishop. These parents are discovering—just in time and through painful life experiences—that if they want to raise children who have a strong, sound relationship with God, they must

- work on rebuilding their relationship with God.
- communicate honestly with their children and encourage them to communicate honestly.
- forgive and receive forgiveness.
- never use God as a threat.
- respect their children's emotional boundaries.
- build warm memories in their children's hearts.
- become involved in their children's spiritual education.
- discipline with love and consistency.
- give their children the gift of *time.*

"For me, parenting is all about breaking the cycle," says Rick Hanks. "It's about saying, 'The cycle of pain stops with me.' I've made a promise before God that I won't do to my kids what my father did to me. I don't keep that promise perfectly, of course, but it's my goal as a father and I give it my best shot. The payoff for me is when I listen to my children pray, and they just pour out their little hearts to their heavenly Father. Those prayers are so honest and trusting. It's the sweetest sound you'll ever hear."

As a Christian parent, you want your children to experience a close, warm relationship with God. The key to your children's image of God is *the way you live* and *the way you parent.* You are God's earthly representative to your children. God is counting on you—and your children are counting on you—to give them a hug from God every day. Every hug, every kiss, every affirming, tender word you give your children is given on behalf of a loving God. When that becomes the way you view your task as a parent, it will transform your view of parenting from a duty to a *ministry.*

Jesus loves the little children—and He loves them through you and me.

Chapter

13

Summer Strategies for Self-Esteem

I think summer, when the kids are out of school and on the borderline of boredom, is a great time to focus on some fun family activities that have the express purpose of bolstering self-esteem. Of course, don't think you can't do these all year long—you can. Helping your child develop a good image of himself and his abilities is something you can do every day for a lifetime!

Just having fun with your children boosts their self-esteem. But in this chapter from Sanity in the Summertime, *we're talking about having fun to teach them about the concepts of inner beauty, positive thinking, and appreciation. With these ideas, songs, and activities, even your little ones can grasp that "they are special."*

Linda Dillow and Claudia Arp
Sanity in the Summertime

Several young people were asked to write ten conclusions for the sentence beginning, "I am . . ." One wrote, "I am ugly. I am not very smart. I am sad." Another wrote, "I am a child of God. I am happy. I am a good painter." What would your children's responses be?

One of our children came home one day and told about a new friend in her class. Most of the children didn't want to be her friend because she looked different—she was a head taller than the others in the class. A friend laughingly told us about her thirty-year-old husband who only wears long-sleeved shirts (even in summer) because as a high school student he was teased about his skinny arms. Another friend remembers being called "stupid" by her aunt. It's amazing how we remember seemingly insignificant statements made years ago.

BEAUTY AND BRAINS

One of our favorite books, James Dobson's *Hide or Seek,* contends that the two most admired qualities in our society are beauty and brains. (Perhaps for boys, brawn could be added.) The child who is naturally attractive and has above-average intelligence often has smooth sailing through life. He or she has built-in advantages over the tall ten-year-old girl, the skinny-armed boy, and the child who is a slow learner.

The whole thing is grossly unfair! Why should our appearance and brain power or achievement orientation have so much to do with how we see ourselves and how others see us? We try to teach our children that it's the "inner qualities" that count, yet "beauty and brains" is the message they hear from all sides. They need to hear a different message from us!

The first thing our children need to hear from us is how God sees them. Psalm 139:13–16 is an excellent passage to share with children of all ages.

> You made all the delicate, inner parts of my body, and knit them together in my mother's womb. Thank you for making me so wonderfully complex! It is amazing to think about. Your workmanship is marvelous—and how well I know it. You were there while I was being formed in utter seclusion! You saw me before I was born and scheduled each day of my life before I began to breathe. Every day was recorded in your Book! (TLB)

Be sure to emphasize the words *wonderfully complex, marvelous,* and *amazing*. We parents are God's tools to help our children see and accept God's viewpoint of their appearance, abilities, intelligence—of their total being. God says the issue is not how many talents or how much intelligence we have, but faithfulness with the abilities and intelligence He has given us (1 Cor. 4:1–2).

A sizable proportion of a child's self-concept emerges from the way he thinks his parents "see" him. When a child is convinced he is greatly loved and respected by his parents, he is inclined to accept his own worth as a person.

Understanding the problem is important; realizing that each child needs our love and admiration is important; but what can we as mothers *do* this summer to help our children see their uniqueness and accept themselves?

Have an "Inner Beauty" Discussion Time

Why not plan a Children's Day or a family night to set personal goals for inner beauty?

The key verse is 1 Samuel 16:7 (TLB): "But the Lord said to Samuel, 'Don't judge by a man's face or height . . . I don't make decisions the way you do! Men judge by outward appearance, but I look at a man's thoughts and intentions.' "

1. Inner Beauty/Outer Beauty

Begin the time together by talking about two kinds of beauty. Identify what makes a person outwardly attractive (good looks, nice clothes, strong body, good figure, etc.). Then help family members define characteristics of inner beauty (love for others, kindness, patience, willingness to help others, etc.).

Compare God's statement in 1 Samuel 16:7 with 1 Peter 3:3–4. What do these two Bible passages say about God's view of inner and outer beauty?

2. Beautiful People We Know

Have family members identify people who have true inner beauty. Decide why family members feel these people have this special beauty.

Also name two or three people who are attractive from an outer beauty standpoint. Do inner and outer beauty sometimes go together? Why or why not? Can a person be unattractive outwardly but still have real inner beauty? Why?

3. Enjoy a Family Snack

As you eat, talk about which is best for a person to focus on every day—inner or outer beauty? Why? What would the world be like if everyone focused on outer beauty? Would the world be better or worse if everyone concentrated on inner beauty? Why?

4. Personal Beauty Plan

Give each person a sheet of paper. Allow time for everyone to write out *one* way he or she wants to try to be more beautiful in outward appearance. Then each person should plan for at least *two* ways to work on improving inner beauty. Decide together if you want to share your goals or keep them secret as each person's private plan.

HAVE A POSITIVE PICTURE

"Finally, brethren, whatever is true, . . . honorable, . . . pure, . . . lovely, . . . if there is any excellence and if anything worthy of praise, let your mind dwell on these things. . . . and the God of peace shall be with you" (Phil. 4:8–9 NASB). We are instructed to think about positive things. A person is a by-product of what he/she thinks about; if our children hear positive things about themselves, they will begin to think positively about themselves. The positive needs to be in their minds and in their hearts. A good place to begin is to encourage and help your children to memorize Scripture portions about how God views them (1 Sam. 16:7, 1 Peter 3:3–4 and portions of Psalm 139 would be excellent to use).

For younger children, plan a special time to listen to Sandi Patti. *Psalty Agapeland; Sandi Patti's Friendship Company;* or *Patch the Pirate* are good tapes to use. Listen, learn the words, and sing them together. If a stereo is not readily available, learn the songs as poems. The messages of the Bill Gaither Trio's "You're Something Special" and "I Am a Promise" are fantastic and have had a tremendous impact on our children.

VERBALIZE APPRECIATION

With Notes

A favorite note at our home was "Have a Happy Day! I'm so glad Jesus gave you to me. You're so very special to God and to me. I love you. Mommy." Summertime is a perfect time to express love through notes dropped in a picnic lunch, hidden under a pillow, or tucked in a bathing cap. We don't write notes to get notes, but it can happen. After years of writing notes Linda received one from her eleven-year-old daughter. "Dear Mommy, I'm so glad that Jesus gave you to me for my mommy. You are so special to me. I love you. Joy."

With a Gift for No Reason

A gift could be some cute stickers, a bucket and shovel, a soccer ball, sunglasses, sugarless gum, or anything (anything cheap, that is!). The gift itself is not important; it's the message of saying, "I love you just because you're you." You could even get "artsy" and write a poem, like the one a child found attached to new colored markers.

> Because you're special and neat
> I bought for you a little treat!
> May you have fun as you draw today
> And your talent and creativity display!

The poem may not win any literary awards, but the child will feel delight in the fact that he or she is special enough to merit not only new markers but a poem too!

If poetic ability is not your strong suit, just write a note expressing your love. We used to keep several three-by-five cards handy in our kitchen cupboards, along with cute stickers. A "card" is quickly made with one of these three by five cards, a sticker, and a felt pen. It is much cheaper than buying a commercial card. Again, it is not the gift or the poem or a lovely card that is important; it's that you took the time to buy or make a small gift and express your love for your child.

Be a Secret Pal

To emphasize how special each family member was, one summer we drew names for a "secret pal." The idea was to do something often for the secret pal (in secret). Evidences of "secret pals" were found in the above poem pinned to the refrigerator (complete with "lovely" picture!), Dad's pajamas and slippers by the bed and the sheet turned back for him, and Mom's dresser neatly cleaned. Secret pals remained secret for one week and then everyone guessed who his or her pal was.

Have a Special Person Party

How better to help one child feel special or important than by letting him/her feel like "queen or king for a day"!

One family chose to have a party in honor of their oldest son when he began his first summer job picking strawberries. Hot, bone weary, and aching from head to toe, he stumbled into the house one evening to discover posters, presents, and poems—all with his name on them. It was a party to express his family's love and to show him that they were on his team.

The walls were decorated with posters that said, "My brother is great! He wins the Strawberry Picker Award!" "We love Sam." Silly gifts had been wrapped and were stacked at his place at the table. With each gift was a poem or note to express appreciation. The meal was his favorite, the dessert extra special.

After dinner each family member gave Sam a coupon saying what they would do for him the following week: "I will empty the trash for you." "I will make your bed for one week." After dinner a slide show was given in his honor, showing pictures of his life from the first year to the present. He was the "star" for one night.

Think for a moment how you would feel if your family spent the time to plan a Special Person Party in your honor. That is exactly how each of your children or your husband would feel.

Here are some ideas for Special Person Parties.

a. Use a Children's Day this summer to plan a Special Person Party for another family member, special friend, or elderly neighbor. The day can be spent together cooking the food, making "We love you" posters, drawing pictures, wrapping silly gifts, preparing a slide show and letting the children write a script, practicing a song to sing, thinking of special things to do the following week as coupon gifts. Let your imagination run wild, or better yet, ask your children (their imagination is *already* wild) what they would like to do for the special person.

b. Use a Children's Day or "Just-Me-and-Mom" time to plan a Special Person Party for one child. The perfect time to plan this is when one child is visiting relatives or friends or is away at camp and the other children are home with you. What fun it is to plan a special surprise party for the brother or sister who is gone!

c. Choose times when Special Person Parties are in order even though it is very inconvenient for you.

· When Dad worked hard on a project at work for months, and he just called to say it has all fallen through.

· When the neighborhood kids laughed at your child because of his/her new braces and he/she says he/she's not smiling for two years.

· When your child studied hard for his/her exam but studied the wrong things.

· When a super summer week has been planned and your child gets the chicken pox.

· When Mom "gracefully" trips over the sidewalk curb and breaks her ankle. *She* needs a party! (Give the book to spouse and children and mildly suggest, "It's *my* turn!")

Note: If you feel overwhelmed by "a slide show—so much work!" then don't have a slide show! We may sound redundant, but it's not how fancy, how much, or how expensive, but the fact that you cared enough to take the time to say, "I love you."

Other Ideas

For other fun and simple-to-do ideas, see Dave and Claudia Arp's book, *60 One-Minute Memory Builders*—Part One "You Are Special." If you are a single and/or working parent, these minute "ideas" will help you find the time to let your child know he/she is special.

READ SPECIAL BOOKS ABOUT SELF-IMAGE

There are many books available on the subject of self-image that can help us help our children.

Hide or Seek by Dr. James Dobson (Revell) is one we cannot recommend highly enough! Put it at the top of your list of books to read. The book explicitly explains the problem of self-image and gives great encouragement to parents. *Your Child's Self-Esteem* by Dorothy Corkille Briggs (Dolphin) is another good book for parents. Others include: *The Blessing* by Gary Smalley and John Trent (Thomas Nelson); *How to Really Love Your Child* by Dr. Ross Campbell (Victor); *My Book about Me* by Dr. Seuss & Roy McKie (Random House); and *My Family, Myself* by Carol Batchelor (Hayes).

Helping our children develop healthy self-images cannot be accomplished in a summer or even in a year; it's a continual process of helping our children see themselves as God sees them. But as you apply some of these projects each summer, it is with the prayer that by summer's end your children's conclusions to "I am . . ." will be, "I am a child of God. I am happy. I am learning!"

Chapter

14

The Training System

Fiduciary responsibility. Even the movie Mary Poppins *spoke of it. Sounds like a hard job—being responsible for teaching our children to manage money. Many of us parents were never taught as children how to manage money; therefore, we often overlook this important aspect of our children's training.*

In this chapter from Raising Money-Smart Kids, *we think we've come up with a simple system to help you teach your children to handle the responsibility of money. But before we get into it, we think there are a few basic precepts that go along with the mechanical system of money management.*

In teaching our children the wise use of money, we must first teach them to remember that (1) God owns it all—we are managers, not owners of the money God gives us; (2) every spending decision a spiritual decision; and (3) the best way to model that God owns it all is to give and tithe freely. With that, let us tell you about our system for making our children wise stewards of God's wealth.

Ron and Judy Blue
Raising Money-Smart Kids

We learn so much from those who have gone before us. For instance, probably the simplest yet most effective approach to managing money can be found in Grandma's cookie jar. That's right! This method is nothing more than putting income received into the jar and taking money out of the jar as needs arise. When the jar is empty, that signals the end of spending. There are no credit advances.

This method demonstrates a basic, but profound, financial planning principle. The cookie jar is not a bottomless pit; therefore, the outgo can never be greater than the inflow. There is no such thing as a credit card or debt. With this method it is not possible to overextend yourself financially.

An alternative to the cookie jar method of budgeting is to use more than one cookie jar. In training our children, we have used multiple "cookie jars," which are merely stationery-sized envelopes with a label on the outside indicating how the cash in the envelope is to be used. These envelopes are kept in a simple file box or recipe box.

The same principles apply for the envelopes as for the cookie jar. The envelope is not a bottomless pit, and the spending can never be greater than the amount originally put in.

Two elements are necessary in any budget, be it a family budget, a business budget, or a government budget. Those elements are a *plan* for spending and a system of *controls* to ensure that the spending is never greater than the plan has indicated. Absolutely every budget must work under these two elements; and the envelope system and the cookie jar system include these elements in their most basic forms.

Credit allows us to live in the short term, as if there were no bottom to the cookie jar and, therefore, no limit to our spending.

The problem in our families, in our government, and in many businesses is that we have become so "sophisticated" in our thinking that we have lost sight of the basic elements. We behave as if these two basics were no longer relevant or necessary in our daily lives. Credit allows us to live in the short term, as if there were no bottom to the cookie jar and, therefore, no limit to our spending.

Deficit funding, at every level, has made the plan almost irrelevant because financing is always available to go beyond what was planned. The problem surfaces only when all sources of credit have dried up, and a life-style has been established far beyond the ability to repay. At this point, the options are so devastating that many couples end up in severe conflict which results in divorce or personal bankruptcy.

I have counseled many godly families in very desperate financial conditions because they had no plan for spending. And the opportunity to fund needs and greeds by using credit cards enabled them to overspend year after year when they ran out of credit, they had to make some tough decisions. Houses and cars had to be sold; children had to be taken out of private schools; clothing budgets had to be readjusted; and the total life-style had to undergo a dramatic reduction in order for them to survive, unless they wanted to declare bankruptcy. Declaring bankruptcy was not a real option, however, because they believe (as I do) that it is unbiblical.

Had they followed the basics of the cookie jar process or the envelope system, they never would have gotten into poor financial shape. Did these people *plan to fail?* No, they merely *failed to plan* and failed to choose to live within a plan. Debt is no man's friend; it will always make you a slave.

THE MECHANICS OF OUR SYSTEM

The system that we use with our children is very simple. Each child, beginning at about age eight, has been given a recipe file box containing five letter-sized envelopes: a "tithe" envelope, a "save" envelope, a "spend" envelope, a "gifts" envelope, and a "clothes" envelope.

The "spend" envelope contains money that can be used in any way they choose. The "gift" envelope is the amount allocated for buying gifts at Christmas, birthdays, and other special occasions for friends and relatives. The "clothes" amount is used to purchase *all* their clothes.

They are given a monthly allowance, in cash, to place in each of the envelopes according to a preset plan. The amount set for each envelope comes from an annual planning session that Judy and I have. We discuss the allowance amounts for each of the five categories, based on what they are required to pay for; then we give them one-twelfth of that amount each month in a lump sum.

Debt is no man's friend; it will always make you a slave.

As they earn money or as they receive gift money during the year, they deposit it into at least three envelopes, and perhaps all five envelopes. When they are beginning to learn about the system, they are required to put 10 percent into the "tithe" envelope and 10 percent into the "save" envelope; the balance can go into the "spend," "gift," and "clothes" envelopes. As they get older and understand the purpose of the system, they are given the freedom to divide the money as they see fit. We try to help them see the value and benefit of giving and saving. That way when they choose for themselves, they enjoy the experience of decision making.

The most important thing is not what children are responsible for buying, but how they handle the responsibility of managing the money.

Each family has to decide what children are responsible for in the various categories. The most important thing is not *what* children are responsible for buying, but how they handle the responsibility of managing the money. They need to know what they are responsible to buy, and that when the money is gone, there is no more. They must learn to live within the designated amount. If you want them to buy their own sports equipment, that's great. Allocate enough money to the "clothes" envelope so that they can cover those expenses, then require them to make the purchase.

If children habitually make the mistake of poor allocation—such as spending all of their money in October for fall clothes and, consequently, having no money left to buy the winter coat that is desperately needed—there are several ways to deal with this problem. First, you may decide to *not* make them responsible for what *you* consider to be the "necessities"—such as winter coats, snow boots, Sunday shoes, haircuts, school lunches, and so forth. *You* provide the money for those things. Second, you can let them do without. Third, they can live with the consequences of wearing last year's coat, shoes, or whatever. Fourth, you can make them earn the extra money needed for the purchase.

You come up with other creative alternatives, but the point is that children should have responsibility for certain budget items, and they must learn to allocate properly within those budget categories.

For a larger purchase, such as a bicycle, a tennis racquet, or a seasonal wardrobe, children may need several weeks or months before they accumulate enough to make the purchase. But when they have saved enough money and are ready to make the purchase, they can take the envelope with them and pay for the item with cash.

We allow them to borrow from envelope to envelope, except for the "tithe" and the "save" envelopes. They need to feel the responsibility for the management of the money, and therefore, we allow them a tremendous amount of flexibility in how they spend their money.

Their "save" envelope accumulates moneys that they deposit periodically in a savings account in their name. As I mentioned earlier, at least once a year I will share with them how much money is in the savings account and show them how the interest causes that account to "grow" without their having to expend any physical or mental energy.

PRINCIPLES AND PRACTICES

Children can begin to manage money at a very early age. We believe that they can be given money to make decisions with, on their own, at age four or five. Perhaps they could have two or three envelopes—a "tithe" envelope, a "save" envelope, and a "spend" envelope.

By the time they have reached age eight or nine, we believe they can have all five envelopes, and become responsible for planning and buying all their clothes and all the gifts they need to buy. The significant purchases—clothes and gifts—will require the greatest amount of discretion and thus provide the greatest value in training, right on through their college years. To say whether children can, or should, spend one hundred dollars per year or one thousand dollars per year on clothes is really a matter of the family and individual priorities and objectives.

When the children reach the teen years, they may choose to have more envelopes, and that is okay. However, we do not encourage our children to have more than six or seven envelopes until they reach college age. The system needs to be simple to work most efficiently.

We have included some completed sample budgets for a thirteen-year-old boy (Charts 1, 2, 3, 4) to help you determine how much allowance per budget category there will be. The amount per category will vary, first, by age, and second, by activities. We have found that even our children of the same sex have different financial requirements. Some children will spend more time participating in sports or taking music lessons than others; therefore, the budget amount should vary to recognize that. As children reach the teen years, they may have earnings they can use to meet some of the budget categories.

CHART 1
BUDGET WORKSHEET—CLOTHES
(Sample for 13-year-old boy)

	Estimated Annual Amount (1)
I. Clothes	
A. Seasonal wardrobe	
1. Fall	$ 100
2. Winter	$ 150
3. Spring	$ 100
4. Summer	$ 75
B. Underwear and socks	$ 30
C. Shoes	
1. Dress	$ 100
2. Everyday	$ 135
3. Sports	$ 75
D. Coats	
1. Winter	$ 120
2. Spring	$ 75
E. Athletic clothes and equipment	$ 200
F. Accessories (ties, belts, jewelry)	$ 40
G. Other	
(band uniforms, stage costumes, etc.)	$ 0
	$ 0
	$ 0

	$ 0	
	$ 0	
Annual total	$ 1200	(2)
Monthly amount needed (annual total divided by 12)	$ 100	(3)
Subtract amount provided by allowance	(80)	(4)
Amount to come from earnings and other sources	$ 20	(5)

1. *Estimate* annual amount for each category.
2. Add the amounts in all categories to get an annual total.
3. Divide the annual total (2) by 12 to get monthly amount.
4. Subtract the amount the parents will provide as a monthly allowance.
5. The monthly amount (3) less the allowance amount (4) results in the amount that must be provided from earnings, gifts, and other sources.

Parents need to make their decision whether a child should work while still in high school, based on their own unique circumstances and desires. Whatever the decision, it will impact the amount of the allowance. We did not require our two oldest daughters to work while they were participating in athletics or in cheerleading, but once the season was over we strongly encouraged them to get a job.

CHART 2

BUDGET WORKSHEET—SPEND

(Sample for 13-year-old boy)

II. Spend	Estimated Annual Amount (1)
A. Food and snacks (school lunches, other)	$ 480
B. Entertainment (movies, sports, etc.)	$ 240
C. Hobbies	$ 84
D. Records/tapes	$ 60
E. Jewelry	$ 0
F. Personal grooming (haircuts, perms, supplies)	$ 48
G. Reading material (books, magazine subscriptions)	$ 84
H. School supplies	$ 24
I. Auto	
1. Insurance	$ 0
2. Gas, oil, maintenance	$ 0
3. Repairs	$ 0

4. Tires	$ 0	
Annual total	$ 1020	(2)
Monthly amount needed (annual total divided by 12)	$ 85	(3)
Subtract amount provided by allowance	(65)	(4)
Amount to come from earnings and other sources	$ 20	(5)

1. *Estimate* annual amount for each category.
2. Add the amounts in all categories to get an annual total.
3. Divide the annual total (2) by 12 to get monthly amount.
4. Subtract the amount the parents will provide as a monthly allowance.
5. The monthly amount (3) less the allowance amount (4) results in the amount that must be provided from earnings, gifts, and other sources.

Each budget category needs to be reviewed for each child on a regular basis because circumstances and needs will change. The budget categories we have presented are not the law. Give yourself time to determine the amounts needed. Be willing to make mistakes.

If this is the first time you have used this type of system, it may take a couple of years before you are comfortable with determining the amounts per category and even with the number of categories. At the end of this chapter are average amounts received and spent for all teens in 1990 according to the Nationwide Survey conducted by the Rand Youth Poll (Chart 5), which may be helpful to you in setting the amounts for your children.

CHART 3
BUDGET WORKSHEET—GIFTS
(Sample for 13-year-old boy)

III. Gifts	Estimated Annual Amount (1) Family	Friends	Total (2)
A. Christmas	$ 100	$ 20	$ 120
B. Birthdays	$ 100	$ 20	$ 120
C. Anniversaries	$ 10	$ 0	$ 10
D. Mother's/Father's Day	$ 20	$ 0	$ 20
E. Special Occasions			
1. Graduations	$ 10	$ 0	$ 10
2. Weddings	$ 0	$ 0	$ 0
3. Valentine's Day	$ 10	$ 10	$ 20

4. Easter	$ 0	$ 0	$ 0
5. Other	$ 0	$ 0	$ 0
F. Other	$ 0	$ 0	$ 0
Annual total	$ 250	$ 50	$ 300
Monthly amount needed (annual total divided by 12)			$ 25 (3)
Subtract amount provided by allowance			(15) (4)
Amount to come from earnings and other sources			$ 10 (5)

1. *Estimate* annual amount for each category.
2. Add the amounts in all categories to get an annual total.
3. Divide the annual total (2) by 12 to get monthly amount.
4. Subtract the amount the parents will provide as a monthly allowance.
5. The monthly amount (3) less the allowance amount (4) results in the amount that must be provided from earnings, gifts, and other sources.

Those averages, however, do not include the total clothes budget for a child or any amount for a tithe. Therefore, your numbers will no doubt be higher in total than those averages. There are also two sets of blank forms you can use to begin the system. Remember, the *purpose* of the envelope system is not to have the system down pat, but to teach your children the basic tools of money management.

How frequently the allowance should be given will depend upon the ages of the children. If you begin the system with very young children, it probably should be given weekly because they cannot fully comprehend how much time is in a month or a year. When children reach age eight or nine, we believe that they should be given the money on a monthly basis. For example, their clothes money for the year is divided by twelve, and given to them monthly. They then have the responsibility for the money in the envelopes, the freedom of decision making, and the freedom to fail. Sometimes for clothes for our teenagers, we have given amounts on a semiannual or even annual basis in a lump sum, so that they can plan for and buy a wardrobe for a season.

The purpose of the envelope system is not to have the system down pat, but to teach your children the basic tools of money management.

Many parents are concerned that children will spend unwisely if they receive a large amount on a monthly basis. They may in the beginning, but that is how they are going to learn. After a series of mistakes, they will plan much more wisely. They must have the freedom to make their own decisions and the freedom to fail.

CHART 4

MONTHLY PLAN

(Sample for 13-year-old boy)

		Monthly Amount Needed	Allowance	Earnings Etc.
Clothes	(1)	$ 100	$ 80	$ 20
Spend	↓	$ 85	$ 65	$ 20
Gifts		$ 25	$ 15	$ 10
Total	(2)	$ 210	$ 160	$ 50
Save (10% of total)	(3)	$ 21	$ 16	$ 5
Tithe (10% of total)	(4)	$ 21	$ 16	$ 5
Total monthly plan	(5)	$ 252	$ 192	$ 60

1. Copy totals from appropriate Budget Worksheets for "monthly amount needed" [*worksheet line (3)*], "allowance" [*worksheet line (4)*], and "earnings, etc." [*worksheet line (5)*].
2. Add to get total for each category.
3. Multiply (2) by 10 percent (or another desired percentage).
4. Multiply (2) by 10 percent (or another desired percentage).
5. Add the total (2), the save (3), and the tithe (4) amounts to determine the total monthly plan.

Once the amount for each category has been determined and you are comfortable that it is a fair amount, you should not change it without a serious discussion. Our caution is to be wary of being manipulated by your children. If they learn that they can constantly change the amount by arguing, pouting, scheming, or just asking, the whole system of spending *limited* resources has been destroyed. In fact, there are no limits on the resources when you vary them according to the children's protests or desires.

CHART 5

INCOME AND SPENDING
Boys Aged 13 Through 15

Income

Allowance	$15.25
Earnings	17.10
TOTAL	$32.35

Expenditures

Food and Snacks		$11.05
Clothing		6.05
Movies and Entertainment		4.80
Records		1.65
Personal Grooming		1.00
Hobbies		.85
Books, Paperbacks		.45
Magazines		.40
School Supplies		.35
Coin-operated Video Games		.20
Greeting Cards		.10
	TOTAL	$26.90

Savings:

$5.45 a week towards athletic equipment, cameras, video games, radios, watches, computers, hand calculators, bicycles, and so on.

Note: The above and following figures on teen-age spending are based on weekly averages.

The world is bent on teaching you and your children to get all you can now—no matter what the cost will be in the future.

The world is bent on teaching you and your children to get all you can *now*—no matter what the cost will be in the future. Both credit card companies and advertising firms have this motivation. You have an awesome job to try to teach your children delayed gratification through good money management and long-range planning. Don't add to the problems they already face each day by allowing them to have unlimited resources to meet their wants and desires. Help them learn to be responsible, mature individuals by being able to put off today's desires for future benefits. On the other hand, remember to be flexible. There must be a proper balance.

Girls Aged 13 Through 15

Income

Allowance	$16.90
Earnings	18.80
TOTAL	$35.70

Expenditures

Clothing	$11.50
Food and Snacks	7.05
Movies and Entertainment	3.80
Cosmetics	3.60
Records	2.00
Jewelry	1.60
Fragrances	.55
Hair Products	.45
Beauty Parlor	.40
School Supplies	.40
Magazines	.35
Hobbies	.30
Books, Paperbacks	.25
Greeting Cards	.25
Coin-operated Video Games	.05
TOTAL	$32.55

Savings:

$3.15 a week towards radios, accessories, athletic equipment, bicycles, hand calculators, cameras, and so on.

A woman once explained the money management system she had her children using. I couldn't believe it—they were required to keep track of *every* penny they spent on a daily basis. That kind of record-keeping system would be appropriate for a CPA, but not for children. Her children rebelled against the rigidity of the system, which is not surprising.

Boys Aged 16 Through 19

Income

Allowance	$27.20
Earnings	47.05
TOTAL	$74.25

Expenditures

Clothing		$12.10
Movies, dating, entertainment		11.95
Food and Snacks		11.80
Gasoline and Auto		10.05
Personal Grooming		6.00
Records		1.60
Hobbies		1.15
Books, Paperbacks		.65
Magazines		.60
Coin-operated Video Games		.60
School Supplies		.45
Greeting Cards		.25
Cigarettes		.15
	TOTAL	$57.35

Savings:

$16.90 a week towards education, motor vehicles, TV sets, computers, radios, hand calculators, video games, stereos, cameras, typewriters, sporting equipment, stocks, and so on.

Children should not be required to keep track of where they spend the money within each envelope. The envelope is the record of how much they spent and how much is left. If children want to know why they are running out of money each month in a particular envelope and want to keep track of how they are spending it, that's fine; but they should not be required to keep track of every penny spent on a regular basis.

The amount given to children as an allowance should *definitely not* (1) *be withheld as a discipline* or *to influence behavior,* (2) *be based on performance of chores,* or (3) *vary once the agreed-upon amount has been determined to be fair and reasonable.*

Girls Aged 16 Through 19

Income

Allowance	$28.80
Earnings	48.60
TOTAL	$77.40

Expendit ures

Clothing		$25.90
Cosmetics		9.05
Food and Snacks		8.00
Movies and Entertainment		5.50
Gasoline and Auto		5.40
Jewelry		3.10
Records		2.30
Fragrances		2.00
Beauty Parlor		1.25
Hair Products		1.25
Books, Paperbacks		.85
Hobbies		.70
Magazines		.60
School Supplies		.50
Greeting Cards		.50
Cigarettes		.45
Coin-operated Video Games		.05
	TOTAL	$67.40

Savings:

$10.00 a week towards education, marriage, vacations, travel, typewriters, hand calculators, cameras, radios, telephones, TV sets, and so on.

SOURCE: Nationwide Survey, Rand Youth Poll, 1990.

This system is to teach children money management; it is not to be used, at the same time, as a disciplinary tool. For example, what happens if their grades go down? Do you take away their allowance? The answer is no. You are not using the system to motivate them to get good grades; there are other ways to accomplish those results.

CHART 6
BUDGET WORKSHEET—CLOTHES

	Estimated Annual Amount (1)	
I. Clothes		
A. Seasonal wardrobe		
1. Fall	$_____	
2. Winter	$_____	
3. Spring	$_____	
4. Summer	$_____	
B. Underwear and socks	$_____	
C. Shoes		
1. Dress	$_____	
2. Everyday	$_____	
3. Sports	$_____	
D. Coats		
1. Winter	$_____	
2. Spring	$_____	
E. Athletic clothes and equipment	$_____	
F. Accessories (ties, belts, jewelry)	$_____	
G. Other (band uniforms, stage costumes, etc.)	$_____	
	$_____	
	$_____	
	$_____	
	$_____	
Annual total	$_____	(2)
Monthly amount needed (annual total divided by 12)	$_____	(3)
Subtract amount provided by allowance	(_____)	(4)
Amount to come from earnings and other sources	$_____	(5)

1. *Estimate* annual amount for each category.
2. Add the amounts in all categories to get an annual total.
3. Divide the annual total (2) by 12 to get monthly amount.
4. Subtract the amount the parents will provide as a monthly allowance.
5. The monthly amount (3) less the allowance amount (4) results in the amount that must be provided from earnings, gifts, and other sources.

CHART 7

BUDGET WORKSHEET—SPEND

II. SPEND	ESTIMATED ANNUAL AMOUNT (1)	
A. Food and snacks (school lunches, other)	$_____	
B. Entertainment (movies, sports, etc.)	$_____	
C. Hobbies	$_____	
D. Records/tapes	$_____	
E. Jewelry	$_____	
F. Personal grooming (haircuts, perms, supplies)	$_____	
G. Reading material (books, magazine subscriptions)	$_____	
H. School supplies	$_____	
I. Autos		
1. Insurance	$_____	
2. Gas, oil, maintenance	$_____	
3. Repairs	$_____	
4. Tires	$_____	
Annual total	$_____	(2)
Monthly amount needed (annual total divided by 12)	$_____	(3)
Subtract amount provided by allowance	(_____)	(4)
Amount to come from earnings and other sources	$_____	(5)

1. *Estimate* annual amount for each category.
2. Add the amounts in all categories to get an annual total.
3. Divide the annual total (2) by 12 to get monthly amount.
4. Subtract the amount the parents will provide as a monthly allowance.
5. The monthly amount (3) less the allowance amount (4) results in the amount that must be provided from earnings, gifts, and other sources.

Also, the allowance is not a payment for chores. We believe that chores are of two types and are to be handled separately from teaching money management. Some chores are *expected;* as members of the family, children should perform certain chores, such as doing the dishes, cleaning their room, making the bed, or carrying out the trash. Our children have to meet their responsibilities as members of the family, and one of those responsibilities is helping with chores around the house. We are a "team," and all members of the team must do their part. Others are *optional;* these chores are not expected of them, such as mowing the lawn, helping with the ironing, baby-sitting, or doing things above and beyond the normal expectations of the household.

As discussed earlier, it will take some time to come to a decision as to a fair and reasonable amount for the allowance. This may be as little as six months or as much as two years before you are sure of the amounts. Once the amount has been determined, however, you must not vary it, or you will teach children that there are, in reality, no boundaries. For that reason, we feel strongly that the amount should not be adjusted unless circumstances convince you that the amount is incorrect.

CHART 8

BUDGET WORKSHEET—GIFTS

III. Gifts	Estimated Annual Amount (1) Family	Friends	Total	(2)
A. Christmas	$_____	$_____	$_____	
B. Birthdays	$_____	$_____	$_____	
C. Anniversaries	$_____	$_____	$_____	
D. Mother's/Father's Day	$_____	$_____	$_____	
E. Special Occasions				
1. Graduations	$_____	$_____	$_____	
2. Weddings	$_____	$_____	$_____	
3. Valentine's Day	$_____	$_____	$_____	
4. Easter	$_____	$_____	$_____	
5. Other	$_____	$_____	$_____	
F. Other	$_____	$_____	$_____	
Annual total	$_____	$_____	$_____	
Monthly amount needed (annual total divided by 12)			$_____	(3)
Subtract amount provided by allowance			(_____)	(4)
Amount to come from earnings and other sources			$_____	(5)

1. *Estimate* annual amount for each category.
2. Add the amounts in all categories to get an annual total.
3. Divide the annual total (2) by 12 to get monthly amount.

4. Subtract the amount the parents will provide as a monthly allowance.
5. The monthly amount (3) less the allowance amount (4) results in the amount that must be provided from earnings, gifts, and other sources.

Once a year Judy and I take each child out to dinner as a birthday treat. During that dinner we discuss the child's goals for the next year as well as the goal accomplishments over the past year. To facilitate that conversation we keep a journal containing the goals. Those goals might be making a new friend, buying something of "significance," making certain grades in school, achieving something specific in a sport, or spending time daily reading God's Word.

CHART 9

MONTHLY PLAN

		Monthly Amount Needed	Allowance	Earnings Etc.
Clothes	(1)	$_____	$_____	$_____
Spend	↓	$_____	$_____	$_____
Gifts		$_____	$_____	$_____
Total	(2)	$_____	$_____	$_____
Save (10% of total)	(3)	$_____	$_____	$_____
Tithe (10% of total)	(4)	$_____	$_____	$_____
Total monthly plan	(5)	$_____	$_____	$_____

1. Copy totals from appropriate Budget Worksheets for "monthly amount needed" [*worksheet line (3)*], "allowance" [*worksheet line (4)*], and "earnings, etc." [*worksheet line (5)*].
2. Add to get total for each category.
3. Multiply (2) by 10 percent (or another desired percentage).
4. Multiply (2) by 10 percent (or another desired percentage).
5. Add the total (2), the save (3), and the tithe (4) amounts to determine the total monthly plan.

We also review what the allowance will be for the next year for each of the five categories. We review the chores the child will be responsible for, both those that are *expected* and those that are *optional* for which they can earn compensation. If we did not set aside this predetermined time, which is extremely valuable but never urgent, we probably would not go through this process with each child.

CHART 10

BUDGET WORKSHEET—CLOTHES

	Estimated Annual Amount (1)	
I. Clothes		
A. Seasonal wardrobe		
1. Fall	$_____	
2. Winter	$_____	
3. Spring	$_____	
4. Summer	$_____	
B. Underwear and socks	$_____	
C. Shoes		
1. Dress	$_____	
2. Everyday	$_____	
3. Sports	$_____	
D. Coats		
1. Winter	$_____	
2. Spring	$_____	
E. Athletic clothes and equipment	$_____	
F. Accessories (ties, belts, jewelry)	$_____	
G. Other (band uniforms, stage costumes, etc.)	$_____	
	$_____	
	$_____	
	$_____	
	$_____	
Annual total	$_____	(2)
Monthly amount needed (annual total divided by 12)	$_____	(3)
Subtract amount provided by allowance	(_____)	(4)
Amount to come from earnings and other sources	$_____	(5)

1. *Estimate* annual amount for each category.
2. Add the amounts in all categories to get an annual total.
3. Divide the annual total (2) by 12 to get monthly amount.
4. Subtract the amount the parents will provide as a monthly allowance.
5. The monthly amount (3) less the allowance amount (4) results in the amount that must be provided from earnings, gifts, and other sources.

Of course, there is nothing biblical or magical about the birthday date, but it is a time that is special for each child. It is an occasion that few parents and virtually no children ever forget. With a large family it is easy to treat children as a group rather than as individuals. This technique allows us to deal with them individually in terms of their allowance, chores, and goals; it is very important to us that we treat each child as an individual.

WHAT THE SYSTEM TEACHES

The system we use is not the only system available. Feel free to take what we have shared and adapt it to your unique situation. We have found that the envelope system is a tool for teaching our children many things, and we have reviewed them here for you.

Tithing

In 1 Corinthians 16:2 we find the principles of giving, which are applicable for the New Testament church: "On the first day of the week let each one of you lay something aside, storing up as he may prosper, that there be no collections when I come."

The book of Proverbs says, "Honor the LORD with your possessions, / And with the firstfruits of all your increase; / So your barns will be filled with plenty, / And your vats will overflow with new wine" (3:9–10).

The tithe is the recognition that God owns it all. If your children put money into a "tithe" envelope on a regular basis and then give it, they are learning the habit of tithing. This will become ingrained in their minds as recognition that God owns it all.

Rewards for Work

By having a limited supply of money, children must earn additional money for the discretionary items they want. Then when they make a purchase, they are learning a significant reward for work.

Savings

Saving teaches the principle of delayed gratification. Putting money into a "save" envelope on a regular basis is an important discipline to ensure financial success. Allowing some of the savings amount to be spent periodically for significant items will begin to teach delayed gratification. Remember the definition of financial maturity—"giving up today's desires for future benefits."

Opportunity Cost of Consumption

When the money is gone, you cannot buy anything else. There is no more dramatic way to teach the opportunity cost of consumption. The cost is not dollar-for-dollar, but multiple dollars taken out of the future that could have been available had the money not been spent. The system makes that principle a reality.

God is the only One who never has, and never will, exhaust His resources.

Limited Supply of Money

The whole system is built around the principle that there is a limited supply of money. When the cookie jar or the envelope is empty, the only way to get funds is to work. Contrary to the world's philosophy, there is an end to what can be spent. God is the only One who never has, and never will, exhaust His resources.

Decision Making

Dealing with a limited number of resources and an unlimited number of choices on which to spend those resources requires that decisions be made.

Budgeting

Budgeting is a one-year financial plan, and the whole system is built as a one-year financial plan.

Wise Buying

Children do not have to be wise buyers for the system to work, but they will quickly learn that by buying wisely they will have more money available to do other things.

CHART 11

BUDGET WORKSHEET—SPEND

II. SPEND	ESTIMATED ANNUAL AMOUNT (1)	
A. Food and snacks (school lunches, other)	$______	
B. Entertainment (movies, sports, etc.)	$______	
C. Hobbies	$______	
D. Records/tapes	$______	
E. Jewelry	$______	
F. Personal grooming (haircuts, perms, supplies)	$______	
G. Reading material (books, magazine subscriptions)	$______	
H. School supplies	$______	
I. Autos		
1. Insurance	$______	
2. Gas, oil, maintenance	$______	
3. Repairs	$______	
4. Tires	$______	
Annual total	$______	(2)
Monthly amount needed (annual total divided by 12)	$______	(3)
Subtract amount provided by allowance	(______)	(4)
Amount to come from earnings and other sources	$______	(5)

1. *Estimate* annual amount for each category.
2. Add the amounts in all categories to get an annual total.
3. Divide the annual total (2) by 12 to get monthly amount.
4. Subtract the amount the parents will provide as a monthly allowance.
5. The monthly amount (3) less the allowance amount (4) results in the amount that must be provided from earnings, gifts, and other sources.

Goal Setting

Our boys began realizing at ages 9 and 11 that if they do not spend the money they earn during the summers they will have saved enough money to buy a car when they are age sixteen. The system teaches the wisdom and value of setting long-term as well as short-term goals.

CHART 12
BUDGET WORKSHEET—GIFTS

III. Gifts	Estimated Annual Amount (1) Family	Friends	Total (2)	
A. Christmas	$_____	$_____	$_____	
B. Birthdays	$_____	$_____	$_____	
C. Anniversaries	$_____	$_____	$_____	
D. Mother's/Father's Day	$_____	$_____	$_____	
E. Special Occasions				
1. Graduations	$_____	$_____	$_____	
2. Weddings	$_____	$_____	$_____	
3. Valentine's Day	$_____	$_____	$_____	
4. Easter	$_____	$_____	$_____	
5. Other	$_____	$_____	$_____	
F. Other	$_____	$_____	$_____	
Annual total	$_____	$_____	$_____	
Monthly amount needed (annual total divided by 12)			$_____	(3)
Subtract amount provided by allowance			(_____)	(4)
Amount to come from earnings and other sources			$_____	(5)

1. *Estimate* annual amount for each category.
2. Add the amounts in all categories to get an annual total.
3. Divide the annual total (2) by 12 to get monthly amount.
4. Subtract the amount the parents will provide as a monthly allowance.
5. The monthly amount (3) less the allowance amount (4) results in the amount that must be provided from earnings, gifts, and other sources.

CONCLUSION

The most critical issue regarding the envelope system is that children must have *goal ownership*. In other words, it must be *their* system rather than your system imposed upon them. Help them set up the system and understand what they can learn by it. Then allow them to have control of the money and freedom to work within the system.

Children may change the system to fit their needs. Karen was having trouble with the system when she was ten or eleven years old because she prefers to live spontaneously, and our system made her feel too confined. She told Judy that she was fed up with the envelope system. As Judy talked with her, she discovered that Karen did not "feel" free to spend. She was trying to live, if you will, under the law. What she really wanted was to have some money to "flit" away if she chose to do so.

Judy, with great wisdom, suggested to her that she add a sixth envelope and call it her "flit" envelope. Money in the flit envelope could be used any way that she chose. In reality, she had that freedom with her "spend" envelope, but she didn't feel the freedom. Merely by setting up another envelope and labeling it the way she wanted, she experienced tremendous freedom to operate within the system.

Money is nothing more than a resource, and money management is nothing more than a tool to use that resource.

Although she does not enjoy discipline as a way of life, Karen has become a very disciplined young lady in certain necessary areas of her life—her school work and her money management. She does an excellent job of managing her money, and I believe that is because she had the freedom to learn when she was allowed to design the system. The "flit" envelope taught me something I needed to remember: Money is nothing more than a resource, and money management is nothing more than a tool to use that resource. Neither is an end in itself!

Our challenge to you is as follows:

1. Discuss the system with your children and make sure they understand the extent of their responsibility.
2. Review the Budget Worksheets and set the allowance amounts for each of your children.
3. Give your children the file box with the money already inserted in the envelopes for the first month.

4. Be flexible!
5. Watch your children take responsibility for this very important area of their lives.

CHART 13
MONTHLY PLAN

		Monthly Amount Needed	Allowance	Earnings Etc.
Clothes (1)		$_____	$_____	$_____
Spend ↓		$_____	$_____	$_____
Gifts		$_____	$_____	$_____
Total	(2)	$_____	$_____	$_____
Save (10% of total)	(3)	$_____	$_____	$_____
Tithe (10% of total)	(4)	$_____	$_____	$_____
Total monthly plan	(5)	$_____	$_____	$_____

1. Copy totals from appropriate Budget Worksheets for "monthly amount needed" [*worksheet line (3)*], "allowance" [*worksheet line (4)*], and "earnings, etc." [*worksheet line (5)*].
2. Add to get total for each category.
3. Multiply (2) by 10 percent (or another desired percentage).
4. Multiply (2) by 10 percent (or another desired percentage).
5. Add the total (2), the save (3), and the tithe (4) amounts to determine the total monthly plan.

Chapter

15

Give It Away

Ron and Judy Blue touched on it—giving. And I'd like to expound on it—giving our money and our "stuff." It's an attitude of life, and I think an important one, especially for teenagers. I wrote How to Rearrange the World *to give teens some great ideas on how they can help fix the planet and its people. It takes* being *different to make the world different, and I think the teenage years are a great time to start to encourage habits and attitudes that can make a difference. This chapter is written to the teenagers in your family, so you just might want them to read the chapter; but, then again, you might find it inspiring too—especially if you're into wanting to rearrange the world into just a little bit better place.*

Todd Temple
How to Rearrange the World

Life starts out so simple. You show up naked, dimpled, tiny. But within moments, they're piling possessions on you: a name, a diaper, clothes, toys—and one of those mobiles that hangs over your crib, just out of reach, driving you absolutely crazy.

It doesn't stop there. Your life becomes an endless consumption of *stuff*—new clothes to replace the ones you grow out of, new toys to replace the ones you broke, lost, or ate. Then it's trikes and bikes, books and tapes, and still more clothes. By the time you're a teenager, you're a full-time consumer: shoes, clothes, jewelry, CDs, tapes, videos, stereos, phones, TVs, VCRs, computers, mountain bikes, skateboards, skis, cars. And you're still just getting started; you'll be acquiring stuff for the next sixty years.

I'm sure you've seen the bumper sticker, "He who dies with the most toys wins." It's a silly idea, yet lots of people live as if they believe it. Cheering you on are the countless commercials showing you what you'll need to buy to "win." Commercials make up about 20 percent of television programming. The average teenager watches twenty hours of television a week. So by the time you're eighteen, you've seen about 350,000 commercials. No wonder you can't get those stupid jingles out of your head.

Even if you don't watch TV, you're still getting hit over the head with advertising: on the radio, in magazines and movie theaters, on buses, benches, billboards, and the back of your cereal box.

The ads are working. Teenagers are spending more money (theirs and their parents') on "stuff" than ever before. For example, 50 percent have their own TV; 44 percent own a VCR; 33 percent of those aged sixteen and older own a car. Teenage girls spend over $5 billion annually on cosmetics, $16 billion on clothes.

In 1989 alone, you and your twenty-three million friends spent over $71 *billion.* The big question is, *What are you getting for your money?* Not peace: the number of suicides, homicides, and cases of depression keeps increasing despite all the toys that should make life more pleasant. Not fulfillment: no matter how much you buy, how many clothes in your closet, how fast your car goes, you cannot fill the emptiness inside you.

WORLD CHANGERS ARE BIG GIVERS

The bumper sticker would be correct if it read, "He who *tries* for the most toys loses." I think the only way to win the race is to run *backward.* Instead of trying to collect wealth, try to give it away.

Give Money

"Wait a minute! I don't have enough money to afford giving some of it away," you say. I beg to differ. Almost all of your parents' income has to go toward rent, utilities, taxes, insurance, food, medical bills, and your clothes. You, however, can spend most of your money any way you please.

Sure, you spend lots of your money on food and clothes, but you wouldn't starve or go naked if you didn't—the closet and refrigerator at your house are subsidized by your folks. Unlike them, you spend most of your money on wants, not needs. Compared to most adults, you're rich. Which means you're able to give away a greater percentage of your income.

Sometimes you see TV preachers who say that if you're "faithful" and give money (to them, it's assumed), God will make you wealthy. I think this is a stupid idea. One of the best reasons to give money is to help *other* people, but these guys turn the act of giving into a selfish thing. I think if that's the motive, it's better to just keep the money and leave God out of it.

Giving to a worthy cause *does* have its rewards. You feel that you're doing something to change the world—which is a wonderful feeling. If you give regularly, you sense a feeling of accomplishment —it takes discipline to do this. And when you give to a cause, you have more authority to speak out on it—you're now an *investor* in change. (I don't have much respect for people who complain about hunger or homelessness or the environment yet won't give their time or money to change the situation. It's put up or shut up.)

In one way, those "prosperity preachers" are right. Giving can make you richer because in order to give regularly, you have to learn to manage your money. And the better you handle your money, the more you'll save. For example, if you don't have any obligation to give, you can spend freely on CDs and food and movie tickets. But if someone is counting on the $30 you give every month, you're going to think twice about blowing your paycheck on "stuff."

Give Smart.

Lots of people and organizations would like for you to give your money to them. Unfortunately, some of them are crooks. The crooked ones not only "steal" your money. They also steal your desire to give, so legitimate causes lose out because you fear you can't trust anyone. When you give money, it's *your* responsibility to know where that money is going. Ask questions.

Is it a nonprofit organization? If an organization is authorized by the government to accept tax-deductible donations, it's called a 501(c)(3) corporation, which refers to the paragraph in some tax code that explains this. That doesn't automatically make it legitimate, but you know it has to follow certain rules that make ripping you off more difficult.

What percentage of your money goes toward "the cause"? Like any corporation, nonprofits have to pay rent, utilities, phone bills, postage, salaries, and so on. Some also have large advertising costs—TV ads, brochures, and mailings. Most respected organizations are able to put at least 80¢ of every dollar into the cause.

Warning: beware telephone fund-raisers. Crooked or questionable organizations often call and announce they represent such-and-such association, a name that sounds an awful lot like the name of a legitimate organization but isn't. Those who do lots of telephone soliciting often pay a for-profit company to do the calling—and give it a percentage of every dollar they collect. If you're interested in giving, don't pledge on the phone. Instead, tell the person to send you some literature that explains where the money will go, in what percentage, and so on. If he's legitimate, he'll understand. If he's crooked or being paid a commission on every telephone pledge, he won't like your idea at all. In that case, say good-bye.

Give Every Month.

The best way to give is to donate a set amount each month to one or more organizations. That way, they can count on your money month after month (imagine an employer who paid you "whenever she felt like it"). It's also easier for you to budget your giving. Treat it like any other monthly expense such as rent or a car payment. The difference is that this is a payment you *want* to make.

Lots of people give a percentage of their income—5 percent, 10 percent, 20 percent, 40 percent. At the end of the month you add up all your income, figure out the portion that you will give away, then write the checks. If you made lots of money and have some gift money left after making your regular contributions, give a one-time gift to a special cause.

I believe the simplest and most effective monthly gift is to support a needy child. I cannot think of a better use for your money than to provide food, education, and hope for a kid in another part of the world. For about $21 a month, *you* can change the world for one other person. That's two cassettes or four movies or five trips to McDonald's. For lots of kids, $21 is a big sacrifice. Is it too much to pay to save the life of a child? Give it away. If you're interested in child sponsorship, contact Compassion International, P.O. Box 7000, Colorado Springs, CO 80933, 719-594-9900.

Give Up.

The best part of percentage giving is upping the percentage each year! Chances are, your income has increased, so you can give an extra percentage point and still have money left over. Let's say you start with a commitment to give 5 percent of your income each month. After the first year (or six months, if you're gutsy), raise the commitment to 6 percent. Or if you start at 10 percent (much better), graduate to 11 percent. The goal is to keep doing this each year.

I know what you're thinking: *If I do this every year, by the time I'm sixty I'll be giving away over* half *my income every month!* Yes! That's the point. You can't even begin to imagine the impact you'll have on this world by investing so heavily into changing it.

Give Stuff

The first time I moved away from home, my worldly possessions fit into a backpack and a couple of duffle bags. At the next move I had added a couple of cardboard boxes of stuff to the baggage. By the time I moved again, I filled a VW van with junk acquired since my last migration. Now when I move, I need a twenty-foot U-Haul truck and three buff friends to help me load it—and I can't even *find* my backpack.

How did my life get filled with so much stuff? Then I remember: I brought it in myself. Not all at once—I would have noticed such shameless materialism. I acquired it one piece at a time.

A lot of the things I have are necessities: my toothbrush, sleeping bag, and Spiderman pj's. Some of my possessions are *almost* essential: my Craftsman socket wrench set and pink polyester tuxedo. But most of the stuff is pure luxury—bicycles, surfboards, stereos, backpacking gear, and enough clothes to outfit a family of twenty-seven.

Lately I've been thinking that I don't need all this stuff. I don't need the clutter. I don't need the headaches and expenses of fixing and mending—something is always breaking. I don't need the worry of its being stolen. So I've begun a nonaccumulation policy.

Here's how it works. Whenever I want to get something new, I have to get rid of something like it. If I want a new shirt, I go to my closet and pick out a shirt to give away. A pair of new shoes costs me one pair of old shoes given to Goodwill. Christmas is the toughest because I get lots of clothes as gifts and have to give away as many items.

Okay, so there are a few things I *don't* do this with. Socks and underwear, for example. Fourteen pairs of underwear mean I can go two weeks without doing laundry. My goal is sixty pairs. I also don't give away books, which are an investment I can use again and again in my writing. At least that's the excuse I use when I'm at the bookstore.

The biggest problem with the nonaccumulation policy is that I hate to give away things that mean a lot to me—an old baseball glove, an address book, my first baggy swim trunks. I put these things in a keepsakes box where they stay exempt from the rule. (Now if I can just figure out how to fit my old VW van into that box . . .)

No More Piles.

Why not adopt a nonaccumulation policy in your life? Start by pulling out of your closet, dressers, and shelves all the stuff that's just taking up space. Box it up and take it to the Salvation Army, Goodwill, or some other agency that can use your old clothes and toys. Warning: since your parents probably bought you a lot of this stuff, it's wise to let them look through the pile before you give it away.

Now abide by the rule. If you want a new pair of pants, pick out the pair it will replace. A new toy? What will you swap for it? After a while, your buying habits will change—getting a new toy will cost you money, and it'll cost you an old toy you like as much.

The best part about this policy is that it compels you to attach the act of *receiving* to the act of *giving*. If you *want* something, you must *give* something. And the people you give it to will appreciate it.

Merry Christmas

I think one of the reasons why Christmas is the biggest holiday is that it is the one time of the year when virtually everyone, regardless of religion, *gives*. It's not people's wallets and checkbooks that do the giving—it's their hearts. And when they do, it changes them.

The sad thing is, many people wait until December to do what their hearts would have them do all year if they stopped to listen.

World changers listen to their hearts. They give away their time and money and possessions to people and causes they care about—all year long. In a way, they make every month December and every day Christmas. Pass the eggnog.

Giving Week

MONDAY	Hide twenty nickels in your little brother's pants—don't tell him you did it.
TUESDAY	Slip $2 in coins through the slots of a friend's locker.
WEDNESDAY	Give $5 to a total stranger.
THURSDAY	Do a monthly budget to figure out how much money you earn and what you spend it on. Decide to give away a percentage.
FRIDAY	Fill out the form in the back of this book and send it to Compassion International to find out about sponsoring a child.
SATURDAY	Begin a nonaccumulation policy. Give away the stuff you don't need.
SUNDAY	Give an hour of your day to someone who could use it. Run an errand for a neighbor, mow the lawn for someone, clean out the garage, scrub the kitchen floor, or pick up trash at a park.

PART THREE

Wisdom for the Tough Times

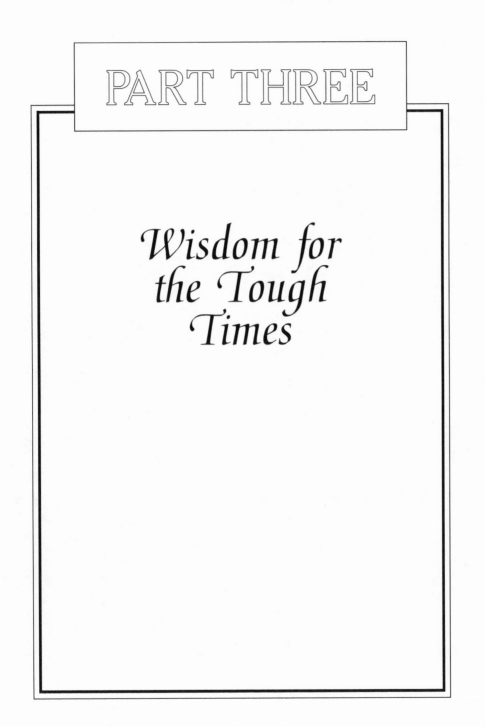

Chapter 16

I'm Not Me, But I'm Not You: The Terrors of the Teen Years

Which brings us to teenagers . . .

If ever there were God's extra-special children, it would have to be our teenagers. They're invincible, aren't they? They know everything, *don't they?*

Would you believe that underneath that false bravado and sometimes obnoxious behavior lurk some fears as big as—well, big enough to be called terrors!

Now, you want to help them, don't you? Sure you do. Can you see past their behavior to their fears? How about your own fears? Can you get past your own fears to be able to help them? And more importantly, will you know how *to help them? From our book* Things That Go Bump in the Night, *we'd like to share a little insight into the terrors your teenagers are facing so you'll be able to help them, if you want to, that is—and we know you do!*

Dr. Frank Minirth, Dr. Paul Warren
Things That Go Bump in the Night

Dear Hector,

I am a grown man. This is absolutely, utterly stupid. Foolish. I am writing a letter to a dog.

Can't help it. My son has the cat sewed up.

Speaking of sewed up, Hector, how are your stitches? You haven't been scratching them lately, so I assume they've quit itching. The vet assures us you're just fine. You'd better be, after all that money for neutering.

I guess Paul Warren is doing a good job on Jimmy. I mean James. Apparently he prefers to be called James. Maybe he's reading Ian Fleming. You know: "The name is Bond. James Bond."

No you don't know. Of course you don't. You're a dog, for crying out loud.

Warren says I can help James by doing this, so I shall. I'm supposed to air my feelings with these letters. Anything I want to write. There's some TV show about a teenager who's a doctor. Talk about fantasy! And he puts all his thoughts on a computer. The new medical criterion, apparently. Very well. Here I go.

James was telling me about the way the kids mock him and call him a scaredy-cat. A sissy. He can't possibly know how deeply his stories hurt me.

Because I am James. His stories are my story, his youth my youth. I remember, and ache. Their jeers echo in my memories.

You look at your newborn baby, hold him tight against your heart, and picture him growing up to conquer the world. Invictus! *He will become all the things you dreamed of being and never were. All the heroic deeds you imagined for yourself, your child will accomplish in your stead. I never foresaw when James was born that he might merely repeat my own painful childhood. Will he repeat my pitiful adulthood too?*

O God of deliverances, I pray You deliver my son from the misery of my own youth!

Dr. Roger Tanner

GROWTH AND CHANGES

James's father was finally coming to terms with his own unresolved childhood fears. He recognized them now. As he worked on them, he would be able to tackle the fears of the teen years too.

I'm Afraid of Growing Up

They were *goyim,* these two gentlemen—men outside the Jewish faith. They were watching a synagogue from across the street as the happy participants of a bar mitzvah came streaming out.

One man shook his head. "Look at the kid. He's what? Thirteen?

'Today I am a man.' Hmph. He was a kid this morning and he'll still be a kid tomorrow morning, and no religious mumbo-jumbo will change that."

The other man nodded sagely. "Say, doesn't your son get his driver's permit soon?"

The first man beamed. "Next Monday I take him down. He can't wait and neither can I. My kid, behind the wheel." He paused and smirked. "Think I'll look okay in gray hair?"

Every culture on record has a death rite. A marriage arrangement. And a rite of passage from childhood to adulthood. For example, the bar mitzvah ushers a Jewish boy into the beginning of a man's life. It is a door, a step, a chasm jumped. It is definite. Other cultures observe a wide spectrum of rites, but each, in the end, becomes that very same door. The two gentlemen observing the bar mitzvah from afar did not realize they were also discussing the modern American's rite of passage: the driver's license.

The neophyte driver whose father beamed so proudly will be a kid on Sunday. He'll still be a kid on Tuesday. Getting his permit on Monday won't change a thing. Rites of passage do not perform magical transformations. They mark progress, exactly as do the milepost markers along a hiking trail.

That does not keep either them or the progress itself from being very scary.

Let us look at the underlying fears experienced by children from eleven to about fifteen. We will examine how to resolve those fears and concerns. Then we'll discuss the noble task of setting the child up for the future, planting the seeds for separation years hence, and providing emotional support from ourselves and from others.

I'm Not Me Anymore and You're Not Who I Thought You Were

Observe the progression in a child from infancy to now. From fear of slogs of slime through fear of others, then fear of others' opinions, and fear of personal success, now comes the ultimate fear: the child's fear of himself. A lot of life-changes herald that fear. Hormones, both growth and sexual, change the body and the thoughts. The emotions change, wildly swinging side to side on their way to adult stability. Well, semi-stability.

Change is scary! I am not the same person I was two days ago.

Children this age joke a lot about how nerdy their parents are, and how parents are so behind the times. Beneath the veneer of joking lies fear.

Two major blows in the child's life generate that fear. One, the child is entering adulthood uncertainly, without a track record of adult achievement with which to evaluate success as an adult. For a hypothetical example, let's imagine a young man who wants to be an illustrator. He dreams of creating artwork for magazine stories, for book covers, perhaps for fantasy-film promotion. But as he begins to pursue this career he has no portfolio, no work he can cite to show, "this is what I can do."

He takes any job that comes along, building a portfolio, a track record. As his name becomes known in the business he no longer has to carry his portfolio into an art director's office and sell himself face to face. He can phone the art director with an idea. Once he has proven himself across a span of time, art directors phone him.

Similarly, children on the cusp of adulthood have absolutely no way of knowing whether they will succeed as adults, or how well. Ideally, as they build their track records as adults—achieving the grown-up successes of living independently, driving a car, getting a job, advancing, falling in love—they become more confident in their adulthood. The fear abates. But that comes later. How does one deal with that fear now? One way is to build oneself up at the expense of someone already built. Thus the jokes about parental incompetency.

Another is to stay little as long as possible. For example, recently a worried mother brought us her twelve-year-old daughter, Renée. Renée ate ice compulsively. Mama feared for Renée's teeth ("You know what your dentist says about eating ice cubes!") and her very sanity ("It's just not normal!").

When we probed to the seat of Renée's fears, we found her terrified of growing up. The ice tightened her alto voice into a more child-like soprano. She had no conscious desire to sound younger. The gimmick was a ploy to prolong her childhood and avoid the unknown terrors of being an adult.

The second major blow in a child's life is the inevitable, devastating realization that Mom and Dad aren't perfect. Only a few short years ago, they were. They were not always obeyed, not always listened to, but that was the child's shortcoming, not theirs. Now the child learns to his or her horror that Mom and Dad perhaps ought not to be obeyed in every single matter. Just when the child needs perfect, divine guidance most, the traditional guides are proved fallible.

Santa Claus has been unmasked and he is a government bureaucrat. The tooth fairy is dead. Life is bitterly unfair.

A lot of children at this stage fear they won't make it because they feel they don't really have parents walking with them anymore, leading the way. They are afraid of what they might do without perfect parents to offer guidance and control. Children are very black and white, right and wrong, remember. Parents are either right or wrong, black or white, perfect or poops. No shades of gray. No middle ground. No partial guidance or limited relationship.

This is an age where chronic problems such as serious health impairments, dyslexia, epilepsy, cerebral palsy, attention deficit syndrome, and other difficulties gouge their deepest wounds and scars. Children are already uncomfortable with who they are, and if they have a measurable, visible difference, they will have a difficult time both internally and externally with self-image. In our counseling we find that this is the classic time when kids with chronic problems become resistant to treatment. They have an emerging sense of omnipotence, and they will use that powerful feeling to handle—rather, to mishandle—their future.

Omnipotence is a universal coping mechanism to deal with the fear of inner changes every child suffers. *I can do what I want. I'm diabetic but I don't need insulin.* Denial is a dandy response (and potentially deadly at times) in children and adults both to that nagging fear of what may come tomorrow, and of what may forever stay away.

Will Rogers said, "We're all ignorant, only in different areas." What children fail to realize is that every single child has some disability. If all emergent adolescents were omnipotent, no one would be hampered by a disability. It's not rational, but then so few attitudes are.

"I tend to have trouble with mechanical things," Dr. Warren admits. "Call that a disability, if you will, compared with the mechanical prowess of many people. But I could still get through school being a mechanical klutz. A few laughs, some jokes and teasing—but I made it. It's embarrassing now and then, but not debilitating. But if you have trouble with letters and words and numbers, you're in real trouble. My mechanical clumsiness is nothing like the kid who is in a wheelchair or dyslexic. The only criterion adults see is school, and if your disability affects you academically . . ." He wags his head.

"When children have a disabling situation, their parents are going to have to be prepared to go through the whole grief process to deal with problems because there is very real loss. Omnipotence won't save the day."

How can someone who is not a trained counselor see these fears that are hidden so deep?

Recognizing Fears in Their External Forms

"Yes, I know the law requires Burton to go to school until he's sixteen. Yes, I know if he doesn't get a diploma he's not going to do well in life. Yes, I know it's not good for him to sit at home all day watching TV." Burton's mother, frail as a songbird and thirty pounds underweight, perched on the edge of a chair in the police precinct's booking room. Her discolored cardigan hung listlessly from sloping shoulders. She looked from face to face at the officers around her.

"I tried everything," she continued. "I begged and pleaded, I teased him, I threatened him. I yelled at him till I was blue-faced. Couldn't bribe him—I don't make enough money but to buy food and rent. But I doubt that would've done much good. Burton flat out refuses to go." Her voice dropped to a murmur. "And Burton's bigger'n me."

At age twelve and a half, Burton presented an extreme case of school phobia, a common manifestation of fear. Burton and his mother had other problems also, severe problems. Sadly, although a brilliantly competent social worker tried to help them both, in this case the problems won.

Why does school phobia peak around Burton's age? As Burton entered junior high he faced a new school with new teachers and a new way of attending classes (moving from classroom to classroom for the different subjects). His old fears of childhood were still largely unresolved, making change and strangeness especially fearsome. Most of all, this is the beginning of individuation time, the close of childhood as Burton makes the shift from Mom's little kid to independent adult. Individuation is scary under the best of circumstances. Burton's circumstances were chaotic. He and his mom lived in a small apartment, his father having long since abandoned them. To that situation add Burton's fear of self just now developing, a natural and necessary part of growing up.

But Burton's mom had just as many problems. She feared letting go of her boy, the only person close to her. Her voice and her actions said, "Go to school." Her heart and her subliminal attitude were, *Don't leave me. Don't grow up and go away.*

Burton's case was larger than life, but the kernel of his problems exists in every child. Thus we so often find a reluctance in children to move away from their parents by attending school.

The fears of this age also manifest themselves in rigidity. The more rigid the child's attitude, the more we worry about him or her.

" 'Not only do I not do drugs, I would never be tempted to! And I'd like to beat up every kid who does,' " Dr. Warren says, quoting a boy in his counsel. "That boy was thirteen when he spoke those words just about verbatim. He was rigidly, adamantly against any idea that drugs might be a temptation to him. We are seeing him now because he is hopelessly addicted. He'll be fifteen next month."

The young man desperately feared himself and all the terrible things that the world's temptations and his own impulses might lead him to do. He feared his own unpredictability and vulnerability. He no longer knew himself. He adopted a rigid, inflexible stance to build a stone wall between himself and destruction. His attitude might be pure, but his defenses were not flexible enough to guard him against being human. Assaulted, they shattered.

"An appropriate approach," Dr. Warren explains, "is an attitude flexible enough to give a little when it has to, to mold itself to the human being. One way to put it into words, perhaps, is: 'I'm not going to do marijuana, but I know it's a temptation, and I recognize that I could.' The kid who recognizes both the danger and his fallibility will probably be all right."

Kids may build a rigid defense against any temptation—sexual acting out, alcohol, or other deviant behavior. Their parents and society may even applaud the solidity of their convictions. But beware the defense that disregards human nature.

Kids so rigidly guarded against any of these experimental behavior impulses are depending upon internal defenses. Parents form the primary external defense. They play the major role in helping their children survive this time and thrive and grow, and they do so in several ways. Their attitudes toward rules, toward oversight of their children's lives, toward the eventual wrenching pain of letting go, all help or hinder the child's growth.

The Lure of Lockstep Rules

Talk about rigid. Two recent cases in our counsel come to mind.

Joyce was fifteen when her parents brought her to us. Her mother sat ramrod straight on the sofa as she talked rapid-fire staccato, like a typist putting out 150 words a minute. Call her Mrs. Jones.

"Everything was fine when Joyce was growing up." Mrs. Jones

looked like a woman who had not washed her own hair in twenty years. She had it professionally styled, probably several times a week. She wore designer-perfect clothes and maintained a designer-perfect complexion. Every detail of her appearance suggested she left absolutely nothing in this world to chance.

Across from her, Joyce slouched in the wing chair. A charming girl with her mother's clear skin and rich brown hair, she scrunched in a corner of the chair with her legs crossed demurely and her long, graceful fingers gripping the chair arms the way Scrooge clung to his gold.

Mrs. Jones continued. "Joyce made very good grades. All A's. Then she went into junior high and things sort of fell apart."

"Explain," we requested.

"Well, uh, it sounds so trivial now. But . . ." Mrs. Jones frowned. "It seemed so incredibly important then. She started being late getting home to supper. School is out at 3:10, and she wouldn't get home until 5 or 5:30 sometimes."

"Did she offer some reason for not coming straight home?"

"Oh yes. One night she stayed after for some club she was in, and another night, she said, all her friends went to this burger place and so she went along."

"Why did you feel this was unusual or wrong behavior?"

"Well, uh . . ." Mrs. Jones laced and relaced her fingers in her lap. "I called the school to verify the club meeting, of course, and that Joyce had been present. Her father investigated and it seemed like an appropriate club for a girl. But the friends. The burger business. No way to check that. We could just see her being led astray. The age, you know. Those teenage boys."

"She worked within a rules system?"

"Oh yes! Doctor, a child that age knows nothing about the world, or about—you know. It is our duty to protect her. All these girls running around unsupervised, it's no wonder there are so many teen pregnancies."

Joyce sat before us seven months pregnant.

Joyce's parents had set up an airtight control system. After school was out, Joyce was required to check in every fifteen minutes by phone—just in case, her mother explained, she would get some impulse to do something she shouldn't. She was forbidden to sit next to boys or to talk to them on the phone.

Supposedly, this young lady in a family way never had a date or talked to boys.

The mother of another of our cases, Margaret Rissoto, was absolutely convinced she was being fair with her Robert, aged fifteen. She let him ride his bike anywhere within half a block of their house but he had to come home every fifteen minutes to check in. He was not allowed to talk on the phone, to have friends over, or to go to others' houses lest he be contaminated by kids who weren't very good.

"The only way Robert Rissoto could grow," Dr. Warren explains, "was symbolically to get into a Mack truck and drive over the rigid boundary. He ran away from home. When the police finally found him out in Midland he had hooked up with a marijuana dealer and was doing drugs."

Unusually gifted with words, Robert told us, "I learned a long time ago, when I was twelve, that it was far easier to come home with my tail between my legs, begging forgiveness for breaking Mother's rules, than to ever ask her permission for new rules."

Emerging adolescents are volatile and unpredictable—unknown personalities to both their parents and themselves. Parents are understandably tempted to lay down close, solid strictures.

Obviously, a rigid system controls an emergent adolescent like a picket fence controls an angry bull. The more they try, the more parents find themselves out of control and alienated. By trying to keep a lid on everything about this budding teen, they sabotage any chance of a healthy relationship. Growth is inevitable. It's programmed into the child. And yet, parents may be tempted to sacrifice growth for rules.

COPING WITH THE FEAR OF GROWING UP

Children this age will cope better with their fears if the parents take three important steps: letting go, monitoring surreptitiously, and allowing other adult journeymates into their children's lives. None of the three is easy.

Letting Go

Researchers conducting an ambitious survey in Richardson, Texas, schools asked kids this age, "What would you like parents most to know about your opinion of rules and limits?"

Their response, paraphrase, was: "We would like them to understand that at our age we need parents who let us go and at the same time watch us carefully."

Wise children.

"Think about a child—let's say a girl—growing up on a small farm," says Dr. Minirth. "She doesn't really have time to worry about whether she's getting appropriate responsibility. In her childhood she's out weeding in the garden, taking care of the chickens. Her parents taught her how to do it by modeling and showing her how. Years before she's old enough for a driver's license she's out driving the tractor. If for some reason she can't handle that, let's say because of a physical problem, she's shunted into other jobs. She always has something to do that's basically an adult job. She's learning the same skills her farming parents use every day.

Children this age will cope better with their fears if the parents take three important steps: letting go, monitoring surreptitiously, and allowing other adult journeymates into their children's lives.

"Letting go won't be quite as hard for her parents because she has a good handle on the future. She knows what the job is and she knows she can do it. So do they. Her parents see her as a child but also as a co-worker."

"I've said this before, but it's worth repeating," adds Dr. Warren. "Parents have to be able to let go by degrees while kids are young and failure isn't going to be as terrible as it would be later on. And every child, every family, is different. What's too liberal in one situation might be too conservative in another. It's a case-by-case situation."

Monitoring the Child's Choices and Well-Being

When Mr. and Mrs. Jones called the school about the club their daughter attended and investigated its aims and structure, they were monitoring. Monitoring is everything from keeping an eye on the odometer and gas-gauge readings if the child drives to running background checks on all the kid's acquaintances. Not all monitoring is healthful or helpful.

Mrs. Jones, trying to piece together what went wrong, looked confused and dubious. She shook her head. "I can see where letting go and monitoring are sort of a balance . . ."

"Exactly. A very delicate balance, requiring wisdom," Dr. Warren said, nodding.

"And I was a little fearful of letting go. We both were."

Dr. Warren knows the value of not agreeing out loud with everything a patient says. He listened.

"All right, I can see now where we were monitoring Joyce a little too closely. What is too close? Where's the line?"

The line varies with every child.

"Common sense," Dr. Minirth constantly preaches. "Stop and think and use your native common sense."

"Common sense," Dr. Warren agrees. "To find an acceptable line to draw—not necessarily the best and not the worst, but an acceptable one—give the matter some perspective. Sit back and think about it. Would your control measures have been appropriate a year ago? How about a year from now? When you were a child would you have considered it appropriate, or at least livable?"

Mrs. Jones winced. "I would have felt suffocated."

"Compelled to do anything to get out from under?"

"Anything!" And then insight hit her right between the eyes. "Joyce did anything to get out from under it. I asked her so many times why she did what she did, and she wouldn't tell me. She didn't know, did she?"

"I doubt it. She felt compelled but didn't know why. Children don't do well analyzing their own motives and actions; they haven't had enough experience yet with human nature to understand what goes on inside. They do things, sometimes precipitously, and don't always know why they do them."

"But what would be too little supervision?"

"You tell me."

"I suppose setting no rules at all."

"Allowed to come and go whenever she wishes, you mean?"

"Allowed to do anything."

"If you had been given that freedom, so to speak, in your own childhood, how would you have felt?"

Mrs. Jones had to think about that awhile. He gave her the time. She frowned. "Frightened, I suppose, with no guidelines to work within. I wouldn't know what was okay and what was dangerous. But you've talked about letting her fail. What do you mean, let Joyce fail while it's safe to do so? Obviously, she made a wrong choice and it wasn't safe."

"Good question."

Monitoring does not mean protecting the child from failure, from the consequences of wrong choices (within reason). You monitor to keep a potentially dangerous situation from getting out of hand or causing lasting harm. Pregnancy and parenthood, drug and alcohol misuse, riding a skateboard on Route 30, getting in with a crowd devoid of ethics—from these the child needs protection and a wise guide. But for his or her own growth, the teenager must learn to handle all the non-ruinous slings and arrows of outrageous fortune, painful though they may be.

During our conversations, we learned that Mrs. Jones wanted everything just right for Joyce. The mother operated from the best of intentions. She and her husband worked hard to protect Joyce from many dangers. But they neglected to give her the necessary experience of responsibility while it was safe to fail. Specifically, they interviewed not just Joyce's friends but the friends' parents before she could talk on the phone to them. Joyce was allowed to associate only with kids whose parents were friends of Joyce's parents. Mrs. Jones worked so hard at protecting Joyce from failure that she would call around before school to find out what other girls were wearing so that Joyce would be dressed like the others that day. *Honey, we don't want you to feel the pain of other kids rejecting you,* she said not with words but with actions.

Ultimately, Joyce was unable to fend for herself. She was easily swayed by smooth words and got her feelings hurt by rough ones. She felt depressed and lonely with her life. Kids—yes, even the children of her parents' friends—joked around with her and about her, tittering over her naivete, acting like geese, as kids that age will do. Joyce wasn't prepared for real life. Thoughtlessly—that's how peers treat you. Because she could not experiment with friendships early, taking her knocks and learning about the thoughtlessness and perversity of human nature, by the end of early adolescence Joyce was critically damaged. The window of opportunity to learn had passed unused, never to pass again. Joyce would play catch-up, but she would never quite succeed in actually catching up.

Mrs. Jones presented another important question. "Very well. We monitor from a distance, so to speak. And we find something very wrong. How do we handle it?"

"Actual wrongdoing?"

"For starters, yes. Let's say actual wrongdoing."

"Let me tell you about Brandon."

Brandon was what his harried mother called "all boy," Dr. Warren told her. Into everything. Inquisitive. Creative. Inventive. Those attributes are dandy if you're Thomas Edison, but in a fourteen-year-old they can cause havoc. One night Brandon and some buddies did a tour through an alley behind Eighty-fourth Street, pegging rocks through garage windows. All six kids got caught.

In the past, Brandon's transgression would have earned him a spanking, but a fourteen-year-old is too old to spank. His father demanded restitution. With Dad waiting and watching from twenty feet away, Brandon knocked at each door on Eighty-fourth Street. He confessed his deed and promised to make good. Placing himself in financial debt to his father up to his ears, he borrowed to buy the replacement glass. His father helped him reglaze the garage windows—thirty-seven of them. Brandon learned the most important lesson a child this age can learn: You are responsible for your actions.

"I read a magazine article once about appropriate enforcement. That's what you're talking about. Discipline, right?" Brandon's mother said.

"Right," Dr. Warren agreed. "But at this age, discipline is also another tool to dispel fears, an important one."

"How?"

"Remember, children fear themselves, fear they'll lose control of these uncontrollable urges. They fear what they might do if they stray from the limits; they might even lose their parents' love if they stray too far. Discipline says, *You just blew it, buddy, but I love you anyway.*"

"That's like Brandon's father did. He stayed with him right through his discipline." Mrs. Jones shook her head. "But if Brandon's father had kept a closer eye on him and set an earlier curfew, Brandon wouldn't have done it in the first place, maybe."

"Maybe. But quite possibly he would. Had he been prevented from misadventure, he would not have learned the lesson in responsibility. It was costly, yes. And embarrassing. But by seizing the opportunity, his father helped him through important growth. Brandon feared what would happen if he went out of control. Then he did go out of control and he did not lose his father's love. That was an even greater lesson than that of responsibility."

"Can't you supervise closely—stringently, I suppose, is a good word—and just teach the precepts? Does it have to be object lessons in life all the time?"

"You don't have to look for object lessons. Kids being what they are, the lessons will come. You yourself know that a child can get into serious trouble despite the closest supervision. Our advice is control what you can control and drop the rest."

"What can I not control? Obviously, behavior."

"Right. You cannot control what your child says, her attitude, or what she does when you're not there. But you can control the consequences of behavior, as Brandon's father did. Particularly at this age, when you try to control what you cannot control, you reinforce, in a funny sort of way, their fears of growing up. By trying to control what you cannot control, you're saying, in effect, 'I don't trust you to mature; I don't trust your control of yourself.' Kids have got to face who they are, which means they have to feel they are in control of what they do and say."

Mrs. Jones wagged her head sadly. "I'm still in the dark about how to respond when Joyce does wrong, or does something I don't like."

"Again, there are no absolute rules. Every child differs. Let me suggest a repertoire of responses."

Responding to the Inevitable Goofs

One response is, simply, no response. If you can keep your wits when friction erupts, pause to think, *Why is the kid doing this?* The child may simply be frustrated or out of sorts, as we all are on occasion. It might be wise to let a minor infraction (such as speaking disrespectfully) slip through, particularly if you sense the child is trying to hook you into a battle. Children may pick a fight to let off steam, just as older people (who ought to know better) do.

Another response is to invoke a loss of privileges. If the child chooses to engage in certain behavior, so-and-so privileges are forfeited as a direct result. Cause and effect. The opposite cause-and-effect is even more powerful: the child who behaves in a positive way gains specific desirable privileges. In short, children receive the fruit of their choices. Is this bribery? Not really. The lessons of cause and effect are crucial to responsible behavior now and later. Children need those lessons.

A third response is grounding. Many parents use this response much too broadly.

"Dad, I'm sorry I threw my brother through the back screen door. While it was closed. It was an accident. Sort of."

"You, son, are grounded for the rest of your natural life."

It's better to reserve grounding for when children say with their behavior, *I feel like I'm out of control,* or, *I feel I am trapped in circumstances beyond my control,* or, *I'm in over my head.* In other words, when the children need help and protection. What behavior says this? Every time a boy is allowed to be with a certain group, he becomes involved in a fight or in trouble. Every time a girl associates with a certain boy she comes home in tears. A child is caught joyriding in a "borrowed" car, a potentially lethal situation. Grounding is *always* for protection, not for punishment. With grounding the parent sends the message, *I don't think you can handle this; therefore I need to protect you.* It helps immensely here if the parent and child enjoy an open relationship in which to talk about it.

It's better to reserve grounding for when children say with their behavior, I feel like I'm out of control, *or,* I feel I am trapped in circumstances beyond my control, *or,* I'm in over my head.

An ultimate measure may include professional help. A child who is out of control may require no less. Some options are counseling, hospitalization, unusual discipline, placement elsewhere (such as in an alternative residence or group home), or restitution handled by a third party (for example, a court may require appropriate community service of a teen convicted of vandalism). The underlying feeling is, *I'm going to do whatever I have to do to help this kid, to turn it around.*

We caution parents never to *threaten* kids with drastic action. The mind-set must be, *This child has big problems. I'll go all the way to help.*

There are a number of actions that should never be in the repertoire of responses.

One is physical, corporal punishment at this age. Brandon's father did not spank him, although Brandon had received his fair share of spankings when he was small. Children become more physical in their reactions during this early adolescence. Boys are pushier, girls are more into movement and contact. When you push an early teen, the teen pushes back instinctively. Besides, you want to teach teenage children ways to solve problems themselves, and a swat teaches nothing. Kids this age say, "I don't worry about getting in trouble. I'll just get some licks and burn it off." Not a good lesson. Negative consequences alone may extinguish inappropriate behaviors but do nothing to teach the child appropriate behaviors.

Positive restitution, such as Brandon's father used, beats physical response because it is physical in some way but is nothing the child can react to. "So you got in trouble for spray-painting fences and smashing bottles, eh? We won't spank you. We'll make you responsible for picking up the glass and for repainting."

Mrs. Jones wrinkled her nose, not in disdain but in serious thought. "Now what about this adult journeymate business? I mean, Brandon's father was a journeymate. He walked through it with his son. What more does the boy need?"

Encouraging Other Adult Journeymates

"Quite a bit," Dr. Warren explained. "The child is starting to move from the dependence of childhood into the independence of adulthood. It's not a smooth transition. It happens in fits and starts, just as the child's growth and maturation occur by fits and starts. Children this age are not ready for strong peer relationships, yet they're pulling away from their parents. During this lag time, so to speak, a healthy adult best fills the gap. This is someone who's willing to invest time in the child. Also, we hope, it's someone the parents do not feel jealous about."

A few days later, Elaine and James Tanner were in for a periodic visit. Elaine, James's mother, did not take well to this idea of other adult journeymates. Why? Because Elaine's brother was John, the baseball-card shop owner who never grew up, the one person in the world James should not have as a role model.

"It's not like John is a convicted felon or a bum out on the street or a shark in the business world. It's just that he's so . . . so flaky. So immature. What if James latches on to him a couple of years from now?"

"James very well might. I perceive that he idolizes his uncle."

"Oh, Doctor! You could have talked all day without saying that. I mean, really. What would we do? This is serious!"

"Not quite as serious as you see it, perhaps."

"Oh, no? You don't know John. He makes his whole living off

baseball cards and comic books! You want a 1957 Batman? He can get it for you. Did you know that in the early fifties, there was a line of comic books about the Lone Ranger's horse? Not the Lone Ranger. His horse—Silver. Before he met the Lone Ranger, I guess. John didn't want anyone handling them; they're collector's items apparently; but he photocopied them all for James. Every page."

"Wholesome comics?"

"Well, yes. How many adventures can a horse get into? But that's beside the point. You see, James and his father are not close, not really. But James and John could be. Frankly, they're the same age, as far as I'm concerned."

"And you're secretly afraid that if Roger doesn't spend more time with James, he'll abandon you, his parents, in favor of Uncle John. At least, emotionally."

Elaine gaped a moment, then sat back. She drew a deep breath. "I keep forgetting that your profession is knowing what makes people tick. Yes. That's what I'm afraid of."

These new journeymates must enter the picture, not just to provide approval, but to talk deeply.

"The first step for a child reaching out to other adult journeymates is having his own parents as journeymates. The picture is getting much better, but up until now, James hasn't had that."

"He's behind."

"Way behind."

Elaine brightened. "Like you say, that's getting better, though. Roger and James are going out on a hike in the country this weekend. Remember, you recommended that?"

"Something of that sort. I'm glad to hear it. Little things will make a big difference in James's attitude toward himself—things perhaps as simple as going down a scary water slide, jumping in the deep end of the pool, playing ball. The journeymate relationship, whether it is your husband or Uncle John, can validate the new feelings about himself. Soothe some of the old fears. Give James new experiences. Ideally, Dad is the one to do that, now and later."

She darkened again. "But about John . . ."

"I urge you to relax, Elaine. As James enters adolescence and begins the process of separation, and then adopts an adult journeymate other than you, his parents, his uncle will do just fine. You see, the adoption is temporary—a few months, a year at most. It's a stepping-stone, a transition. The outside relationships do not take the place of parents but augment them.

"This, too, will be in the interest of allaying James's fears of himself. James will need affirmation that he really is okay, and that affirmation should come from people other than his parents. Or rather, in addition to them."

"An outside opinion."

"Exactly. Parents have to approve of you. But as you move into adolescence and separation begins, you think you don't want their approval. James will need other adults—other kids, too—for approval."

In addition, some fears are too scary to share with one's parents. This is part of God's plan to help children fledge the nest, to spread their wings and leave home. If they could always talk about everything with their parents, the camaraderie would pose a powerful temptation to never grow up.

In other words, these new journeymates must enter the picture, not just to provide approval, but to talk deeply.

Forging Friendships

Elaine's worries about the influence of Uncle John aside, Elaine and Roger are the primary teachers of friendships in their children's lives. With their own adult friendships they model what friendship is all about.

Here is where "like father like son" can be literal. A recent example is a girl we'll call Melanie. Melanie's mom brought her to us because Melanie, excessively shy, had no friends. Mom was deeply concerned, for although she could get Melanie to school, the child remained essentially isolated. She never went to others' houses, never played in others' yards, never invited others home. "How," Mom wanted to know, "can I get Melanie over being so painfully shy? She seems so fearful of social contact."

As we got to know Melanie's mother, we learned that she literally sat at home all day. She herself had no friends. Melanie's father worked all day and had no friends, either. Although he did not act withdrawn or shy, Melanie's older brother had no real friends either. He played team sports and knew none of his teammates except on the most casual, shallow basis.

Here were four separate people in this house with no outside contacts. But the problem ran deeper because the emotional growth in the parents was stunted as much as it was in the kids. Inwardly directed, the parents were shy, themselves, though they claimed they were not.

Parents need friends for many reasons. A major reason is to teach the kids of this age how to be friends by modeling adult friendship. However, it goes a giant step past merely modeling. Because outside friendships are stimulating—the catalyst of other people promotes growth—parents who are committed to friends are committed to growth itself. This is what the child "hears" below conscious level.

Parents also make an important contribution by guiding their children into choosing healthy friendships.

Joyce Jones's distraught mother insisted, "But that is exactly what my husband and I were trying to do! What went wrong?"

"I suggest," Dr. Warren responded, "that you were trying to control what you could not control: every specific friendship, every social contact, every minute. You can't choose your child's friends, but you can control what you can control. The method of that control is to teach children about positive and negative friendships."

"Kinds of friends, instead of specific friends. Generalization."

"Exactly. Consider this: You might say 'I'm not going to give you permission to be with that kid or this kid.' But you can't follow your child around to enforce it."

"You can say that again."

"Neither can you say, 'It's that nasty other person's fault if you get in trouble.' "

"I understand. We have to hold her responsible for herself, for her own actions."

"Right. So, although you cannot choose your child's friends, you can say, 'Such-and-such child is not welcome here in my home,' and you can have a reason for saying so."

"Being social. Do you realize how many problems are linked to being social? We would escape so much heartache if everyone were normally solitary."

Dr. Warren laughed. "On the other hand, good friendships are one of the ways children conquer their fears about their changing bodies and personalities. The friends accept them. The friends treat them like real people, hurting and helping. The friends present a united defense against the buffeting of the world."

"What is a good friend? How do I teach Joyce to tell good from bad?"

"Another excellent question!"

When we discuss friendships in counseling with young clients, we offer the children these criteria for a good friendship:

· Good friends tolerate each other's weaknesses instead of tearing each other down because of those weaknesses.

· Good friends, especially at this age, enjoy an active sense of humor. They appreciate a good time, with lots of laughing and fun and being silly.

· Good friends express a healthy respect for parent-child relations. Good friends don't encourage you to get in trouble with your parents; they don't try to destroy or damage the parent-child link. Your biggest asset in getting through this life is a strong bond with your parents, even if it doesn't seem that way on the surface, and good friends honor that. Good friends have that bond themselves.

· Good friends are supportive. They stick by you.

We find that children understand and react to these criteria pretty much instinctively. "Yeah," we hear again and again, "that's the kind of friend I want. Except maybe about the parent part."

"You want someone to wedge in between you and your family?"

"Naw, I guess not."

In these sessions we also characterize bad friendships:

· Bad friendships are centered around negative things. What holds these friendships together is not fun but negative, destructive behavior and hatred. Skinheads and gangs are two examples.

· Bad friendships are based on poor boundaries. It is not the job of one friend to carry another's burden completely. It should never be the responsibility of one kid to keep another alive. For example, we frequently see, mostly with girls, a case where a girl will tell her supposed friend, "I'm going to commit suicide but don't tell anybody." Where does that put her friend? The friend carries a terrible burden. If she tells anyone, she betrays her friend, and if she doesn't her friend might do something awful. What does she do? It's a problem to vex older people, and this girl has no life experience to help her make a wise decision.

· Bad friendships damage the parent-child relationship. For example, a so-called friend might say, "Don't pay attention to what your parents say."

The Prime Advocate—the Parent

But amid all the friendships and significant other adults and guidelines and lessons, the child's biggest support remains the parents.

We have in our counsel now a young man of fourteen named Josh. Not Joshua. Josh. He insists on that. His personality shines bright even if his scholastics don't. He has a gap in his front teeth, "like Terry Thomas and Omar Sharif," he'll be quick to tell you. "Movie-star stuff, huh?"

Josh's scores run under the rug clear across the floor. His years in schools have taught him only that it's all his fault he's disruptive. His disruptions aren't vicious or bitter; he's a pain in the patoot for teachers, but in a genuinely kindly way. He's certain he is dumb. He thinks all he can do at school is be the troublemaker. It's the role he's always taken because he can't handle symbols of any sort.

He has survived because his mother won't quit. He's welcome at home regardless of the grades he makes. The school hates her; she's always in there. She holds Josh accountable to get certain jobs done around the house. She does not hold him accountable for things he's not capable of doing.

He's great at doing stuff with his hands. He can do just about anything that does not involve marks and symbols. With Mom behind him, we're helping him see that he has strong points—they just don't show up on the tests—and value. In a few years he'll be able to go into vocational training and find a spot for himself. Right now, his strongest advocate is a mother who won't give up.

James had a strong advocate, too, although neither he nor his mother realized it at first. Elaine Tanner almost became a dentist once. It was what she had always dreamed of doing. She pictured herself in a clown suit, serving little children who were afraid of the usual dentist in a white tunic. She pictured herself on an Indian reservation or in some emerging third world nation, serving as a missionary dentist to people who needed the service desperately. She pictured herself as the boss of a support staff, paying them all a little more than she had to, giving them their birthdays off, keeping morale high with her gentle spirit and servant's attitude.

Elaine Tanner never told anyone about her dream, not even Roger. It takes money and dedication to complete the schooling.

She got married instead—the safe way out for a woman. It takes guts to travel out into a hostile world. Elaine couldn't quite bring herself to do that. It takes poise and self-confidence to practice in that profession. Elaine was hardly a powerful authority figure.

And so the dream withered, leaving a residue of bitterness deep inside her, the dry, scratchy little remnant of a flower gone with the season. Fear, like a killer frost, had nipped her dream in the bud.

Now fear stood a good chance of nipping James's dreams too, and Aubrey's, just as it had destroyed hers. Through counseling, Elaine was beginning to see how her children's primal fears had not been allayed, just as her own had not. One night when Roger was late at work and the children had been put to bed (now that Aubrey was doing better about monsters, life was so much more pleasant!) Elaine sat by the fireplace sipping tea. She thought about fear, and about its effects.

And that night she determined that fear would not cripple her children. She was uncertain yet just what she would do about it, but she would not let history repeat itself. Her children would flower, frost free.

Chapter 17

Depression in Adolescents and Older Teens

Depression is among us in full force these days. You can find it in all ages, from infancy to old age. In Depression Hits Every Family, *I write about the symptoms of and the cures for depression for each age group. But I particularly want to share this chapter on depression in teenagers. Depression can be the calling card for serious drug and alcohol abuse, and even suicide, one of the leading causes of death in our teenagers today. I do not mean to say that all depressed teenagers consider suicide, but we would do well to be able to recognize the symptoms of depression in our teens, to be able to discern depression lookalikes and know how to react to all of them.*

Dr. Grace Ketterman
Depression Hits Every Family

In only two decades, suicides of young people between ages fifteen and twenty-four have increased by 250 percent.[1] Each year I must try to deal with the repercussions of the suicides of some ten to twelve teenagers. Each death has an impact on other youths who may see the death of a friend as a taunting temptation to escape their own despair. Every person in the mental health field will replicate my experiences again and again.

In a very careful piece of research, Robert Kosky and others studied over six hundred children who were depressed and/or suicidal.[2] They discovered that children who thought seriously of suicide were more likely to have disturbed relationships with their fathers and siblings than those who were simply depressed but not suicidal. But both depressed and suicidal young people had disturbed relationships with their mothers. The disturbance was characterized by persistent discord, persecution, hostility, and some form of child abuse.

So Parents, look carefully at the relationships within your families. I have learned that few parents *ever* want to hurt their children; they do so out of unconscious frustrations, severe stress, and inadequate resources for help.

DEPRESSION IN ADOLESCENTS

His face, lined in sternness beyond his thirteen years, was downcast. It was embarrassing for Curt to show his tear-filled brown eyes to me—an unknown adult. But I could count the accelerating teardrops on his worn blue jeans. His sandy hair, though long and unruly, was clean. His nervous motion revealed the restless energy that drove him.

Another bright, capable student was failing most of his courses. And I, with my trusty magic wand, should make him better. But Curt had another, more serious, problem. He had confided in a friend that he was feeling "pretty down" and that he often felt like he'd rather not be alive. He spoke at other times of running away.

In getting to know Curt and his parents, I learned that they had discovered in kindergarten that he was unusually intelligent. He was also charming, good-looking, and fairly well accepted by his peers. Therefore, his parents had high expectations. They wished for him a higher level of success in life than they had achieved. So they were not content with *B*'s and *A*'s. They expected straight *A*'s. And despite Curt's ability, he did not give evidence in his intelligence tests of his ability to make straight *A*'s.

Feeling that his very best efforts were not good enough for Mom and Dad, Curt finally gave up. He decided to quit trying. He withdrew into his own sullen world of anger and sadness. He felt helpless

2. Robert Kosky et al., *The Journal of Nervous and Mental Disease,* vol. 174, no. 9, March 18, 1986, pp. 523–528.

and finally began to believe there was no hope. Curt was approaching despair—a situation that concerned me greatly.

Before I could reach his frustrated parents, Curt did indeed reach desperation. He swallowed a number of aspirin tablets, hoping to find release from an unbearable life in suicide. Fortunately, he did not take enough to do serious damage, but he certainly got the attention of his family!

Because they truly wanted the best for him, Curt's parents could not see their role in his problems. They believed that the school was too easy on him, that I was promoting "permissive parenting," that relatives were taking sides and just feeling sorry for him. And there was a little truth in what they said. But they could not accept that their input—of unwittingly expecting the impossible—had been a negative influence on Curt.

In almost all depression there are a series of losses—often forgotten and rarely gigantic. But because they have been unrecognized or forgotten, the grief work surrounding them has rarely been completed. It gradually collects until its weight breaks down the youth's defenses, leaving him sad, helpless, angry and, often, guilt-ridden.

Curt is a good example of a collection of such losses:

· He lost his carefree status as a child when he entered junior high and those "terrible teens."

· He lost his usual successes in elementary school to face stiffer competition and less help from teachers.

· He lost a trusting, secure relationship with one primary teacher to face a series of teachers who had large groups of students for less than one hour a day. He could find no way to know any of them well enough to feel understood or safe with them.

· Due to his depression and sullen withdrawing, he lost most of his friends. He didn't have the energy to care, really. He was too "down."

· Curt lost his parents' pride in him. The competency he had shown in elementary school was not evident to them after junior high. They believed he was just lazy, and they nagged, prodded, and punished instead of recognizing his need for comfort, reassurance, and encouragement. Curt needed to have study time established and responsibility enforced—but in a loving, supportive, and firm manner.

· Perhaps most painful of all was Curt's loss of confidence in himself. He came to believe that he could never make the leap to adolescence and that he would never again know success.

In addition to these losses, Curt's misery was compounded because he did not possess the physical stature, prowess, or coordination of many of his peers who can cruelly tease anyone who is significantly different from themselves.

Depression in adolescence has several main causes, although its expression is similar for all of them. The expression, by the way, differs mainly according to each adolescent's temperament and the response of the adults involved with the individual.

1. A universal factor in depression is that of *some kind of loss.*
2. Almost as common in adolescents is a sense of being a *social misfit.* Feeling isolated or different from classmates is excruciatingly painful to a young teen who developmentally needs to identify with or belong to a group.
3. Being *physically different* from others is another focus of teen depression. The tall girl or the noticeably short boy (especially when he still has a boy-soprano voice) is going to attract attention.
4. Being *unable to compete* with some degree of success in sports or gymnastics is another cause of depression. In a culture that is almost as sports focused as it is sexually preoccupied, young people often seek peer acceptance and recognition through prowess in physical contests.
5. Depending on several factors, some young people who feel they *can never measure up* in other areas of life may try to compensate through academic success. If this, too, fails to be possible, even more severe depression may set in.
6. Experiencing a *lack of parental encouragement and support* may serve as a distorted mirror to reflect the young adolescent's existing sense of ugliness. An affirming attitude from the family is always important, but to the adolescent, it is absolutely necessary.

DEPRESSION LOOK-ALIKES

Although depression is extremely common in junior-high young people, they may behave at times as if they are depressed, but they actually are not. If you are to recognize and understand true depression, you need to know some of the attitudes and actions that resemble it. The following are five major look-alikes of depression.

1. Fatigue Due to Rapid Physical Development

As their bodies develop into adult, sexual ones, a great deal of physical energy is burned up. This process makes nearly all early adolescents somewhat lethargic at times.

Parents who fail to understand the physical aspects of adolescence may become impatient or worried. Sensitive, alert adolescents, even though they may *appear* lackadaisical, will quickly sense their parents' concern and will certainly react to parents' irritation. Any negative reaction by parents during these difficult months, and even several years, will complicate matters, often by precipitating needless depression.

I do *not* mean to imply that parents should "walk on eggs" or pamper adolescents. Nor should they give in to them in order to keep peace. Young teens desperately need parents who are wise enough to know when to extend limits and when to be firm enough to hold those lines tight.

Another priceless asset of parents is the ability to set limits and hold firm without *unnecessary* anger. Also avoid treating a teen in a childish manner. You need to rearrange your priorities very carefully as your child is approaching puberty in order to have time to zero in on her needs and respond to them.

Before reacting to your child, consider these things:

- Is my son truly rude or rebellious, or is he trying to cover up the confusion and fear that belong to the no-man's-land between child and adult?
- Is my daughter defying me or testing me to see if I'm strong enough, wise enough, and caring enough to stand firm when I must?
- Am I reacting to my son in fear, holding him so tightly he'll have to rebel to get free of me at all?
- Do I ever correct my child by shaming her, even if I *intend* that to motivate her to try harder?
- Do I see my child as being lazy, pouty, or moody instead of truly fatigued and anxious about strange new thoughts and emotions?
- Have I complimented my child today?
- What am I doing today to prepare my child for successful adulthood?

If you answer as few as three of these questions in a manner that is unsupportive of your child, I urge you to think before you react the next time. Your motives are almost certain to be positive, but your attitude may defeat the very help you intend to provide. If you cannot find an affirming, positive, loving frame of mind, seek help.

2. Disturbed Family Relationships

A friend brought his adolescent daughter to me for help. His shoulders inside his professional navy blazer were set in a firm line. His clean-shaven face depicted anger and resentments that nearly covered the anxious, tender look in his eyes. I occasionally detected the moisture of restrained tears as he related the struggles he and Melissa had endured. She was now depressed, he revealed, and at least 90 percent of the time a problem!

Believe me, I was eager to see a young teenager who was so extremely "bad." To my amazement, Melissa did not spit at me, swear at me, or act anything like a profoundly angry, depressed young woman. She was, in fact, very quiet and soft-spoken. Her long brown hair did cover her blue eyes, and she had a great deal of difficulty looking at me.

Over some weeks, Melissa and I became well acquainted. The problems her father had described were real, and they troubled her at least as much as they did him. She was perceptive enough to understand, as he had not, that the two of them were very alike. Such similar parent-child personalities often clash and result in severe misunderstandings.

When adolescents cannot resolve such difficulties through discussions, soften their parents with tears, or in any way known to them find harmony at home, they do one of three things: (1) withdraw to their rooms in moodiness, (2) spend more and more time away from home, or (3) resort to angry retorts. Melissa did all of these!

No wonder her father believed her to be depressed and just downright *bad!* But Melissa was not feeling helpless or guilty because she understood the situation fairly well. She knew she was no more at fault than her father. By her actions, she was proving she was *not* helpless (though she *was* at times misguided). She was frustrated at what she diagnosed as her dad's stubbornness. She was a bit sad because she really loved and admired her father but could not break through their barriers.

One of the joys of my profession as a therapist is that of helping restore harmony in dissonant families. As I sat one day with Melissa's father, I eagerly recounted Melissa's many assets, and I commented that he had raised a bright, loving daughter.

He looked incredulous. Surely she had "conned" me. She was still away from home or on the phone a lot; they could not communicate. Realizing I was not convincing him, I asked if he still believed Melissa to be 90 percent bad. Miserably enough, he nodded yes.

With a prayer for guidance I then suggested, "Bob, will you try for three weeks to ignore that 90 percent and react lovingly to the beautiful 10 percent?" After some thought, he agreed to try that as best he could.

I continued to see Melissa, encouraging her to react appreciatively to his efforts. A gradual change began to crescendo into a truly harmonious melody in that home.

These events took place some twenty years ago. Only a few months ago, I again saw my friend. With a grin, he thanked me for restoring his daughter to him. He had found that the more positively he reacted to her, the more open, loving, and appropriate she became. He couldn't quite give her 100, but he did say that she became 90 percent good. And I believe that's very good!

Parents may see their children as depressed when actually the young people are feeling shut out by their parents' unrealistic expectations. Believe it or not, teens want parental love and approval most of all when they act their very worst. And as I understand it, that's what the heavenly Father gave us—acceptance and forgiveness at our very worst.

3. Temporary Moodiness—The Blues

Cindy, eyes intently focused on her mirror, was a reflection of misery. Quietly, her mother watched for a while, then commented, "You look terribly unhappy, dear! What's bothering you?" She put down the clean laundry and sat expectantly on her daughter's rumpled bed.

It was a long wait, but worth every minute when Cindy finally broke away from her self-inspection. Wavy strawberry blonde hair in disarray, freckled cheeks wet with tears, and shoulders heaving with sobs, she threw herself into her mom's arms. At fourteen, that was, in itself, something of a task! Hugging her tall, gangly adolescent daughter was a not-so-common event, and both mother and daughter treasured the moments when they could recapture earlier times.

After her sobs quieted enough to permit words, Cindy began to explain. "Mother, why do I have to have curly hair and freckles? *No* one has such terrible hair. (The style was for long, silken, *straight* hair.) And not one of my friends has freckles. I'm fat and flat in all the wrong places. No boy will ever want to be seen with me. And I'm just *so* miserable!" The tears flowed again.

Mother rocked Cindy in an awkward teenage replica of her preschool nap-time manner. She reminded her child that she, too, had freckles but that had only endeared her to Cindy's father when they were young. She offered hope that as Cindy continued to develop, the hated flatness would develop its curves, and with exercise and a careful diet she could help nature balance out a lovely figure.

Best of all, her mother pointed out, Cindy's own hurting was helping her to become kind and compassionate to others. It is, she said, not so much how one looks on the outside, but who one is becoming inside that counts. And it was clear to her mother that Cindy was pretty special—inside. Cindy was soon chatting away and smiling happily.

Certainly there were more grim tête-à-têtes with her mirror, more tears, more moods of both sadness and irritation, but Cindy would not be truly depressed. She was always sure of a wise confidante in her mother; she had enough friends, enough achievements, and enough common sense to remember the last time she felt "down" and her recovery.

All young teens have moments and sometimes hours of the "blues." Their own self-comparisons seem to leave them hopelessly beneath their peers. And because teens share their successes more easily than their sadness or fears, they may never realize that most of their classmates feel *exactly* the same way.

Fortunate, indeed, is the youth who, like Cindy, can turn to an understanding and available parent for comfort and counsel. Moments of pessimism can be transformed into realistic self-confidence and genuine compassion for others who have pain of some sort throughout life.

Adolescents suffer, often dramatically, over failing a test, being cut from the team, finding only a minor (or no!) part in a school play, being snubbed by the tragically snobbish cliques of their school. These and many other events create temporary disappointments and even moods of despair. But these are transient, lasting from a few hours to a few days, and they are interwoven with happy phone calls and plans for next weekend or next year.

The truly depressed person stays unhappy or even miserable for many days. Two to three weeks of constant hopelessness are usually necessary for a diagnosis of major depression.

4. Minigrief Episodes

One of the most common look-alikes of depression is grief. In fact, I must repeat that unresolved grief episodes accumulate and form the basis for most depression.

Whether it is a move away from a familiar existence, the loss of a grandparent, the divorce of a best friend's parents, or simply the lack of straight hair and clear skin, grief is the result—the common denominator of them all.

You parents need to recognize grief and distinguish it from depression. The main difference lies in the ease with which you can track down the grief's origin. You need to understand the concept of minilosses and the little grief that attends them. For these experiences, comfort and reassurance are all that are usually needed—along with time—to heal them.

In true depression, the victim can rarely recall any events that caused the sad feelings. And parents or school faculty members can rarely offer additional clarity. Professional counseling may be needed to unearth the beginnings of a lengthy, true depressive episode.

5. Chemical Addiction

Most serious drug and alcohol abuse, in my experience, is the result of underlying depression in young people. Even elementary-school children are enticed into the use of chemicals partly because they are bored or "blue." And with all the stresses of the turbulent early teens, it becomes almost irresistibly tempting to feel good quickly—with the help of a pill, a smoke, or a drink.

Many other youngsters, however, experiment with drugs or alcohol to be "in" with their so-called friends. They often become dependent on these chemicals and realize, too late, that they are caught in a web of stealing, engaging in sex-for-pay, and drug dealing to support a habit they feel they cannot break. This vicious cycle will almost surely end in depression, but there is grief, too—over the loss of freedom, individuality, and integrity. And these are tragic losses.

Parents, you must familiarize yourselves with the signs of chemical abuse: red eyes; dilated or pinpoint pupils in the eyes; a watery, itchy nose; the burnt-hemp odor of marijuana; lethargy and excitement occurring in cycles dependent on drug availability; long sleeves worn to cover needle marks; the unmistakable odor of various forms of alcohol. The school or your physician can supply you with literature on the subject. Obtain it and memorize it. Don't accuse your teen without good evidence, but never be lulled into the belief that such a tragedy cannot happen to your child.

REVIEW OF SIGNS OF DEPRESSION IN ADOLESCENTS

Let me summarize the major symptoms of serious depression in young adolescents.

1. *Their work suffers.* Adolescents' work is primarily academic, and usually the grades of depressed young persons suffer. Depression impairs the ability to concentrate, memorize, organize thoughts, and speak clearly.

If they have job responsibilities around home, they have real difficulty getting even routine work done because of their preoccupation with their emotional pain and the energy drain it creates.

2. *Their social lives are damaged.* No one enjoys being around depressed persons, so friends often drift away. Furthermore, depressed young people stop reaching out to others. Even phone calls, the main joy in life to many adolescents, are cut off.

Many depressed young people retain confidants, but they place those trusted friends in a serious bind. They swear them to secrecy, even about suicidal plans, but those friends are not equipped to carry such a heavy responsibility alone. Young persons who seriously consider suicide may give away special possessions or write notes about the disposition of prized items.

3. *Their emotions are different.* A young person who has been relatively quiet may become silly or clownish as a cover for depression. A youth who has always been effervescent may become irritable or silent. And these changes persist for weeks, in contrast to common moodiness of a few hours.

4. *Their physical habits change.* Eating habits seem to go to an opposite extreme from the "norm." Many depressed youngsters eat frequently and gain weight, but others refuse to eat and lose weight rapidly. The same holds true for sleep habits. Some sleep excessively, but others have great difficulty falling asleep, awaken with terrifying nightmares, or awaken early in the morning.

The facial expression is a variable mix of anger, sadness, and anxiety. The shoulders usually slump, and the resting posture is strongly suggestive of depression. The weight of the world seems to rest on the young shoulders.

WHAT TO DO IF AN ADOLESCENT IS DEPRESSED

In this era of drug abuse, suicide, and all sorts of aberrant behaviors in youth, the very word *depression* strikes terror in the hearts of many parents. In fact, concerned parents often overreact and misinterpret normal adolescent development and behaviors.

1. I urge you, parents, to *observe carefully,* wait watchfully, and seek input from others who are close to you and your children before you give in to anxiety. The symptoms listed are reliable, but your interpretation of them may be a bit out of proportion. Counsel from trusted friends, school counselors, a pastor, or your family doctor can verify your fears or reassure you.

Remember the rule of thumb regarding the duration of the symptoms as well as their meaning. Your plump adolescent daughter may simply be slow in maturing to the level that she can control her eating habits. The door-slamming withdrawal of your angry son may simply be the only method he knows to avoid hitting his "crummy" kid sister.

If you are uncertain about your child's possible depression, ask what's bothering him. Don't blurt out a question in the midst of an angry confrontation. But perhaps at bedtime you can make a gentle comment: "Bill, I've been noticing that you are quieter than usual and you look sad. Can you tell me what's going on? I remember when I was just fourteen, life could seem awfully grim. If you can talk with me, I daresay I can help."

You may have to wait a long time for a truly depressed or even a moody child to talk. But that wait is well worth your time because it can release the pent-up pressure and cut short the mood. It may even be a positive turning point up and out of depression.

2. If the adolescent has at least four signs of serious depression that have lasted for as long as two weeks, by all means *consult with a counselor.* (See list at end of this chapter.) Locate one who truly knows family counseling and can help all of you to understand and overcome the problems together. It is widely recognized that the person in a family who seems to have "the problem" may be, like the tip of an iceberg, the smallest part of that problem. It always pays to check it out together.

3. *Use medications appropriately.* Many therapists these days de-

pend on medications alone to relieve depression of patients. And believe me, medications can play an important part in treatment. They can be lifesaving if a person is considering suicide.

Many medications will relieve the signs of anxiety, worry, and depression. I frequently prescribe medications, but I believe that I have only begun my job when I write a prescription. My most vital task is to discover what caused the anger, sadness, guilt, fear, or helplessness that underlies the depression.

The old losses need to be understood, and the grief must be completed. The misunderstandings that create rifts between parents and child must be clarified; usually forgiving must take place. New insights must be acquired, and new choices need to be taught. Most people do not realize they have the power to choose how they will act or react or even how they will feel. Parents often fail to understand that their intended discipline may have been ill-fitting for a special child, resulting in estrangement and rebellion.

If you find a counselor who *only* medicates, please ask for or seek a second opinion. You and your child deserve the kind of help that will teach you how to recognize and cope successfully with stress without *forever* relying on a pill to do so for you.

4. In the process of counseling, I caution you to *avoid two common extremes.* At one extreme are families who stop too soon. It can feel so good to see some problems being solved that they may believe they have reached the end of the road to recovery. It usually takes some months to achieve the awarenesses family members need to prevent relapses.

At the other extreme are families who become so attached to the therapeutic process (or the therapist) that they become almost helplessly dependent. One primary goal in counseling is that of developing a trusting relationship with a person who cares about you and can help you. Equally important, sometimes painfully so, is the goal of personal growth in wisdom and loving strength that will result in independence from that therapist.

5. *Seek* as a counselor someone who will *help in your spiritual development* as well as in your understanding and communications. If you cannot find such a counselor, I urge you to meet regularly with a member of the clergy of your faith to keep your total life in balance. For a long time good counselors have been taught to avoid getting into the field of religion or faith. Fortunately, many therapists are learning that we are all spiritual beings as well as emotional, physical, and psychological ones. Many members of the clergy are

also becoming aware of the need for good counsel along with spiritual growth. Keep your family well balanced by getting the help you need.

DEPRESSION IN OLDER TEENS

Each year news stories report the tragedies of young lives wasted through suicide. In 1984, over five thousand young people (ages fifteen to twenty-four) took their lives, according to the studies of the American Association of Suicidology in Denver, Colorado. At least three times that number consider suicide, according to a study done at the University of Kansas at Lawrence, Kansas, in 1986.

Personally, I have interviewed a great many seriously depressed, potentially suicidal young people. The causes of their depression are many, but some broad categories of causes may help us understand these youngsters who have lost hope.

Physical Changes

Puberty begins in junior high or sometimes even in elementary school. No specific time for its beginning and ending holds true for all people. The biological stress of physical development causes great changes in young people that can affect their lives.

When one person's change does not compare favorably with another's, that young person is at some risk for depression. A girl who is not as well developed as most of her peers is almost certain to suffer some degree of depression. The same thing is true of a young man whose pubertal changes lag far behind those of his friends. Skin problems, emerging sexual feelings, and ultimate body height and shape are physical issues that may contribute to late adolescent depression.

Social Factors

Being part of a group is a high priority among young people. Some established groups could become a place to belong, but due to social influences, many of them are not open to every young person. Only a select few can make it into a variety of athletic teams. A few more may belong to debate, drama, or music groups, and a very few become cheerleaders. Where do the vast number of teens belong? In many communities, there simply is no place for them.

True enough, many older teens find a niche in part-time jobs. The associates they find at work become friends and offer a social outlet. The money they earn provides some evidence of self-worth and offers the fun of spending the fruits of their own labors.

A tragically large group of young people find their place of belonging in groups of vandals, drug addicts, or alcoholics. The false highs and sophisticated pleasures these groups offer are tempting to youths who know too little success and have no self-esteem.

Our society has an extremely permissive attitude about sexual mores. Many youths in all sorts of groups become sexually active and even promiscuous at an early age. For many young people, sexual encounters are characterized by an intense, almost desperate quality. They think if they are considered "sexy," they will become popular.

Certain modes of dress and styles of hair have become symbols of the group to which teens belong. No single "look" prevails today. No longer is there a generalized appearance of shabbiness that characterized the teens of the sixties, and the designer labels of the late seventies and early eighties that robbed families' budgets are less conspicuous. Now we have the smartly dressed, affluent group, the counter-culture groups in army garb or "ethnic" wear, and the punk-rock youths with extreme hairstyles and rock-group attire.

Each group has its levels—those who are leaders with some success and confidence, those who are followers and have some security in simply belonging, and those who simply don't fit, who feel strange, confused, and depressed. When these people find it impossible to locate a place for comfortable belonging, they are likely to consider suicide as the only escape from loneliness and futility.

Family Conflicts

As I've noted earlier, several studies show that troubled parent-child relationships contribute to depression throughout life. The disturbances may be of several kinds—neglectful, abusive, or overprotective. They often include divorce of the parents, alcoholism, or mistaken forms of discipline that weave the ugly strands of false guilt into the fabric of a child's personality.

Children who suffer pain from parents' mistakes are helpless in their misery. They learn to feel angry because it gives them a sense of some power. One adolescent confided that she had survived the almost unbearable pain of her earlier years by imagining taking her life. Considering life to be otherwise beyond her control, she found a measure of confidence in the capacity to decide to end it all if she needed badly enough to escape.

Other young people become depressed and contemplate suicide out of anger. Strangely enough, these youths actually know their parents care about them. They typically say, "I'll just kill myself! Then you'll be sorry!" Most young people who threaten suicide, and even those who attempt it, do not actually want to die. They are screaming out the anguish of their frustration at life—and often specifically at their families.

They very often take a handful of whatever prescription drug they find in the medicine cabinet or just common pain relievers. Some of them carve lines across their wrists or over a vein elsewhere, and many cut designs of some sort on their bodies. Thankfully, most instances of self-mutilation and pill swallowing are only gestures, dramatic cries for help or attempts to escape imagined or real threats of punishment.

But such actions should *never* be dismissed lightly. Whether or not their lives are at stake, they are asking in the best way they know for help. And they may accidentally take too many pills, cut a bit too deeply, or miss out on the anticipated "rescue" if help does not arrive. Life is a precious gift to be saved and restored to joy!

Academic Stress

Pressures to achieve academic success are strong in a great many families and schools. In fact, there is an upsurge in visits to therapists during times when grades will be released. Only a few years ago, a friend's youngest son disappeared from home one evening in late spring. My friend and her husband adored their son, and they tried to provide the proper balance in tough and tender love that would make him a secure, well-balanced person.

They were incredulous, then, to hear from his friends that he had run away from home shortly before he was to graduate from high school. During the hours he was gone, they suffered immeasurable anxiety. Desperately, they reviewed their imagined or real mistakes in an attempt to understand why he would leave home.

After what seemed like an endless day to the parents, their wandering son returned. His story was simple. During the last quarter of his senior year, he had become careless about studies. Frankly, he didn't know what he wanted to do with his life, and he was somewhat anxious and depressed. When his grades came out, he was appalled at their decline. He simply panicked, imagined his parents would be devastated, and could not face their disappointment in him. They were upset about the poor grades, but they were able to reassure their son that they would always love and help him through anything.

When teens are unable to succeed academically, they are likely to become depressed. The more depressed they are, the less effectively they can study, and their grades fall even more. When parents yell and punish truly depressed young people, they further complicate those problems and estrange their children.

Our schools, to complicate matters further, do not help the problem. Over the years, they have rigidly attempted to press all young people into one academic mold. Certainly all people need basic skills in reading, mathematics, and communications. All students, however, are not college-bound, nor should they be. Many trades demanding a variety of skills are just as essential as academic excellence. Mechanical work of all sorts is fundamental to the maintenance of our civilization, but schools fail to emphasize this. The trades are still relegated to positions of less respect in some families and reserved for those who can't go on to college.

If your teenager can't concentrate on English or has difficulty with math, help him to learn these basics the best he can, and then introduce him to a variety of career opportunities, such as carpentry, plumbing, tailoring, or food service, among others. Let your teen discover the future for which his inborn talents and natural interests fit him. You can help him avoid depression by finding fulfillment and a focus for his skills.

Drugs

The hard young face opposite me was almost frightening. Dick was only sixteen, and he was already an angry failure. His high IQ was denied by the list of *F*'s on his grade report. His eyelids drooped, and his speech was not always audible. When I finally aroused him enough to talk, he verified my guess. He had been smoking "pot" with friends before school that very morning.

His gang came to school early and gathered, of all places, under the stairs of a nearby church. They took turns providing marijuana and believed they were putting one over on both their parents and the school staff. This boy had no idea that the drug was slowly taking control of him. It was making him lose motivation, hampering his ability to concentrate and remember, and giving him a false sense of power.

Marijuana, speed, cocaine, and all illegal drugs are deceptive, and they breed a vicious cycle. Many young people start taking drugs out of curiosity or to get an easy "high." Before they realize it, they become drug dependent, and then they become frightened and depressed.

Other teens start on drugs because they are unbearably depressed, and the chemicals help them feel better—for a while. But then they become even more depressed because they run out of money to buy the substance and are afraid their parents will find out. Their suppliers promise help if they will sell for them, and a complex fear-and-need-based system is established.

Parents and school faculty must join resources to recognize the depression that makes students vulnerable to drug dealers and dealing. Courses should be developed about drugs and about depression. And counseling and support should be required before such tragic addiction destroys our young people and our culture. All too often, parents believe depression is just a phase and fail to seek help. They may punish their child's behavior and fail to understand and support his sagging self-esteem. Many schools now offer excellent help for both depressed teens and their parents. This should be used.

Broken Relationships

In the late teens and early twenties most young people form relationships of permanence. (At least we used to consider them permanent!) Dating develops much more seriously, and the possibility of engagement and marriage becomes a probability at this stage.

When everything goes smoothly and progress is made toward a commitment, all is well. But that is not always what happens. In some instances sweethearts change their minds and break their promises and even engagements. A very secure young person will grieve over a rejection of this magnitude, recover, and find a new partner.

However, the broken dreams and sense of rejection that this event involves may throw a person into deep depression. Anyone who has suffered previous fractures in a serious relationship and who has poor self-esteem is a likely candidate for this sort of emotional breakdown.

The devastating part of rejection is the implication that the one who is left is not really a very good person. The one the sweetheart favors is obviously perceived as the better person. So it is not breaking up, alone, that is the problem. It is the unfavorable comparison the rejected person sets up that lands a powerful blow to the ego.

(*Note:* Up to this point, I have addressed parents primarily. But I think that this subject and the one that follows it are more appropriately addressed to the young person.)

At this very point, you may find your greatest resource. Rather than give in to the supposition that the new person is superior, think carefully and evaluate honestly. It is almost certain that you are as capable and likable as the new love. You simply may not fit the personality and meet the needs of your erstwhile sweetheart as well as the new love. Chances are that neither you nor your prospective partner would have been very happy if the marriage had taken place. Another strong possibility is that your onetime sweetheart is fickle, has trouble with choices, and is habitually searching for greener pastures.

Once you establish your basic worth, you will be far better prepared to cope with depression. That does not mean, of course, that you should rationalize away all your faults. You may well have habits or attitudes that do not wear well in an intimate relationship. Use this pain to goad you into a bit of healthy introspection. Whatever you discover that is not as positive as you would like to be can be changed. Ask a friend to remind you when you slip into habitual behaviors that offend others. You can become even more lovable by working on change and growth.

The Future

Rick loved to tinker with tools. Ever since he was a little boy, he had been fascinated with fixing broken things and building new items. A cherished memory was of his grandfather showing him how to use a chisel and saw.

In high school Rick realized he hated books, and he did not make good grades. For many young men, this would have been no serious problem, but for Rick, it seemed a giant issue. He greatly respected his father and wanted to please him. He knew all too well what his dad expected of him. Dad was an attorney and had, in his own opinion, become far more successful than Rick's mechanic grandpa. In fact, Rick believed his father held little respect for the old man who tinkered in his shop and earned little money.

The predicament is clear and is representative of what happens to many young people. Rick wanted to measure up to his dad's expectation that he enter a profession, but he realized he probably could not achieve the academic proficiency to do so. In his heart he wanted to follow his grandfather's trade, but he felt to do so would lose him his dad's respect. The dilemma was constantly on Rick's mind, and the depression generated by his helplessness became serious. To avoid his anxiety, Rick began to drink and, of course, to neglect his studies. Though he entered college, his depression and dilemma were packed with his other belongings into his suitcases.

Whether in high school, college, or the early stages of being out on your own, the challenge is there. When you grow up, who do you want to be? How can you find out? Who will help you? Are you willing to practice the self-discipline and even sacrifices it will take to reach your goals?

The world is changing rapidly. Many jobs that once were attached to manufacturing things in this country no longer exist since we import the items. Jobs now seem to focus on services, but these positions are scarce since so many people are seeking to make a living in service-related industries. Knowledge has exploded in recent decades. How can you master all you need to learn? These big questions may seem to have no answers, and depression is likely to overpower you. The answers to this sort of depression are truly difficult to find. But here are some ideas that can help.

1. Try to forget the ambitions and demands of everyone else for a while. Think carefully about your inner strivings. When you were seven or ten, what did you most enjoy doing? What did you want to be when you grew up? Inner searching may put you clearly in touch with your own best goals and aptitudes.
2. Ask your parents or, better yet, your grandparents what they think you are good at doing. Teachers or friends may also be helpful in this search.
3. Be practical. What education and training opportunities are open to you? Consider your intellectual skills, financial resources, and personal aptitudes. What jobs are likely to be available if and when you complete a specific training program?
4. If you can find no workable solutions, seek out a vocational counselor. In high schools and many junior colleges, services are available to evaluate your aptitudes. They pick up the areas you are likely to be good at and can tell you what kinds of jobs may be available and even what it will take to prepare you for such jobs.
5. Make a genuine commitment to stick with your training until you are prepared to excel in the field you choose.
6. Most career decisions can be changed. Do not get stuck in the

process of choosing by the fear that you may dislike a certain field but then never be able to leave it. Many an initial career choice becomes only the gateway into something an individual would not otherwise have considered.

Even as you investigate some possibilities for your future, I hope you will discover your depression is dissipating. Depression cannot long coexist with decisive action and commitment to excellence. You can choose to become who you want to be as well as how you want to feel and act. Our Creator has given us this incredible power!

Please review the signs and symptoms of depression at the end of this chapter. If you have four or more of these, focus on your life. You may be able to find out what factors are at work to create your disorder. If you know, make a plan to solve the problems. If you don't know, talk about your situation and your feelings with a perceptive friend or a counselor. Never accept the belief that seeking help means you are crazy or weak. The opposite is, in fact, true. It takes courage and honesty to face your needs, admit you need help, and follow through to solutions. The exciting truth is that you can find the answers to your special needs!

Accept the fact that your teenage years will be turbulent. The physical changes are drastic; social adjustments and relationships are changeable and may be disappointing; facing the future with its demands for adult responsibilities is frightening; becoming independent from parents is confusing and difficult.

Parents' need to release older adolescent children to become adults is equally frightening. They often instinctively grasp their children and try to rework their discipline and training, creating needless rebellion. A key to surviving these times is the parents' ability to remember (to recall their own youth), to recapture the good job they actually did (a day at a time) as parents, and to rely on the master plan God designed for them and their young adult child.

SIGNS and SYMPTOMS

Depression in Adolescents and Older Teens

1. A subjective feeling of sadness and hopelessness. *They can seem to find no way out of their maze of stress and inadequacy. This inner feeling can be picked up by careful observers of their facial expression, posture, and tone of voice.*
2. Moodiness. *A clear demonstration of sadness and hopelessness, moodiness may well be masked by irritability or downright anger. Almost all youths have these feelings at some time, but truly depressed young persons will experience them for weeks at a time.*
3. A bleak outlook for the future. *Seriously depressed youths make no plans for next week or next year. I worry about suicide when young people express no hope for anticipated happiness at least after the crisis is over.*
4. Disturbances of eating. *They may eat too much or too little, but there is a prolonged change in eating patterns from their normal ones. Anorexia and bulimia have become common diagnoses and are extremely frequent. These cases involve several emotional and familial issues, but a distinct element of depression is usually involved.*
5. Sleep disturbances. *They may have frightening dreams. They may have difficulty in getting to sleep or awaken early due to the inner stress of the many anxieties and problems in which they feel immersed. Or they may sleep excessively.*
6. Changes in social life. *They are likely to stop spending time with friends. They may even refuse phone calls. Rarely, a usually withdrawn young person may enter almost feverishly into social activities to lift himself out of despair.*
7. Chemical abuse. *Some young people begin using drugs and alcohol out of curiosity or to prove their sophistication, but most of them do so to relieve depression. Before they know it, they are "hooked" and unable to stop.*
8. Suicidal ideas. *Preadolescents often leave notes or drawings around that clearly allude to depression and death. In my experience, this is infinitely more true of adolescents and older teens.*

Chapter

18

Overcoming Addictions—What Parents Must Not Do

One of the toughest issues of parenting has to be drug abuse —your child with an addiction or addictive behavior of any kind (smoking, alcohol, hard drugs, or overeating). I wrote Kids Don't Want to Use Drugs *to help parents see that kids do not like to ruin their lives by using drugs; kids use drugs (overeat, smoke, drink alcohol) because they hurt—it's that simple. The book is a practical book of prevention to help parents understand what their child needs to bolster self-esteem and make him feel secure.*

I also wanted parents to understand that they can, and will, make mistakes. The important thing is to be able to admit your mistakes and be willing to change. In a lot of ways, the "do's" for parents are found in the preceding chapters of this book. If you heed the advice contributed by these well-known authors and counselors, you will be developing a family of love, acceptance, and understanding, which will keep your child protected from needing to turn to drug use to ease his pain.

But what if your child is already hooked? What if your child already uses drugs? What should you do? The two chapters I have chosen to share with you address these two areas: what parents must and must not do.

Dr. Joel C. Robertson
Kids Don't Want to Use Drugs

Parents' first and natural response to their children's drug use generally is not the right response.

If that's the case, what can parents do?

Before I answer that question, I have to answer a different one: What should you as a parent *not* do?

In overcoming addictions, there are almost as many rules about what not to do as what to do. Here is the overall negative principle that I tell parents—a principle I've observed being violated in thousands of instances of parental involvement.

Before you can intervene successfully, learn what to avoid doing.

Here are some what-not-to-do rules for you to think about.

Don't Confront Them Unless They Are Sober

If children are using alcohol or other drugs at the time, the best thing you can do is to say absolutely nothing. At that point, you will be talking to a drug and not to your children.

The day after the episode may not be the best opportunity, either, because they may still be under the drug's influence, or they may feel terrible.

QUESTION: ***When is the best time to talk to your children about their using drugs?***

ANSWER: ***When you don't feel you have to talk to them.***

When you feel angry, upset, afraid, or depressed, don't talk to them. You'll blow it. When you feel you have to get your message across, you will probably come across with a preaching tone or sound like a police interrogator. They pick up your emotions quite easily.

Your goal is to eliminate the drug problem. This goal is best accomplished when you and your children struggle with the problem together. When you feel that you don't have to confront them and you're not compelled to do so by some inner urge, that's probably the right opportunity to communicate with adolescents.

Don't Criticize Your Children for Using Drugs

They use drugs because doing that is less painful for them than seeing themselves as they really are. They have needs that are not being met without drugs, even if they're not fully aware of what they lack. You can help them identify those needs so that they can overcome addiction.

You are the most important person to your children, although they will rarely admit that to you, especially when you need that assurance the most. You are the one who observes the changes in their behavior and attitudes; they do not see themselves accurately.

Approaching your children with a let's-fix-this-problem-together attitude is more effective than asking them why they are disappointing you and hurting themselves. You can have significant impact in helping your children take the step to change.

Don't focus on yourself and your hurt or disappointment. Immediately after you discover your children are using drugs, you'll probably think of how your friends will react or what your pastor, coworkers, and relatives will say or think. Or you'll focus on your failure and guilt. Push those ideas aside and deal with them on your own. Your feelings are not the issue when you have to deal with your children.

Don't Get into Power Struggles

Power struggles take place when parents try to force kids to do what parents want them to do. Parents can't get away with it. Eventually, they run into confrontation. The kids can withdraw mentally by no longer listening, or they can withdraw physically by staying away from home. Trying to win by using parental power will always be a mistake. When it comes to power, the kids always win.

Don't push children into a corner where they have to obey or rebel. That's a power play on your part. The kids are living and responding the best they know how to their felt needs. They are seldom rebelling as such but are trying in their unsophisticated way to say, "Hey, I'm hurting. I need . . ."

Even if you consider their action and attitude as rebellion, you simply won't win when the issue becomes one of power. Rebellion begins when children have unsatisfied needs, and it develops over a period of time. If you can recognize that fact and get on your children's side, you avoid the confrontation.

Don't Try to Be a Special Friend

A parent can't be a special friend and a parent, too. You can (and should) be friendly, warm, and caring, but you also need to remain a parent. Once the children have grown up, you may be able to develop a true friendship, but not when they're still living at home.

Kids need someone who is objective and able to see beyond

their immediate needs and gratification. If you try to become their buddy or closest friend, you end up compromising your values. You want the best for your children, but don't compromise your values so your kids will like you.

If you do, your "little" compromises sound like this:

- "Oh, it's just a beer now and then." *(Drugs)*
- "She knows where to draw the line with boys. We trust her to do the right thing. Besides, these things aren't such a big deal to kids today." *(Sex)*
- "Hey, come on, we used to listen to music our folks called garbage. It didn't hurt us, did it?" *(Music)*
- "I know kids dress different today and with all that symbolism and stuff, but devil worship and witchcraft are pretty far-out and used only by fanatics." *(Satanism)*

When you try to take on the role of peer-friend, you send out messages of inconsistent values. Your behavior lowers your children's self-esteem because they don't have standards to judge against.

Your children are not your friends. They are your children.

Don't Set Up Rules and Regulations Until You Have Looked Carefully at Kids' Unmet Needs and You Can Offer Solutions

Rules and regulations won't satisfy needs the way drugs do. When kids are using drugs, imposing more demands on them is a power play that doesn't work.

If you can provide for their needs, the drugs won't be necessary any longer. You don't want to set up lists of rules to keep them from using drugs. If you remember this one fact, you can then turn them toward a positive direction: *You can never set up enough rules to keep your kids from using drugs.*

Don't Dismiss Satanism As an Act of Rebellion

Satanism is a religion. Most parents view satanism and interest in the occult as rebellious activities. Kids find the occult attractive because they seek a higher power—some being more powerful than they are, than the drug is, and than you the parent are. They want a god who can help them, rescue them, give them peace and hope, and show them how to change.

Occasionally, drug use and behavior are acts of rebellion. Most of the time, satanism and interest in the occult express the need for spiritual development—a need not being met.

The greater the addiction, the greater interest you may see in satanism and the occult. That being true, you need to look at that situation as a search to satisfy a religious need. It is a spiritual search, not simply rebellion against authority.

Since the 1980s, satanism has become a significant ally of drug use. This development partially has to do with the acceleration syndrome—there's the need for more excitement and acceptance.

Although drugs temporarily provide a sense of power, in time that power dissipates. Kids then realize there must be something more to make life worth living. They may look at organized religion but find so many inconsistencies in the people who practice it—people who say they believe in something but don't live their faith—that they turn away from the church.

From there, they tend to investigate the type of spiritual experience that doesn't set standards or levels they have to achieve, yet provides a power greater than themselves.

Adults tend to get into the New Age movement* because of its philosophical bent. By contrast, adolescents may move to the highest statement level of satanism, which often includes devil worship, animal sacrifice and, in some instances, human sacrifice.

Most parents seem ignorant of the significance of satanism. But

* The term *New Age* is a vague one and incorporates a variety of ideas. I refer specifically to the forms that emphasize practices such as witchcraft, channeling, and fortune-telling, and include elements of Hinduism and Buddhism.

police in almost any area of the country—whether urban or rural—have become increasingly aware of the work of these cults. In fact, police academies now provide seminars about this phenomenon. They are also aware that

- adolescents are most often involved.
- adolescents turn to satanism because it reflects their needs.
- adolescents often get into satanism when they become heavily involved in drug use.

Estimates of the number of kids involved with satanism vary with the geographic location. Estimates in the early 1990s are that 10 percent of the kids involved in heavy drug usage turn to satanism and the occult.

If you suspect your children are involved in satanism, a few of the obvious clues include

- the way they dress (any change from their normal styles).
- the symbols they use or have on their clothes or bodies.
- attitudinal changes such as increasing hostility and unwillingness to communicate, mystical references, and using phrases such as "the Power of the Darkness."

Turning to satanism is more than having harmless fun. It can progress to violent activities.

Chapter

19

What Parents Must Do

In the previous chapter, I presented my don't list. This chapter discusses what parents must do. *These items are not options.* Any statements on this list, if neglected or ignored, can develop into more serious problems.

Focus on Children's Needs and Not on Their Drug-using Behavior

Unmet needs have to exist for drug addiction to occur.

Offer Your Children Unconditional Love

No strings, no conditions, and no rewards for compliance, and no laying of guilt for noncompliance ("If you really loved me, you would . . .").

Show love for your children—not for their actions but for who they are. Especially if they're already using drugs, they need to know that you love them.

Don't use love to manipulate them.

Don't withhold love because they're not doing what you like.

Do let them know that there is nothing they can do to make you love them less, even when you dislike the way they behave.

Accept Your Children Where They Are and As They Are Right Now

Don't accept them for who they may become or what they may one day achieve.

All of us—and especially children—need to know we are all right, just as we are without making changes.

The situation may be such in your home that you honestly don't like your children as they are. Then you have to do some work on yourself first. You may need to learn that differences in the way they look or the way they do things aren't related to the depth of your love for them.

You can't help your children change if you don't like who they are right now. If children justify what they're doing, yelling out, "Everybody does it," and "Hey, I can quit any time I want to," they have no apparent reason to change. They are justifying to you who they are because they want your love and acceptance now.

Learn to Communicate

You can learn to communicate only if you spend time with your children. Parents can argue all they want by saying, "I'm interested in quality time, not in quantity." That's a fallacious argument.

Suppose you're absolutely starved. You go to a fine restaurant and order a steak. As you sit there, you say, "I can't wait to be fed, I'm so hungry."

At last the server brings you a steak. It is one-inch wide, one-inch long, and one-inch deep. "Here's your steak."

You stare at the meat for a few seconds and then take a bite. In two bites, it's gone. You tell the server, "I'm still hungry. I want more steak than that!"

"I'm sorry, but it's the best quality meat you'll ever find. Didn't you like what you ate?"

"Yes, very much, but I want more."

"Sorry, we serve only top quality products here. We don't deal in quantity orders."

Silly? Of course. But the quality of your time with your kids, if given in small doses, won't satisfy their needs.

Spend time dealing with your children and their problems today, or spend time later dealing with the consequences of their drug use.

Teach Your Children about Emotional Hassles

That is, instead of teaching children that it's not good to be angry, to feel guilty or depressed, let them know that it's all right to have such feelings, that everyone does, and that they are natural. More important is explaining how they can cope with those emotions when they occur.

Most parents tend to say, "I don't want you to get angry when other kids call you names." That's not what children want to hear. If they've been hurt at school, belittled, insulted, and bullied, they already feel angry and hurt. *Now* what can they do about such emotions?

Instead of discounting their anger, say, "Of course, you're angry. I would expect you to feel that way. Here's what you can do to get over those feelings. You can give in to that anger. Stay with your anger and remember every bad thing that other person did. If you do that, the other boy controls you.

"*Or* you can decide that you need to be a normal boy. It's all right to feel the way you do. And I understand that you have a problem. Now that you're going to do something about it, you're no longer under that other boy's control."

Use this time for discussion. What can he do now to relieve his anger? Think about it together.

Teach Your Children about Fear

All children have fears. Kids fear

- going to school the first day.
- not being liked by the other kids.
- not getting good grades and feeling stupid.
- not being pretty enough or big enough or strong enough.

Like all other human beings, kids have fears about everything in life. Wise parents help them learn to face up to those fears.

If a nine-year-old girl is afraid that she's not as pretty as several other girls in her class, a wise mother won't say, "You're pretty. So you shouldn't feel that way."

Here's a better response: "You know, some days I don't feel very pretty either. And when I don't feel pretty, I look at myself in the mirror and say, 'Oh, well, this feeling will pass. Tomorrow I'll probably look better.' "

Or the mother can say, "You'll always find somebody prettier. I like the way you look. Besides, let me tell you something else I like about you. You're a sensitive, caring person. You can read well." (Name whatever the child can do well.)

First, emotions change from day to day. Feeling ugly today doesn't mean she will feel like that every day. Second, you can't build up a false security if your daughter isn't pretty on the outside. Everyone is going to be insecure in certain ways. Help your child focus on her strong points.

Teach Them about Priorities

You demonstrate priorities, no matter how little you teach directly. Your kids see what you do when you're pressed for time. There are occasions when you can't spend the amount of time with them that you want to. When the family is going through a financial crisis, Dad may have to work extra hours, or Mom may need to go to work. Or a crisis at work may need attention right away. Or there's a death and you need to go to the funeral home.

If you tell them directly and honestly, most children understand. For example, you may say, "For the next two weeks I'm going to have to work a lot more hours than I want to because of this situation."

Or you may say, "The choir at church is planning a big Christmas musical. For the next three weeks, I'll have to leave right after supper two or three nights each week."

If your children know ahead of time that such things will end, that it's important for you to be away, they don't feel rejected. They feel a part of the solution, and they can be encouraged to help. Let them help clean up the kitchen after supper or wash the dishes or stack them in the sink if they're fairly young. They are then part of what is going on.

I recall when I had a deadline on a book. I said to my family, "I'm going to have to work every night this week. I don't want to, but I have to. I'd like you to be aware that I can't spend my usual time with you. Let's make sure when this is over that we take off three or four days together."

Instead of complaining about my not being around, which was normal for the children, they brought me coffee and wanted to bake things for me so I could have enough energy to go on. Even my three little daughters became part of the solution because it was a family issue.

It's a three-step idea: (1) When you take time to describe the problem to your children, (2) and you allow your children to be part of the solution, (3) they know that they hold a high priority in the family.

When you have priority conflicts, and we all do at times, life is not ruined. You simply need to reevaluate your life.

Teach Your Children Responsibility

That learning happens gradually because you can't suddenly expect kids to make a drastic change. If they weren't responsible before they turned to drugs, they won't be more responsible if they're not using drugs. Discuss with your children responsible behavior from their point of view. Together, determine consequences, and follow through if they fail to live up to the expected behavior. For example, if your daughter borrows the car but doesn't follow through with prearranged responsibilities, she can't use the car again for a realistic period of time.

Set Realistic Goals with Your Children

You and your children need to set the goals together. Agree on the behavior (results) that can be reasonably expected. These must not be standards that you set up for the children to respond to as if there is a new set of regulations.

The purpose of these mutually agreed-upon goals is for your children

- to expect realistic, obtainable results by their cooperative behavior.
- to achieve a sense of responsibility.
- to live with a style of behavior acceptable to them and to you.

These goals must be simple. Toddlers take one tiny step, pause, and then take the next. Even one baby step in the right direction is important.

I'll illustrate what I mean. Alex is using drugs. Sometimes he doesn't come home all night. Along with his parents, Alex agrees that he will come home by curfew time, say, midnight, no matter how much he is into his drugs.

Helen, on the other hand, stays away so often that a curfew isn't realistic. The first goal that Helen and her parents set up is that she will come home each night. She will not stay out all night. It may be 3:00 A.M. when she comes in, but she will make it her first step just to come home.

Once Helen and her parents have decided together that she will come home sometime before morning, they need to ask,

- "Do you think this is an appropriate goal?"
- "Do you think you can achieve this goal?"
- "Do we need to look at this more before we agree?"

If Helen agrees, they accept this first goal: She will come home. The parents promise not to complain, grumble, or lecture, no matter how high she is. If she reaches the minimum goal, she has done what she has promised.

Of course, once Helen consistently comes home (say, after two or three weeks), they talk again about goals. "Can we set a curfew hour, Helen?" asks her dad.

"Not yet," she answers.

When Helen is ready and says, "Yes, let's do that," they mutually agree on the time she will come home.

"Suppose we make it 2:00," her mother says. "You've been coming in consistently now between 2:30 and 3:15 every morning. Think you can do that?"

If Helen agrees (her agreement, remember, is the key to success), they can gradually set the curfew earlier.

If this procedure is done correctly, adolescents like Helen and Alex will be willing to take the next step because they are now feeling a sense of responsibility. They are being respected and trusted. They have a sense of being important. They often realize, as never before, how much their parents actually love them.

Set these goals at a time when children aren't trying to manipulate—that is, when they are not answering and agreeing to what they know you want to hear from them.

Adolescents will fail to live up to their goals, even though they helped to set them and agreed to follow them.

"Now what?" you ask when they don't live up to their agreement.

Adolescents need to determine for themselves the consequences of goal setting. If parents set the rules and the consequences and the children fail, then what? The kids can justify their action by telling themselves that the goals were unrealistic and inappropriate.

They can't be allowed to get away with this form of manipulation. The failure to reach their agreed-upon goals must have consequences. "This is what will happen" is the answer.

The consequences must

- be enforceable.
- be realistic.
- be appropriate.
- be set up by the children.
- be agreed to by the parents.

Kids don't need harsh punishment. The tendency of parents is to punish for not being responsible. It's more important to *enforce the consequences.* Let's see how this works by going back to Alex.

Alex has said that he will come home by midnight every night. If he doesn't, his father can withhold his allowance. On the third, fourth, and fifth nights Alex doesn't come in before 3:30. Normally, what would his father say? "You're grounded for a week." However, Alex hasn't been coming home at midnight, so his father has no control. If Alex doesn't want to come home, he won't.

Instead of grounding Alex (a harsh response), the father could say, "All right, Alex, I won't give you the money to go to the Bon Jovi concert next week." Or perhaps, "I will not give you the money to buy the new CD by La Toya Jackson."

A loss of reward (not getting a ticket or a CD) is not harsh rule setting that Alex can break. The father's action also enforces a reasonable curfew.

Once Helen and her parents settle upon realistic and obtainable goals, the parents must be consistent. If they have agreed to withhold a reward, they must consistently withhold it every time Helen fails. If they need to change a goal or consequences, they must do so the *next* time, not now, and only after discussion with Helen.

If the parents change the goals and consequences as they go along, the kids will see no consistency, and they will have no idea what to expect. They won't know if parents will enforce their action. They will feel insecure—one of the reasons kids turn to drugs in the first place.

Teach Your Children to Cope with Disappointments

Everyone feels let down at some time in life. When children are running a race and they lose (that is, they didn't come out number one in the race), it doesn't help for Dad to say, "It's all right. It really doesn't matter."

It *does* matter to the children involved. It matters to those who did not win.

Mom can say, "You really tried your best."

Dad can say, "You probably feel bad about that race. When I was a kid and our team didn't win, I felt terrible."

Parents can also discuss the issues that relate to whether it's important to run fast or to practice more. But don't discount their disappointment.

Teach Them Balance

These are the major areas in life: social; job and vocation; health; spiritual life; and relationships. You can spend too much time on relationships or the job or any of the other areas.

I know one father who is so caught up in physical fitness that he seems obsessively preoccupied with his exercise programs and diet. He does much of his exercising at home, but he might as well be on another continent. Many of us know people who spend too much time with church activities. They see needs and feel they can do them. But they fail to see that they're putting church involvements ahead of their families.

A balanced life is comprised of five priorities or commitments: social, health, spiritual, vocational, and relational.

If I give 80 percent of my life to one commitment, such as my job, it's out of balance—that is 80 percent of my life is in conflict. I will feel insecure and misperceive what's going on, and I will confront an array of struggles. Such problems won't develop if I am balanced.

You may be saying, "If I spend equal time on each area of my life, and there are twenty-four hours, I have to give almost five hours to each area." No, that isn't what I mean. I am talking about equal commitment and priority.

Other than sleeping and working, where do I spend my time? Do I spend it reading alone, which would be decreasing my relationships? Do I spend time with my family because I enjoy them? Do I spend time with my friends?

For example, let's say my job takes up eight hours a day. I can give more time to my work than I do to any of the other areas, but it doesn't have to be the number-one priority in my life. I have to give my work eight hours a day because that's what it takes to make a living.

However, when the job is done and I've completed my eight hours, perhaps my relationships become more important. Or maybe it's my physical health, so I say, "I need to run now." I move away from relationships and make health a priority that day. Although my priority to health may be ahead of my job, I may give it only fifteen to twenty minutes a day, four days a week.

We make the mistake of trying to categorize or balance by the number of hours we devote to something. *Keeping balance in life has little to do with committed time;* it has to do with *free time.* It's a matter of internal priorities. It's what we give ourselves to.

Let's go back to health. Let's say I spend fifteen minutes four times a week—that's one hour a week—to take care of my health. No matter how busy my schedule, no matter how hectic things get with the family, I find a way to squeeze in my quarter hour. That determination to put in my fifteen minutes shows to me and to my family that my physical health rates a high priority. My family time may require four hours a day to achieve the same level of priority.

Families need to work together so that each member learns to achieve a balanced life.

Designate and Develop a Support Person or Couple Outside the Present Family System

When it's feasible, if both parents are in the same household, you need to enlist another couple whom you respect. This couple will help you deal with your expectations and value systems.

You are not asking them to approve of your children or their behavior. You are asking them to help you deal with realistic expectations. All too often family systems are based on what was done by or expected of the previous generation. Such expectations may not be realistic. Outsiders can be more objective and point out this situation.

If you are a single parent, or if stepchildren are involved, find at least one support person who can look objectively and realistically at your family. Family systems can become dysfunctional. Getting outsiders involved is essential to developing a proper perspective of what is going on.

Have Fun Together

This firm principle says that you must have fun together if your children's lives are important to you.

Nothing is more significant than having children say to you, "We had fun together today. We had a neat time. Let's do it again."

Parents who enjoy being with their children and like doing things they enjoy tell the children without words, "You are important. Your needs count, too."

Having fun together may mean that you will have to learn how to participate in activities different from your usual ones. Often parents have a hobby, and they ask their kids to participate in it. If golf is your favorite sport and hobby and you invite your children, but they don't want to play, ask, "Okay, what would you like to do?" When they hear that question and know you mean it, they will also know they are important to you.

Adolescents figure out quickly who accepts them, who likes them conditionally, and who loves them unconditionally. If you fail your children here, your kids will still get the support and acceptance they need—but they'll get those things from the drug culture!

As a caring parent, you must learn to demonstrate love and acceptance. It's not up to your children to decide to change to get those needs met from you. All children have the right to be accepted and loved by their parents.

Remember this: If you don't give your children unconditional love and acceptance, they'll find them elsewhere. It's definitely to your advantage to communicate and demonstrate that you love them unconditionally and accept them. If you can learn to do that, your children have a chance. If you can't, the drug culture and drug addiction are going to overwhelm and take advantage of them. Your children end up winning the war. You end up losing your children.

But it doesn't have to be a sad ending. You can make a difference in your children's lives.

Ten Commandments to Prevent Addiction

If you follow these ten commonsense commandments, your children are less likely to use drugs than children who are allowed to grow up on their own and have to figure out for themselves such things as how to relate to others and learn problem-solving skills from society.

1. *Spend time with your children.*
2. *Share your failures and successes with your children.*
3. *Allow your children to make mistakes, and don't be disappointed with them when they do.*
4. *Accept your children as they are.*
5. *Love your children regardless of their actions.*
6. *Stand up for your values, and share them.*
7. *Submit yourself to God—not your church or your friends or your own preferences.*

8. *Once your children know the rules, follow through on the agreed-upon consequences.*
9. *Look for teachable moments with your children.*
10. *Show your children your love for your God, your spouse, and them—daily.*

Kids Don't Want to Use Drugs
Dr. Joel C. Robertson

Chapter

20

Freeing Our Children from Alcoholism

In my book, Hand-Me-Down Genes and Second-Hand Emotions, *I present extensive research about the genetic predisposition and environmental factors that underlie depression, suicide, obesity, and alcoholism. Many times our society, even the Christian society, is prone to look upon drug use or alcohol abuse as the problems of "everyone else" or "someone else's" children. But statistics show that more than likely the problems are in your church, and, possibly, in your home.*

This chapter on freeing our children from alcoholism is essential because alcohol is one of the most accessible drugs, and accessibility plays an important part in any drug abuse. Alcoholism has reached epidemic proportions in our generation and in our children's generation, with more than fifty million practicing alcoholics in America today. It is important to know there is a difference between alcohol abuse and alcohol addiction. "Abusive drinking may, indeed, be almost entirely a result of problems in character or environment, learned behavior, or destructive patterns of thought. That does not seem to be true for alcoholism. Alcoholics are trapped in an escalating and devastating progression and may not have any idea that they are addicted to alcohol." *The signs of addiction are preoccupation with a substance, increasing tolerance of the substance, withdrawal symptoms if the substance is removed, a debilitation of normal physiological and social functioning.*

Alcoholism runs in families. (At least 31 percent of alcoholics have a parent who was an alcoholic. . . . for most, the parent was the father.) A certain set of inherited personality traits in childhood may indicate predisposition to alcoholism later in life. Dr. Cloninger, in his continuing research on the heritability of alcoholism, . . . reports that children possessing the following traits by age ten are more likely to have developed an addiction to alcohol by age twenty-eight. The more intense the traits by age ten, the more likely alcoholism will have developed by age twenty-eight. High-risk traits are as follows:

1. The children need to be constantly occupied and challenged and are easily bored.
2. The children compulsively avoid any negative consequences of their actions.
3. The children crave immediate and external gratification as a reward for their efforts.

(Dr. Cloninger's suggestion to parents whose children may have these traits is that they create an environment full of challenge but also highly structured, and that they surround children with plenty of personal support, security, and strict, consistent discipline.)

"If we or someone we love has a drinking problem, there is only one reason not to get help. It is the killer disease of denial. We must see the reality of the problem and break through all of the emotional reasons to deny what is there. We must accept our responsibility to deal with the situation before us. God will provide us with the strength we need. The pain of change is never greater than the pain of looking back with regret on lost opportunities and wasted lives when it is too late to do anything."

Stephen Arterburn
Hand-Me-Down Genes and Second-Hand Emotions

Over the past few years there has been a decline in the use of drugs by most segments of the adolescent population. That would appear to be good news to most parents. Sadly, it is not. With the decline in drug use in general has come a dramatic increase in alcohol use in particular. What is even more alarming is that kids do not drink like they used to. Today they drink to get drunk. They see no reason to drink if it is not to completely obliterate reality with a drunken stupor. Not all of these kids are alcoholics and not all of them will be, but every one needs help before there is loss of life or limb. Now more than ever parents need to reach out to their children and help them stop drinking before the devastation gets even greater.

The following tips offer the greatest hope available of initiating change within our children and our families. Each one relates to either preventing the problem or arresting it once it has started.

STARTING WITH OURSELVES

Our attitudes and actions play an important role in children's decisions to use or abstain. If we are heavily involved with the drugs of our culture, we have no credibility when asking children to avoid the drugs of their culture. If we reach for a Valium or a drink when under pressure, we must change our behavior to set the best example.

If there is evidence of alcoholism and heavy drinking on the family tree, we have to provide special education to our children. They need to know that a high tolerance may be a family trait that has led to many others being involved in alcoholic drinking. We must do our best to see that heavy drinking is *not* portrayed as a virtue.

Additionally, we must examine our behaviors of excess. If we are overweight or workaholics, we send a message that excess is okay. We may need to obtain professional help for our obsessions and compulsions before we can adequately help our children with a compulsive drinking problem.

BUILDING A SOLID FOUNDATION

Every treatment center, even the most secular, discusses the vital role God plays in the recovery process. Alcoholics and drug addicts can't recover without turning their lives over to the One who created them. If God is so vital in treatment and recovery, surely God is essential in the prevention of a problem. Raising our children to know that God deeply cares about every decision they make is the strongest foundation we can provide.

In our society we see drugs and alcohol filling a values vacuum.

Some kids are raised not knowing the difference between right and wrong. It is no wonder we have lost this generation to rampant immorality. We as parents must do what the government cannot. We must provide a foundation of morality that is a guiding force in each thing our children do. If we do not have a strong faith in God, there is little chance our children will. The strongest motivator of kids who remain abstinent is their belief that God created them and their bodies and their desire to do only those things that bring honor to God.

BUILDING SOLID CHILDREN

Children who search for meaning, acceptance, and self-worth easily succumb to peer pressure. We need to provide these things for our children so they won't seek them from someone else. If parents are negative, critical, and rejecting of children, they will turn to peers who will be positive and affirming, or they will do anything to get praise from those potentially negative peers. It is only natural that rejected children will drink if that brings a feeling of acceptance.

To avoid this setup, we must encourage our children. We can emphasize the positive, catch them in the act of doing something right, and let them know we are deeply concerned about each decision made and hope that each decision will produce positive results. We can let them know that our love is not conditional, that whatever they choose, we will be there for them with love and acceptance.

TEACHING OUR CHILDREN

Too often parents leave education to someone else. When that happens, it is usually someone from the street. We must start early teaching children the dangers of drugs and alcohol. We must teach, starting at kindergarten, the harmful effects of alcohol and the harmful effects of all irresponsible behavior.

If we wait until they are in junior high, we are probably waiting too late. Children will make the decision of whether or not to drink between the ages of ten and twelve. I think those ages are getting younger every year. That is why we must start early, so when the children choose, it will be an informed decision.

MOTIVATING OUR CHILDREN

Short-term rewards and short-term restrictions are the best prevention tools. Children will not refuse to drink because of the possibility of cirrhosis of the liver. But tell them that if they're caught drinking, the driver's license and the car go away, and we'll tell them something that will have an impact. Being able to tell a peer that parents will take the license away provides an excuse to say no. It is not the cure-all to the problem, but as one component, it provides an added edge.

IDENTIFYING ABUSE EARLY

Any parent actively involved in a child's life will be able to notice evidence of drinking. Experiencing radical mood swings, hanging around friends who drink, smoking tobacco (ten times greater chance of smoking marijuana), defending the use of drinking by others, and possessing strange paraphernalia are all symptoms of drug use and drinking. If children are doing some sort of drug, there is a 99 percent chance of drinking, heavy drinking, to go along with it. The natural thing is to deny the problem exists and try to cover it up. But we must break through the denial, see the reality, and act on it. The sooner we see it, the sooner we can stop it. Remember, we must be involved with our children to see the need for change.

INTERVENING EARLY

Intervention is the process of confronting children with consequences of alcohol use, abuse, and alcoholism. We may come to a point where we have to make a serious decision. In extreme circumstances, we may have to decide whether we will continue to act as suppliers or ask them to move out unless they are willing to obtain treatment. It is very tough to confront, but the alternative is to enable the problem to grow and addiction to set in deeper. The fear of sending children out into the streets must be overcome by the fear of being primary enablers of a growing addiction that will eventually kill them.

Adolescents often progress through the stages of alcoholism more rapidly than adults. While adults take from five to ten years or longer to manifest the full range of the disease, adolescents may take as few as one or two years. Teenagers often use other substances along with alcohol. This may accelerate the progression of alcoholism.

Hand-Me-Down Genes and Second-Hand Emotions
Stephen Arterburn

FINDING THE BEST TREATMENT RESOURCE

Wars are won because people seek wise counsel. Treatment involves waging war on addiction. But not all resources are equal. A center with a strong reputation for quality care, a place that goes out of the way to help us face the problem, is the place for us. A quality center will always involve the family in treatment. Each family member must make adjustments if treatment is to be effective. The least we can do is call and discuss what kind of program is available.

At New Life Treatment Centers we have a journey program for kids. It is a fifty-two-day wilderness program that enables kids to experience the consequences of the behavior immediately. This program is staffed with a field team and therapists. If children do not wear dry socks to bed, they experience cold feet that night. If they do not prepare their own food, they do not eat. The consequences are immediate and sure. This program has changed lives more intensely than any program I know of.

SUPPORTING RECOVERY

Tremendous barriers to children's recovery are parents who do not support the recovery process. Parents must forgive children for not meeting the expectations of being perfect (or at least wonderful) children. Facing the reality of an addict in the family is hard for many parents to bear. Eventually, children sense the resentment, and they end up in a no-win situation. Feeling the pain of failure, they return to drugs, playing out the feelings of worthlessness perceived from the parents. Parents who have difficulty supporting recovery should seek counseling for themselves.

REACHING OUT

Rather than wonder about our children and drug problems, we should talk to someone experienced in dealing with these problems. We can't afford to hide or deny any longer. If anonymity is important, we can call anonymously. The worst thing we can do is to do nothing. We have the power to change children's lives. The pain may intensify in the short term, but the long-term rewards of healthy children will be worth the price of the pain.

CONCLUSION

There aren't many things worse than parents on a guilt trip. I certainly have not wanted to put parents on one. I hope we will feel the need to accept responsibility to do everything we can to help our children. That means we will have to do the painful thing of helping ourselves first. Too often parents don't help their children because they are too lazy to help themselves. Please accept the challenge of creating a better generation to follow. Accept the challenge to free our children from some of the pain we have had to endure because we did not know the truth.

> Whatever things are true, whatever things are noble, whatever things are just, whatever things are pure, whatever things are lovely, whatever things are of good report, if there is any virtue and if there is anything praiseworthy—meditate on these things.
>
> —Philippians 4:8

Chapter 21

A Conversation with Two Parents

What happens when all the efforts of loving, Christian parents cannot stay a son or daughter from the path of rebellion to abandon his or her parents' faith? I've discussed several reasons why people leave the faith in Why Christian Kids Leave the Faith. *Young people leave their faith, church, and many times their family behind because*

- they have troubling, unanswered questions about their faith.
- their faith isn't working for them.
- other things in life become more important than their faith.
- they never personally owned their own faith.

Is there hope for the return of a prodigal? In an extensive survey, it was determined that 85 percent of faith dropouts return to their parents' religion by the time they reached 24 years old. Yes, there is hope, but there is also much pain. In their own words, here is the story of the parents of a prodigal.

Tom Bisset
Why Christian Kids Leave the Faith

Most parents of prodigals endure their sorrows in painful silence. They pray and trust God. But mostly, they deal with their special problem by not talking about it.

These parents are silent because of the guilt, shame, self-doubt, grief and anger that come with the territory. To bring up the subject with anyone, including family and friends, is to tear off the thin layer of healing that forms each day and to pour salt into the reopened wound.

We who watch from outside this circle of pain are also silent because we understand these feelings instinctively. We're afraid of them. We don't know what to say. We offer brief words of encouragement, a pat on the back and our assurances of prayer and support. These are welcome and right. But for the most part, we too say very little about prodigal children.

The outcome of this uneasy silence is that it prevents parents of prodigals, those brave, weary, anguished souls, from doing the one thing they need to do most: share their burden with others. Going through this most difficult experience alone accomplishes little more than intensifying the emotional trauma of it all.

In the conversation that follows, you will see how one couple endured their own painful silence until at last their willingness to open their hearts and lives to their friends brought help and healing to themselves and to others. The unfortunate part of this story is that these parents lived three years with their sorrow until an event in the life of their prodigal son forced them to decide whether they would continue to remain silent or tell all.

You will also learn how these parents managed to live with a semblance of normalcy during this time, even though they were tormented daily, even hourly, by the total rebellion of their son Sean. And you will learn how God in His mercy and grace brought their son home to them.

Admittedly, this story is one-sided. I have not talked with Sean. Someday I hope to hear what happened from his side of the fence. I have no doubt that at some point and in some unlikely way he heard the tender voice of the Good Shepherd calling him back to the fold. Like multitudes of lost sheep before him, he responded to that loving call and went home to the Father's house.

This is the story of John and Becky and their family, two sons and a daughter. Christian parents now in their middle forties, John and Becky's lives were forever changed by a prodigal son whom they could not control from the time he was twelve years old. During this time, John worked in a parachurch ministry while Becky was employed part time in a secular occupation. Today the family, including Sean, his wife and their baby, live in a large eastern city.

I will let the story speak for itself.

Q. Can you folks sketch in the background of the story for me?

John: Our son was a model child. By the time he was two-and-a-half, he had memorized twenty-six verses of Scripture. He went through various youth programs and typically won awards for being the best student or whatever the goal happened to be. He attended a Christian school and was always a model student.

But when he entered seventh grade, he began to change. The change came when he teamed up with some friends who were interested in other things than school. I think these friends convinced him that sin had more to offer than following the Lord.

Becky: He was physically very mature for his age.

John: Yes, he was bigger than most of the other students. The friends he began to hang around with were also large for their age.

Q. When did you begin to understand that Sean was having problems? What kinds of things started happening?

John: The first indication of trouble was an attitude problem. He didn't want to listen to us. He challenged us. He got into rock music. I remember finding one tape of a group called "The Sex Pistols" which I confiscated. He began to steal things. He was picked up for shoplifting when he was twelve.

Becky: It wasn't that he needed money. He had a paper route and had money in his pocket when he was picked up by the police.

Q: How did you react to these problems and the resistance you were feeling from him?

John: We told him we didn't like what he was doing. I tried corporal punishment at first, but gave up on that. We took away privileges. That slowed him down a little but basically he maintained his belligerence and independence.

By the ninth grade he was beginning to run away from home. He would just disappear for periods of time. Sometimes we would wake up at night and discover that he was gone. One night, when he was fourteen or fifteen, he stayed overnight with a girl and probably became sexually active at that time.

Becky: He would just disappear. That was one of the hardest things. We never knew what to expect next. One minute he was in the house, the next minute he was gone. He would take our car and drive around even though he didn't have a license. One night he went to a friend's house and drank a whole bottle of vodka with Coke. He was so drunk he couldn't do anything.

In the ninth grade we decided to change schools. We sent him to another Christian school which didn't work out. Then in the tenth grade we sent him to a tech school thinking he might be challenged by the change in educational emphasis. He immediately found the worst kids in the school. We learned later that he wasn't even going to classes. He would go in the front door and out the back door with his new friends and go smoke pot. He didn't make it through the semester. He was out of control.

John: He made his getaway at this time. He stole our van and took off with some girlfriends. We called the police and we were able to find out who the girls were. That evening we called our church and asked them to pray for Sean in prayer meeting that night.

Becky: That was the first time we told anyone we were having trouble with Sean. It was just too hard to tell people about it.

John: The next day we were in pretty bad shape. I kept reminding Becky about James 1 where we're told to count it all joy when troubles and testings come. It didn't work very well. We weren't counting anything joy.

That day we got perhaps a half-dozen phone calls from people at church. We were surprised to hear how many other people were having problems like this with their kids. In fact, the pastor's sister had rebelled and had turned her back on the Lord and the church. We never knew it until that day. Those phone calls helped a lot. We felt the comfort of friends and the Lord.

That Saturday night at about 10:30 we got a call from the police saying they had picked Sean up in Florida. He was in jail, charged with grand theft auto and being a fugitive. I didn't know what to do. I was on the phone with the police and others for a couple of hours, trying to figure out whether I should go down there or what.

On top of this, I was supposed to preach the next morning at a church in Philadelphia. My message, which I had already prepared, was on Luke 15 and the Prodigal Son. I remember sitting up there on the platform Sunday morning wondering if I should admit that I had a prodigal. Then I wondered if that would disqualify me from preaching because it would prove that I didn't fulfill 1 Timothy 3 that says a bishop should have his own children under control. I'm sitting up there arguing with myself: Should I do it? Should I not? I knew I wanted to describe what the father felt. So I did it.

What surprised me was that afterwards at the door of the church when I was meeting the congregation, I guess twenty to twenty-five people came to me and said, "I've been through that same thing myself," or "My children are in the same place as your son is right now." Opening my heart increased my opportunity to talk with people about it.

The Lord used that morning in many ways. Later, I was able to talk with a Christian young man who was on trial for attempted murder. He knew about Sean and he was willing to open up and talk to me about himself because he knew about our troubles. He knew we didn't have our act together either. He had never shared anything with anyone before. I see that in many places now. People who are hurting sense they can open up to me.

Q. Were you dialoging with Sean at all during this time? What were you saying to him?

Becky: I was always saying to him, "Sean, when are you going to change? This is so hard on me." I can't describe how I felt. During his rebellion things just got worse and worse. I was talking to a pastor and I said, "I'm ashamed to tell you this, but I wish the Lord would take him. I can't stand the pain anymore."

John: Sometimes he would respond positively to what we said. He would feel bad about what he was doing. But it didn't make much difference for long.

Q. What role did your faith play in your pain? How did it mix in with what you were going through?

Becky (crying): I would be able to deal with it for a while, then it would all come crashing down when Sean would disappear and we didn't know what was happening, whether he was dead or alive. But somehow the Lord got us through. John kept saying, "In everything give thanks." As a mother I can tell you the Lord was good. John helped me so much by constantly reminding me that the Lord is faithful.

God would bring different people into our lives to help us. Once I talked with James Dobson at a banquet. We didn't speak for more than a minute and in that brief moment he encouraged me so much. He said, "I want you to know that you will make it through and that your son will come back to the Lord." I don't know how he could say that. He isn't a prophet, but he said it and it came true.

Q. Did you have feelings of guilt and failure while this was going on?

Becky: Oh yes. You wonder what you did wrong. You think about how you might have done things differently, how you might have changed this or that so that things wouldn't have happened this way.

John: I kept asking myself, "Did I spend enough time with him?" When I looked at it closely, I realized that I spent more time with Sean than my other children. All kinds of questions kept going through my mind. One thing that helped me was the thought that God Himself had prodigal children. Adam and Eve were prodigals.

Q. After you brought Sean back from Florida, did you see any changes in him? Did that experience sober him at all?

John: He was still out of control. He kept running away, sometimes for days. He would steal our money, get the keys to our car and take off. He went to New York once and to a couple of other places. We couldn't handle him. One time he jumped out of the second-story window and ran away.

Becky: It was at this time that my brother offered to take him in. Sean had been through four schools and he was still fifteen years old. We knew we couldn't handle him so we sent him to my brother. He lasted three weeks in school there and after three months my brother sent him back to us.

John: So then we put him into a home for problem kids. It wasn't openly Christian but it was run by Christians. We were really impressed with the place. After a month or so we went away for a little vacation, to get some rest, and we got a phone call: Sean had run away from the home. When we talked to them they said they wouldn't take him back. They said they couldn't do anything with him. So we had to take him home.

At that time I decided to write a contract between us. I told him he couldn't come back unless he signed it and kept his part: no drinking, drugs, running around. I told him, "This gives me permission to put you out of this house if you break this contract." And he said okay.

Becky: We couldn't go anywhere. I literally stayed home all the time. I home schooled him. I hardly went out of the house for a year.

John: We kicked him out three times that year. That was a pretty rough year. He threatened to commit suicide if we didn't let up on him. Then came a break. One of his best friends, a girl, who was just as rebellious as Sean, gave her life to the Lord. She became a ball of fire for God. She went overseas on a summer missions trip and just completely turned around. Sean didn't know what to do.

One night things got pretty bad. We threatened to put him out and he became extremely frightened. He didn't want to go. He was petrified. We found out that he was into witchcraft and the occult. He was hearing things and seeing things in his room.

We called our pastor who immediately suspected occult activity. He came over and began to question Sean. As it turned out, someone had given our son an occult name and had sworn him to secrecy, saying he would die under a curse if he ever told anyone. It took three hours to get that name out of him. Once he said it, he knew the curse wasn't true. He was so relieved to get out from under that.

One time he got high on LSD at an event specifically for Christian kids. When he came home he was incoherent. We sat up all night reading the Bible to him. It was an interesting time to say the least.

He struggled through school and finally graduated a year late. The night he turned eighteen he was gone. It was about that time he started going with this girl. He was drinking and hanging around with her all the time. He would come to our house late at night to sleep if he came home at all. He never ate with us.

One day Sean and this girl came to our home and told us she was pregnant. My first reaction was to tell them they shouldn't necessarily get married just because she was pregnant. We talked about their options but nothing seemed to come of that conversation.

A couple of months later they came over and said they wanted to get married. At first we weren't sure if we wanted any part of it. Then we decided this was a unique opportunity to show our love to both of them. So we decided to be a part of it and do it up right. We rented a fancy place, had the wedding and put together a beautiful reception. All our relatives came. You can imagine what that was like to have a wedding for your son and his bride who was seven months pregnant.

Things got a little better after that. Sean's wife couldn't understand why we treated them so kindly. We tried to help them in different ways. She started coming to our church and brought Sean and the baby with her. Slowly but surely Sean and I started talking more. One night we were talking and out of the blue Sean said to me, "Dad, I led my wife to the Lord." I was speechless.

I'm not sure exactly what happened to Sean during this time, but somehow he got himself right with God and the same day or the next day led his wife to Christ. He never talked to us about it until after it happened. He still hasn't told us the details.

As I look back now, I realize that the day he got things straightened out with God was *four years to the day* from when he got picked up in Florida and put in jail. I don't know if there is any connection, but that is an amazing fact. From the day he told me about leading his wife to the Lord, things have turned around completely. He has been a total joy to us.

Becky: It's been unbelievable.

John: He comes over to our house now and he's the delight of the place. He and his wife come to our house church one night a week. His wife knows literally nothing about the Bible and she loves to study with us. They're totally interested in spiritual things. The Lord is making up for all the pain in a hurry.

Q. As you look back, what do you think was the wisest thing anyone ever said to you as you were going through that experience? Was there anything in particular that was said that helped you handle the pain and suffering and trauma of it all?

Becky: For me, it was John who kept saying, "In everything give thanks," and, "Count it all joy." In all the tears and pain, which no one really understands until they've been through it, those verses held me up.

I was also helped a lot by a woman who told me that she couldn't guarantee that Sean would come back, but she could guarantee that through it all I would become a stronger person who would someday help others. Then she told me her son had done the same thing and was still away from the Lord. She said it was the first time she had ever told anyone. She really helped me by saying I would live through it. Let me tell you, at that time I wondered if I would. You feel like you're going to die of a broken heart. I can't tell you how hard it was. So many tears, so many nightmares, so many times when you're frightened to death.

John: Some friends really helped me too. One guy in a pastoral ministry sat me down and said, "The same thing happened to us when our son was fifteen. The greatest mistake I made was not telling anyone about it. I just kept it quiet." He encouraged us to share our burden with others.

A lot of people told me they were going to pray for Sean every day. In that church in Philadelphia, where I first went public about

Sean, there were at least twenty-five people who promised me they would pray for him *every* day. That was so encouraging, just knowing that we weren't in this alone.

My parents stood behind us. They were not shocked or negative about the fact that our son—their grandson—was so messed up.

Becky: That was so encouraging.

John: My father said in a kind of quiet way, "Sometimes young men have to go their own way to learn what God wants to teach them." That was surprising for me because he never had any prodigals in his family. I don't know how he knew to handle it that way.

Q. Have you got anything to say to parents of prodigals?

John: I would say there is hope. All kinds of hope. God is at work in your child's life. He can use the strangest things to convict kids, to get into their thinking.

Becky: You've got to let your prodigal children know that you still love them no matter what happens. I think that's the one message that got through to Sean. We were constantly telling him, "We hate what you're doing, but we love you, Sean, and we'll go right on loving you, even though you reject us and the Lord."

John: We wanted him to know that no matter where he went, no matter what he did, he couldn't get away from our love. We were still coming at him with love.

That night the Florida police called me, they asked me if I wanted to talk with him and I said yes. They said, "Here he is," and handed the phone to him. I said, "Sean, I want you to know that I love you and I have forgiven you for what you've done. I want to help you in any way I can."

I didn't feel like saying that, but I knew it was the truth and I just chose to be like the father in Luke 15. Sean's response was negative. He said, "Oh yeah." His response was still negative even when I picked him up at the jail. Despite your child's reactions and your feelings, you choose to do and say what you know is right.

Q. Any final comments?

John: One of these days I'd like to go to that church in Philadelphia where all those people prayed for Sean. I'll have him with me but not tell them. Then I'll have him play, "Jesus Loves Me" on the piano for special music and just before I begin to preach, I'll say, "By the way, before I get into my message this morning, someone here wants to say something." Then Sean would come up and stand in front of that congregation and say, "I'm Sean. I want to thank all of you for praying for me."

PART FOUR

The Broken Family

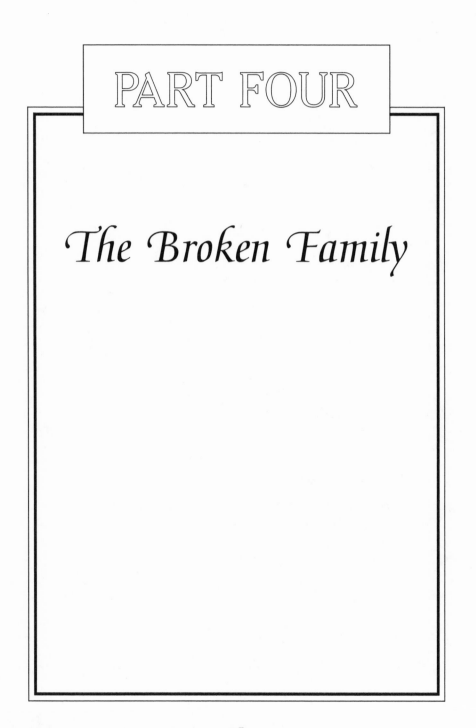

Vital Information

Your child should know the following information by the time he or she is three years old and should be able to give it to an adult in authority in a clear, loud, easily-understood voice:

Full name (first and last names)
Home address (house number, street, and city)
Home telephone number
Mother's name (first and last names)
Father's name (first and last names)
Doctor's name (last name)
Mother's employer (company name)
Father's employer (company name)

Your child should be able to identify these adult authority figures:

- *A police officer*
- *A store clerk*
- *A school-crossing guard*
- *A fire fighter*
- *A doctor*
- *A security guard*

Your child should be able to identify

- *A stop sign*
- *A do-not-enter sign*
- *A danger sign (skull and cross-bones)*

52 Time Savers for ON-THE-GO MOMS
Kate Redd

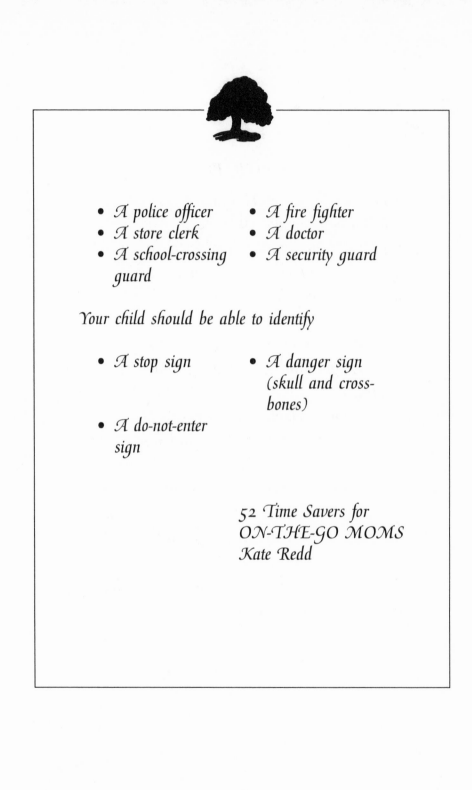

Chapter

22

How Divorce Affects Children

It is possible for you, as a single parent, to help your children survive the trauma of divorce with high self-esteem. A lot of it depends upon the emotional health of your child: Does she feel loved, secure, worthwhile; take responsibility for herself and her actions? And a lot of it depends upon the relationship between the parents: Do you put the needs of the children before your own needs? We all know the scars of divorce will always be with them, but, yes, it is possible for you to actually produce happy, responsible, well-adjusted, fully-functional children.

We open this section on the home that is broken with a chapter from Divorced Kids *to speak for the children. They will tell you the feeling responses they are having as they react to divorce. We then hope to show you how you can respond to meet their needs.*

Laurene Johnson and Georglyn Rosenfeld
Divorced Kids

I was real young. I didn't know what was going on. I knew Dad was missing, but I didn't know why.

Eight-year-old girl

I was very mad at my father and I wanted him to die so I could remember him the way he was before he left us, not what he had turned into.

Nine-year-old boy

My dad didn't leave us. My mom took me while I was sleeping and she left him. I didn't even know about it.

Five-year-old girl

I currently reside with my grandparents. I have lived with them since I was nine. My mom and dad have both divorced three times. I went through the first divorce and my mom's second divorce. My grandparents sheltered me from the other divorces.

Eighteen-year-old boy

If the nuclear family can be likened to a small, quiet pond, its waters unruffled and at peace, then divorce is a large boulder hurled violently into its middle. The shock waves surge across the entire surface, leaving no edge untouched.

Virtually every American's life is touched by divorce . . . from the upper echelons of society to the homeless on the streets. Watching the rich and famous divorce has practically become a spectator sport in America. Like other sporting events, someone wins and someone loses. In divorce, unfortunately, the real losers are the children. Divorce legally severs a marriage, but it also frequently severs the parental relationship, making the children feel that their parents not only divorced each other, but also divorced them.

Although adults experience a significant amount of trauma while going through a divorce, children not only suffer during the process but continue to suffer long after the final papers have been signed. Children of divorce battle fear and humiliation for many years, their perception of themselves drastically altered by the loss of their family. This stigma follows these children throughout their lives, making them feel like "divorced kids." Struggling to find their own way to cope with the trauma, some children strike out with behavior problems while others succumb to cripplingly low self-esteem. In their weakened emotional condition, divorced kids often blame themselves for the divorce.

No one escapes the trauma of a fragmenting family—parents, children, grandparents, and extended family are all affected.

Unfortunately, kids are often the forgotten element in a divorce.

Parents are truly in the driver's seat, with access to friends, divorce recovery groups, support groups, church groups, lawyers, and counselors. Children are all too often left to fend for themselves. To an adult, a marriage—even with children—may be a relatively recent event in life's time line. To children, however, the family unit is all they have ever known. It is their world, containing their earliest and most profound memories. The split in the marriage cracks the deepest foundations of their life, and suddenly everything is unstable. What can they depend on? Can anything be trusted?

VARIETY OF RESPONSES TO DIVORCE

There seem to be as many different reactions to divorce as there are different kinds of children. Nevertheless, most fall into several well-defined categories. And not surprisingly, the feelings children have are similar to the grieving process that adults experience during a tragedy. In addition, they suffer from a devastating loss of self-esteem, a feeling of responsibility for the divorce, and other emotions that are frightening in their intensity.

In this chapter we will attempt to grasp the enormity of this problem, using many actual comments from children of divorce and taking a look at the way children react to divorce in general. First, let's consider a sampling of the most common responses children have to divorce.

Sadness

A four-year-old girl said, "I cry at night when I'm in bed, but my mom never knows."

One twelve-year-old boy wrote, "I wouldn't miss my dad so much if I didn't hear my mom crying so hard every night. It's not fair my dad isn't here to do his job."

"It really hurt," commented a teen. "It was hard for me to accept not being able to live in the same house with both parents."

Many teenagers drew pictures of their feelings, sketching simple broken hearts and sad faces. Several drew dark clouds with a drizzling rain or eyes with tears pouring out. Others drew hearts being torn in two or stabbed.

Even children who welcomed their parents' divorce as an end to bitter fighting and distress still felt upset. "I felt glad," wrote one child, "but it was like losing a good friend too." Another said, "I felt sad at the time but realized later it was best for everyone."

No matter what other reactions children may demonstrate toward their parents' breakup, a deep, pervasive sorrow is always present. Sadness and despair can dominate their lives.

And sometimes children cling to this sadness because letting go of it feels like a betrayal. Children may feel that if they are sad for "long enough," what they had will come back; by giving up the sadness, they are giving up the chance of a happy ending, as well as betraying the object of their loss.

What children need to know is that their sadness is not a "contract" that will bring back their lost parent, home, or family structure. At the same time they need to understand that it's OK to feel sad, and they will ultimately feel happy again.

One of the best things you can do for your children is allow them to express their grief. Prolonged crying and preoccupation with the lost relationship are normal responses. They can actually help the child move through the adjustment period after the divorce. Parents who are trying to deal with their own trauma, however, may find it difficult to deal with a grief-stricken, despairing child who is acting out feelings the parents may be trying to avoid. But children need to be assured that they will not drive their parents away if they act sad or angry. Parents frequently try to hide their own grief from their children, but by expressing it in front of them, they can validate their children's pain.

Doug never saw his father express any grief or sadness over the divorce. He was always told, "Your mother was the cause of all our problems and now the cause has left. We are going through a few adjustments and some hardships, but life goes on." Although Doug felt devastated by his mother's departure, he thought, "Look how strong Dad is. I should be strong too and not feel bad about it." When Doug grew up, however, he found out from his grandparents that his father was actually severely depressed over the divorce and even contemplated suicide. Realizing that his father's stoic attitude had all been a façade, Doug felt totally disillusioned and doubted whether his father had ever been emotionally open and aboveboard with him.

Contrast Doug's father with Jerry, a psychiatrist friend of mine, who was devastated when his wife of twenty years filed for divorce. For more than a month he had frequent crying spells, which usually occurred when he was alone. One weekend when his teenage sons were visiting, they started watching a movie that reminded Jerry of his courtship days with his estranged wife, and he was overcome with sadness. First, tears ran silently down his cheeks, then he started crying, then he sobbed uncontrollably as the memories of twenty years of happiness and love, pain and sorrow came crashing down on him. His sons had never seen their father cry. Nothing they did or said could console him. Unable to handle seeing their father lose control of his emotions, they called their mother and asked her to come pick them up.

At the time, it was a scary experience for the kids, but later they told their father that it validated their own feelings of sadness and helped them realize that it was all right to cry sometimes when they felt like it. After all, if their father, a well-known psychiatrist, cried over the divorce, it must be the mentally healthy thing to do.

It is important for all of us to know that we do not have to be sad all the time or carry our grief around forever. We will always keep our memories. And the sadness for what we have lost will always be available if we need to feel it again.

Feelings of Abandonment and Isolation

A ten-year-old boy described divorce this way: "It makes me feel like my arms and legs aren't attached."

"Daddy left. Will Mommy leave me too? What will happen to me?" an eight-year-old girl wondered.

"Even when your dad is bad," an eight-year-old boy said, "you don't want him to leave because he's still your father."

"I thought it was my fault at first and I thought they hated me. Then they fought about custody and I thought nobody wanted me. The second and third times I was relieved about the divorce and had no negative feelings," wrote one tragic child.

Dr. Ken Magid, a psychologist, and Walt Schreibman, a marriage and family counselor in Evergreen, Colorado, collaborated in 1980 to produce a book called *Divorce Is . . . A Kid's Coloring Book,* which has proved useful to many children of divorce. All the panels contain a boy and his dog. One of them shows the pair in front of the refrigerator. On the door is a note that says, "Be back in a year or two, love Mom."[1] This fear, strongest among younger children, is quite literal. They feel they will be left to fend for themselves—after all, if one parent walked out, what's to keep the other from doing the same? Some recently divorced mothers even report that whenever they come home just five minutes late from work, they find their children hysterical.

The fear of abandonment often manifests itself as loneliness.

Some of the pictures children drew for us describing divorce depict empty rooms with closed doors and windows, empty boxes and squares with nothing in the middle. One student caught the wrenching pain in a picture of a mangled dog lying in the street with tire treads over it and a car speeding away.

Children also feel abandoned when parents begin dating. A triangle of Dad, me, and his girlfriend creates much confusion. A child feels replaced by the girlfriend. Randy, an adolescent, closes the door to his room, listens to the stereo, and cuts off communication with Dad. Dad doesn't understand why Randy has stopped talking to him and says, "He's just a teenager—they're all like that." Randy experiments with new friends and drugs—he medicates himself to escape. Randy doesn't understand his feelings—he just knows he feels empty.

Confusion and Disorientation

Far and away the most common problem for children of divorce is an inability to understand what in the world has just happened to them. In their resourcefulness and intelligence, they arrive at a number of conclusions—many, unfortunately, that are wrong—in an effort to simply find answers and just try to cope.

"I really didn't understand at first," said one teen, looking back on his parents' divorce when he was five, "but as the years went by, I thought it was my fault. It was a very confusing time for me."

A nine-year-old boy remarked, "Divorce is like two lions in a den attacking each other. You know somebody is going to get hurt real bad. All kids can do is sit behind a window and watch it happen."

A group of teenagers were asked to draw pictures of what divorce felt like to them. Many of the pictures contained turbulent, chaotic scribbling—some surrounding a brain, some enveloping a heart. One picture showed an out-of-control car careening toward a tree. One teen drew a giant question mark with arrows, like turn indicators, pointing in opposite directions as if to ask, "What do I do now?"

One boy, who had experienced five separate divorces, confessed, "It was scary the first time and also confusing. The other four times it was almost like old hat."

Children's lives revolve around their family—it is all they have ever known. To hear from Mom and Dad that they will no longer be living together is more than a child can comprehend.

Feeling Torn between Parents

This is perhaps the most wrenching feeling kids have to struggle with, and many times parents do nothing but add fuel to the fire.

Pictures describing these feelings included many houses that were being cut in two . . . some even split by lightning. One picture showed four children trying to push the house back together while it was splitting down the middle. A teenager drew a circle with a jagged line down the middle, dark on one side and light on the other. Another drew two houses separated by a giant mountain range. One boy drew a picture of Washington and Arizona with himself in the middle and arrows pointing toward each state. Several kids drew pictures of themselves with outstretched arms, Mom pulling on one arm and Dad pulling on the other.

"Dad couldn't really be as bad as Mom says he is," said a nine-year-old girl.

"My mom cries when I tell her about Dad's girlfriend," one twelve year old said. "I can't help it if I like her just a little. She's nice to me."

"I looked at my dad's check from his boss. He makes lots of money and tells my mom he's poor. He's a liar. I can't tell him though, because he might not like me," a sixteen-year-old girl told me.

Frequently, innocent remarks by the child become a battlefield for the parents. Kids soon learn that they can no longer share things with Mom or Dad. They just get bounced back and forth between vengeful parents, and everyone ends up in trouble.

A group of children, parents, lawyers, and psychologists were asked to name events they believed had a significant negative impact on children in broken families. Some of the events included:

- When one parent tells the child that he or she doesn't like that child spending time with the other parent.
- When one parent asks the child questions about the other parent's private life.
- When one parent says bad things about the other.
- When relatives say bad things to the child about his or her parents.
- When one parent tells the child not to tell some things to the other parent.

· When parents talk to children about which parent they want to live with.

· When parents make children feel like they have to choose between Dad and Mom.

A nine-year-old boy summed it all up when he said, "I don't care who I live with, I love you both. Please don't make me choose—just tell me."

Forced Adulthood

A surprising number of the high-school students who put their feelings into artwork drew pictures of nuclear holocausts or cataclysmic storms—the end of life as they knew it. No matter how old or young the child, divorce usually means experiencing grief and emotional trauma much sooner than most children would have. Several students drew pictures depicting death or self-destruction. One drew a tree with a hangman's noose on it.

Divorce shatters the safe, secure fantasy world of childhood, and children are suddenly forced to replace a parent's missing marriage partner and provide companionship for someone much older than themselves.

"I hate it when my mom asks me how she looks," said one fifteen-year-old boy. "I don't like being put in that situation. I wish my dad were here to do it."

"My mom doesn't think she's a good cook. I don't want her to feel bad." Then this eight-year-old girl added, "So I tell her it's good, just like Daddy used to do."

The need of a parent for an adult partner is revealed in this boy's comment: "My mom acts sexy in front of me. She just needs a boyfriend."

Divorce also imposes worries and responsibilities on children that are far beyond their age.

"I always check the liquor cabinet in the morning after they've been fighting. I measure it," a little girl tragically confessed.

One insightful nine-year-old boy said, "I hate my mom's boyfriend but I don't tell her. After all, she'll be alone someday when I'm gone, so I pretend I like him."

Arnold Lopez, a therapist in Phoenix who specializes in codependency, says he sees major lifelong issues develop when a child is placed in a parental role after a divorce. He works with adolescents who have been placed in the surrogate parent or spouse role and later find themselves in need of therapy.

Some children of divorce, after reaching adulthood, say that they feel like they've missed out on childhood by being forced to become their parents' missing partners, which is frequently regarded as a form of codependency. The most common form is when a child becomes a "surrogate spouse."

Codependency

According to Lopez, when the other spouse is missing, the single parent's needs for love, belonging, and support are going unmet. This is why single parents tend to become emotionally enmeshed with their children. They discuss the details of financial burdens, daily exhaustion, loneliness, disappointments, anger, and depression with one of their kids. And the children begin to see themselves in the role of a spouse. Moms in particular tend to treat a son as a spouse, a confidant. And the sons, therefore, wind up feeling as if they have to fill Mom's needs. What a burden!

One boy said, "Dad left so suddenly that if I don't take care of Mom, she might leave me too." In later years children resent this role, and sometimes the resentment turns into anger in adolescence.

When discussing his resentments, a fourteen-year-old boy said, "I think I felt I had to be strong for my mom and my little sister. I had to be strong to help them through it . . . even though I was only five at the time."

All too frequently single parents have limited financial resources and a weak support system of family and friends who are willing, able, and close enough to help. When this situation exists, the parent may end up not only being a poor parent, but may set up a situation in which the child ends up parenting the parent.

While discussing divorce, a nineteen-year-old woman remarked, "In one day I could be a college student, my mother's therapist, my dad's escort, and my brother's mother. Small wonder I was a little ditzy that year."[2]

When I share my concern about this with my clients, they bend their heads in shame. Most parents innocently put their child into this role. They don't knowingly set their children up for enmeshment. It's just that their needs are not being met and they don't see other choices at the time.

In his book *Bradshaw on the Family,* author John Bradshaw says,

> Codependence is the most common family illness because it is what happens to anyone in any kind of a dysfunctional family. In every dysfunctional family, there is a primary stressor. This could be . . . Mom's hysterical control of everyone's feelings; Dad or Mom's physical or verbal violence . . . the divorce. . . . Anyone who becomes controlling in the family to the point of being experienced as a threat by the other members initiates the dysfunction. This member becomes the primary stressor. Each member of the family adapts to this stress in an attempt to control it. Each becomes outerdirected and lives adapting to the stressor for as long as the stress exists. Each becomes codependent on the stressor. . . . My belief is that codependence is the disease of today. All addictions are rooted in codependence, and codependence is a symptom of abandonment. We are codependent because we've lost our selves. . . . Codependence is at bottom a spiritual problem. It is spiritual bankruptcy.[3]

HOW LONG DOES THE EMOTIONAL TRAUMA LAST?

In our workshops, when we asked children the question, "How long did it take you to get over the divorce?" some of the responses were:

"You never get over it" (fifteen years after the divorce).

"I still haven't" (twelve years afterward).

"It's been four years but I'm still not over it."

"It took me about seven years to really get over it."

"I wasn't upset at the time. About a year later it hit and it lasted for a year."

"A few years of therapy."

"About five years."

"Four years."

"I still haven't gotten over it yet. I may never."

"I'm still trying to get over it" (ten years later).

The only "positive" response was:

"Not long. My dad was pretty mean."

Clearly, the injuries sustained in a divorce heal slowly, if ever. One of the great tragedies of divorce is that children come to assume that the whole world operates like their own. They don't feel that "living happily ever after" is possible. Many feel destined to repeat their parents' mistakes. One college student said, "To me, getting married is like walking over a mine field; you know it's going to explode . . . you just don't know when!"[4]

A young boy said, "I'll probably grow up and get married and have babies, and then I'll get a divorce. Everybody does." When asked what advice he'd like to give to his mom and dad, the eighteen-year-old previously mentioned who had survived five divorces said, "Don't get married."

Divorce may be the most catastrophic event the average American family is forced to overcome. For children, it violently interrupts the already tempestuous process of growing up. The adults involved in a pitched battle with each other have the advantage of a certain amount of control, even if it's minuscule, but children have none. This leaves the child in a wait-and-see posture, forever trying to adapt to changing conditions, torn between two parents, resiliency tested to the utmost.

Children are survivors by nature. With proper guidance their survival skills can be greatly improved. Parents are in the best position to help their children, but unfortunately, they are usually consumed by their own struggle for survival. Extended family, friends, and other interested adults can work with the parents to provide emotional support and minimize long-term damage to the child's mental health after a divorce.

Chapter

23

Long-term Effects

Now that you have seen the short-term responses to divorce, let's look ahead to the long-term effects that have been documented. What we have found is that many times our own relationship or life problems are a result of having grown up as children whose needs were not met during the divorce of their own parents. I hope this chapter from my book Innocent Victims *will do three things: (1) inform you that there* can *be long-term negative effects of divorce if your children's emotional needs are not met during this traumatic time; (2) give you insight into your own life or relationship problems if you, indeed, were a child of divorce whose needs were not met; and (3) show you that there can actually be tremendous* positive *long-term effects as told to us by the children themselves.*

It is with these positive outcomes in mind that I hope this chapter will help you in your efforts toward understanding your children's fears and meeting their needs before, during, and after divorce.

Thomas Whiteman, Ph.D.
Innocent Victims

Cindy had problems with relationships. She had broken off four serious relationships in two years. For each of them, the pattern was always the same. Cindy would grow closer and closer, until some type of commitment was implied. Then the difficulties would start. The specifics were different each time, but the basic issues were always the same.

According to Cindy her partners couldn't be trusted. She would usually set up some type of trap in which she tested the character of her boyfriend. Sometimes it would be checking his whereabouts, even though he told her where he would be. Other times it was merely whether or not he could account for all of his time when asked, "What did you do today?"

I can remember one specific incident in which Cindy was incensed by her boyfriend's so-called dishonesty. It seems that when she asked him about what he had done that day, he failed to mention that he had called for her earlier in the evening and talked briefly with her roommate. Cindy suspected there was something going on between her boyfriend and her roommate. Needless to say, the relationship did not last much longer, and her friendship with her roommate became strained.

Cindy, who is now twenty-five years old, came to counseling to find out why she seemed to have such poor luck in relationships. As you may have guessed, Cindy came from a divorced home. She first found out about her father's indiscretions when she was about ten. Her parents did not divorce right away. But Cindy remembers a series of incidents in which her mom and dad had prolonged arguments over suspected affairs. Finally, when she was seventeen, Cindy's parents got a divorce. Her mom continually reminded Cindy about how devious her father had been, even though Cindy still saw him a couple of times a month.

This is a typical example of a divorce that has long-term implications. Today we are seeing more and more published about the long-term effects of divorce on individuals. In one of the more popular works on this topic, Judith Wallerstein followed children of divorce for over fifteen years. This book, along with many followup articles and books, seems to have given adult children of divorce the courage to come forward to tell their stories. The comments I hear repeatedly proclaim, "I'm glad someone is finally recognizing and documenting the long-term effects of divorce. It has had a significant impact on our lives and relationships." One of the greatest proofs of the impact of divorce on children is found in talking to the adult children of divorce. Every one of them, and I've talked to hundreds, has said, "I'll do everything I can to be sure I don't do this to my children." The sad truth is that children of divorce actually have a slightly higher divorce rate than the rest of the population.

Many of you probably are aware of the interest there is today in establishing support groups for those who have come from dysfunctional families. These groups most frequently include adult children of alcoholics and adult children of incest and abuse. Now, more and more, we are seeing adult children of divorce as one of the recovery groups offered. At our own counseling center, just the mention of such a support group will usually initiate many calls of interest from potential participants. As one caller recently stated, "I know my parents' divorce, and the following years of conflict, have affected me. I'm not quite sure of all of the ways I have been affected, but I'd love to talk to others who have been through the same type of experience. Just to know that I'm not alone in my feelings, and to gain insights into some of my behaviors, would be well worth it."

LONG-TERM VS. SHORT-TERM

Many ask, "What's the difference between the long-term and short-term effects of divorce?" The short-term effects of divorce are those reactions that begin immediately and can last for a number of years. The short-term reactions don't truly end, however, until the children reach a point of acceptance. Beyond that, even though the children have worked through the grieving of their family breakup, they still have to work through the implications of growing up in a divorced home. These effects, which are what I consider to be the long-term effects, have been documented to last up to fifteen years for some adult children of divorce, and may very well be permanent.

Approximately one-third of the children of divorce never seem to recover from the trauma of their parents' divorce. These are the most seriously affected children of divorce, both from long-term and short-term perspectives. They don't learn healthy coping skills, and lead lifestyles of continuing struggle, depression, anxiety, and difficulty in personal relationships.

The children, who after a period of adjustment are able to cope and move on with their lives, are the ones who seem normal to those around them, and outwardly lead healthy, productive lives. Yet as is true for all of us, what they grew up with has a considerable effect on how they live today. Divorce shapes our personalities and characters, our interests and ambitions. These are the subtle changes that will be covered as part of the long-term effects of divorce on children. As might be expected, this will only be a general review of the research, and a personal review of my experiences. Time and practicality do not permit us to discuss all of the subtle changes that take place with your children. You can observe your own children to see how they change over time.

FACTORS TO BE CONSIDERED

There are a number of factors to be considered when discussing how your children will be affected over the long-term. Let me list a few of the more prevalent factors.

1. The age of the children at the time of the divorce. Researchers estimate that most of your children's personalities are developed by the age of six. This does not mean that there are not changes in their personalities beyond that time. But for those children who witness their parents' breakup at a young age, there is a greater chance that it will have an effect on their personalities. The longer your children live in a single-parent or blended family, the more likely it will affect their personalities. This does not have to be a frightening statistic for those of you who have young children. It merely indicates that you will need to be even more aware of how your children might be affected, and how you might compensate for specific losses. (Note: Most of the long-term studies have started with young children, and may be overly pessimistic, since these children spent a greater percentage of their lives in a divorced home.)

2. The number of changes that result from the divorce. The impact of divorce on children is greater when you add other life stresses; such as, a new home, new church, new school district, new spouse, or a blended family. All of these changes are difficult for children if they are experienced on separate occasions. But when they are heaped together, as is the case in many divorcing situations, the effects can be lifelong. Wherever possible, parents need to control the number of changes, and perhaps even make sacrifices in order to limit the upheaval.

3. The adjustment of the custodial parent in the divorce. While both parents are of key importance in the eventual well-being of the children, research indicates that the emotional health of the custodial parent (usually the mother) is the greatest predictor of the children's adjustment. It is important for both parents to get the help they need to resolve the anger, resentment, depression, or anxiety produced by the divorce, and to conclude any ongoing squabbles as quickly as possible. Almost all couples have conflicts during the early stages of divorce. But if these continue beyond the actual divorce settlement, they can suck all participants back into the black hole of divorce for more years than necessary.

Since children spend the majority of their time with the custodial parent, it stands to reason that parental attitudes will influence the children. No matter what the circumstances, the custodial parent must choose an attitude of reconciliation and desire to do whatever is best for the children, particularly when it comes to the relationship with the other parent.

4. The relationship with the noncustodial parent. For years we have tended to ignore the importance of the relationship with the noncustodial parent (usually the father). Within the past five years or so, we have seen more and more research which points to the fact that the noncustodial parent is also a key player. (Any of you dads out there who might be thinking about giving up on seeing your kids, please read this carefully.) Many researchers have found that a primary reason for negative effects of divorce on children was the loss of contact with one of the parents (usually Dad). And in fact, the traditional visiting pattern of every other weekend has created feelings of intense dissatisfaction, and at times reactive depression, among children, particularly the boys.

Consistent and frequent contact with the noncustodial parent has repeatedly been shown to correlate with well-adjusted children, unless the father is abusive or otherwise unfit. The relationship with the father has been linked to identity with the opposite sex for girls, ambition and motivation for boys, and overall adjustment and relating abilities for both sexes. The well-being of the children has proven to be particularly strong when the custodial mother encourages the continued contact with the father.

If the relationship with the noncustodial parent is so important, then why is it that two years after the divorce only 40 percent of the fathers have regular visits with their children? This is an alarming and discouraging statistic. Having talked with many fathers who have actually given up, I have found that many become discouraged by their lack of input into the children's upbringing. To put it in their words, "Why should I continue paying, when I have little or no say in how the kids are raised?" Perhaps this is the reason joint custody arrangements have a much higher rate of involvement by the father. When they have more input, they are more likely to stay involved, and more likely to have well-adjusted children.

5. Other specific traumas that accompany the divorce. Research for this is incomplete, but it is my opinion that most of the children of divorce, who fall into the one-third of the children who never seem to recover from their parents' divorce, are also the ones who have to contend with other specific traumas. These traumas include, but are not limited to, physical abuse, sexual abuse, severe emotional or verbal abuse, extended neglect, drug or alcohol addiction of one or both parents, and mental illness in the family. For children exposed to these factors, the long-term implications of divorce are greatly complicated by preexisting conditions and compounding problems. This is a general statement, and does not imply that if your children were exposed to one or more of these traumas, they will end up basket cases. This factor merely indicates a greater propensity for long-term problems. You need to be particularly sensitive to your children's needs and emotional condition.

LONG-TERM EFFECTS

Jason, who is now twenty-four, first came to see me when he was fifteen. At that time he had long hair, torn jeans, a punk rock T-shirt, and a sour look on his face. Jason was actually referred to me by his mom because he had decided to drop out of school. Mom said she would permit it (she had actually lost her ability to control him anymore), if he would go to three counseling sessions.

Imagine yourself in my position. Here's this big, fifteen-year-old punk rocker, sitting in your office glaring at you, as if to say, "I dare you to get through to me." He didn't want to be there. To be honest, I didn't either.

Every topic I brought up was met with silence, or an occasional "yep" or "nope" (mostly "nope's"). Finally, I decided that my only option, and one that I found would work as a last resort, was to talk to him about something *he* was interested in: music. This was not just any music, but punk rock and heavy metal music. Now you have to understand that I detest punk rock or heavy metal music. In fact, I encourage parents to keep it away from their kids. But in this case, I felt it was my only way to connect.

Suddenly Jason became very animated and talkative. He was surprised that I had shown any interest. (Believe me, it was tough.) He later stated that no other adult had ever taken an interest in this topic, which he valued so highly. Adults usually walked away or told him to turn it off (both the music *and* his conversation about it).

Jason went on to tell me about all the groups, the most popular songs, and the meaning behind the lyrics. (As if anyone could actually hear the words.) He offered to bring his tape player next week, along with a couple of his favorite cassettes.

I survived his tapes, and Jason continued coming, by choice, for the next six months. During that time, he began to tell me about his family, his life, and his feelings. Jason was a very angry young man. His father had left home when he was about nine years old, and moved in with another woman. The new woman had children of her own, and was soon pregnant with Jason's soon-to-be stepbrother. As Dad gradually broke off contact (and financial support) with his former family, Jason felt more rejection, resentment, and anger with each passing week. He eventually withdrew emotionally, and isolated himself in his room with his music and an occasional marijuana cigarette.

Jason's main problems were his attitude and motivation. He had given up on life by the time he was fourteen. After all, life wasn't fair, and he couldn't even sustain his father's love. This inability to have a sense of control over his own life is what researchers have identified in approximately 45 percent of the male children of divorce. As in the case of Jason, even though children might be intelligent and talented, there is a higher tendency for them to show little direction or purpose in their lives. Dropping out of school, not attending college, and being under-employed, are all typical signs of the phenomenon in the male, and a few female, children of divorce.

Today, Jason works in a factory. He finished high school, but went no farther even though he has above-average intelligence. He is socially active, and appears to be much happier today. His hair is still long. (Fortunately his taste in music has moderated.) To his friends, he's an average twenty-four-year-old. But to me, he is a victim—a victim of divorce.

Alice is a twenty-six-year-old adult child of divorce. Her parents split up when she was seven, and she gradually lost contact with her father over two years. Her mother remarried within that time, but was divorced again when Alice was eleven. Since the second divorce, Alice's mom has had a series of boyfriends, but has not remarried again. After a period of adjustment, Alice seemed to come through both divorces fairly well. It was in adolescence, as is often the case, that Alice began to have difficulties. She found her first "true love" when she was fifteen, and was convinced they would eventually marry. When that relationship broke off, Alice found, in disgust, that she could get boys to do what she wanted them to do, by offering sexual favors. Throughout high school and college, Alice was sexually active, but soon after graduation had a born-again experience, which led her into a new lifestyle. She became active in a church singles group. She now believes in a heavenly Father who loves her unconditionally, and for whom she does not have to perform. The new difficulty is in finding that same kind of loving relationship with an eligible man.

Whether it is the reaction found in Alice, or the lack of trust found in the example of Cindy (from the first paragraph of this chapter), researchers have documented this sleeper effect in approximately 66 percent of the female children of divorce. This has been called the sleeper effect because it has been found quite often in the women who previously seemed to be well-adjusted. It occurs most frequently at a time when women are making important decisions about their lives.

The common element in the sleeper effect, as seen in the two women presented, is fear—fear of commitment and fear of betrayal. For some, fear may lead to the coping strategy of control. "If I can learn how to control men, or the situation, then I won't be hurt again." I have seen this numerous times in the lives of adult children. While I can empathize with the feeling, I'm afraid the coping strategy can become quite unhealthy.

The common element in the sleeper effect is fear of commitment and fear of betrayal.

Another coping strategy, which is used by both men and women who are experiencing the sleeper effect, is avoidance. This can include avoidance of significant relating, or avoidance of any kind of commitment. Usually patterns of relating are developed, and unconsciously repeated, in which relationships only reach a certain level, and then self-destruct before they can go any farther. This pattern includes inability to communicate deeper than at a superficial level, inability to make a commitment, or inability to allow the relationship to grow beyond a friendship or a purely sexual basis.

The combination of control and avoidance can reach extreme levels among some adult children of divorce. This is evidenced by a disproportionately high number of both men and women who experience divorce in their own marriages in spite of vows that it will never happen to them. Without insights into their pattern of relating, and help in overcoming these patterns, these difficulties may follow them the rest of their lives.

Another documented long-term effect of divorce is commonly referred to as the over-burdened child. When marriage breaks down, it is common for both the mother and the father to do less parenting. The mother, or custodial parent, is often worn down by the changes in her life, including moves, job changes, new financial responsibilities, and parenting alone. The father, who feels guilt because he is not there for the kids as often as he'd like to be, just wants their times together to be enjoyable. So both parents tend to discipline less, spend less time with their children, and may be less sensitive to their needs. The adults may be struggling with their own reactions and recovery.

Another documented long-term effect of divorce is commonly referred to as the overburdened child.

Unable to meet the challenges of parenting as a single, many parents begin to lean on their children to pick up the slack. We have all heard of latchkey kids, who must take major responsibilities in the home well before they might otherwise have to. The children's roles may include housekeeping, babysitting younger siblings, being the man of the house, becoming the mediator in arguments, being the parent's confidant, and emotionally supporting the parent. While most of this is not intentional, it is a fact of life in many single-parent families.

The first time I met Sarah, I was amazed at what a responsible, mature child she was for fourteen. Her mother was proud of the fact that teachers and friends all commented on what a good job she had done in raising her daughter alone. The present problem was that they were having difficulty in choosing a college. Even though it was early, Sarah was anticipating a problem when it came time for her to go away to school. You see, she wanted to go *away* for school. Her mother, on the other hand, felt that Sarah should stay home so that she, the mother, could continue to provide the proper guidance to her daughter.

Since college was still three years away, and Sarah was so responsible, I was confused about why this was such a burning issue. As we explored it further, it became evident that the reason Mom needed Sarah to stay home was to help Mom keep it together. Sarah was the one who kept the house in order. She prepared the evening meal, and then would ask Mom all about her day when she got home from work. Sarah did not go out socially during the week or on weekends because she didn't want her mother to be alone at home. If Mom did happen to go out on a date, which was rare, she always solicited Sarah's approval on her choices. "Sarah," she stated, "is a better judge of character than I am."

Whenever she returned from a date, she would confide in Sarah everything that she liked and didn't like about the person so that together they could come to some conclusion about any future relationship. The truth of the matter was that if Sarah went away to college, neither one of them were sure if Mom could make it on her own. What a role reversal!

Sarah is a good example of the overburdened child. The children's role becomes instrumental in maintaining the well-being of the parent. The divorce itself may not be to blame, but serves as a catalyst for bringing to the surface specific emotional difficulties. As with any type of dysfunctional family, the results of the children taking on so much responsibility, so early in life, is generally twofold. Either they react by going the opposite way and become overly irresponsible, or they continue in their overburdened lifestyle, and are at risk for perfectionism, nervous breakdowns, overly nurturing relationships, overparenting, and losing their own identity for a cause or another person.

Preliminary studies have indicated that approximately 15 percent of the children of divorce are overburdened. Some have indicated that this estimate is low, since there are increased responsibilities for nearly all children of divorce. A balance of responsibility may be the key, since increased responsibility can actually have a positive impact on some children of divorce.

Whether it is diminished motivation, the sleeper effect, or the overburdened child syndrome, it is hard only to point the finger of blame at divorce. Divorce never stands alone as a one-time traumatic event, but is experienced on a continuum. It begins with an unhappy marriage, goes through custody battles and court hearings, and begins ripple effects that continue for generations. The biblical phrase from Exodus 20 comes to mind: "The sins of the father are passed on through many generations."

Do these predictions of gloom mean that parents should stay together for the sake of the children? Even though research is troubling and needs to be taken seriously, there are situations in which continuing the marriage would be intolerable. And to stay in a bad situation for the sake of the children would probably only lead to more resentment, and possible violence. Even though there are few comparisons of children from divorced homes with children from unhappy homes, all known evidence points to the fact that children exposed to parental fighting and the pressure of relentless conflict turn out to be less well-adjusted than many of the children of divorce.

If divorce is undertaken with thoughts of the children's well-being, and if both parents work together for the sake of the kids, then there are many things that can be done to lessen the negative effects on your children.

Let's look at some of the long-term positive effects.

POSITIVE EFFECTS

It is hard to believe that anything positive could be written about divorce. In fact, in reviewing the literature, it is hard to find anything positive. But if divorce is viewed as a handicap to children, then we must consider the fact that many have taken the worst kinds of handicaps and used them to build character and personality, which become the envy of others. So it is with the long-term effects of divorce. I have met many teenagers and adults who have shared how their parents' divorce has built strength of character and moral resolve. Janet, a sixteen-year-old child of divorce, explained it to me.

"It is hard to find anything positive that can come out of the divorce when it first happens. My dad left when I was only six, and I know that it has been difficult on me and my mom. But I wouldn't trade anything for the things that I have learned from growing up in a single-parent household. I was forced to face the realities of life at an early age. Realities, like "life isn't always easy," and "there are no guarantees," have forced me to be more practical and down to earth. I know that I'm a more responsible and resourceful person today because of the divorce."

Crystal, a seventeen-year-old, echoed similar comments.

"It definitely takes time, but you do work through it. When you do, you find that you are much more understanding than other kids your age. You have to be! After all, you've seen your parents fail. Everything they taught you has fallen apart. So now you have to decide how you're going to live your life, what you are going to believe in. For me, it has strengthened my faith in God. He is real in my life, not because my parents told me so, but because I needed a source of strength that was greater than I could be on my own, and greater than my parents. I've found that now, so I consider myself luckier than other kids my age."

David, a seventeen-year-old survivor of two divorces, put it this way.

"Something about the divorce forces you to view life differently. It somehow puts every other life event in perspective. When your mom or dad leaves you at age five, and your whole world seems to fall apart, then you are better able to deal with other crises as they occur. You're wiser and more mature. I see some of my classmates who fall apart over bad grades or college entrance exams or something. You even read about kids who kill themselves because they didn't get accepted to the college of their choice. Things like that upset me, but I know it's not the end of the world. I always figure I've survived my parents' divorce, I can certainly get through this one."

Here are some of the common themes I have heard when interviewing children of divorce about the positive aspects of divorce. First and foremost, they all indicate that there is nothing good about it in the beginning. But over a long period of time, some of the following characteristics may emerge.

1. Children of divorce are more sensitive to other kids and their problems. When you've been through a significant life trauma and have felt like no one else understands your pain, you are bound to be more compassionate toward other people and the difficulties they might face. I have seen this firsthand whenever our counseling center sponsors a program to help others who are struggling with some life crisis. Adult and teenage children of divorce are among the first to volunteer to help.

Julie, a sixteen-year-old girl, expressed it like this: "Having cried myself to sleep many times, I realize the depth of pain a little girl can feel. Now, when I have the opportunity to share my healing with someone else who is struggling, I feel like it was almost worth it. A lot of my friends come to me with their problems, because they say I understand them and can really relate. You know, I think they're

THE CAPABLE KID TEST

Step 1. Think of a situation that your child or teen has experienced as stressful. It could be sharing a room or the car with a sibling, having a favorite weekend or a date cancelled, flunking a test, not making the school team or play, being shunned by friends, being embarrassed, etc.

Step 2. Think about how he reacted and whether that is his typical response to that type of situation.

Step 3. Choose one statement from the following list that best describes his reactions. (Select the first one that strikes you as appropriate.)

1. *"Things like this always happen to me."*
2. *He becomes unreasonably quiet and walks away.*
3. *"I never get what I want. Nobody cares about me." (May become belligerent and verbally abusive.)*
4. *"Boy, am I disappointed." Then a few seconds later, "Oh, well, maybe it will work out the next time."*
5. *"This is no surprise. I was expecting something cruddy like this to happen." (Then becomes withdrawn and preoccupied.)*

6. "That sure makes me angry, but I didn't know. Is there anything I can do about it now?"
7. "That is not fair. It's just not fair!" (And proceeds to have a child's or adolescent's temper tantrum.)
8. Doesn't visibly react, but just withdraws. He won't talk about it and tends to isolate himself.

Step 4. Now, find the description of your teen or child as indicated below. (Remember, the description you select should be his typical way of responding.) This will clarify for you the level of ability your child or teen has to handle stress.

#4 or #6—Either of these responses indicate a capable person. He handles stress well. This person will express his disappointment or anger and then quickly figure out what to do about it. He will be disappointed rather than greatly upset and it will last for only a few minutes.

#1, #2, or #7—This is a slightly vulnerable child or teen. He has upset reactions, but they don't last long. He soon calms down, becomes less preoccupied with himself, and begins to make statements about how he can handle the problem. He could *learn some new ways of coping so he wouldn't be so reactive.*

#3, #5, or #8—This person is seriously vulnerable. His response usually lasts more than twenty-four hours, and symptoms of being vulnerable are evident in his life.

Antoinette Saunders and Bonnie Remsberg,
The Stress-Proof Child
New York: New American Library (1984) pp. 31–32
Adapted for Helping Your Kids Handle Stress
H. Norman Wright

right. But it's taken a long time for me to get to the point where I can help anyone."

2. Children of divorce tend to be more mature and responsible than their peers. Even though this maturity comes from the school of hard knocks, many of the children of divorce that I have spoken with seem to have a wisdom beyond their years. This comes from having to grapple with issues that other kids don't have to face until they are much older—issues like loyalty, betrayal, adultery, child support, court hearings, and rejection. Although you would probably prefer to have your children avoid these issues, they do help children move from concrete to abstract reasoning.

One teenage boy put it this way: "I used to just think about me and my needs. Now I'm more concerned about my little brother. I've tried to support him through this mess, because I know how much I hurt when I was his age. I sometimes just take him fishing, or something, so we can get away and talk. We cry together, laugh together. We're closer now than ever."

Since your children inevitably take on more responsibilities, either they fight the changes, or eventually become more responsible people. They stop blaming, or looking to others for the solution to their problems, and realize that they've got to take responsibility for their own futures. Many people don't learn this until they are adults. But the pressure cooker of divorce has a way of maturing children more quickly than might otherwise be expected.

Margie, a seventeen-year-old, said, "Before the divorce, my life was fairly secure. Everything was taken care of as far as my schooling, my welfare, and even my future. Then, when everything fell apart, I learned that the world wasn't secure at all. While in high school I had to work, take care of my brothers and sisters, cook and clean. I feel like I got a taste of motherhood. I'm leaving for college soon, and I know that I'm going to have to work my way through. But I know I'll value my education more, and not take things for granted as much. After all, it's my education and my future."

This increased level of responsibility may include the children's moral development. Children of divorce are faced with their parents' moral failures—lies, manipulations, maybe even cheating and stealing. Obviously, this forces children to think more about what they believe and how they are going to live their lives. It is no longer enough to believe something because "my mother told me so."

After a sometimes rebellious transition, children of divorce settle down to a belief system that is based on what they have concluded about life, rather than what their parents have taught them. Even though this may be a scary thought to parents, it is actually a more mature and enduring belief system. Nancy explained it the following way.

"All my life my parents taught me right and wrong. Then I saw my mom and dad break just about every one of their own rules. It forced me to really examine what was truth. Today, I have a strong faith in God, which helps me in every area of my life."

3. Children of divorce are better able to put life experiences into proper perspective. "When you've been through some of the worst things at age eight that can happen in life," John said, "everything else that comes your way seems so much easier. You've survived divorce, and now you're determined that nothing else is going to get you down again. I still have difficult times, but I always go back to my parents' divorce and compare it to that. Then I know I'm going to be just fine."

Growing up in a storybook life many times leaves us with the expectation that we are going to "live happily ever after." It can be a real shock when we discover that the fairy tale is not true. I have seen adults come apart because they were not prepared for the realities of life, realities that children of divorce learn much earlier. Even though we would rather shield our kids from such difficulties, they have a way of teaching lessons that last a lifetime.

4. Children of divorce are very motivated to succeed in marriage. Having experienced firsthand the effects of divorce, children usually are determined that it won't happen to them. Even deeper than this determination is the realization that you can't take certain things for granted, such as someone's love.

"If my divorce helps to keep my daughter from having to go through the same thing someday, then it was worth it!"

Having grown up in a happy, secure home environment, it wasn't until after college when I learned that the world isn't always a fair place and that bad things *do* happen to good people. This was a difficult lesson, which many of us learned after stumbling into relationships with people whom we thought were trustworthy and good. Children of divorce learn at a very young age that good people (their parents) still hurt them, and perhaps can't be trusted. When looking for a mate, they tend to be much more cautious.

Children of divorce (especially women) tend to delay marriage because of their fear of betrayal. This may be healthy, if we consider that they may avoid a future divorce by not marrying the first man they fall in love with. In fact, there is some preliminary evidence in Judith Wallerstein's longitudinal study which suggests that even though children of divorce are afraid of commitment, they eventually settle into relationships that last. She says, "I'm predicting that after a lot of trial and error, after a lot of getting hurt, a significant number of children of divorce will find a relationship that will stick."

When I interviewed teenagers of divorce for this book, I asked the question, "How do you think your future will be affected, particularly your getting married?" Every one of them responded that they would be more cautious about whom they chose to marry. This usually included a list of qualities that they would need to see. One teen put it this way: "I don't mean to be picky, but I am certain I want to know someone for a long time before I marry them. I want to be sure they're not going to change later on. I want someone who is kind and compassionate. But most important, I want someone who has a strong faith in God and knows the meaning of commitment."

One parent summed this point up best: "If my divorce helps to keep my daughter from having to go through the same thing someday, then it was worth it!"

Chapter

24

Your Hidden Hungers Along the Way

The trauma of a breaking up of a family, either through death of a mate or divorce, has brought you face to face with raising your children by yourself. I know the pain can be deep and intense; the confusion can be overwhelming. I have been along this path many times before, first by myself, then with hundreds of single parents. I hope you will trust me when I say you need to take care of yourself first. You must always remember that it is important for you to take care of your needs also so that you are in optimal physical, emotional, and spiritual health to take care of your children's needs.

Just like the airlines instruct you in case of an emergency to put the oxygen mask first on your face, then on your child's—it's the same thing in this emergency. You must take care of yourself first. It is by knowing yourself and taking care of your needs that you will be able to know your children and meet their needs.

In this chapter from my book Parenting Solo, *I want to help you learn how to deal with the severe emotions that attack you at this time: shock, fear, denial, anger, guilt. You can survive them and grow through them to become a more whole person because of and in spite of your trauma.*

Dr. Emil Authelet
Parenting Solo

You have some pretty heavy emotions to deal with, so before diving into this chapter I want you to take a good, deep breath. It may take a little while for your feelings to allow you to surface for another one. May I suggest you pull out the following promise, which God gave to Israel during a troubled time:

> Do not cling to the events of the past, or dwell on what happened long ago. Watch for the *new thing* I am going to do. It is happening already—you can see it now! (Isaiah 43:18,19)

Every time negative emotions threaten to hold you under, return to this promise and claim it as your own. The Lord is doing a new thing in your life and, according to Philippians 1:6, He *will* complete it.

THE DEATH OF A MATE

You knew throughout the years of your marriage you had some deep emotional needs. Like many others, though, you buried them under an avalanche of activities: keeping a home, relating to a husband, raising three children who came along within the first ten years, and being busy in the church. You knew that someday you would have to get serious about those inner needs, but at the time things seemed to be in balance. At least you were keeping your head above water for the most part. Then it happened.

The police officer at the door tried his best to soften the blow but there was no way around it. Your mate had been in a terrible accident, and he was pronounced dead at the scene. Your whole world suddenly caved in. You, "Mrs. Dependent," as you perceived yourself, were suddenly faced with widowhood, single parenting and being alone, which meant a zillion problems you never expected to have to face at thirty-two years of age. The emotional needs you had packed away suddenly burst forth and came tumbling down on you with all the force of a house collapsing around your ears.

A DIVORCE

Or . . .

You knew things had not been going well in your marriage the past three years, but his work and your involvement with the family, house, job, church, and other activities kept the two of you from talking much about it. During this time your emotional needs had been put on hold as you tried to keep the relationship going. Then it happened.

He wanted out of the marriage, and your world turned upside down. You weren't sure how you would get through it, and the needs you tried to ignore before hadn't gone away. They had been hidden and now what had been a little hill grew to become a mountain. You were in trouble and you knew it. Suddenly you felt something you hadn't experienced since you were a little girl—you were weak, shaken, confused—and *scared.*

EMOTIONAL NEEDS

All of us have emotional needs, and to deny we have them is to court disaster. When you deny an emotion or repress it, you bury it alive. It continues to grow and fester, and it poisons your entire system. (*Repression* occurs when a strong, usually negative, emotion is subconsciously blocked from the conscious mind because the pain is so intense the person cannot accept it. It is still present in the subconscious, though, and very much alive.) What I want you to do right now is assess your needs so some realistic plan of action can be worked out to meet them. Coming through the death of one's spouse or through a divorce takes an emotional toll on everyone involved. Even if you wanted the divorce, sought and pushed for it, you still have an emotional upheaval to deal with.

A TIME FOR REFLECTION

Take a moment and reflect on this question: *What am I feeling right now about the divorce, (or death of my mate), being a single parent or being me?* Get in touch with the feelings that are there. For example, if you have gone through a divorce, you may be feeling scared about where everything will end up, fearful of being a single parent, dependent on others due to a feeling of powerlessness, and angry that it all has come to this. You may feel very unchristian toward your Ex, or like begging for things to be put back together somehow. You have a kaleidoscope of constantly changing feelings, with some that show up more often than others. All these feelings tell you something important about yourself. They reveal your emotional needs. The greater the need, the more complex and intense the feelings. You are struggling for emotional survival.

Here's another question: *What has all this done to me?* The initial shock of sensing your life is about to end is a natural one. But you have gotten through it this far—do you still feel the same way? Or has it lessened? If your emotional needs have not been met in the past, you may still feel life is over for you. Like the prodigal son in the far country, you have been brought to yourself. It *should* put you in touch with what is going on inside you, what your resources are, how well you are able to cope, and how much you can rely on the Lord to see you through. But if the emotional needs are too deep through neglect or a lack of self-awareness, all your needs have been compounded. (See Luke 15:11–32, especially verse 17.)

Another question to consider is: *Where am I now?* You may be stuck in the denial stage even though the death or divorce took place long ago. If you were divorced a year ago and are still wearing your wedding rings, or if your mate died a couple of years ago and you are still saying "we" and "us," you probably are stuck in denial. Your emotional needs have not allowed you to move through this stage toward recovery and adjustment. How does one recover? Each of us takes a private journey into this jungle; however, God's grace is all-sufficient for every need, including this one (2 Cor. 12:7–10), and if it is allowed to work in us, we can travel *through* the tangles to a meaningful resolution.

WHAT DO OTHERS THINK?

One question we all have asked is: *How do others see me? What do they think of me?* If you are widow or widower, they may have a lot of sympathy, understanding and genuine concern. On the other hand, it may seem like some people you thought you understood have gone crazy. Your very close friend suddenly drops you without any real reason. She just is no longer available. Maybe she is insecure in her own marriage and fears you will steal her husband. If you're divorced, maybe she senses a loyalty to both you and your Ex so is staying away from both, not wanting to take sides.

Other people may move toward you because they want to get out of their own marriages and are envious of your new situation.

In addition, unfortunately, in most every congregation someone will come along and tell you he will do "anything" to help you, but he doesn't mean fix your car, stay with the children, or do the laundry so you can have a Saturday at the park.

You need to realize you cannot control how others see you, or what they think of you, or if they mentally consign all divorced persons to the local leper colony. What matters is how *you* see you—what *you* think of you. If your perception of yourself is within the boundaries of reality and you work at a healthy emotional balance, the Lord will lead you through this with a solid sense of growth and maturing.

If you are too concerned about how others see you, you may isolate yourself from the people who truly care about you. If you need the approval of all those around you, you will be in real trouble because divorce is not easy for everyone to handle. In some circles it is still the "unpardonable sin." In others it is acceptable only if you are the "innocent partner." By giving others the power to tell you whether or not you are worth loving and accepting, you give away something that belongs only to the Lord of your life. Better take it back from them, surrender it to Him and believe what He tells you about you.

HANDLING YOUR ANGER

Now let me ask you: *How do you feel about having to go through all of this?* With the death of a mate your other feelings may be accompanied by anger. You loved him and miss him terribly, but you are also angry.

Normal Anger

You need to know that this anger is natural and normal. You had plans, dreams and needs. With him gone, the plans and dreams are gone too, and the needs are worse than before. More than that, he went before you did. He died on you. That wasn't part of the "unwritten agreement" you had when you married. Now you have to deal with all these enormous emotions, especially the negative, conflicting ones, and he is not there to talk them out with. You *can* love someone and be angry with him at the same time. You know that. Deal with that anger as a natural feeling—but do deal with it.

Or you have gone through a divorce and are angry. She walked out on you, left you with a pile of bills and two children to care for along with a whole sack of emotions to sort out. What I want to ask you is: What is the real emotion hiding beneath your anger? Is it guilt because you were not a better husband or more attentive to her needs or a better listener? Is it fear that others will see you as a failure, think less of you, question your lovability since she didn't want to stay married to you? Is it hurt because all your dreams have been shattered, your pride stabbed, your ego cut? Maybe it's jealousy over her freedom to walk away from all the responsibility and carve out another life for herself. Or frustration when you think of two children to raise and how you will answer their questions—"Daddy, why did Mommy go away? Did Mommy stop loving you?"

To hide all these things under a blanket of anger is to keep yourself from facing the truth. Maybe you really feel the anger toward yourself, not her. We meet angry people often who never have been able to face the pain inside them, and the anger oozes out of them into every potential relationship. They have never forgiven themselves so they go around continually cursing their Ex. They frustrate the grace of God in their lives. Can you be honest enough about your anger to allow the Spirit of Truth to deal with it?

Anger and Sin

Anger is neither right nor wrong. What you *do* with it is right or wrong. Paul states in Ephesians 4:26, "If you become angry, do not let your anger lead you into sin, and do not stay angry all day." Verse 27 goes on to add, "Don't give the devil a chance."

Look for the deeper thing, the emotion that is crippling your recovery. If you get locked into your anger and never get beneath it, you can spend the rest of your life nursing it and sharing it with others.

Your "normal" anger can "lead you into sin" if you continue to vent that anger. You can sin by dumping it all over another person, threatening your relationship. You can sin by swallowing it, making yourself sick. Anger is a signal that something else is wrong. Your emotional system has been thrown out of balance.

Dangerous Anger

I remember well the woman who told me she would not forgive her Ex because to do so would get him off the hook. The doctor called me in to counsel with her because he was losing her and saw no medical reason. She was dying following a surgery that was not that critical. What was killing her, literally and figuratively, was her spirit of revenge and her bitter desire to keep her Ex on the hook. (I'm not sure what that hook is. Maybe it's a cross.)

She needed to realize that her Ex was off building a new life for himself and she was the one on her own hook. She was contaminating her relationships with her children, and she was killing herself.

The children continued to relate to their father, but she embittered herself to where she couldn't even stand to be alone with herself. The day she decided to let him off the hook was the day she was free to be healed—physically, emotionally and spiritually, and every other way as well. When the Lord heals, He heals totally!

Fear, anger, and guilt can get so mixed up you don't really know which is which. You act angry because you don't want anyone (not even yourself) to know you are afraid. Or, you feel guilty over your lack of meeting another's need so you cover it up with anger. You may be feeling angry toward another person when, if you examined it, you would discover you really are afraid that person will reject you. Yet your anger keeps that person at arm's length. See how confusing it can be? Whenever you experience anger in a relationship, especially a significant one, always ask yourself: *What is beneath it? What am I trying to hide that I would rather not face?*

ANOTHER QUESTION

What will it take to lift you up again? Your are in a pit because of your divorce. What will you have to do to get out of this pit? What will you have to allow the Lord to do in your life? One thing is certain. You can't stay here. You owe the Lord more than this, and you owe your children and family more. You owe yourself more. How can you make the adjustments that will allow Him to change you? Now, at least, your focus is on the sky above rather than on the bottom of the pit, worrying whether it will hold you or allow you to sink deeper.

With that change of focus you notice something you hadn't seen before in your despair. The Lord has carved neat little notches in the side of the pit, going all the way to the top. With your desire and with His strength you're going to start climbing out. This pit is no place for a child of His love to be living in. You're on your way!

I find 2 Timothy 1:7 a real help at this point: "For God hath not given us the spirit of fear; but of power, and of love, and of a sound mind"(KJV).

Fear here means those inner fears we create to keep us from having to face life or other people. (Normal fear is a reaction from an obvious threat. Pathological fear is a fear of rejection based on self-rejection.) *Power* is strength, the ability to cope. It is the power to live as He has called you to live, to face and overcome the difficulty. *Love* is the ability both to care for others and to allow yourself to be cared for. *Sound mind* means right thinking that leads to proper self-control and self-discipline. Memorize this verse along with its meaning and keep it on hand for quick use.

THIS WAY UP

You have already begun the climb out—you have looked up and you have seen God's blue sky. You feel the warmth of His smile beckoning you to come. The first thing you need to do is what Paul admonishes when you are about to run a race: Jettison the excess baggage (Heb. 12:1–3). By that I mean, take a good look at your emotional past and get rid of the garbage that is weighing you down.

The climb isn't an easy one and you don't need any hindrances. You need to feel good about being you. Spend time with people who truly love you and allow yourself to feel their love and warmth. The church is to be a mutual affirmation society. If you don't find love and warmth in yours, look for one where you can. Whatever you do, don't let yourself sit in a "judgment corner" while others hack away at you because you've been divorced. Let the Lord deal with them. Find yourself a "love seat" among His true saints and let them love you. You are on your way up, into His joy for you. He's the one inviting you out of the pit, so keep climbing, no matter what.

FACING FACTS

The next step is to come to grips with your stuff in the marriage that didn't work out. This is hard and will take a lot of prayerful insight, but it needs to be done. I know I'm asking you to lance a boil and it hurts like sin, but if you don't, the pus will remain inside and the infection will spread. Claim the Lord's full grace. Take the scalpel of the Spirit and carefully peel back the affected areas. Ask Him to expose the core by pointing out to you where you were wrong, where you failed, where you need to ask forgiveness, where you need to make amends. Don't load your stuff on your Ex and don't allow his or her stuff to get dumped on you. Assess the full relationship and your part in it honestly. No marriage breakup is the fault of just one. It is a shared responsibility.

If you are getting a divorce or have been through it, stand in front of the mirror, look yourself squarely in the eye, and say this to yourself: "I am divorced. This is a fact. My marriage is over. For whatever reasons, it did not work out. I am willing to accept the full blame for my part in its breakup. I have asked for forgiveness and I am learning to forgive myself. I know God has forgiven me. I know He loves me. I am on my journey out of the pit I have been in. I cannot do it alone but He is with me. Together we will make it."

If you lost your husband in death, go back and see what the relationship was like during the years of the marriage and see if there was anything you need to own up to. Your healing will be retarded if you fail to own your part of the relationship. All need to do this, but when a death has terminated the relationship you sometimes end up with a whole lot to face all at once. If your relationship was not doing too well at the time of his death, or if you have had deep struggles throughout the marriage, you may be in real trouble right now. You may have more emotions rattling around in you than you can possibly handle alone. *Get help!*

In both cases, divorce or the death of a mate, how well you relate to your children will be determined by how well you handle your part of the problems in your relationship with your spouse. Your children don't need you putting your stuff on them, either, through discipline or holding back from them because you fear they may discover your inadequacies. It is time to face your hidden hungers, resolve them, and move on up to the next step.

FORGIVENESS AND FORGIVING

One of our deeper struggles centers in the need for both forgiveness and to be forgiving. No element is more intrinsic to our spiritual well-being. You have made as honest an assessment as you could. You have allowed the Holy Spirit to show you your part in all of it. It has not been easy, and the picture that emerged may not be one you want to frame and hang in the living room. You know now, though, that you were a good mate, if less than perfect. You have examined that imperfectness and are ready to deal with it. You can flog yourself with it, wear it around your neck like an albatross, or deny it.

Or you can *deal with it in an effective, productive manner, possible only because of the cross of Christ.* You can forgive yourself, thus releasing it to Him and allowing Him to nail it to His cross on your behalf. To forgive yourself is to first *own your imperfectness* (it is yours alone)—and to *fully acknowledge your part* in the problems. Then you must *turn it all over* to the One who died for you.

Why keep yourself on the hook when God doesn't keep you there? Why condemn yourself when He does not condemn you? Only forgiveness can free you to live differently. It alone is the key to change. In John 8, Jesus said to the woman, "Go and sin no more," but only after He had forgiven her. You will change after you have accepted His forgiveness and have forgiven yourself (John 8:1–11). You will be freed to become forgiving of all others, no matter what (Matt. 6:12; 18:21–35).

Now you need to forgive your Ex. I want you to let him or her off the hook for whatever was done to you, *no matter what,* even though he may have cheated on you and abused you and the children. Your emotional health is at stake.

Forgiving doesn't mean not fighting for custody if it is needed. It doesn't mean not demanding child support payments on time. It doesn't mean not standing up for your needs. What it does mean is dealing with the past so it can *be* past. It means clearing the relationship of any balance of unmet needs so you can live again. It means giving Jesus any spirit of revenge. It means being free to recover, to grow, to rebuild, and it means having your present unshackled from the spirit of bitterness. Whatever that person owes you, it is nothing compared to what you owed God. And He forgave you *all!*

It may be helpful to write your Ex a letter, sharing your feelings, hurts, disappointments and regrets. You may want to write several and tear them up. But, in time, write one that expresses what is deep inside you. If you can't bring yourself to write anything else, just say, "I forgive you." Let it go. The time has come for healing, and the price of healing is the granting of forgiveness.

I do not say "forgive" as though it were easy or even simple. It may be the hardest step you have to face. Forgiveness is a process much like an oyster goes through when it forms a pearl around an irritant of quartz. Day after day the oyster secretes a milky substance that gradually covers the sharp edges until at last the pain diminishes.

As you go through your process day after day, you will eventually come to where it is easier. The beauty of the final result causes you to forget the pain, and it is a prize which, as God's child, you may one day lay at His feet. In the process of creating that priceless gift for Him, something wonderful also happens to you. It is not by accident that the apostle John pictures the entrance to glory as having gates of pearl.

Forgiveness involves more than forgiving seventy-times-seven sins, or the same person seventy-times-seven times. Every time the offense pops into your consciousness, you need to apply another layer of that milky substance, God's grace. When you relive that experience in your dreams, you need to apply God's grace to it all over again with your first waking moment. You never forget, but you do not have to be forever locked into the icy grip of your memories. Forgiveness frees you from their power. That is the good news of the gospel.

GOD'S PERCEPTION OF YOU

Your major emotional Source is the One who dares to call you His own. It is essential, as noted before, that you understand His perceptions of you. He knows you as you truly are. When you do see His vision of you, *accept it as your own.* Match your feelings to that perception; begin to feel the feelings that grow out of it; then emotionally you will be made whole.

When you finally can believe God's view of you as His child, it also frees you to become what you are designed to be. Through this you learn to love and be loved. There's no better passage for you to examine in regard to this than 1 John 4:7–21. God is love. When you plug into that source, His love flows first to you, then through you to others. Your emotional stability is in direct measure to the ability you have to love and be loved.

Your deep need is to be loving, yet the person with acute, unmet emotional needs is not able to love. Look around in the church where you worship. How many people do you see who are emotionally unable to love or be loved? Most of the people around you are content to stay as they are. What they do is up to them. If you want your emotional needs met, though, you will have to do something more than just sit there and be one of the bunch. You will have to be assertive in seeking sources, helps, information and nourishment that will meet your need in good measure. What you accomplish is up to you and the Spirit's working in your life. There are excellent resources available to you today. Some are listed at the end of this book. Ask your pastor if you can borrow a commentary on 1 John and explore in depth the meaning of 4:7–21. Its truths are profound.

THREE TASKS OF THE SELF

There are three tasks for the self to accomplish as a whole, mature Christian person. The *first* is to *discover who you are and to know fully whose you are.* Without knowledge of your true self you will be dealing with a "me" you do not understand. If you can't understand you, how can you ever understand another? (*True self,* as used in

Scripture and psychology, refers to that person you are in reality, not the one disguised with layers of defenses whom you share with others in safe ways. It is the person God knows.)

The *second* task is *to enhance the self.* You have discovered who you are so you can know yourself; now you need to become, by His grace, the best you that you can become. You have spiritual gifts but you need to enhance them. You have a personality but it needs to be enhanced. You need to grow toward completion as 1 John 4 points out. God gave you life but your enhancement, what you do with it, is your gift to Him in response.

Then comes the *third* and final task, the task that marks true maturity and emotional balance. You are to *give the self away* in love, service, ministry, caring, helping, and whatever He calls you to do. You are learning to spend and be spent for others.

NOT LEVELING OFF

There is no plateau of growth you may achieve that is worth leveling off at. You may be head and shoulders above all those around you, but that plane is easy to reach. Just settle in among a bunch of "spiritual pygmies," and you can look like a giant.

But put the overlay of Christ's full stature against your life. Now who's the "spiritual pygmy"? You are to grow up into Him and this growth is what your children need to see in you. As long as you continue to grow, you will be what they need you to be. Leveling off would rob you, it would rob them, and it certainly would rob Him. So continually re-evaluate your needs, resources and growth to make sure you are moving along well in the emotional and spiritual process of maturing.

REFLECTING ON THE SPIRITUAL

You will not mature emotionally without maturing spiritually, nor will you mature spiritually without maturing emotionally. You cannot separate the two. You will never find a spiritual giant in an immature personality because the emotional limits the spiritual. John says, "Perfect [mature] love drives out fear" (1 John 4:18 NIV). Love has to do with maturity—fear has to do with immaturity. Both are spiritual, but both involve the emotional as well.

As you mature and become stronger in your relationship with the Lord, what happens in your relationship with your children? Do you become more understanding and patient? Is it easier to listen and give of yourself to them? As you move closer to Him, you move closer to them, don't you? At the same time you also feel better about being you—you have moved closer to your true self. You can tell how you are doing emotionally and spiritually by how you relate to Him, to them, and to yourself.

You may find the following prayer helpful:

"Lord, there are times when the emotional struggle all but overwhelms me. Did it ever seem that way for You? The Word tells me You were tempted in all points such as I am, but at times it is hard to imagine You ever felt like I do. I need to know my feelings are not strange to You and that, even though I may not understand them, You do. Then I can trust You to interpret them to me and to lead me through them to where You want me to be. Help me find answers to my emotional needs. Help me let You be my primary Source. Help me be open to the love of others for me. Help me to be loving. I want so much to be whole. You who are holy and whole—make me whole too. In Jesus' name. Amen."

TAKING ACTIO
EMOTIONAL NE

There are people in your lif you, or hinder you, in mee emotional needs. List those perso of the following areas and identif helpers or hinderers. Then note v responses mean in terms of h emotional needs are or are not b through these relationships.

1. *Emotional security, feeling loved nc what.*
2. *A sense of belonging.*
3. *A sense of freedom to be me.*
4. *The discipline to set limits on myself*
5. *Feeling accepted.*
6. *Having the approval of significant ot*
7. *Being affirmed.*
8. *Being independent at times by depen on myself.*

9. *Being responsible for myself.*
10. *Dealing with my fears, keeping them at a minimum.*
11. *Growing in my ability to love and be loved.*
12. *Having a true sense of having been forgiven.*
13. *Having a sense of worthwhileness.*
14. *Feeling good about being me.*

Chapter

25

Parenting As a Single

Lemonade anyone? If you're a single parent, you've probably been handed some lemons in your life. What we'd like to do in this chapter from Innocent Victims *is show you how to make lemonade out of your lemons. We'll give you some practical advice on coping with the nitty gritty, everyday ins, outs, and issues of being a single parent. We'll give you some important keys to your parenting that will help mend the broken pieces of a family. And we hope to answer a* really *important question—how can you actually enjoy the life you now have?*

Thomas Whiteman, Ph.D.
Innocent Victims

"As a single parent of two preschool boys," the thirty-two-year-old woman said, "I found my life going through an overwhelming set of changes. At first, I was too depressed to be any good to anyone, including my boys. Later, I determined that I was going to overcome my circumstances. That led me into my superwoman role, where I tried to do everything by myself. I took a full-time job, arranged daycare for the boys, ran the home, and tried to maintain a social life. I wanted to take the place of their missing father. But I was becoming more and more frustrated, and the boys were usually mad at me. What a terrible feeling!

"Now I'm just trying to be a decent mother. I no longer need to be superwoman. I don't even have to be good. I'm settling for doing the best I can, and spending whatever time I can with the boys. It's like I wanted 100 percent before, and now I'm settling for 75 percent. But at least I can preserve my sanity this way. And who knows, maybe I'll even enjoy a few days."

Even though the preceding quote seems a little gloomy, it is a fairly accurate portrayal of how most single parents feel at least some of the time. There is a sense that "I can't do it all myself" and "What do I really have to look forward to?" There is no question about it; parenting as a single is an extremely challenging task, especially if you have little or no support from the other parent. Yet I know of many single parents who not only make it on their own, but appear to be happy, fulfilled, and are raising children who are well-adjusted. In this chapter, we will look at ways to help you become more effective as a single parent—not only at raising your children, but also at enjoying the life that you have.

Two of the keys for successful single-parenting, which we want to focus on in this chapter, are the way that you raise your children, and your own attitude toward your circumstances. In the first half of the chapter we will discuss the parenting keys. Then we will conclude with the ways in which your own attitude toward your circumstances affects the entire single-parenting process.

KEYS FOR PARENTING AS A SINGLE

The Fresh Start Single-Parenting Workbook focuses on healthy parenting skills for the single parent. What I will focus on in this section is an overview of the issues. In addition, I will provide a list of other resources, which might be helpful to you if you would like to look more closely at a particular parenting skill.

Parenting as a single is not a whole lot different from parenting in general. Both require loving discipline, guidance, modeling, nurturing, teaching, and a full range of emotional supports. The greatest difference for the single parent is two-fold. One, your children tend to be more emotionally needy because of their sense of loss. Two, you don't have the additional support of a second parent with whom you can share your decisions and frustrations. So you need to focus on a few critical skills that you can commit to working on. Here are some of the most important areas.

Provide a Loving Environment for Your Children.

Everyone would agree that providing a loving environment is one of the most important gifts you can give to your children. But many would disagree as to what a loving environment entails. Should we be firm or compassionate, foster independence or reliance on the family, give in to their wishes or force them to do without? These are all questions that have different answers, depending on the circumstances and the personality of your children. The important point is that you assure your children of your unconditional love for them.

Unconditional love for children of divorce must come in the form of constant reassurance of your love and commitment to their well-being. They need to know you will be there for them, and they are a top priority, even though you have additional responsibilities which require your time. They need to see concrete expressions of that love during good times and bad.

Practical expressions of love should include the following:

- Verbal reassurance of specific things that you like about each child.
- Physical contact with your children, which includes hugs, kisses, back scratches, etc. (I still remember my mom waking me up on school days by gently scratching my back.)
- Notes and cards, which express pleasure with something they have done, or something you like about their personality. (This is particularly helpful for the noncustodial parent to do.)
- Spend individual time with each child. Find a hobby or activity you can share with them alone.
- Actively listen to your child. Focus on them and what they are saying. Stop what you are doing and give them good eye contact. Do not give advice, or simplistic answers, but try to view the information through their eyes.
- For the noncustodial parent, make frequent phone calls during the week, which focus on them and their day. Also, give them a number where you can be reached at almost any time. They need to be assured that they have easy access to you when they feel they need to talk about something.

No one is capable of displaying unconditional love at all times. However, if this is your goal, then you need also to be able to ask for forgiveness when you fail with your kids. If you grew up in a home that was less than loving, then you might have particular difficulty expressing this love to your children. For a more in-depth look at learning how to love your children, I would recommend the following books: *How to Really Love Your Child* by Ross Campbell, *The Art of Loving* by Eric Fromm, and *Unconditional Love* by John Powell.

Rebuild Trusting Relationships.

One of the casualties of divorce is the ability to trust again, at least immediately. This is just as true for children as it is for adults. As a parent, it is primarily your responsibility to rebuild your children's trust, since you are probably the most influential adult in their lives. You may also be the target of their distrust, if you were the one who left, or if you are perceived as having betrayed the family in some way.

Rebuilding trust takes time. Above all, it requires complete honesty from you. This is demonstrated in the way you explain divorce to your children, whether or not you are willing to admit your own mistakes, how honest you are with your feelings, and whether or not you keep promises to the children. In an effort to compensate children for losses experienced in divorce, some parents compound the mistake by making promises to the children that they are not sure they can keep. Vacations and extravagant toys do not tell the children you love them. More often than not, they are reinforcement of the belief that Mom or Dad can't be trusted.

Even if you got away with minor unfulfilled promises before the divorce, what you must realize is that now your life is under a microscope. Your children are testing to see if they can trust you again. You must take special care to measure your words before you speak.

These promises include the negative ones, too. If you tell your children, "If I hear you whine one more time, I'll send you to your room for a month." Don't say it unless you can follow through. This might seem like a minor infraction, for which we have all been guilty. But now, more than ever, it is imperative that you think before you speak.

Consider the following statements: "If you do that one more time, I'll kill you!" "If you don't clean up your plate, you won't eat for a week." "If you don't get in the car right now, I'll never take you to Grandma's again."

Besides the fact that you shouldn't make such harsh statements, think about the message these words convey to your children regarding their ability to trust you again. I know we've all sent these messages, or not followed through on a commitment merely because it slipped our minds. When we become aware of these mistakes, it is important that we speak the truth as lovingly as we can.

You might say something like this: "I'm sorry I said that. Mommy didn't really mean that she wouldn't feed you for a week. I only said that out of frustration. You need to finish your meal, or you won't get any dessert." Or, "I know Daddy said he would take you fishing this weekend, but I forgot that I had to get the car inspected. It was my fault for not remembering. I know you're disappointed, but I'm sure we will be able to go some other time. How about if we try . . ."

Provide Firm, Yet Loving Discipline.

Another casualty in many divorcing families is a continued level of loving discipline. As you lose touch with your children, or lose the energy to keep up with their immaturity, many parents take the easy way out, which is to give in or react in haste. Yet consistent discipline is key to the children of divorce feeling secure and loved.

It is not within the scope of this book to cover the full range of disciplining techniques. I will review a few guidelines, and then recommend some books.

Make the punishment fit the crime. This takes a great deal of wisdom, and no one can be there to tell you how to handle each new situation. But don't overreact to minor infractions, and take seriously the mistakes that carry long-term implications. The way this is played out in many homes is for parents to let things slide until they've had enough. Then they react with the back of their hand, or a threat that everyone knows they will not follow through on. Logical consequences make the most sense, and also teach valuable lessons.

"If you don't put away your toys, I'll have to take them away for a couple of days." "If you don't turn off the Nintendo now, you won't be allowed to play with it tomorrow." "Since I don't like to see you act that way, why don't you sit in the other room until you're done pouting?"

The consequences to each situation require thought and patience. This means you need to stay calm, and not react in anger. The easiest thing to do is not always the best.

Pick your battlegrounds. You need to decide which areas are important enough to battle over. This is particularly true of teenagers. Since discipline takes a lot of thought and energy, you may decide not to fight over cleaning up every bite on the plate, or whether your daughter can wear makeup to school. You need to decide in advance which issues are important, and on which you need to show some latitude.

Distinguish among accidents, disobedience, and defiance. Even though accidents may be devastating to you personally, you don't want to deal with them as harshly as disobedience or defiance. For example, if my daughter spills her juice on my computer and ruins it, I'm going to be very upset. (Especially if I'm at the end of a chapter that I haven't saved to the disk yet.) Her seeing how upset I am may be punishment enough. In fact, I'd probably end up hugging her and assuring her, "It's okay, I realize it was an accident."

But if I tell her to sit in the kitchen and drink her juice, and instead she walks into my office and spills her juice, now I need to punish her for disobedience. Perhaps sitting her in her chair for a while would be sufficient penance, even though my anger at the moment might tempt me to do more.

The most serious infraction is defiance. This is evidenced by my daughter looking me right in the eye and pouring the juice on my computer, right after I told her to take her juice back to the kitchen. For this, a young child could be restricted to her room. An older child might have to work in order to replace the computer they ruined, which would be a logical consequence of their action.

As you can see from the example, the result is the same. My computer is ruined. The difference, which needs to be distinguished, is, was it an accident, disobedience, or defiance?

Explain to your children the difference between your feelings toward them and your feelings about their behavior. In other words, tell your children, "I love you, but I don't like the way you are behaving."

Remember when your parents used to say just before they spanked you, "This is going to hurt me more than it will hurt you"? Even though that used to drive us crazy at the time, the message behind the words is, "Because I love you, I have to do this. But it hurts me, too."

Think about the following statements, and how they should be said.

"You're stupid," might become, "I know you are very capable, but the way you're acting right now isn't very smart."

"Shut up!" could be stated, "I want to listen to you, but could you please stop talking right now so that I can think?"

"I hate it when you do that!" might need the minor modification to, "I love you, but I don't like it when you do that."

These changes seem obvious in the calm reality of the present, but they take great willpower and thought when you reach the height of your frustration. I guess that's why people say, "Parenting is hard work!"

Some books that take a closer look at issues of disciplining your children are *Dare to Discipline, The Strong-Willed Child* by James Dobson, and *The Key To Your Child's Heart* by Gary Smalley.

Foster Healthy Relationships.

As a single parent it is very important that you promote healthy role models for your children. These usually include monitoring whom they hang out with, finding positive opposite-sex and same-sex adult relationships, and providing exposure to healthy, intact families. Here are a few guidelines to help you accomplish this.

Insist on meeting your children's friends. Even if they are teenagers, you are entitled to know whom your children are hanging around with. Try to be friendly and open-minded toward all of them. Be cautious about disapproving of any of their friends, since this can make the relationship even more important. Remember, you can't pick your children's friends. Even to suggest a person can sometimes be the kiss of death for that relationship. Usually, the most you can do is to put your children in places where they will be in close promixity to more desirable peer groups; such as church, the YMCA, clubs, civic groups.

Find adult role models for your children who will be a stable and reliable influence. This is especially important if your former mate does not provide that type of support. If the other parent is not very involved with your children, then a role model of the opposite sex is critical. This should be a family friend, a grandparent, an uncle—someone whom they can count on to be there for them over the long haul. This is not a series of boyfriends or girlfriends who might be in and out of your life.

If it is a friend, then it is best when the person is interested primarily in helping your children, and not trying to get closer to you.

If no one has shown real interest in fulfilling this role, you might want specifically to ask a friend or relative to help out. They might not realize the need, and would be flattered that you turned to them.

Maintain relationships with some healthy married couples. Even though many of your friendships will evolve away from married couples and toward singles, it is important that you and your children observe some happily married couples, so that you don't lose your perspective. One teenager recently told me, "I don't know if I'll ever get married. I don't know of a single family where there hasn't been a divorce, or one that isn't headed in that direction."

Another girl told me, "I'm really nervous around men. I've never lived in a home with a man, because my dad left when I was three. Whenever I'm around couples, I always check out the husband and wife to see how they act. I want to know what a normal family looks like for when I get married; that is, if that ever happens."

Times with relatives and friends who are married, both during holidays and when they're just doing their daily routine, can be a very important part of your children's development.

Build a Positive Sense of Self-worth.

No matter what your job, your most important responsibility is raising your children. And probably one of the greatest gifts you can pass on to your children is a balanced self-image. Of all of the problems I face in counseling, and in day-to-day contact with people, the most prevalent and pervasive are those of insecurity and poor self-image. To some extent, we all struggle with these from time to time.

Each of us must ask, "What does our society value in a person? What values do I reinforce in my home?" Unfortunately, in most settings, children see that they are valued primarily in four areas: beauty, brains, brawn, and bucks. Our society reflects these values in everything from advertising and cartoons, to who gets elected to the local school board or women's club.

If children are not good-looking or smart, they often feel like failures and may be treated that way by classmates. This is particularly true for girls, who must look like a Barbie Doll.

Boys can get away with not being exceptionally handsome or smart, as long as they are good at sports, or are among the strongest kids in the class.

You may be surprised at how important money is to children's popularity and standing with peers. Our children must wear the right clothes, have the latest games and toys, and even have the correct label on their sneakers. Children are also keenly aware of who lives in the right neighborhoods, and whose parents are influential in the community.

If children do not have at least one of the four ingredients—beauty, brains, brawn, or bucks—then they are destined to an uphill struggle in order to achieve acceptance in our society. One difficult truth, which complicates this problem, is that no matter how blessed we may be, there is always someone out there who is a little prettier, smarter, stronger, or richer. No matter how many of the ingredients we do have, we will still struggle from time to time with a negative self-image.

Given these difficulties, how can I help to develop a positive self-image in my children? Let me describe briefly some general guidelines, and then recommend a few books which expand on this topic.

You need to love yourself before you can love others. If you do not have a good self-image, then your first task is to get help for yourself, so that you can model a positive self-image for your children.

You need to counterbalance what their peer group values. When your children are with you, you need to show them a more secure kind of love. This is a love not based on how they look or act, but one that values and loves them all the time. Show them love that is unconditional.

Nurture your children with physical attention and concrete expressions of love. Be sure to mention specific things that you like about each child.

Encourage your children to be open and honest with their feelings. Don't negate their feelings, even when you disagree with them. You need to be an example of open and honest communication.

Foster independence in your children. Remember, your goal is not to create obedient clones, but responsible adults. You must encourage their decision-making and willingness to try things on their own, even when you think it might lead to failure. When they do fail, allow them to suffer the consequences, but then be there for them emotionally, encouraging them to try again.

Some additional guidelines can be found in the following books: *How to Really Love Your Child* by Ross Campbell, *Hide and Seek* by

James Dobson, *The Key to Your Child's Heart* by Trent and Smalley, and *Raising Positive Kids in a Negative World* by Zig Ziglar.

Give Your Children a Sense of Purpose or Meaning in Their Lives.

This is a parenting skill that is vastly overlooked, and yet is critically important for your children's healthy development. Children and adults need to have something in their lives that gives them meaning and purpose. For some it is their work, for others it may be in serving society, while others seek a personal relationship with God. Whatever your priority, you have probably come to find that living solely for self is an unfulfilling quest. Many have found greater fulfillment when they live for something beyond themselves.

One of the failures of the yuppie generation was their pursuit of wealth and power, devoid of ethical considerations. King Solomon, one of the richest and most powerful men of his time, said, "All that the world has to offer is a vain pursuit." As we teach our children how to make their way in this world, we must not forget that a faith or belief system should be part of the fabric of our lives.

I hear many parents almost apologize for what they believe. This sends a message to our children about how important our moral values are to us. Many don't want to offend others. But with our children, we have an obligation to present a firm set of values, which tell us who we are and why we are here. Young children will not understand these concepts, and teenagers will rebel against them, so many parents ask, "Why bother?" The answer is one you have heard before. Children may not understand it now, or may not want to hear it later, but the seeds you plant today will have a big influence on how they live as adults. Solomon put it this way in the book of Proverbs: "Train up a child in the way he should go, and when he is old, he will not depart from it."

There are many things you will want to teach your children as they grow up. The best way to teach a belief system, or your faith, is to live it. You don't want to preach it without living it. That would only create an opposite reaction. If you don't have meaning or purpose in your own life, that needs to be settled first. For this, I recommend the book *Power for Living* by Jamie Buckingham.

YOUR ATTITUDE TOWARD YOUR SITUATION

Let's shift the focus from our children to ourselves and take a closer look at how your attitude toward your circumstances can affect your entire life.

The parents' attitude about their situation has a bearing on how they interact with their former spouse, how they relate with their children, and the speed at which their own recovery takes place. Let's contrast two situations.

Both Mrs. A and Mrs. B are suburban housewives. As they were approaching their fortieth birthdays, their husbands left them for younger women. Both women were devastated by the loss, as were their children. Neither women were educated beyond their high school degrees, and neither worked since getting married. Mrs. A views herself as a victim. She is angry with her ex, and boasts about giving him a hard time. She got full legal and physical custody of their three children, along with four years of alimony, so that she could train for some type of new career. Currently, about two years after her divorce, Mrs. A is working as a receptionist for little more than minimum wage. She has no plans for her vocational education. She says, "I'm really not very good at anything. Besides," she explains, "I never wanted this divorce in the first place. I don't think I should have to work, when I have three kids at home."

Mrs. A has very few social outlets, and many of her married friends are drifting away from her. She is feeling more isolated, and tells her children about how unfair all of this has been for her. Her children feel sorry for her, and feel guilty when they want to visit their dad. He has been sporadic in his visits, and late with many of his payments. But, as he puts it, "At least I'm still there for them when they need me."

Mrs. B, on the other hand, seems to be doing a lot better. She went back to school. Now, two years later, she is well along in completing her business administration degree. She has already started her own small business, doing word processing out of her home. She also has physical custody of her two children, but she and her Ex have joint legal custody. Mrs. B requested this arrangement because she knew that her husband would stay more involved in the kids' lives if he had some continuing input into their upbringing. As she put it, "I may not be married to him, but he is still their father. Even though he didn't turn out to be such a good husband, he was always a good father—and I believe he still is."

THE TWENTY MOST STRESSFUL THINGS TO A CHILD—AS RATED BY THEM

1. *Losing a parent*
2. *Going blind*
3. *Being held back a year in school*
4. *Wetting pants in school*
5. *Hearing parents quarrel*
6. *Being caught stealing*
7. *Being suspected of lying*
8. *Receiving a bad report card*
9. *Being sent to the principal's office*
10. *Having an operation*
11. *Getting lost*
12. *Being made fun of in class*
13. *Moving to a new school*
14. *Having a scary dream*
15. *Not getting 100 on a test*
16. *Being picked last for a team*
17. *Losing in a game*
18. *Going to the dentist*

19. *Giving a report in class*
20. *Acquiring a baby sibling*

Helping Your Kids Handle Stress
H. Norman Wright

Mr. B has a good relationship with his children, and they enjoy their visits with him. They feel good about leaving for his place, and good about telling Mom all about their weekends, because they know that their mother encourages this.

Mrs. B is very involved socially. She has found a new support system, with friends who have been through similar life changes. Yet she still stays friendly with one or two of the married couples with whom she was formerly acquainted. Mrs. B describes her life in this way.

> I wouldn't wish divorce on my worst enemy, but I wouldn't trade anything for what I have learned, having gone through a divorce. I have more self-confidence and feel more fulfilled now than I ever have. I never would have thought I could make it on my own while I was married, but now I know I can. I understand more about myself and other people. I think this has made me a better friend to my friends, a better parent to my kids, and a better person. Sure, I get lonely sometimes, but there are worse things than being single and lonely, and one of them is being in a bad marriage. Besides, now I have much stronger friendships, with people whom I know I can count on when I need a listening ear.

In our Fresh Start Seminars, we describe a poster that features a man with a funnel in his head, and a spigot where his nose should be. In the funnel is a bunch of lemons, and out of the spigot, lemonade is pouring into a pitcher. The caption reads, "When life gives you lemons, make lemonade."

This is a perfect illustration of how divorce affects our lives. We have all been given some lemons in our lives. (Some of us married them.) Yet, in spite of these bitter experiences, we still have the ability to choose our own attitude toward our circumstances. Will we choose to become bitter, to squeeze those lemons and serve other people lemon juice? You know what happens when someone serves lemon juice. The sour taste turns people away. We alienate our friends, our children, and even ourselves.

Or will we choose to add some sugar to that lemon juice, and serve lemonade? The sugar, which we all possess, is a sweet disposition, the ability to forgive, to love, and to uplift others. When we add this to the bitter experiences of life, we find a perfect combination of sweet and sour, which attracts others, like lemonade on a hot and thirsty day.

Charles Swindoll, in his book, *Strengthening Your Grip,* explains this concept as follows (pp. 205–206):

> The colorful, nineteenth-century showman and gifted violinist Nicolo Paganini was standing before a packed house, playing through a difficult piece of music. A full orchestra surrounded him with magnificent support. Suddenly one string on his violin snapped and hung gloriously down from his instrument. Beads of perspiration popped out on his forehead. He frowned but continued to play, improvising beautifully.
>
> To the conductor's surprise, a second string broke. And shortly thereafter, a third. Now there were three limp strings dangling from Paganini's violin as the master performer completed the difficult composition on the one remaining string. The audience jumped to its feet and in good Italian fashion, filled the hall with shouts and screams, "Bravo! Bravo!" As the applause died down, the violinist asked the people to sit back down. Even though they knew there was no way they could expect an encore, they quietly sank back into their seats.
>
> He held the violin high for everyone to see. He nodded at the conductor to begin the encore and then he turned back to the crowd, and with a twinkle in his eye, he smiled and shouted, "Paganini . . . and one string!" After that he placed the single-stringed Stradivarius beneath his chin and played the final piece on *one* string as the audience (and the conductor) shook their heads in silent amazement. "Paganini . . . and one string!" *And,* I might add, an attitude of fortitude.
>
> Dr. Victor Frankl, the bold, courageous Jew who became a prisoner during the Holocaust, endured years of indignity and humiliation by the Nazis before he was finally liberated. At the beginning of his ordeal, he marched into a gestapo courtroom. His captors had taken away his home and family, his cherished freedom, his possessions, even his watch and wedding ring. They had shaved his head and stripped his clothing off his body. There he stood before the German high command, under the glaring lights being interrogated and falsely accused. He was destitute, a helpless pawn in the hands of brutal, prejudiced, sadistic men. He had nothing. No, that isn't true. He suddenly realized there was one thing no one could ever take away from him—just one. Do you know what it was?
>
> Dr. Frankl realized he still had the power to choose his own

> attitude. No matter what anyone would ever do to him, regardless of what the future held for him, the attitude choice was his to make. Bitterness or forgiveness. To give up or to go on. Hatred or hope. Determination to endure or the paralysis of self-pity. It boiled down to "Frankl . . . and one string!"
>
> Words can never adequately convey the incredible impact of our attitude toward life. The longer I live, the more convinced I become that life is 10 percent what happens to us and 90 percent how we respond to it.

The question remains, "What will *my* attitude be toward *my* circumstances?" Will it be bitterness, self-pity, and immobilization, as with Mrs. A? Or will you choose forgiveness, hope, endurance, and determination, as Mrs. B described? What kind of music are you going to play on that one string of yours?

I know you're thinking, "Yes, but you don't understand how much I've been hurt." Or, "You can't imagine what a creep I was married to." Look again at the life of Victor Frankl. You could not have suffered as much as he did. Are you going to be a victim, or a victor? Before you answer that you'd rather remain in your self-pity, think about your children. Do you want *them* to overcome their circumstances? What attitude would you like for them to choose? Research has demonstrated that the attitude of the parent, especially the custodial parent, is the biggest predictor of the children's adjustment.

The title of this book does not convey the attitude that you and your children need to adopt. Even though you have had some terrible things happen to you as a family, I believe there is still great hope. You *can* serve lemonade, and your children can, too. It's your choice!

Chapter

26

Encouragement: Sometimes I Want to Resign

Encouragement. We need encouragement. We need lots and lots of encouragement! Whether you are a mother trying to raise sons (or a single dad trying to raise daughters)—or you are a two-parent family engaged fulltime in raising your children—all of us need encouragement to keep going. In this chapter from Single Mothers Raising Sons *I want to show you a few ways to hang tough, hang loose, and hang in there. Here's some more much needed, down-to-earth, reality check advice on how to survive the throes of single parenting. Believe me, you* can *take charge of your life!*

Bobbie Reed
Single Mothers Raising Sons

The process of training up children in the way they should go is tough. There are so many times when mothers want to resign, to quit, to give up. A lot of single parents I share with have one complaint in common: "I didn't sign on for this!" they exclaim. Few of us fantasized ourselves as single parents during our growing-up years.

Parenting isn't all that it is cracked up to be. One of the current books on parenting claims that babies have the best press in the world, and that's true. Who can resist a sweet, tiny baby all wrapped in a fuzzy blanket? But babies grow up, we discover, and the process of growing up is a very long one. Often moms find themselves thinking, "Wait a minute! Where does it say that just because I have a son that I also have to raise him alone, contend with his teachers, listen to the neighbor's complaints, handle all of the crises . . ."

There's Just Too Much to Do

Do you start each day with a list of things to do and find that regardless of how hard you work you never seem to finish? So you add the leftover items to the next day's list, which also never gets done?

A sense of being overloaded is common in a single parent home because one adult is trying to do all of the tasks of home maintenance, which is at the very least a two-person job. It can be done, of course, but the cost may be too high. Whenever one person attempts to do a two-person job for a sustained period of time, the results are fatigue, tension problems, high blood pressure, irritability, lack of energy, a diminished capacity to perform in all areas, and a loss of self-esteem. It is often better to decide what is reasonable for one person to do and then try to attack only those duties. Helpful hints for smart moms include:

- List all the tasks you have to do.
- Rate each as "must do," "should do," "would do if there were time."
- Prioritize the "must do" list.
- Focus only on the top priorities from this list.
- Find time for some of the "should do's" and "would do's" by delegating tasks to the children, reducing the frequency of some tasks, combining some tasks, and learning shortcuts.

Of course, sometimes you will wish that you had done everything on all three of your lists, but most of the time you will be glad that you have made time to be a person instead of a slave. Persons make better parents than do slaves or robots.

Coping with Stress

"I feel stretched to my limits. I can't take another problem with the children!" Sharon sighed wearily at the end of a horrible week.

At one time or another we each experience symptoms of stress overload, caused by having to cope with too many changes, problems, or demands within a short period of time, or by having a few severe stressors continue for too long a period of time. Since we live in a world of accelerating progress and changes, we are all subject to increased opportunities for stress overload.

A certain amount of stress is good for us because it provides the push needed to overcome inertia. However, too much stress is dangerous and can cause *distress*. People experience stress overload when they no longer maintain balance in their lives. When this overload occurs, energy is diverted from various areas in the body to support the stress response. If the situation is short-lived, the body quickly returns to homeostasis or equilibrium. On the other hand, if the stress is prolonged, sufficient energy to maintain a healthy body is no longer available and illness may occur.

People tend to live to the limits of their resources. We spend all of our incomes. We schedule all of our time so that we can't accommodate unexpected delays or demands very easily. Often we accept more stressors (demands) than we can handle with our reserve energies, so when we encounter unexpected stressors, we are unable to cope effectively because we have no extra energy.

We need time to learn stress management skills. Just as stress overload builds up over a period of weeks, perhaps even years, we learn to take control of the internal responses to external demands over a period of time.

The following list offers some steps to help with stress management.

- Keep a written record of things that cause you stress. Try to eliminate as many as you reasonably and practicably can.
- Set priorities, then devote your energies to those top priorities in your life.
- Live consistently with your beliefs so as to eliminate inner tension.
- Learn specific interventions for coping with those things that cause you the most stress and that you cannot eliminate from your life.
- Set up a reward system for yourself when you are functioning well and coping with life in the midst of stress.
- Follow the rules for good health: get enough sleep and rest, eat a balanced diet, exercise, maintain a balanced schedule, talk out negative feelings, have regular medical checkups, and avoid self-medication.
- Take frequent breaks during periods of high stress.

· Learn to physically relax.
· Use biofeedback.
· Take classes in stress management.
· Engage in a highly reinforcing activity upon arriving home from work.
· Limit the amount of work you bring home from the office.
· Learn to make decisions and then not to worry about whether or not you made the best decision.
· Obtain closure on unfinished tasks, relationships, and situations in your life.
· Be assertive.
· Practice acceptance and forgiveness.

Trying to be a supermom is unreasonable. Do your best, and accept not only your own limits but those of others. It is possible to live with stress—without distress.

When the going gets tough, hang tough. You can make it through.

YOU'LL ALSO NEED TO HANG LOOSE AT TIMES!

Hawaiians have a hand signal by which a fist is made with the three middle fingers while the thumb and little finger stick out. Waved about, this means Hang loose! Be cool! Relax! The message is Don't try *too* hard.

Do you ever feel as if you are trying so hard but getting nowhere? Trying too hard to ensure that your sons are happy and enjoying themselves is a common mistake single moms make.

When I took my two boys camping for the weekend, I packed the frisbee, the battery-operated television, food, and swimsuits. For two days the boys argued, refused to participate in any of the activities offered by the campground, enjoyed nothing I had planned, and complained of being bored.

Earlene planned a "See America" car trip for her teenagers one summer. All she heard was, "How many more days before we get home, Mom?"

Carla insisted that her boys participate in Little League baseball. Every other day, they argue about going to practice, ending up angry with one another.

Most of us have had the experience at least once of having our perfectly designed plans for the family fall apart because our needs, desires, or preferences don't match those of our sons, or because we miscalculated when we planned what we thought would interest them. This can be particularly frustrating when the arrangements were complicated and expensive and other people were also involved. Perhaps there is a better way.

We must remember that we cannot force our children to be happy or enjoy something. It is usually best to involve the boys in what we are planning for family activities rather than to spring a surprise on them, because the surprise may be ours instead, when the whole experience turns out to be a flop. We must not try too hard to do it all. It is not always the big things that make children remember family times with nostalgia.

When I was first divorced, I lived in a low-income housing apartment complex and my sons were in a child care center there. It wasn't a very good one because at five o'clock they simply closed and sent the children home. If I could have afforded a better option, I would have found one, but since I got off work at 4:15 and only worked six miles away, I didn't foresee a problem. Each day I rushed home and was almost always there by 4:35. Then one day it rained and there was an accident on the freeway that tied up traffic for two hours. While I sat in my car, frustrated and angry, I imagined my two little boys being sent home alone. It was getting dark, and it was cold and rainy outside. I felt sick at my stomach and helpless to do anything about getting home any sooner. Finally the accident was cleared and we were allowed to proceed. I hurried home and my worst fears were realized. There on the step sat the boys, huddling together, scared, and soaking wet. They had obviously been wading in the five or six inches of water along the curb.

Feeling awful, I hurriedly bundled them inside, gave them warm baths, prepared their favorite supper, and cuddled and coddled them all evening. In fact, I spent the next several weeks making it up to them. Also, I immediately found a different child care center. For a long time I felt like a failure as a mother for having put my children through such an ordeal.

Guess what Michael's favorite story was as he grew up? The big flood in Sacramento when he and Jon had to swim home and Mom couldn't get home all night! Today's disasters may turn out to be tomorrow's favorite stories.

I asked several adults who grew up in single parent homes what made it good for them and came up with the following three attitudes.

1. Mom's Attitude Toward Our Situation

If you are angry, frustrated, resentful, bitter, or unhappy about being a single parent, you will pass on those attitudes and feelings to your sons. Your boys will grow up feeling deprived, cheated, and angry toward one or both of their parents.

In contrast, if you face reality with a possibility-thinking attitude you communicate the positive side of life to your sons. Even children who grew up in homes that never had enough money, let alone any luxuries, did not always feel that they had been "poor." Their perceptions usually depended on the attitude and atmosphere created by the mother.

2. Mom's Relationship with Us

"Mom used to play games with us in the evenings," Joel remembered.

"Mom used to trust me as if I were grown up," Artie said.

If you take time to be with your sons, sharing together, laughing and having fun as a family, as well as talking through serious subjects, your boys will grow up feeling good about their childhoods. If you are too busy working, working, working, to ever have time for the boys, they will grow up feeling that they were deprived.

3. Mom's Attitude Toward Dad

The lack of a good relationship with the absent parent seems to leave the deepest scars on children from single parent families. Whether this lack is due to death or divorce, the pain feels like rejection and the loss of a beautiful "what might have been." If the other parent is alive, there is usually a natural curiosity to get to know him. The mother's attitude toward the father and his relationship with the boys will often color their perceptions of the growing-up years. "Mom never minded when I called or visited my dad," David said. "I could see him as much as I wanted. Some of my friends used to have to sneak around to meet their fathers or call them from a friend's house. But not me. Even though my folks were divorced, I still grew up with two parents. We didn't have any big problems."

An ideal family? No, just a single mom with the right attitude.

IT IS YOUR LIFE!

Do you ever feel you aren't getting from life all that you had hoped for? If you do, then stop right now and decide to take charge of your life:

1. Determine where you are now and where you want to be.
2. Recognize that the difference between what you are and what you will become is what you do.
3. Accept the realities in your life that cannot be changed, such as your height, age, single state (at this time, at least).
4. Identify what can be changed.
5. Identify what *you will change.* Write realistic, measurable, and dated goals.
6. Implement your action plan and evaluate your progress.

Doing a self-assessment every few months is an important part of growing. In this way you will know where you've been, where you are going, and how far along you are. The abundant life can be yours. If you aren't one of those people who are enjoying the adventure of being a single mom, make some changes.

It is your life! Make it worth living!

Jesus said in John 10:10 that He came that we might have an abundant life. Go for it!

PART FIVE

The Aging of the Family: Yours, Your Parents, Your Children

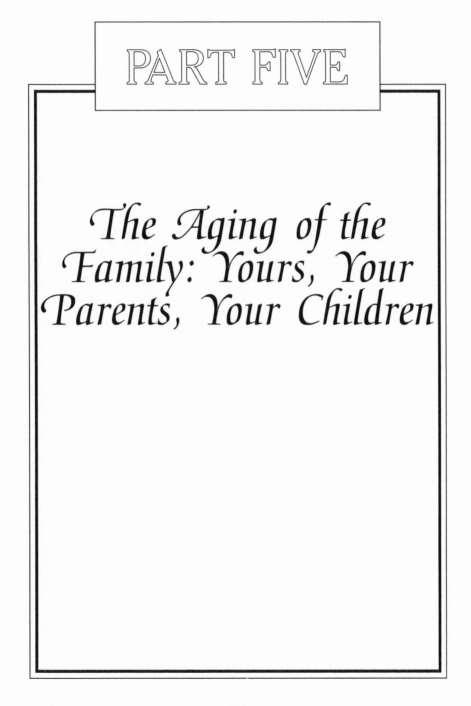

Chapter

27

Visiting and Communicating with Elderly People

As we age, so do our parents. With our increasing longevity, our generation is now more than ever forced into a new role of parenting our parents. My book A Guide to Caring for and Coping with Aging Parents *is a record of my wife, Carolyn's, and my experience of decision-making for our older loved ones, Anna and Paul. They required our help first through home care and retirement centers, and finally to long-term skilled and institutionalized care. Paul Lewis Young was my father-in-law, born in 1893, and a missionary all his life. Anna Batutis Gillies was my mother, a Lithuanian immigrant who, in 1924, married another Lithuanian immigrant, Anton, who had just been graduated from the Northern Baptist Seminary. For more than three decades, Anna lived in a nursing home because of severe brain damage. Paul also lived in a nursing home, suffering from aphasia caused by a massive stroke the day before he was to be married again at 83 years of age.*

What we would like to share in this chapter is a universal love and caring you can show for all aged and elderly people—especially if they happen to be your parents.

John Gillies
A Guide to Caring for and Coping with Aging Parents

These days, when I visit, Anna rarely recognizes me as her son. As I have aged, I look more like my father, and I think Anna often thinks I am Anton, her husband of many years ago. Perhaps this should be expected despite her disability; she has known me as an adult for more years than she knew Anton as her husband.

Anna accepts Carolyn and appears grateful for her attention, but she doesn't know Carolyn is her daughter-in-law.

Paul does recognize us for who we are. He knows his other daughter, Esther, and her husband, Wally. He identifies his grandchildren and great-grandchildren from the pictures on his wall. Most of the time he can place the name of someone who writes to him. He receives information, but can't always respond. Aphasia shackles his tongue. His speaking vocabulary is limited, and sometimes they are not the words he needs to express his thoughts.

Anna and Paul live with severe communications handicaps; in this chapter I will describe some of the specific ways we have discovered to share life better with our parents.

It is often equally difficult to communicate with disabled people who are neither senile nor disoriented nor affected by a speech disorder. Experts in gerontology say depression is the primary emotional ailment of our aging relatives and friends. It, like pain or disability, can hinder the process of communication.

But when they are lonely, bewildered with surroundings, enduring discomfort, suffering pain, and perhaps trying to cope with a frustrating handicap, these are the times visits can be most helpful and meaningful.

Here are a few suggestions for relating to older friends and loved ones, particularly those who live in nursing homes or other institutions.

REALITY ORIENTATION

Social workers recommend that older people be "kept in touch" by way of "reality orientation" or "reality therapy," a fancy name for a rather simple procedure.

Whenever you visit a parent who is becoming more confused about himself or herself and life, at some point in the visit turn the conversation to some reality. Establish what day and date it is. Ask the person his or her name; if possible, get your parent to write it. At any rate, let your parent know by mentioning his or her name that you know the name and the name is theirs. Discuss the season of the year and the weather outside. Underscore where the parent is living —in what city and in what state, as well as the name of the nursing home. You might want to chat about some headline of the day. Establish who is president of the United States. Call attention to upcoming anniversaries.

A calendar on the wall—the bigger the better, perhaps a large one where you tear off each day's date—and pictures of the family help establish time and relationships.

Repeat these kinds of questions during each visit. It isn't childish or irrelevant. This is the substance of reality, and for a person who is disoriented the repetition is necessary and helpful.

To be sure, not every resident of a nursing home suffers from brain damage or some handicap that restricts communication. For those who are blessed with clear or clearer minds, conversation is no problem. All you need to do is ask a question about the home town or a garden or grandchildren, and you can sit back and listen. Your visit and the opportunity to share is no less important.

NEGOTIATION AND FORGIVENESS

I strongly believe that elderly people should be treated as adults and not as children. However, this is easier to believe than to practice, particularly when senility brings on *childlike* (not necessarily *childish*) behavior.

It's also difficult to maintain this adult-to-adult relationship as we assume the role of parent for our parent.

There may be a need for *negotiation,* when it is clarified that you must assume certain responsibilities for the other. This is a new relationship for both of you, and it may be necessary to make clear that you are no longer a child (you are probably in your fifties) and that your parent is no longer a parent in the way he or she once experienced that role. Treating each other and visiting each other as adults will help establish a foundation for this new kind of family partnership.

It's essential to come to new understandings in this emerging relationship with our parents—in other words, to negotiate—because we as children carry so much emotional baggage with us.

We remember our parents as they used to be. Perhaps we still think of ourselves as we used to be. We remember past slights and misunderstandings and instances of our own erratic behavior. We remember things we said and situations that haunt us. We need to forgive our parents, and often we may feel that our parents still need to forgive us.

Perhaps we can discuss these things with our parents. On the other hand, the event that so sears our memory may long since have been erased from theirs. This is not their problem or tragedy; it is ours.

This is when we must negotiate with our Creator, who knows us and our relationships. If we are to establish healthy, supportive ties with our aging parents, we as believing adults must turn over our residual or actual guilt and anger to God. He does forgive and He does heal. Only in this way can we go forward; indeed, how can we express and share love with anyone until we experience God's love?

For many of us this has been the beginning of hearing and accepting the good news.

PERSONS OF WORTH AND DIGNITY

While your parent is still alert and involved with life, keep in mind that you are the visitor to his or her residence. When parents are confused or handicapped, it's easy and often necessary to "take charge." I must do so now where Anna and her care are involved. But I must not be as quick to check Paul's closet and drawers to see if things are in order, without first explaining to him what I want to do and asking his permission to do so. This is also part of having adult relationships with older people. Their dignity is fragile, and we must not damage it.

BE CONSISTENT AND REGULAR

Maintain a definite schedule. This doesn't mean you always have to visit on Mondays at four; there will be times when you'll need to visit on Tuesdays at noon instead. Some elderly people are still quite conscious of time and the clock; Paul is one of these. Deviations in schedule can be explained. It is the conscious decision and commitment to visit two or three times a week—or once a week, if the distance is considerable—that is good discipline for the visitor and fulfilled expectation for the person being visited.

Regularity is important, whether you visit in person or by telephone, letter, or cassette tape. Content may be important; I'm rather sure that quantity and verbosity is not. And I now suspect that in this area of fading relationships Marshall McLuhan is correct: The medium (the visit) is the message.

Don't give up visiting merely because visiting is difficult. Without your visit your parent or loved one would become more withdrawn and more depressed. You don't visit to be appreciated; you visit to demonstrate by your presence that you still care, to be of whatever help and support you can be.

A FEW SUGGESTIONS FOR VISITS

1) *Take advantage of nostalgia.* Prepare a book of snapshots relating to your parent's life. Ask for explanations or descriptions, and write these under the pictures. This could become a kind of "This-Is-Your-Life" album that you can review whenever you visit, and that your parent will find captivating and amusing when alone. This is good reality orientation as well. Perhaps staff members will enjoy seeing it and getting to know your parent better.

An old magazine—one that's thirty or forty years old—can sometimes serve the same purpose. Looking at old advertisements and pictures, seeing the old styles and old cars, can trigger happy memories. The recently reprinted *1908 Sears Catalog* makes a great gift!

2) *Get your parent to talk about those memories.* When did Mother meet Father, and how? Where was their first home? What was it like? Build on past interest in sports or hobbies or vocation. Get your parent to talk; one of the best things you can do as a visitor is to listen. Patients are constantly being told what to do and where to go, and they don't have much opportunity to chat.

Bring a map with you once in a while—perhaps one of the United States or the world. Let your parent point out those states where he or she lived, or the countries visited.

3) *Share some exercise.* A walk down the corridor (outdoors is better if the weather cooperates) is always helpful. If your parent is handicapped, massage unused muscles.

4) *Work on a gift.* There may be a small craft item you could work on together for a grandchild's or great-grandchild's birthday. You can choose from easy-to-make, economical leathercraft items, simple embroidery items, or paint-by-number posters. Working together can be fun, and the project might occupy part of several visits. If there isn't interest in making something, or you are between projects, bring a simple puzzle along.

5) *Bring something to read.* If your parent is aphasic or with-

drawn, remember that if you can't chat, you can at least read. Bring something that will hold interest and that can be read in small segments. Continue that reading with each visit. While cassette tapes of many fine books are available through libraries, your personal reading will bring special pleasure. If it's an old favorite, so much the better. Repetition is desirable. Reading can provide structure and substance to your visits. (Pastors might keep this simple hint in mind. When words fail them—and they do—pastors can read, too.)

6) *Memorize a joke or two, and share these.* Visits among church-related people like Paul and Anna sometimes tend to be overly somber and even pompous. There is a line in the "Old Hundredth" psalm-setting about "Him serve *with mirth,* His praise forth tell!" Why not? There is precious little laughter in the lives of the sick and the handicapped. Bring back some joy into their lives. Carolyn and I have found the *Reader's Digest* invaluable for short articles, anecdotes, and humorous stories. With all due respect to Scouting, *Boy's Life* jokes are corny enough and simple enough to almost always guarantee a chuckle.

7) *When you speak, you don't necessarily have to shout.* Sometimes it seems that we think every older person is deaf.

8) *Be prepared to be silent.* Planning things to do or say is desirable, but your visit won't be a disaster if nothing is said or done. Your parent may be drowsy or may not be feeling well. Or both of you may suddenly be caught up with past memories.

This is where tactile communication—speaking by way of touch —may be needed. I say very little to Anna as I push her wheelchair up and down the corridor or outside her building. There is little we can say to each other now, but I massage her back, I hold her hand, I brush her hair. The silent times are many.

Paul often seems content to be left alone. This was true when he lived with us, and I think it's still true in his new residence. He needs time to be alone, to meditate, to pray, or just to doze. It is his privilege.

Your parent may be morose, despondent, and withdrawn. At times you may even sense resentment. Accept these silent moods. All these things will pass.

Be content with the "now." Some older people may remember more of the distant past than the immediate past; they may remember little, if anything, of what transpired yesterday. But they do experience the immediate moment. They may perceive it differently than you do, but it is being experienced. The present is the common denominator, so enjoy it; this may be all that will be granted to you.

9) *Be bright.* Many things may be going wrong in the world, in your family, or perhaps even in your perception of the quality of care being given to your parent. I don't believe that a visit to a parent is the appropriate time or place to ventilate such concerns. If your parent raises questions about family or care, then of course they should be faced and answered. But don't overload your kin with a lot of unnecessary worries or concerns. I certainly would avoid criticizing institutional staff or administration in front of parents. Such problems should be dealt with at the level where solutions are achievable, not where anxieties will be increased.

Be satisfied with the act of visiting. No great emotional, intellectual, physical, or spiritual breakthrough may occur. If it does, thank God for the serendipity—and return another time expecting again only the opportunity of being together for this particular and immediate moment.

10) *Those of us who are Christians find special strength in reading Scripture and in prayer.* Familiar biblical passages can be repeated. Prayer can be shared. I wish we would always feel free to pray. Not only is this valid "reality orientation," but it is precisely at such times that one can sense God's Spirit close by.

11) *Make your visit brief.* Sometimes it will be obvious that you shouldn't stay longer than ten minutes. So be it. At other times, things will go well for half an hour. Don't overdo and don't overextend. Leave something unsaid for the next visit; leave something to be completed the next time you're together. In my view, short, frequent visits are much better than long, occasional ones.

12) *Get to know some of your parent's friends in the nursing home and visit them.* Get to know the relatives of those friends, and visit them. Perhaps, in time, you could trade off visits; this will add visitors to both sets of parents. This could prove extremely helpful when you are away on vacation or are caught in an emergency and you need someone to look in on your parent.

There are many lonely souls in nursing homes who have no one to visit them. We can't carry the entire burden, but there may be one or two people besides our parent or parents who need us as a friend.

GIVING GIFTS

Gifts do not have to be limited to anniversaries and birthdays. In fact, as time goes on the significance of these occasions may be lost upon your parents. But the excitement of opening a gaily wrapped package never totally disappears.

We sometimes make a special event of giving a needed item of clothing—a new dressing gown or pair of pajamas, a colorful flannel shirt for colder days, perhaps a pair of slippers. Cologne or shaving lotion can be presented as a gift. Belts and wallets often need to be replaced.

Flowers are enjoyed. One rose from your garden can bring delight. A growing plant—preferably one that will blossom—makes a good gift. So might a flowerpot with potting soil and a hyacinth or tulip bulb or some seeds.

Some practical gifts might include a "blanket support"—a device to support a blanket over one's feet, giving a bit more room for movement—or a tray table that fits over the arms of a wheelchair. A hand massage unit or a small hydromassage unit for feet or bath would make a practical and therapeutic gift.

Mobiles that turn and reflect light, pictures, large photographs of family members, and posters can decorate a room and provide pleasant moments of diversion and thought.

Tabletop FM radios with easy-to-handle controls and cassette playback units make good gifts. Perhaps a small window fan would be helpful. If a television is not readily available, a personal TV set—preferably one in color and with a remote control device—would be a long-term, ongoing (and expensive) gift.

VISITING IS YOUR RESPONSIBILITY

The burden of visiting your loved one in a nursing home is yours and will likely be carried out by you alone. If your parent lives with you at home, whatever socialization occurs will most likely depend upon what you design and engineer.

"Burden" may seem to be a harsh word, but I think it's reality. It doesn't have to mean hardship or vexing obligation. The burden can be light; it can become a challenge and an opportunity for growing compassion. But this responsibility also can become tedious and frustrating, and to me that means "burden."

I think it's healthy to recognize this fact.

Carolyn and I are the only persons from the "outside" who now visit Anna. Paul has made a few new friends at Trinity Home; some are residents and some are residents' relatives who have adopted him. However, he receives few visits from friends of previous associations.

TRUST YOUR INSTINCTS

Our threshold of pain and frustration is easily lowered as we review checklists, listen to suggestions, and even read books such as this one. We ought to consult the experts. We should try to listen to what friends are saying.

But we live with a daily reality that doesn't always conveniently fit the categories we read about. It's easy to become bewildered and to feel guilty. Since the responsibility of caring for our parents is ours, there may come a time when we have to square our shoulders and do it our way, risking setbacks and perhaps even failure, but finding some strength and confidence in the knowledge we have gained about our own loved ones. This is when we have to trust our own instincts.

Example: Some experts claim that one-to-one visits are best, that when there is more than one visitor a group is formed and the closeness of two people conversing and sharing is lost. Perhaps. But Carolyn and I have often visited our parents (and other friends in hospitals and nursing homes) together, and we have not sensed that a diverse climate was created. The important thing was the visit.

Another example: Well-meaning friends can throw you a curve. They don't often visit your parents, but when they do they'll telephone to report. Of course this is thoughtful and welcomed. I think these friends want us to feel good; they want to give a positive report. But sometimes it's difficult to recognize whom they are describing!

I've indicated that Paul is aphasic. Occasionally I've received a call that began, "Paul is really improving; I understood almost everything he said."

The first time this was reported, it troubled me greatly. Was this person talking about the same Paul I knew? He had lived in our home for nearly two years, and we had had daily contact. Now I was visiting him several times a week. I knew *I* couldn't understand everything Paul was trying to say. Was I insensitive, or too close to the situation?

You see, conversing with Paul is often like playing a game of "twenty questions." One tries to determine subject (is it animal or vegetable?), the geography of the subject, and the time frame. I have probed and pondered for half an hour over something I thought was deeply theological or financial, only to discover finally that Paul was merely concerned about having some extra dollar bills in his wallet or knowing where his handkerchiefs had gone. This kind of conversation can wear you out, but afterwards you can laugh about it together.

I think Paul's well-meaning friends are so relieved to hear an occasional word from Paul that they understand that they grasp this as something symbolic, perhaps making more of it than they should. Or they may be so disturbed by their own inability to communicate and to understand that they leave after the first recognizable word, wanting to feel as good as possible about a frustrating experience.

A third example: Once you have decided upon long-term care for your parent (usually after consultation and urging from your physician), a friend with raised eyebrow will ask in a tone that sounds accusing, "Well, how *is* your Dad?" Most likely, we've misinterpreted his gesture and tone. But we must learn to live with the risk of some people not fully understanding our decision and misinterpreting our motives.

A final example: It's easy to be overwhelmed by the professional hierarchy in long-term health-care institutions. You can so easily be "put down" as a mere layman. If you observe conditions and practices that you question and that affect the care of your loved one, be assertive. Some things in life are too important to entrust totally to the hands of professionals. Trust your instincts.

Over the months and years, Carolyn and I have acquired a sixth sense in communicating with Paul and Anna. Both are different people with different problems, but somehow we do reach them from time to time, and they reach out to us. Perhaps this sixth sense is really instinctive among people sharing love.

COMMUNICATING WITH APHASICS

Aphasia is defined as a total or partial loss of the power to use or understand words. It is often the result of a stroke or other brain damage, and presents special problems for both visitor and victim.

Expressive aphasics are able to understand what you say; *receptive* aphasics are not. Some victims may have a bit of both kinds of impediment.

Paul is an *expressive aphasic*. We are able to read to him, he watches television, and he tries to participate in singing and in the repetition of familiar Scripture passages. His difficulty is communicating to us those feelings and words that are important to him. Our difficulty is trying too soon to anticipate what he wants to say, completing sentences for him without allowing him enough time to struggle with his own words.

Perhaps you remember how it felt when a word or name eluded you; you explained your embarrassment by saying that the word was "on the tip of your tongue." It probably was. This is the condition expressive aphasics experience most of the time; most of the words they want to speak are on the tips of their tongues, but they cannot be called forth.*

Speech therapists attack the problem by working with phonics and those sounds the patient has greatest difficulty with. Large picture cards are used to help rebuild vocabulary; often the therapist identifies synonyms that the aphasic patient can speak more easily. It is a slow and precise process. Some speech therapists do not welcome extra "drill work" by nonprofessionals; others encourage this, but want to direct and monitor your work.

Picturegram grids are sometimes prepared for aphasics. These are used as "fill-in" answers to the requests of "I need" or "I want"; the patient merely points to the appropriate drawing. This tool has not worked out for Paul.

To help Paul communicate with visitors and fellow residents, I wrote up a kind of ID card for him. We discussed the draft, and I typed the text on a three-by-five index card. (In fact, I typed up two copies—one for his pocket and another to keep as a spare.) This is the text we agreed upon.

> My name is Paul Young. I was born near Pittsburgh in 1893. I accepted Christ as my Savior in my teens and felt called to serve Him. In 1918 I went to Ecuador as an evangelist and pastor. I am ordained as a Baptist minister and served the Christian and Missionary Alliance. Later I directed the United Bible Societies' work in Ecuador.
>
> In July, 1976, I suffered a stroke that has left me with two

* A most helpful book for me in understanding the brain damage of Anna and Paul was *Stroke* (New York: W. W. Norton, 1977) by Charles Clay Dahlberg and Joseph Jaffee, both physicians (one of whom is a psychiatrist who suffered a stroke with resulting paralysis and aphasia).

handicaps: a paralyzed right side and "aphasia" (a speech problem). I do understand you when you speak. You will have difficulty understanding me, but as we talk together you may understand a few of my words and thoughts.

I have two daughters (and seven grandchildren and five great-grandchildren). Esther Howard lives in Columbia, Maryland. Carolyn Gillies lives nearby in Austin.

I do appreciate your visit. Talking to people has always been a big part of my life. Tell me about yourself. Tell me some news. Tell me a good joke. If you have time, I would be grateful if you would read something. Perhaps we could have a prayer together.

God bless you. And thank you.

The message, typed double-spaced, fills both sides of the card. Paul seems happy with this conversational tool. It allows him to tell others who he is and what is important to him. It keeps him from becoming a non-person, which is easy to become when you are bound to a wheelchair and are unable to communicate readily. It opens opportunities to look at books or scrapbooks or mementos.

Since Anna now speaks only gibberish, she too is a kind of aphasic.

For her, Carolyn and I prepared a small photo album with pictures of herself and Anton, our family, her grandchildren, various places she lived during her lifetime, and some of her friends. We also typed captions beside each photograph.

Anna is sometimes amused by the album, but probably doesn't relate to it much anymore. However, the album has been invaluable in the nursing home; many nurses and aides have looked at it and in this way have gained respect for Anna's life and accomplishments. I think it provides her with a measure of status and dignity she might not otherwise enjoy.

VISITING THROUGH CORRESPONDENCE

Writing is a real ministry of love and sharing. Many of the preceding suggestions relating to personal visits apply equally well to written correspondence.

It is necessary for Carolyn or me to read Paul's and Anna's mail, since they cannot. I am grateful for the small cadre of friends who continue to write even though they receive no response from either Paul or Anna except as Carolyn or I write to them.

We maintain a list of some one hundred names for both Paul and Anna. At least twice a year, either Carolyn or I mail some kind of communication to these friends. We want to inform them about Paul and Anna, but we also hope our writing will "prime the pump," resulting in some kind of written response.

Each has a dozen or so faithful friends who do take time to write letters and remember anniversaries.

Often only a card is sent, but this is signed by members of a prayer group or a Sunday school class or some organization with which Paul or Anna once had contact. Paul especially enjoys trying to place names with faces in his memory.

Some of the letters are outstanding. They are written in the style of personal conversation. In chatty fashion, the correspondents tell of their experiences or they recall some past shared event. Memories are awakened, and friendships are reaffirmed.

A few letters never should have been written and mailed. Fortunately, there are not many of these and I use considerable editorial judgment when I read them, *if* I read them. These are the letters that go into pages of detail about family who are unknown to any of us. Some convey gossip or minutiae of dissension in family or local church. Some catalog personal ailments. A few decry the abuses of government or ventilate their suspicion of conspiracies everywhere. Sad to say, I've even seen a letter or two in which the writer questioned God's dealing with Paul or Anna, wondering what evil was done or what demon may still be in control. These are modern-day "Job's friends."

Of course, letters do not have to contain only "sweetness and light." There is a place for relating significant news, some of which may well be tragic or disappointing. It may be that a situation is so serious that the writer desires to request prayer for its solution or resolution.

But potential letter-writers should try to avoid the doom-and-gloom habit, the petty, and the irrelevant. Goethe asked that we spare him our doubts; he had enough of his own already. St. Paul urged us to rejoice *always*.

The White House, with volunteer help, has been sending birthday greetings to persons eighty years or older (and to couples celebrating fiftieth wedding anniversaries). Send your request, with the name and address, thirty days before the birthday or anniversary date to Greetings Office, The White House, 1600 Pennsylvania Ave., Washington, D.C. 20500.

RECORD YOUR CORRESPONDENCE

Instead of writing a letter, consider recording a cassette tape. Your voice makes it a kind of personal visit.

If you've never recorded a "living letter," make a trial recording and listen to it before mailing your first tape. The microphone is a sensitive instrument even on the cheapest recorders and it may reveal more of your feelings than you realize. If you're tired and depressed, you will *sound* tired and depressed. If you're happy and enthusiastic, your smile will be heard. Take time to use this medium effectively. You'll improve with practice; everyone does.

Cassette tapes should be conversational, lively, and brief. Imagine the person sitting in front of you as you speak. That's the secret of good announcers who sound so natural. Be brief; even professional narrators can put a person to sleep within half an hour.

I recommend that you discipline yourself by using the C-20 type of cassette, which provides ten minutes per side or a total of twenty minutes. You might even experiment with the idea of conversing and/or reading for five minutes or so, and then saying something like this: "Why don't we stop the tape here for today? Just leave everything the way it is, and we'll continue our visit tomorrow." Include some humor, anecdotes, and perhaps some continued story or book reading.

Even though Carolyn and I visit our parents regularly, we too are beginning to use cassette tapes. Both of us are recording books that Paul can add to his other listening. Because we are reading material we know interests him, we think we can extend our visits beyond the time we are physically present.

Chapter

28

Giving the Blessing to Your Parents

Giving "the blessing" is giving words of love and acceptance—genuine acceptance to your spouse, your children, your parents, and friends. In our book The Gift of the Blessing, *we explain five parts of the blessing as it has come down through the centuries: meaningful touch, a spoken message attaching high value to the one being blessed; picturing a special future for them; and promising an active committment to seeing that the blessing is fulfilled. In this chapter from the book, we talk about the blessing coming full-circle. As parents we give the blessing to our children, and as the adult children of our parents, we must give the blessing to them. If that seems that it is a hard or impossible thing for you to do given your family circumstances, we hope this chapter and God's help will offer special strength to you.*

Gary Smalley and John Trent, Ph.D.
The Gift of the Blessing

Helen had been physically abused by her father the entire time she was growing up. He was an alcoholic whose changing moods left her insecure, fearful, and distressed. The first chance Helen had to leave home, she was out the door. From her perspective, she didn't care if she ever saw her father again, an attitude that was confirmed when he and her mother were divorced while she was in college. Helen had absolutely no reason to go home now and refused even to consider the thought.

Then Helen met a coworker named Karen, and her whole life began to change. For the first time, she heard about and received God's blessing of salvation and His provision of a spiritual family at church to help meet her needs. With spiritual fathers galore at her church, Helen felt even less of a need to make peace with her natural father.

Gradually, Helen began to notice that some areas of her spiritual life were lagging behind. She had grown by leaps and bounds, but still had a tendency to criticize others. She had come a long way, but her temper still needed control. For a long time, Helen thought these nagging tendencies did not disappear because of a lack of faith or knowledge of God's Word. Countless times she had committed herself afresh to study God's Word. Yet her struggles continued.

Then one day Helen discovered what was at the heart of her problem. She did not lack faith; she was not willing to honor her father. The deep bitterness and resentment she felt still had an iron grip on part of her life, an area she had not opened up to God's leadership, healing, and love.

When Helen looked closely at her life, she found she was becoming more and more like the person she hated most in life—her father. Until and unless she dealt with the stranglehold he still held on her life, she would find a continuing struggle in her spiritual life and possible destruction in her personal relationships.

At first, Helen tried to push away the growing conviction that she needed to deal with her relationship with her father. Even thinking about him again hurt her. This is always the case when we remember something painful from the past. Memories bring back with them feelings, and sometimes those feelings are the things we don't want to face. However, Helen knew what was right. While her emotions didn't agree, she knew that God honored those who honored their parents. By remaining at enmity with her father, she was doing what was wrong and was draining herself of life.

Helen went to see her pastor and explained what God had been showing her over the past several months. After several sessions of prayer and counsel, Helen decided to visit her father. Whether he would respond or not, she was determined to bless and honor him.

On June 14, sitting in the pastor's study, Helen made the most difficult call of her life. She had found out her father's phone number from an old family friend and, after praying with her pastor, picked up the phone and dialed the out-of-state number.

She made the call at 3:00 P.M., and secretly Helen hoped her father would be at work and not be there to answer the phone. But on the fifth ring, her father answered the phone. God gave Helen the strength to choke out, "Hello, Dad?" After a long silence on the other end, he replied, "Helen?"

In a short conversation, Helen told her father she was going to be flying to his city and asked if she could see him. "Please do, Helen," her father said. She got directions to his apartment and hung up the phone.

The first skirmish had been won, but the battle still lay before her. A hundred times in the four days before her flight Helen talked herself in and out of going to see her father. Yet each time she decided to back out, that still, small voice within her convicted her of what was right. If she received nothing from her father except the pain she had gotten in the past, she knew she still needed to go for *her* sake and do what was right.

Helen did board the plane, and her pastor and several friends came with her to the airport to encourage her and see her off. The flight was both the shortest and longest airplane fight of her life. Helen rented a car when she arrived at the airport and drove the thirty minutes to her father's home. With a deep sigh and a short prayer, Helen walked to his apartment and knocked on the door.

An old, tired-looking man opened the door. (Why had she remembered him as being such a giant?) Sitting on the couch with her father, Helen poured out her heart to him. She told about becoming a Christian and the difference it had made in her life. Then, hardest of all, she admitted the anger and hatred she had carried toward him for years and asked his forgiveness.

By the time Helen finished talking, they were both in tears. For fifteen years Helen's father had denied the burning conviction of his wrongs against his daughter. He asked her to forgive him for being such a terrible father and lamented over all the pain he had caused in her life.

After four hours that seemed like only four minutes, Helen left. At the door she put her arms around her father and heard herself say the words that she never thought she could say: "I love you, Daddy." All the hurt he had caused in her life had not stopped her from loving him. Even during the times when she hated him the most, she still felt an attachment to him and a love for the man who had brought her into the world. Where once she could not express that love or even feel it, now she felt compassion, pity, and warmth for a man who had shattered his own life when he shattered hers.

Helen went back to her home, her office, and her church a new person. Not looking different on the outside, but knowing that on the inside she was more free than she had ever been in her life.

When she had come to know Christ, He had freed her from the guilt of every sin and unlocked the shackles that kept her chained to the past. By having the courage to face her father, to honor and bless him, Helen finally took off the shackles Christ had unlocked. She walked away from her father's house that day free to truly live in the present, because she was at last unchained from the past.

THE FIRST COMMANDMENT WITH A PROMISE

What Helen was willing to do in facing her father took a tremendous amount of courage. However, Helen had a God who understood her fears and gave her the strength to face them.

Is it only those like Helen, who have such a hurtful past, who need to bless their parents? Certainly not. In fact, the Scriptures direct every child to give the blessing to his or her parents.

In the book of Ephesians, Paul goes into detail about what it means to have healthy family relationships. He gives a beautiful picture of God's design for the husband/wife relationship. With the man as a loving leader and the woman as a highly valued partner and responder, the stage is set for children to come into a loving home.

Paul's next instructions are for those children. While under the roof and protection of one's parents, children are to "obey your parents in the Lord" (Eph. 6:1). Then Paul gives a general admonition for children of all ages: " 'Honor your father and mother,' which is the first commandment with promise: 'that it may be well with you and you may live long on the earth' " (Eph. 6:2–3).

What does it mean to honor your parents? We can see that if we will look at the word *honor* in the Scriptures. In Hebrew, the word for "honor" is *kabed.* This word literally means, "to be heavy, weighty, to honor."[1] Even today, we still link the idea of being heavy with honoring a person.

When the President of the United States or some other important person speaks, people often say that his words "carry a lot of weight." Someone whose words are weighty is someone worthy of honor and respect. However, we can learn even more about what it means to honor someone by looking at its opposite in the Scriptures.

The literal meaning of the word *curse* (*qalal*) is "to make light, of little weight, to dishonor."[2] If we go back to our example above, if we dishonor a person we would say, "Their words carry little weight." The contrast is striking!

When Paul tells us to honor our parents, he is telling us that they are worthy of high value and respect. In modern-day terms, we could call them a heavyweight in our lives! Just the opposite is true if we choose to dishonor our parents.

Some people treat their parents as if they are a layer of dust on a table. Dust weighs almost nothing and can be swept away with a brush of the hand. Dust is a nuisance and an eyesore that clouds any real beauty the table might have. Paul tells us that such an attitude should not be a part of how any child views his or her parents, and for good reason. If we fail to honor our parents, we not only do what is wrong and dishonor God, but we also literally drain ourselves of life!

WHAT HAPPENS WHEN YOU HONOR (OR DISHONOR) YOUR PARENTS?

Paul goes on to remind us in this passage in Ephesians that a promise is available to all those who will keep the commandment to honor their parents. However, we need to understand something about the promises of God before we look any further. The first thing to remember is that God's promises are always fulfilled. What God promises, He will see come to pass.

The second striking reality we need to see about this promise is that it is conditional. If you fulfill the conditions of the promise, God will honor that in your life. God's promise to you cuts both ways. If you will honor your parents, this promise will apply. But if you dishonor them, you will have to live life apart from God's promise.

Paul tells us that two aspects to this promise relate to those who would honor their parents. The first reflects on our relationship with God.

"That It May Go Well with You"

In New Testament Greek, this entire phrase is captured in the tiny word, *eu*. In ancient Greece, this word was used to salute someone with the words, "Well done! Excellent."[3] When you honor your parents, the first thing you can know for sure is that God is saying to you, "Well done! Excellent!"

For God's people, doing what was right before God has always included doing what was right by their parents. In Leviticus 19:3, Moses commands the people, "Every one of you shall revere his mother and his father, and keep My Sabbaths: I am the LORD your God." Linked with the importance of setting aside a special Sabbath day each week to honor God is the command to be consistent in revering and honoring your parents.

Jesus felt just as strongly that the actions you take toward your parents reflect your heart toward God. If you are dishonoring your parents, you are following the tradition of your times, not the Word of God. Listen to the strong rebuke Jesus gave the Pharisees and scribes who willfully chose to dishonor their parents:

> "Why do you also transgress the commandment of God because of your tradition? For God commanded, saying, 'Honor your father and your mother.' . . . But you say, 'Whoever says to his father or mother, "Whatever profit you might have received from me is a gift to God"—then he need not honor his father or mother.' . . . Hypocrites! Well did Isaiah prophesy about you, saying:
>
> 'These people draw near to Me
> with their mouth,
> And honor Me with their lips,
> But their heart is far from Me' "
> (Matt. 15:3–8).

For Jesus, doing what was wrong in dishonoring your parents could never be linked with what was right in God's eyes. Anyone who urges you to dishonor your parents speaks words of hypocrisy and falsehood. You will only hear a "well done" from your heavenly Father when you honor your parents, not if you dishonor them by treating them as a speck of dust.

Not only does it affect your relationship with the Lord when you follow what is right in honoring your parents, God promises that it will affect your own life in a positive way as well!

"That You May Live Long on the Earth"

God promises that those who will honor their parents actually receive life! How can this be? Just ask many physicians, counselors, or pastors. They have seen in their offices the shattered lives of those who dishonor their parents, with their strength drained away as a result.

Each of you has only so much emotional and physical energy, and you choose how you will spend it. What physicians and researchers are finding out more and more clearly today is that a close link exists between what we think and how we physically react.

Positive attitudes have been linked with positive physiological changes while negative attitudes can open the door for illness or disease.[4] When persons choose to hate or dishonor their parents because of anger, bitterness, or resentment, they pay a spiritual, emotional, and physical price.

The Scriptures have shown the strong connection between the words we speak and how they affect us physically. In Proverbs 16:24 we read, "Pleasant words are like a honeycomb,/Sweetness to the soul and health to the bones," and in a later passage, "A merry heart does good, like medicine,/But a broken spirit dries the bones" (Prov. 17:22).

When you decide to honor your parents, you are placing high value on them. God says such actions will increase your life on the earth. However, if you decide to see your life dried up by holding on to bitterness or resentment toward your parents (attitudes of dishonor), you eat up your strength and shorten your very life.

Some people have been dishonoring their parents for years. If that is something you have been doing through your actions or attitudes, you need to deal with it as soon as possible and begin the process of making things right. Otherwise the words of King David can ring true in your life, "When I kept silent about my sin, my body wasted away/ Through my groaning all day long./For day and night Thy hand was heavy upon me;/My vitality was drained away as with the fever heat of summer" (Ps. 32:3–4 NASB).

Paul's words have clearly demonstrated to us that we need to honor our parents. Yet, practically, how do we do this? Once again, we find ourselves at the doorstep of the blessing.

HOW DO YOU HONOR YOUR PARENTS?

The book of Proverbs was written to teach us the skill of right living. We have already seen that honoring your parents is the right thing to do, but how is it done? You honor your parents by acting as wise people, not as fools.

Many of the Proverbs talk about and illustrate different kinds of fools. All are people who are not applying God's principles for right living. One vivid description of a destructive fool is found near the end of the book. Look at this description of a worthless, treacherous man. Then go back and see what heads the list of things that characterize him:

> There is a kind of man who curses his father,
> And does not bless his mother.
> There is a kind who is pure in his own eyes,
> Yet is not washed from his filthiness.
> There is a kind—oh how lofty are his eyes!
> And his eyelids are raised in arrogance.
> There is a kind of man whose teeth are like swords,
> And his jaw teeth like knives (Prov. 30:11–14 NASB).

The man pictured above brings pain to those at home and those outside the home. As we have already seen, he also robs himself of life by cursing his parents. However, he is not only being rebuked in this passage for cursing them, he is also being scolded because he did not bless them.

If you want to be a person who honors your parents, you will be a person who blesses them. In providing the blessing to your parents, you truly honor them, do what is right in God's eyes, and even prolong your life.

Each one of the five elements of the blessing can be a useful tool in honoring your parents.

To begin with, your parents need you to *meaningfully touch* them. Even if they have struggled with hugging and touching you when you were young, as they grow older they need the reassurance that comes from being touched.

They also need *spoken words* from their children. Isn't it interesting that Mother's Day is the busiest day of the year for interstate phone calls! For many mothers, these will be the only encouraging words they hear from their children until the next year. Unfortunately, many fathers will hear fewer words of praise. You need to be consistent in your contact with your parents. They need to hear your voice and the spoken words of blessing they carry.

It is common for a parent to think back in guilt on the past. The things that often seem to stand out to a parent are not the many positive things they did, but the times they spoke out in anger or did something that accidentally hurt their child. When you bless your parents with words that *attach high value* to them, you can be a tremendous encouragement in their lives. You do not have to pretend a wrong was never committed, but you can forgive them and keep them from self-pity. You can decide to value them highly, to honor them because of the great worth they have to you and to God.

Parents need words that picture a *special future* for them. In fact, for many parents the reason they can only look back to times past is because they do not feel a sense of a future in their lives. You can point out useful and beneficial aspects to your parents' lives, even if those useful qualities are different from when they were younger. You can also point them to the Scriptures and the encouragement that their future with their heavenly Father and spiritual family does not end when this life does.

Something that can help is assuring your parents of their important place in the family as the years go by. In some homes with older parents, the grown children will take over the finances and all major decisions and toss aside an older parent's advice or input. Nothing is wrong with providing a helpful service to your parents, but you should be sure you still honor them in the process. By continuing to ask for their wisdom and advice, you can provide them with a picture of a special future.

One last thing that can encourage a special future for your parents is letting them be a part of your future, the future wrapped up in your children. Providing the time for grandparents and grandchildren to meet and interact can be a tremendous tool for providing your parents with a special future. If you will let them know how they can be and have been a blessing to your children, you honor them in a very valuable way.

Of all the ways you can bless your parents, the genuine commitment to walk with your parents through each step in life is particularly important at the end of their lives. Particularly when one parent dies, the other will need an extra measure of your love and commitment to lean on in his or her journey through life.

BLESSING OUR PARENTS WHILE MAINTAINING HEALTHY BOUNDARIES

Thus far, we've talked about giving the blessing to our parents in a positive, honoring way. But it's important to state that honoring a parent does not mean that we have to drop all healthy boundaries.

For example, my (John's) father had an explosive temper that came out many times when I was with him. In fact, the very first time I ate dinner with him at a nice restaurant nearly turned into a brawl!

My father had re-established a relationship with us, and after closing a large business deal, took us out to a nice restaurant to celebrate. While World War II had ended twenty years before, in many ways my father had never left the battlefield. And one evidence of that was his thinly veiled hatred for anyone of oriental descent.

It didn't matter that our waiter was of Chinese, not Japanese origin. With each round of drinks he ordered, he became more upset with his "slanty eyes," his "poor" service, and "smart #@$#" attitude.

Finally, when the waiter was slow getting us our check, my father blew up in anger. He stood up, challenged the man to fight and started towards him. I feel sure that if my older brother Joe hadn't grabbed him and forced him outside (even then Joe was 6′ and 220 lbs.), we'd have witnessed the battle of the Pacific all over again.

Keeping his explosive nature in mind, I put strict boundaries around his behavior when he was in my home. He could say or do anything he liked when I was at his home. But like everyone else who came over to my house, if he chose to smoke it would have to be outside. If he chose to drink before he came over, he should hold off on coming that night. And at all times, his words should be civil and without profanity in front of the children.

As you might imagine, the first time I sat down with my father at a Denny's restaurant and explained these family "rules" was an invitation to an explosion. However, we had just moved back from Texas to Arizona, and I knew the time to set loving boundaries was then.

Without judgment, and without a doubt, I wanted to make sure he knew that I loved him. I didn't preach, or condemn him in any way. But I also had a wife and little ones to consider, and a home where I didn't want anyone, even my father, to cross the line into dishonor.

Healthy boundaries with a difficult parent aren't incompatible with giving them the blessing. I'll have to admit there were times when our family boundaries acted like a wall to him. But every stone was built from his side of the fence.

If you have a parent who consistently "crosses the line" into dishonor, you too may have to establish clear boundaries with them, and have the strength to enforce them despite their reactions.

COMING FULL CIRCLE WITH THE BLESSING

In honoring our parents as very valuable, we have come full circle in our look at how the blessing in the Scriptures can enrich and encourage healthy relationships. Many of us have never thought in terms of providing our parents with the blessing. But if we will, we can leave them a tangible gift of love that they can carry throughout their lives, just as Don and his brother and sisters did for their parents.

Cindy and I (John) have been to some very creative parties over the years. From "re"gressive dinners to "Roaring Twenties" nights, we thought we had seen them all. Then an invitation came that really caught our attention. We were being asked to attend a surprise, "This Is Your Life" party for an older couple in our church.

The party had been planned by the children in this family specifically to honor their parents for years of loving care and sacrifice. It wasn't anybody's birthday, nor was it tied in with an anniversary. It was simply an evening to remember and say thank you for years of commitment to friends and family.

There was not a dry eye in the place by the time the evening was finished. Thanks to the oldest son's, Don's, initiative, their parents had received an evening of blessing from their children. As we left this older couple's house, you could see in their eyes that their hearts were bursting with pride, appreciation, and love. These children had provided their parents with an evening that was worth far more to them than any department store gift from their children ever could be.

Please don't assume that "my parents would never let us do something like that for them." If Don's parents had known what was coming, they would have probably tried to talk their children out of the evening. Yet regardless of how difficult it can be for some parents to let their children give back to them, we need to make an effort to bless them. Has it been too long since you honored your parents with words of blessing? All you need is an active commitment to give back to them what God has already richly given you.

Chapter 29

The Empty Nest

In our book Managing Stress in Marriage, *we try to cover the many stages of stress in a marriage, from the newlywed overtures to the golden chorus of retirement. The two of us have made our forty years together joyful and adventuresome by learning how to manage and survive marital stresses and family crises. We learned how to enter into a partnership together, establish God-centered priorities, utilize the stress-reducers mentioned in our book, and hang tough together during family troubles.*

Then just when you think you've learned from all the crises in the past and you're going to make it through child-rearing, along comes the stress induced by the empty nest. In this chapter we'd like to help you deal with the stress of the empty nest so that you can prepare for all the fulfilling and exciting opportunities God has for you in your retirement.

Bill and Vonette Bright
Managing Stress in Marriage

Vonette and I were helping our youngest son, Brad, pack his car. He was leaving home—moving across the country to Washington, D.C., to work for Senator William Armstrong from Colorado.

Just before he left, the three of us got down on our knees in the living room to pray. When we rose, he embraced each of us. My eyes misted as I silently thanked God for such a wonderful son.

As we walked outside, my mind wandered back to the first day I left him at boarding school . . .

First we had helped Zac, by this time a seasoned college student, settle into his dorm room at Life Bible College in Los Angeles. Then, a few days later, I flew with sixteen-year-old Brad to Stoneybrook, a Christian preparatory school in New York, where through the generosity of dear friends he was given a scholarship.

When the two of us arrived, we lugged his bags to his room. Later, I met the faculty and spoke at chapel.

When the time came for me to go, I could see that Brad was anxious to get settled and meet the rest of the boys. I felt unneeded. And lonely.

The thought of saying goodbye made my throat tighten. A flood of tears threatened to spill down my face. Wiping away the dampness, I hurriedly prepared to leave. I didn't want to embarrass him.

By the time I reached the car, my tears flowed in earnest, and in the privacy of the rental car I told the Lord how much I would miss him . . .

I felt the same ache in my throat now. As Brad drove away toward Washington, D.C., we waved valiantly. I forced a smile and stemmed my tears. *My little boy isn't little any more,* I thought as his car disappeared around a bend. *He's on his own now.*

And so were we. Zac had already left our nest and was soon to begin a family of his own, but I missed him just as much when he left.

I treasure these heartwarming memories of Zac and Brad. We'll always love our sons, and look forward to spending time with them whenever possible. But they are independent now. They don't need us like they did when they were young.

The empty nest stage of life can be the most exciting and creative time for couples. With the stress of child rearing only a memory, their marital relationship can grow deeper and richer. Even so, spouses face new challenges—those special stresses of the golden years.

PREPARING FOR THE GOLDEN YEARS

No matter how we approach life, we age. Feeling older, however, doesn't always match the number of years a person has lived.

The legendary baseball player Satchel Paige used to challenge,

"How old would you be if you didn't know how old you was?" If we think we are ancient, we will be. But if we live creative and adventurous lives, we defy the stereotypes of old age.

How can we live a full life despite the pressures of aging? By preparing for the years ahead. And by utilizing the lessons we have learned from the stresses of our past.

This gives us a distinct advantage. Unlike a bride and groom setting out into the unfamiliar territory of marriage, we who reach the golden years have gained some wisdom from our many pressure-filled circumstances. We can use this wisdom to manage or reduce the stresses of our senior years, and thus enjoy happy, fruitful lives.

STRESS OF THE EMPTY NEST

The "empty nest syndrome" is a recent phenomenon created by increasing life expectancy. Before the medical advances of the 20th century, parents often did not survive long after their children left home. Today, however, many spouses live thirty to fifty years after their children are grown.

The empty nest brings with it a special set of stressors which can destroy a relationship. Many divorces occur at this period in the marriage cycle. This is so tragic, for these are the years when partners need each other for encouragement, comfort, and care.

Let's look briefly at three of the major "golden age" stressors:

1. Loneliness

Without children in the home, a marital relationship undergoes radical change. Couples who have centered their lives around their children find the empty nest a particularly painful period of adjustment. Over the years, their marriage may have lost its vitality. They discover their relationship is merely a hollow shell, with nothing between them to prevent the loneliness.

2. Boredom

During this period, many spouses realize that their mate will never change those irritating habits nor conquer his weaknesses.

With children out of the nest, parents are forced into relating to each other. Spouses see their partner without the covering of parenthood. The only person to talk to at the dinner table is their mate. No energetic teenager livens their long evenings at home together. As a result, they find themselves wallowing in boredom and depression, resenting their bleak future and nurturing bad attitudes.

3. Painful Midlife Adjustments

Expectations and roles during the empty nest period change radically.

With her children gone, the wife is now free to pursue her occupation or ministry full time. She may enter the job force or a ministry area for the first time in many years, eager to attain the goals she has put off for so long.

At the same time, her husband has discovered his limitations in the work world. His career has become routine and dull. With his wife at work, he no longer feels the center of her attention. Her new excitement and awareness makes him realize how tired of the corporate rat-race he is. With occupational stress at a peak, he wants a change.

Thus, emotional stability is threatened. With no children at home for companionship and nurturing, the empty nest couple must reorganize their pattern of home life.

Yet the empty nest can be the beginning of a richer, fuller life. Many couples find profound satisfaction during this period. If they planned ahead, they have more financial resources and fewer expenses. They have fewer demands on their schedules. They have more time together and can concentrate fully on each other's company.

I encourage you to consider this time of life a gift from God to help you deepen your love for each other.

MAKING THE TRANSITION LESS STRESSFUL

Vonette and I dedicated Zac and Brad to God before they were born. Our sons have belonged to Him all these years. We were just responsible to rear them in the love and fear of our Lord and to give them the best training we could.

Even so, that final break when they left our nest was hard to accept.

Perhaps you are about to enter this difficult period. Or you are already experiencing the empty nest. Let me share three important principles that will help make your transition to the empty nest less stressful.

1. Let Go

As our children grow into their teens and become mature adults, we must consciously give them back to God's care. Letting go is no easy task, as you may have discovered. Accepting the empty nest with a positive attitude in the power of the Holy Spirit helps to lessen the pain of separation.

As your nest empties, no doubt you will shed tears as did Vonette and I when we released Zac and Brad to independence. But as you let go, God can fill the void with exciting and fruitful new opportunities and relationships. We have found delight in pouring our lives into each other in order that we may be more effective in our ministry for our Lord. We have also found more time to invest in the lives of many other young men and women and other adults as well.

2. Accept the Change

Sadly, many couples respond to the stress of an empty nest in the same negative way they learned to handle other critical situations. They try to keep the status quo.

We can, however, develop new strategies for adapting at any stage of life.

Instead of holding onto old patterns of living, embrace new ways of doing things. Cultivate an open, teachable spirit. Rebuild your empty home through the power of the Holy Spirit.

Recognize that both you and your partner have also changed over the years. Don't expect that "newlywed couple" to re-emerge after the children leave. Rather, begin reorganizing your relationship on the basis of who you are *now* instead of what you were years ago.

3. Adopt a Positive Attitude

Attitude makes all the difference in how couples adjust to the empty nest.

Self-pity and inflexibility only lengthen and aggravate a difficult transition. But a positive outlook opens our hearts and minds to the Lord's healing and helps ease the pain.

Vonette and I keep a positive attitude by welcoming the years ahead. We started alone, and once again we are enjoying "just the two of us." Though we believe the greatest investment we've made through the years is in the rearing of our sons, these present years in many ways are our most productive. We believe the best years of our lives are before us.

We urge you to taste the same joy. Rejoice in the partner God gave you. Plan to reap the benefits of your fruitful, godly life. Appreciate your life as it is. Look for the many positive results of growing older together.

DEVELOPING A FULLER LIFE IN THE EMPTY NEST

Think of what's happening to older couples in our society. A greater number of wives are entering the job market at middle age, or even later. One mother-turned-grandmother, for example, became a nurse, specializing in pediatrics. More husbands are turning to a second career. We know a successful businessman who became a classroom teacher at forty-three.

You, too, can make the empty nest period an exciting and creative adventure. Let me share several practical suggestions to help you:

1. Step into the Future

Using the empty nest as a stepping stone to the future prepares couples for many rewards later. Determine to live an active, purposeful life—as did a banker who entered seminary to prepare for ministry at age forty-seven; as did a friend who enrolled in graduate school to earn a degree in social work at age fifty-six.

I encourage you to decide which direction the Lord would have you take when your parenting days are over. Then use your extra time, money, and concentration to set out on that path.

2. Expand Your Horizons

Living in an empty nest can be especially tedious if we have too narrow a focus. We must expand our horizons.

One way is to develop new ministries. One couple, for example, looked at their four-bedroom home and wondered what to do with all the space. Then they had an idea. Why not start weekend retreats?

Once a month, they invited ten people to their home on Friday evening through mid-day Saturday. They tried to include at least one person or couple who hadn't committed their lives to Jesus Christ. Guests could choose to sleep over or go back to their homes and return for breakfast. The group studied the Bible and prayed for each other during this time.

With a little imagination, you can think of other things to do. You could begin a ministry to international students. Or use your extra time for discipleship and evangelism. You may wish to travel to a part of the country you have never seen. Learn a new hobby or craft. Teach illiterate adults to read. Plant a garden. Whatever your activity, do something you have always wanted to do but couldn't while the children were at home, and do it for the glory of God.

Above all, keep growing. Use your creative abilities and adventurous spirit to improve your partnership.

3. Enrich Your Friendships

An effective way to reduce the stress of the empty nest is to dedicate your time to helping others. When you pour your life into someone else, the adjustments you make will be easier. The rapport and care you exchange with friends will soothe the lonely days.

4. Enjoy Life with Your Partner

Now Vonette and I view the empty nest as a second honeymoon. Joyful, abundant partnership means receiving our major rewards and strength from each other. It requires sharing our interests and time.

But what fun it is! We laughingly refer to this time of our lives as the "brighter years." And we are looking forward to the rest of our lives with great anticipation.

Chapter

30

Giving the Blessing to Your Older Children

You have done all that you possibly could to raise a family that was honoring to God, to themselves, to each other, and to others outside the family. Is your job done when the kids graduate from college or move out or get married?

A family will remain a family forever. And the blessing is something that you can give forever—to children, to friends, to parents, to each other. In this special chapter from our book The Gift of the Blessing, *we would like to share what we have come to find out is a very important blessing—the blessing we continue to give our older children as they make their way in the world. We have learned that no one is ever too old, too grown-up, or too wise to need to receive the blessing from us. And even as we continue to give the blessing to our older children we free them to give the blessing to us, their parents.*

Gary Smalley and John Trent, Ph.D.
The Gift of the Blessing

When our children were young, Norma and I (Gary) made a commitment to give our children the blessing. We knew that simple acts of unconditional love could make a major difference in their lives. We have seen the fruits of the blessing by watching them mature, leave home, and increase their desire to enrich the lives of others. *But what I never realized, or ever dreamed, was how powerful —and how necessary—the blessing would become to my older children.*

Kari, Greg, and Michael have now grown up and left the house, Kari and Greg to spouses and homes of their own, and Michael to college at an out-of-state school. Our home is much quieter, but not empty. Their laughter, voices, pictures, and love still echo from each wall in our house. And what's more, instead of their growing out of their need for our blessing, they've grown to appreciate it even more. So if you have older children who have moved away from home, they're never out-of-reach of the blessing you can continue to give them. Here are eight important ways you can bless your children to show them your love and appreciation for who they have become as adults.

OLDER CHILDREN FALL BACK ON OUR PRAISE

While we've spoken at length about the need to verbally praise our younger children, I've seen with my own grown children how important affirmation continues to be. In fact, as the decisions they make become more serious, and the trials they face become more real, praise is a tremendous source of security and strength for them.

Children of all ages have an "affirmation bank," that requires constant deposits. When we do verbalize our love, we continue to give them a foundation that operates apart from any trying circumstances they might face.

Recently, I saw two examples of how important words of praise are for older children. First, I met a bright, energetic young woman in her early twenties who, already, is building an outstanding career. She is poised, confident, and always wears a smile. And that's someone who only gets paid commission sales in a highly competitive field, and who faces rejection every work day of the week! What keeps her going as she faces so many closed doors? What is the main thing she credits for her top honors as a sales rep?

"Without a doubt, it's my parents," she told me.

"I deal with rejection from people every day, but I've never gotten anything but acceptance from my parents. For example, I can't think of a single time when I've been alone with my father—and I mean since I was a child—that he didn't verbally affirm me about something. Let me tell you, there are a lot of days that I draw on his praise, and it keeps me going." Now as an adult, facing criticism and stiff competition, her parents' words of praise for who she is, and what she does, are like a lighthouse on a stormy night.

The second example of the power of praise came from my son, Greg. In fact, he taught me a lesson I'll never forget about this important aspect of the blessing.

Last May, Greg married a wonderful young woman named Erin. After their honeymoon, Norma and I had the privilege of traveling a good part of the summer with them before they headed to graduate school and their new home in Colorado.

In my own life, I'm always looking for ways to strengthen my marriage and parenting skills. Perhaps that's why, without realizing it, I began pointing out things that I noticed in Greg's interaction with his new bride.

If he did something I felt was somewhat insensitive, or not completely loving, I found myself taking up Erin's defense. Without meaning to, I made him feel uncomfortable around me, even defensive.

I had no idea how deeply this affected Greg until one night after we'd been traveling for almost four weeks. My son pulled me aside when Norma and Erin were out of the room and we had a "son-to-father" talk.

"Dad," he said, in a serious tone. "I need to have a talk with you."

He outlined his feelings and concerns in a very loving way. But sandwiched in between his words of appreciation for me, was the clear message that my "helpful" pointers were being taken as criticism of him as a brand new husband.

As we talked, Greg reminded me of a crucial lesson. "Dad," he told me. "I'm not perfect, but I'm *trying*. This is all new to me. Do you think that for the first year or so, instead of concentrating on the negative things I'm doing, you could praise me for what you see me doing correctly? I think that would help me a lot more than what you're doing now."

Greg's words made an immediate impact on me. He gave me a reminder that praise is one of the most positive reinforcing tools God has given us as parents!

Since that conversation, Greg hasn't had to come to me one time about my "help." But what he has heard from me is consistent encouragement and praise for the many things he is doing right.

Look for anything your children are doing, saying, acting, or experiencing that you believe is valuable and healthy for them, and that honors God and others. Like the fourth chapter of Philippians says, "Whatever is honorable," these are the things we should think on, and praise in our children.

Remember that even the smallest act of praise can be an encouragement to our children. Michael, our youngest, has even expressed how he appreciates seeing bumper stickers on our cars that read, "Our son and our money go to Baylor University!" I have two other smaller Baylor logos stuck on my car windows as well. Small thing, but to him they say, "I'm proud of you, I'm proud of your college and of the way you're working so hard at school."

Without question, praise inhabits the best of homes. And as our children grow older, their need for our affirmation becomes even greater, not less.

OLDER CHILDREN NEED A WRITTEN RECORD OF OUR WORDS

Written words become a lifelong legacy for a child to keep. In a letter, you can express your pride in them, or share what you're learning from the Scriptures, or what you're doing that fills them in on your life. Whether they're waiting in the mail-line in the military, reaching into their mailbox at school, or thumbing through their letters in their own home or apartment, written words of blessing from a parent are incredibly powerful.

How powerful? John was involved in a wedding several years ago where a young woman graphically demonstrated the power of written words.

At some reception dinners, words of love and blessing are easily spoken from both sets of parents. But in Angie's case, her father was a very quiet, extremely shy person. He did manage to stand up and share briefly—and nervously—how much he approved of the marriage. But then his daughter did something that expressed his love better than any speech he could have given.

Without his realizing it, since she was a young child, she had kept *every* card and note he had ever written her. Somewhat awkward with his spoken words, he eloquently expressed his love for her through written words. And she treasured and kept every one. Even recent letters that expressed how proud he was of her, and how much he looked forward to her marriage.

In front of the entire crowd (whose eyes were all filled with tears), she had her dad come up and stand beside her as she talked about how much he loved her; how meaningful his support had been over the years. And his love for her was all recorded in written blessings, captured in the several thick scrapbooks she had brought to the dinner.

With the kids out of the house, do you find yourself with a little more time? Then why not take some of that extra time and put your blessing for your children into written words. Even if they don't keep every card or letter you write in an album, they'll keep your words of love in their hearts forever. Often, our written words of love become priceless treasures when we're gone—a paper trail of love! a written memorial to our blessing to them.

If you're reading this chapter as a son or daughter, let me tell you how this same principle can be a tremendous encouragement to your parents. For years, I've greatly appreciated my daughter, Kari's, thoughtfulness in leaving Norma and me little notes around the house. Sometimes on a door, sometimes on the sink or refrigerator we'll find the words, "Mom and Dad, I was just thinking about you and wanted you to know how much I love you and look forward to the fun times we'll have in the future!" In many ways, Kari has taught the rest of us the power of written words of encouragement.

WE BLESS OLDER CHILDREN BY HELPING DRAIN ANGER OUT OF THEIR LIVES

I began my book *The Key to Your Child's Heart* by stating that the single most important factor in maintaining harmony in any home is to resolve anger as soon as possible. Even today, the single greatest problem I observe in homes across the world is the epidemic of broken relationships, most destroyed by unchecked, unresolved anger.

Too many people are simply not aware of how much damage anger heaps on any family or friendship. I label this unresolved anger as "closing a person's spirit." The more a family member "closes the spirit" of another, the greater the disharmony and distance in the relationship, and the less interest in spiritual things you'll see. Prolonged anger can lead to depression, ulcers, or high blood pressure. These are just a *few* of the emotional and physical problems that can accompany anger!

Most of us can recognize a closed spirit in another family member. They usually won't talk with us openly or cheerfully, and they dislike our reaching out to hug or touch them. They tend to argue more, and we can sense their subtle (or obvious) avoidance of us. With older children who have a great deal of anger, they may move away at the earliest opportunity, or even deliberately choose any path to take, except the one we've pointed them toward.

For anyone serious about reducing family friction, blessing older children, and dealing with anger in a healthy way, here are five brief, practical suggestions on opening another person's closed spirit. For greater detail, see *The Key to Your Child's Heart.*

Five Steps to Reopen a Child's Spirit

Years ago, I disciplined my son Greg in anger after he was screaming while I was on the telephone. Without finding out the reason why he was yelling, I spanked him and watched his little spirit "close" towards me.

When I realized what I'd done, I applied the five principles (not steps) I'll share with you, and in a matter of minutes I witnessed his spirit reopen.

Today, almost twenty years later, I *still* use these same principles if I see I've done something to put anger in Greg's heart. What's more, I've even used these guidelines to help him deal with the anger others may have placed there over the years.

1. Become Tenderhearted

The first step that I needed to take to open Greg's spirit was to reflect tenderness and softness in my words. "A soft word turns away anger," the proverb says, and gentleness has a way of always melting anger.

We communicate several things to the person whom we have offended when we soften our tone. First it says, "You're valuable and important." Second, it shows that we are willing to slow down long enough to correct what has happened. Finally, by adopting gentleness we communicate that we are open to listen, that it is safe for him or her to share what has happened, and that we don't want anyone to maintain a "closed spirit" in our home.

2. Increase Understanding

The second step to open a person's spirit is to increase our understanding of the pain he or she feels.

As Greg has grown older, when I have stopped to listen and softly ask Greg why he was hurting, I've found his resistance to talking begin to drain away. As my spirit became even softer, I had deeper understanding and could feel his pain. Many times just these two factors—being soft and then understanding a person's pain—will open a person's spirit.

This is particularly important as children get older. The gift of listening with understanding to an older child is often all they need to make the connection between what they're hurt or frustrated about, and dealing with that hurt in a positive way. Avoiding lectures, and increasing careful, honoring listening can be very helpful for a child of any age.

3. Recognize the Offense

The third step to opening a person's spirit is admitting that we were wrong. One of the hardest things for many parents to do is to admit when they are wrong. I find it is especially hard for fathers. I do not necessarily like to find out when I am wrong, and it's not always easy to admit when I am. But I must remember that a hardened, resistant attitude is extremely detrimental to children.

One of my favorite Christian camps is Kamp Kanakuk, in beautiful Branson, Missouri. Jim Brawner was for years one of the directors of the camp (now our National Homes of Honor Director!), and one summer, he made an incredible discovery.

He asked each of the several thousand teenagers who came to camp during the summer, "What is the one thing you wish your parents would do more often?" The answer wasn't, "Say, 'I love you,' " more often, or even, "Spend more time with me." They didn't even say, "Send more money!" The overwhelming number of teenagers said the very same thing: *"I wish my mother and father would admit when they're wrong."*

There is tremendous bonding power when we become strong enough to admit our mistakes to our children. While some children may use our apology as ammunition to shoot back at us, most will be moved to a level of closeness—and a freedom from anger—that would shock you.

Softness, listening, and admitting we're wrong. These three factors are crucial, but there are two more actions that are equally important to making sure the spirit has reopened.

4. Attempt to Touch

The fourth factor is attempting to touch the offended person. Why? First of all, he needs to be touched. If he reaches out and responds to our touching, then we know his spirit is opening or the anger is draining out. This is an extremely important time to take his hand, put an arm around him, or otherwise touch him in a meaningful way. Even with an older child, that touch lets him know that we care, that we love him, and that he is very important.

Second, touching often allows us to find out if the child's spirit is *not* opening. If my child pulls back or moves away when I try to touch her, it is commonly an indication that she isn't ready to open her spirit. She may need more time or greater understanding from the one who offended her.

We encourage you to practice appropriate hugs, handshakes, and kisses with your older children.

5. And Finally, Seek Forgiveness When Warranted

The final step we need to take is to seek forgiveness from the one we offended. When we have offended someone, we must not only be willing to admit we're wrong, but also to give that child a chance to respond. For me, the best way is to say something like, "Could you find it in your heart to forgive me?" When Greg was young, this is when I knew I had reopened Greg's spirit, for when I asked for his forgiveness, he would rush into my arms.

Once they're talking to us again, allowing us to hug them, and speaking to us in honoring tones, we can say at this point that true restoration and forgiveness has been gained. And usually, most of the anger is gone.

Praising our older children; leaving them a written legacy of our love for them; and helping to drain anger out of their life. All three are powerful ways of giving the blessing. And a fourth way is equally powerful.

GIVE THEM THE INHERITANCE OF A GOOD NAME

Not everyone can leave a $100,000 inheritance to their children, even if they want to. I remember when Norma and I were first married, her father took us out to dinner and told us we were going to receive a $100,000+ inheritance very soon. In our minds, that very night we began to spend that inheritance in one hundred different ways! Thank the Lord, we never actually went out and bought things based on his words, because the economy went into a deep slump. Her father lost all the money he had verbally promised (and far more) nearly overnight.

So, while not everyone can leave a monetary inheritance to their child, and we shouldn't always count on that kind of inheritance anyway, every one of us can leave our children the inheritance of a good name.

In Proverbs, we're told that a "good name" is better than jewels. It's a priceless gift that we can pass down to our children, and they can pass down to their children in turn. Our name is something that, no matter what, we will pass down to our kids, and it can either be a blessing to them, or a curse.

Take Darwin Smith, and his son, Darwin, Jr. While this is an extreme example, it illustrates the importance of looking ahead two, and even three generations, on the impact we have on future family members. Darwin, Sr. came from an abusive home, and the home he made for his son was incredibly unstable. He was fired from over a dozen jobs all because every boss he had was terrible. But what his instability led him to do one winter day was even more terrible still.

After being dismissed from yet another job, Darwin, Sr., took a rifle, a handgun, and pockets full of ammunition and killed four people at his former plant, and then killed himself as the police moved in. His father left a name to remember all right, only Darwin, Jr. had to carry it as well. Every day at school, and every time his name was spoken in their small community, the name his father left him became a curse, not a blessing.

How different when we see a person whose parents have loved God and spent a lifetime helping others. The name these people have leaves a sweet fragrance for those who hear it and a powerful blessing to the children and grandchildren who carry it. How is your character today? From truthfulness, to consistency, to Christ-likeness, we need to leave our older children a name they can be proud of, not ashamed of.

WE BLESS OUR OLDER CHILDREN BY TAKING CARE OF OUR OWN HEALTH

While it may sound unimportant, one of the most important ways we can bless our older children is to maintain our own physical, mental, and spiritual health! When we pay attention to what we eat, the vitamins and prescription medications we take, and even exercise regularly, it's bound to help us live longer. And in my case, hopefully, it's extending my ability to be around to bless my children and their children even longer.

In my family, my father died of a massive heart attack at the age of fifty-eight. My oldest brother had a similar heart attack at age fifty-one and has had by-pass surgery since then. My next oldest brother died of a heart attack at age fifty-one.

I have the same genetic tendencies that the other Smalley men do and have had for generations—high cholesterol.

Yet instead of my health's becoming a cloud that my children have to worry about, I've done all I can to maintain a healthy lifestyle. Through the help of my doctors, diet, and regular exercise, I've seen my cholesterol move to a level below even the average risk factor.

For almost twenty years, I've vigorously exercised one half-hour each day—walking, tread-milling, stair climbing, bicycling, and occasionally jogging. And there's a reason. Whether we realize it or not, our children do worry about our health as we get older, even at times, more than we do. That's why actively taking care of ourselves not only blesses us physically—it's a way of giving our children the blessing as well.

Recently, I just went through a procedure, angioplasty, where a camera was literally inserted into my heart arteries, allowing a doctor to see if the Smalley "curse" of high cholesterol had caused any heart damage. The result? To my amazement, and the doctors', all the efforts and prayers I've made over the years seemed to pay off one hundredfold. I was told by the doctor when I finally awoke from the procedure, "Smalley, get out of here and go home! You've got a 'baby' heart, it looks so good. Yours is the best looking heart I'll see in here all year."

Many supportive friends celebrated with me about how positive my health has become, but none celebrated as much as my own spouse and children. Our daughter, Kari, called me in the hospital and said, "Dad, call me the minute you get out of the operating room and tell me everything's OK. Because if it isn't, I'm jumping on a plane and coming out right now!" It's natural for our children to worry about us. However, they've seen me take an active role in doing all I can, not to become a burden on them through ill-health, and to avoid being any kind of burden to them for years to come.

While the previous five blessings for our children involve who they are in their relationships, this sixth blessing can become a tremendous, personal help to them.

TEACH THEM FINANCIAL RESPONSIBILITY

When our children were young, we were responsible for them financially. But in the years that follow, we need to teach them financial independence and responsibility.

There is a tremendous temptation to try to rush in and provide financial help, resources, or even luxuries that a grown child needs. However, at times, this can lead to over-controlling, and even short-circuiting the learning process when it comes to being financially responsible. Rather, like Sam Walton, the founder of Wal-Mart stores, we need to help our children see the value of hard work, savings, and thrift.

Norma and I see each of our children learning to work hard and plan financially for themselves and their own families. We've tried to instill within them an understanding of three important financial guidelines:

1. What do they believe God wants them to do in serving other people? The highest calling for each of us is serving people in love.
2. Once they decided on what area of serving others is best for them, anything from medicine to selling a helpful service, they then need to commit to gain the best knowledge and practical skills possible to become an expert in that field.
3. They must continually practice and increase their skills in their chosen area of service.

I've watched God honor and reward people all over our world who have held to these three guidelines. You'll notice that the focus isn't on money. It's on serving others with an expertise that leads to their efforts being recognized and rewarded.

My children know that they can't depend on others to take care of them forever. They have to find their own plan for satisfying service, knowing that "the greatest among you is the servant of all."

AVOID OVER-CONTROLLING

As we've visited Michael, our youngest son, at college, he's mentioned many times a major problem of parenting—and blessing—

older children. Namely, well-meaning children can find themselves with a parent who is far too controlling for their good.

Mike has actually told us that instead of these parents' being appreciated by their children, they look at them as actually withholding the blessing from them. One example he gave was of a junior in college who still has to call her mother every time she plans to do anything significant, either in-town or out-of-town. Instead of communicating concern, this checking-in has become a control device that her mother uses to live her own life through her daughter.

When our children are young, it's important that we remain in control as their parents. But as they grow older, there's a balance that must come into play. Namely, that we lead them by example and love, encourage them always, and support them with a listening ear or personal counsel—but not control. Rather, we should bless our children out of a desire that they take *positive control* of their own lives as they grow older.

GIVE YOUR CHILDREN THE CHANCE TO RETURN THE BLESSING TO YOU

For me, it's easier to give a gift than to receive it. But as I've learned over the years, it's important that the blessing become a two-way street. While we need to travel the road first and give our children the blessing in every way, they also need to be able to express their blessing back to you.

Without question, one of the greatest rewards of giving your children the blessing is having them grow up one day and return it to you. That's what happened to me a few years ago, when I received something incredibly meaningful from my son.

While it might not catch your eye, if you were to walk into my (Gary's) office, you'd see something hanging on my wall that's priceless. It's not an oil painting, or a bronze sculpture. It's a small plaque that my son Greg created and gave me that carries a picture of the two of us, a father's day card, and his words of blessing returned to me.

All of us have tough, discouraging days at times. But not everyone has the words of love and appreciation I have hanging behind me. Words of blessing returned to me from my oldest son, Greg, that brighten the darkest day.

The Father's Day card that I can't read without mist gathering in my eyes says,

This Is for You

This is for you, Dad, for the father I love,
For the one who has cared all these years,
but has never heard enough about how much I care.
So this is for you,
For the one who has helped me through,
all my childhood fears and failures,
And turned all that he could,
into successes and dreams.
For the man who is a wonderful example,
of what more men should be.
For the person whose devotion to his family,
is marked by gentle strength and guidance
And whose love of life, sense of direction,
and down to earth wisdom,
make more sense to me now,
than nearly any other thing I learned.
If you never knew how much I respected you,
I want you to know it now, Dad,
and if you never knew how much I admire you,
let me just say that I think you're the best father
that any child ever had.
This is a card filled with love,
and it's all for you . . . Dad.

And then added to Adrian Rodgers' beautiful poem are my own son's words of blessing.

> "Father, my wish and prayer on this special day, is that we can share another fifty years of friendship together. To the molder of my dreams, yet still, to my best friend. I love you."
>
> Gregory T.

Greg's words are precious to me because they come out of a commitment Norma and I made years ago to provide our children with the blessing. We've looked at it as our gift to give our children to help them have a wonderful, meaningful life. But it is so humbling and encouraging when they return the blessing to us, it can make our hearts want to burst.

While I've spoken and given Greg numerous examples of my love and commitment (and Kari and Michael as well), I need to be able to receive the blessing from them, too. Not look for it. Demand it. Or pout if we don't get it. But be open to receiving it should they complete the loop by blessing us as well.

While the applications of the blessing may change when they're older, their hearts don't change. Even grown children are waiting for words of love to be spoken and heard.

Eight Ways to Bless Your Older Child

1. *Praise*
2. *Written words of blessing*
3. *Drain anger from their lives*
4. *Leave a positive inheritance*
5. *Teach financial responsibility*
6. *Take care of your own health*
7. *Avoid being over-controlling*
8. *Let your children return the blessing to you*

About the Authors

Claudia Arp is the founder of MOM's Support Groups, a family enrichment resource program, which has groups throughout the United States and in Europe. She is a co-founder and co-director, with her husband, Dave, of Marriage Alive International. The Marriage Alive Workshop is popular across the United States and in Europe.

Claudia is the author of *52 Ways to Be a Great Mother-in-law,* and co-author with Dave of *The Marriage Track* and *52 Dates for You and Your Mate.* Claudia is also co-author with Linda Dillow of *The Big Book of Family Fun.*

Stephen Arterburn is founder of New Life Treatment Centers, Inc., a program for emotional problems and addictive disorders, with treatment centers nationwide. Arterburn is a best-selling author of fifteen books, has appeared regularly on television talk shows such as "Geraldo," "Oprah Winfrey," and "Sally Jessy Raphael," and has been featured in *USA Today.* His books include *The Angry Man; Growing Up Addicted; Drug-Proof Your Kids; When Someone You Love Is Someone You Hate; How Will I Tell My Mother?; Faith That Hurts, Faith That Heals;* and *Addicted to "Love."*

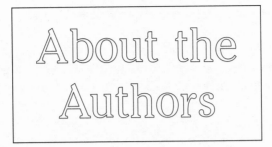

Dr. Emil J. Authelet directs Conflict Management and the Family Ministry for American Baptist Churches of the West, for which he is also an area minister. He has served for 25 years in pastoral ministry and family therapy and holds two degrees from American Baptist Seminary of the West, including a doctorate in pastoral care and counseling. As a popular conference and workshop leader, he specializes in single family ministry.

Tom Bisset is general manager of WRBS-FM, a Christian radio station in Baltimore, Maryland. He is a graduate of Moody Bible Institute, Greenville College (A.B., Th.B.), and Johns Hopkins University (M.A.). He and his wife, Mary Ruth, have two grown children. He has published articles in various Christian and secular magazines and *The Baltimore Sun.*

Judy Blue is a graduate of Indiana University, with a bachelor's degree in speech and hearing therapy and a master's degree in counseling and guidance. Ron and Judy have been married for twenty-seven years and are the parents of five children.

Ron Blue is the managing partner for Ronald Blue & Co., an Atlanta-based firm offering financial planning, investment management, and tax services to individual and corporate clients throughout the United States. Ron received his MBA degree from Indiana University. He is the author of *Master Your Money, Master Your Money Workbook*, and *The Debt Squeeze,* with more than 150,000 copies in print. He is also the developer and creator of two videos: "Master Your Money" and "Common Cents: Training Your Children to Manage Money." He frequently writes for various Christian publications and is a regular contributor to *Moody Monthly* and Focus on the Family's *Physician* Magazine.

Bill Bright, founder and president of Campus Crusade for Christ International, has authored *The Secret, Witnessing Without Fear, Promises, As You Sow* and numerous other books. His special focus is New Life 2000, an international effort to help reach more than six billion people with the gospel by the year 2000.

Vonette Bright, co-founder of Campus Crusade for Christ, has assisted her husband in ministry throughout their married life. She has developed an international prayer ministry (which prompted the setting of a definite date for the National Day of Prayer by Congress and the president) and an International Prayer Congress in Korea. She was chairman of the Intercession Working Group of the Lausanne Committee for World Evangelization for a number of years.

Randy Carlson is the founder and president of Today's Family Life, Inc., and Parent Talk, Inc., the vice president of the Family Life Radio Network, and the cohost of "Parent Talk," a nationally syndicated radio program (the first national, live, call-in program where parents talk to parents). He has written three books: *Unlocking the Secrets of Your Childhood Memories*—a best-seller co-authored with Dr. Kevin Leman—*Father Memories*, and the workbook, *In My Father's Image*. A certified marriage and family therapist, he founded three full-service Counseling Centers, one in Michigan and two in Arizona. He and his wife, Donna, have three children: Evan, 14; Andrea, 11; and Derek (D.J.), 8.

Dr. Les Carter is a nationally known expert in the field of Christian counseling with more than fifteen years in private practice. He is a psychotherapist with the Minirth-Meier Clinic and is a weekly guest on the clinic's popular radio program, "The Minirth-Meier Clinic," heard daily on radio stations across the nation including the Moody Broadcasting Network. Dr. Carter is the author of seven other books, including *Imperative People* and *Broken Vows*. A popular speaker, he leads seminars in cities across the United States.

Carter earned his B.A. from Baylor University and his M.Ed. and Ph.D. from North Texas State University. He and his family currently live in Dallas, Texas.

Jan L. Dargatz has a Ph.D. in education from the University of Southern California in Los Angeles and has written or edited more than seventy books, including *10,000 Things to Praise God For*, *52 Simple Ways to Build Your Child's Self-esteem and Confidence*, and *52 Simple Ways to Help Your Child Do Better in School*. She is also the author of *The Promise*, a dramatic production of the life of Christ, which has been performed in Moscow and featured on TBN.

Jan specializes in the production of curriculum and inspirational materials for and about children through her own creative studio. She also teaches Sunday school at Trinity Episcopal Church in Tulsa, Oklahoma.

Linda Dillow describes herself first as a wife and a mother, and second, as a speaker, author, and marriage seminar leader on being a creative wife. She is author of the best-selling *Creative Counterpart* and *Priority Planner*, as well as co-author of *The Big Book of Family*

Fun. She and her husband, Joseph, live in Hong Kong, training Christian leaders.

John Gillies is a professional writer, playwright, and occasional actor. His background includes twelve years with Church World Service, three years with the Texas Department of Human Resources, and, with his wife, Carolyn, a term in Brazil as a lay communications missionary.

Laurene Johnson is a Certified Reality Therapist in private practice and is director of Successful Living After Divorce in Phoenix, Arizona. She has traveled to eleven foreign countries as an internationally known specialist, lecturer, and seminar leader for divorced families and children of divorce programs. Laurene received her B.A. from the University of Missouri and her M.A. in counseling from Western International University. For seven years, she has been a counselor at the American Graduate School of International Management. She is a member of the American Association of Counseling and Development and the National Speakers Association.

For the past fourteen years, Laurene has been a divorced mother of two children: Cheri, a graduate student in cross-cultural counseling at Western Washington University; and Brad, a history major at Arizona State University.

For further information on seminars, workshops or talks for teachers, churches, or organizations write to 2400 E. Arizona Biltmore Circle, Suite 1400, Phoenix, Arizona 85016.

Dr. Grace Ketterman is the medical director of the Crittenton Center in Kansas City, Missouri, and is the author of twelve previous books, including *Surviving the Darkness* and *Verbal Abuse.* After having received her M.D. degree from Kansas University Medical School, she was affiliated with Menorah Medical Center, Kansas City General Hospital, and Western Missouri Mental Health Center. Undergirding Dr. Ketterman's medical career is her spiritual faith, which she describes as "practical, common-sense, and deeply committed."

Dr. Kevin Leman is the author of fourteen books on family and marriage. His best-sellers have sold millions of copies and include *The Birth Order Book, Making Children Mind Without Losing Yours, Sex Begins in the Kitchen,* and *Unlocking the Secrets of Your Childhood Memories.* A masterful communicator, Dr. Leman is an internationally known psychologist and humorist and is cohost of the nationally syndicated radio program "Parent Talk." He and his wife Sande have five children: Holly, 20; Krissy, 19; Kevin, 15; Hannah, 6; and Lauren, 4.

Dr. Frank Minirth founded the Minirth-Meier Clinic in Dallas, Texas, one of the largest psychiatric clinics in the world, with associated clinics in Chicago; Los Angeles; Little Rock, Arkansas; Longview, Fort Worth, Sherman, and Austin, Texas; and Washington, D.C.

Dr. Minirth is a diplomate of the American Board of Psychiatry and Neurology and received an M.D. from the University of Arkansas College of Medicine.

Founder of Morley Properties, Inc. which in the 1980s grew to be one of Florida's 100 largest privately held companies, **Patrick Morley** has been the president or managing partner of sixty-one companies and partnerships and is a co-founder of The Enterprise Bank, N.A. of Orlando. Morley is the author of the best-selling books *The Man in the Mirror* and *The Rest of Your Life.* The Evangelical Christian Publishers Association selected *The Man in the Mirror* to receive its prestigious Gold Medallion Achievement Award as the best Christian Living book of 1990.

Among other activities, Mr. Morley serves on the Board of Directors of Campus Crusade for Christ and the President's Council of Ligonier Ministries. He and his wife, Patsy, serve as the Host Couple for Executive Ministries in Orlando. He teaches a weekly Bible study to 125 businessmen and is an active member with his family at Orangewood Presbyterian Church.

He lives in Orlando, Florida, with his wife, Patsy, his daughter, Jennifer, and his son, John.

Dr. Brian Newman, clinical director of Inpatient Services at the Minirth-Meier Clinic in Richardson, Texas, is a frequent cohost on the Minirth-Meier Clinic radio program. Dr. Newman is the father of two children, Rachel and Benjamin.

Bobbie Reed, Ph.D. (psychology) is a noted authority on the single life and encourages and counsels singles through her books and lectures. She is the author of thirteen books—including *Single on Sunday, I Didn't Plan to Be a Single Parent!* and *Too Close, Too*

Soon—which offer practical advice and hope for singles and single parents, as well as numerous books on Christian Education.

Dr. Reed has remarried and is a stepmother and an active supporter of the single adult ministry at Skyline Wesleyan Church in Lemon Grove, California.

Dr. Joel C. Robertson, director of the Robertson Neurochemical Institute, Ltd., specializes in neuropharmacology—brain chemistry technology. A pioneer in the use of brain technology for self-help, he is the author of *Help Yourself*™. He is also an internationally known author, lecturer, clinician, and consultant to the psychiatric and chemical dependency fields.

Georglyn Rosenfeld is a freelance writer living in Mesa, Arizona. She received her B.A. in business from Westmont College, her M.A. in business from San Jose State University, and has completed her course work for a doctorate in adult education at Arizona State University. For the past fifteen years she has co-authored books and tapes for numerous motivational speakers. She also teaches workshops for children of divorce.

Her personal experience includes being both a custodial and non-custodial parent, remarrying, and becoming a stepmother to two children. Rosenfeld's son, Nathan Estruth, is now a graduate student at Harvard University, and her daughter, Natalie Estruth, attends Wheaton College.

William Sears, M.D., is a pediatrician in private practice in San Clemente, California, and is clinical assistant professor of Pediatrics at USC School of Medicine. He and his wife, Martha, are coauthors of *The Baby Book,* and he is a contributing editor for *Christian Parenting Today.* Sears also has published articles on child care in *Baby Talk, American Baby, Parenting, McCall's,* and *Redbook.*

Gary Smalley, president of Today's Family, is a doctoral candidate in marriage and family counseling and has a master's degree from Bethel Seminary in St. Paul, Minnesota. His previous best-selling books include *If Only He Knew; For Better or for Best; Joy That Lasts; The Key to Your Child's Heart;* and *The Blessing.* Gary is the father of three children and lives with his wife, Norma, in Branson, Missouri.

Dr. Larry Stephens is a licensed professional counselor and a licensed marriage and family therapist with the Minirth-Meier Clinic in Dallas, Texas. For his Ed.D. dissertation, he conducted a survey of how Christians develop their image of God. Dr. Stephens is author of *Please Let Me Know You, God, The God Who Loves You,* and co-author of *The Man Within: Daily Devotions for Men in Recovery.*

Jay Strack is a prominent national and international crusade evangelist. Having himself experienced the devastating impact of his parents' divorce, he writes with compassion and conviction about the need to build a child's self-image. His work takes him into over 4,000 schools and institutions where he tells his own story: "I grew up through some pretty tough times. My parents split up when I was young and my mother bounced from man to man looking for a security they could never provide. I was alone. I felt forsaken, hopeless, and unloved. My home was not what it should have been—a place of protection, imitation, and affection. But your home can be. Let me tell you how."

Strack has spent nearly twenty years speaking to parents and teenagers on how to find the real purpose in life. Married since 1972, he and his wife, Diane, have two daughters, Melissa and Christa.

Todd Temple is the cofounder and executive director of 10 TO 20, a company that produces national events and conferences designed to get students involved in making a difference. He's written or cowritten nine books, including *Creative Dating* (a reasonably funny book celebrating the notion that there's more to dating than dinner and a movie) and *How to Become a Teenage Millionaire* (which actually is all about how to make, save, and spend money wisely). He's also a frequent contributor to teenage magazines and a motivational speaker to students at schools, churches, and conferences.

Todd holds a bachelor's degree in social ecology from the University of California, Irvine. His interests include literature, computers, theater, surfing, bicycling, travel, and hunger relief. He lives in Del Mar, California.

John Trent, president of his own ministry, Encouraging Words, has a Ph.D. in marriage and family counseling and holds a master's degree from Dallas Theological Seminary. In addition to the "Love Is a Decision" seminars he conducts with Gary Smalley, John Trent holds "Blessing" seminars across the country. He wrote with Gary the best-selling books *The Blessing; The Gift of the Blessing; The Language of Love; Love Is a Decision;* and *The Two Sides of Love.* John has also written two children's books, *The Treasure Tree* and *There's a Duck in My Closet!* He lives in Phoenix with his wife, Cynthia, and daughters, Kari Lorraine and Laura Catherine.

Dr. Paul Warren is a behavioral pediatrician and adolescent specialist and is medical director of the Minirth-Meier Child and Adolescent Division. He is a weekly guest of the radio broadcast "The Minirth-Meier Clinic" and a member of the Christian Medical Society. Warren is co-author of *Kids Who Carry Our Pain* and *The Father Book.* Dr. Warren is the father of one son, Matthew.

Thomas A. Whiteman, Ph.D., is a licensed psychologist and president of Fresh Start Seminars, Inc., which conducts more than fifty divorce recovery seminars a year throughout the United States. He is also founder and president of Life Counseling Services, a Christian counseling center, in Paoli, Pennsylvania.

Dr. Whiteman and his wife, Lori, are the parents of two daughters, Elizabeth and Michelle, and one son, Kurt.

Motivational teacher **Zig Ziglar** is the author of several books, including *See You at the Top, Confessions of a Happy Christian, Dear Family,* and *Zig Ziglar's Secrets of Closing the Sale.* Toastmasters International awarded him the Communications and Leadership Award in 1983, and the Southern Baptist Convention elected him first vice president in 1984. He and his wife, Jean Abernathy Ziglar, live in Dallas and are the parents of four children.

Notes

Chapter 4. Your Marriage: On the Rock or on the Rocks?

1. David Hamburg, "A New Study Promises Answers to an Old Question: What's Wrong with Our Kids? *People,* 15 December 1986, 47.

2. Haddon W. Robinson, *Living God's Will* (Old Tappan, NJ: Fleming Revell, 1976), 16.

Chapter 6. "I Remember Mama—and Daddy, Too"

1. William Shakespeare, *As You Like It,* II.7.139–40.

2. See Dinkmeyer, Pew, and Dinkmeyer, Jr., *Adlerian Counseling,* 19.

3. O. K. Moore, ibid.

4. Carrol R. Thomas and William C. Marchant, "Basic Principles of Adlerian Family Counseling" in *Adlerian Family Counseling,* ed. Oscar C. Christensen and Thomas G. Schramski (Minneapolis, MN: Educational Media Corporation, 1983), 23.

Chapter 12. Giving Your Children a Hug from God

1. Dick Van Dyke, *Faith, Hope and Hilarity: The Child's Eye View of Religion* (Garden City, N.Y.: Doubleday, 1970), 52.

2. Ibid., 41.

3. Ibid., 42.

4. Ibid., 55.

5. Ibid., 42.

6. Dr. Robert Hemfelt, Dr. Frank Minirth, and Dr. Paul Meier, *Love Is a Choice* (Nashville: Thomas Nelson, 1989), 34.

7. See Matthew 18:3; 19:14; Mark 10:14–15.

8. See Ephesians 6:4; Titus 2:4.

9. Van Dyke, *Faith, Hope and Hilarity,* 11–12.

10. Ross Campbell, *How to Really Love Your Child* (Wheaton, Ill.: Victor Books, 1977), 126.

Chapter 17. Depression in Adolescents and Older Teens

1. James P. Comer, M.D., "Young Suicides," *Parents,* August 1982, 88.

Chapter 26. How Divorce Affects Children

1. Ken Magid and Walt Schreibman, *Divorce Is . . . A Kid's Coloring Book* (Gretna, LA; Pelican Publishing Co., 1980).

2. Barbara S. Cain, "Older Children and Divorce," *New York Times Magazine,* Feb. 18, 1990, 54.

3. John Bradshaw, *Bradshaw on the Family* (Deerfield, FL: Health Communications, Inc., 1988), 164.

4. Barbara S. Cain, "Older Children and Divorce," *New York Times Magazine,* Feb. 18, 1990, 54.

Chapter 32. Giving the Blessing to Your Parents

1. *Hebrew Lexicon*, p. 457.

2. Ibid., p. 866.

3. Arndt & Gingrich, *Greek-English Lexicon,* p. 317.

4. Gerald C. Davison & John M. Neale, *Abnormal Psychology* (New York: John Wiley & Sons, 1978), pp. 135ff.